You Mean, There's RACE in My Movie?
The Complete Guide to Understanding Race in Mainstream Hollywood

You Mean, There's RACE in My Movie?

The Complete Guide to Understanding Race in Mainstream Hollywood

Dr. F. W. Gooding, Jr.

• AKA, **The Race Doctor** •

On the Reelz

PRESS

Copyright © 2017, On the Reelz Press, Inc.
All rights reserved. This book, or parts thereof, may not be
reproduced in any form without permission from the publisher;
exceptions are made for brief excerpts used in published reviews.

This title is published by On the Reelz Press in association with The Race Doctor, Inc.,
P.O. Box 6473, Silver Spring, Maryland, 20906, USA.

On the Reelz Press, and the On the Reelz Press logo are trademarks of
On the Reelz Press, Inc.; The Race Doctor, and The Race Doctor logo
are trademarks of The Race Doctor, Inc.
www.theracedoc.com

You Mean, There's RACE in My Movie: The Complete Guide to Understanding Race in Hollywood,
Second Edition

ISBN: 978-0-9778048-7-0
Printed in the United States of America.

While every precaution has been taken in the preparation of this book, the publisher and authors assume no responsibility for errors or omissions, or for damages resulting from the use of the information contained herein.

On the Reelz Press books may be purchased for educational, business, or personal use. E-book editions are also available at www.amazon.com. For more information, contact On the Reelz Press corporate/institutional sales department at http://otrpressinfo.wixsite.com/website.

Special thanks to Sharon.

and of courserous to our #1 fan . . .

DEDICATION

To those who speak directly and don't carry a big schtick

TABLE OF CONTENTS
YOU MEAN, THERE'S RACE IN MY MOVIE?

TABLE OF CONTENTS
YOU MEAN, THERE'S RACE IN MY MOVIE?

ACT 1: Introduction

CHAPTER ZERO: **Behind the Scenes** — 2
Progress, More or Less, 4 • Previews, 5 • It's Showtime!, 7

CHAPTER 1: **What Is a Mainstream Movie?** — 10
Formula for Success, 11 • Mainstream-lined Approach, 14 • The Mainstream Movie Factors, 16 • Special Features, 22 • Don't Get Too Animated, 25 • Independent Films, 28 • Foreign Films, 29 • Mainstream's Universal Appeal, 29

CHAPTER 2: **The Cast of Caricatures** — 32
For Hue? For What?, 33 • Racial Makeup, Please, 34 • Minority Reports, 41

THE BOTTOM LINE #1: *WHITE SCREENS, DARK THEATERS* — 49

ACT 2: CONFLICT & CLIMAX

CHAPTER 3: **The Color Scene** — 52
Now Playing: Same, but Different, 53 • Stereotype vs. Archetype, 54 • The HARM Theory, 56 • But Less is More, 58 • White Beauty Standard, 60 • Approaching Whiteness, 62 • What's in a Name? 67

CHAPTER 4: **The Angel** — 70
Touched by an Angel, 71 • Hot Ticket Items, 74 • Archetype Explored, 75

CHAPTER 5: **The Background Figure** — 84
(Back)ground Zero, 85 • Hot Ticket Items, 87 • Archetype Explored, 87

CHAPTER 6: **The Comic Relief** — 96
Comic Debrief, 97 • Hot Ticket Items, 99 • Archetype Explored, 100

CHAPTER 7: **The Menace to Society** — 108
The Phantom Menace, 110 • Protective Stereotype, 111 • Hot Ticket Items, 114 • Archetype Explored, 114

CHAPTER 8: **The Physical Wonder** — 124
Physical Blunder, 125 • Hot Ticket Items, 130 • Archetype Explored, 130

CHAPTER 9: **The Utopic Reversal** — 140
Reversal of Fortune, 141 • Hot Ticket Items, 143 • Archetype Explored, 143

CHAPTER 10: **White Balancing Act** — 156
As Good As It Gets, 157 • White Balance, 158 • The Arc of the Character, 159 • Majority Rules, 162 • Prototypical Behavior, 164

THE BOTTOM LINE #2: *Color Me Bad* — 195

ACT 3: RESOLUTION

CHAPTER 11: **At a Theater Near You** — 198
Picture This, 200 • I See White People, 203 • No White Crime, 206 • Testing, Testing, 1, 2, 3, 208 • The Sacrificial Sofa, 211 • Just Playing My Part, 214 • To Catch an Audience, 215 • Financing Fantasy, 217 • Image is Everything, 220

CHAPTER 12: **Audience Participation** — 224
Eyes Wide Shut, 225 • The Young and the Raceless, 228 • I, Race Not, 229 • Categorical Denial, 234 • The Greatest of Small-Time, 242 • Act Locally, Appeal Globally, 248 • Total Recall, 250

The Bottom Line #3: *Emotion Pictures* — 253

CHAPTER 13: **The Bottom Dime** — 254
Reading the Writing on the Screen, 256 • The Smokeless Gun, 257 • Presumed Innocent, 259 • The Price of Parity, 260 • Front Row and Center, 264

BONUS FEATURES

GLOSSARY — 270

NOTES — 278

REFERENCES — 302

INDEX — 316

ACT 1: Introduction

CHAPTER ZERO
BEHIND THE SCENES

 *Simply put, the changing face of American society is not being reflected back to the American public by its media.*

Dr. Patricia Heisser Metoyer, former Executive Administrator for Affirmative Action, Screen Actors Guild[1]

CHAPTER ZERO
BEHIND THE SCENES

In the ten years that have passed since the first edition of *You Mean, There's RACE in My Movie?* arrived, numerous and widespread changes within the "racial landscape" require for us to re-evaluate whether this second edition is even relevant! As the first edition was released in 2007, one particular change that must be articulated aloud was the ascension of Illinois Senator Barack Hussein Obama II to the White House as the forty-fourth President of the United States of America. For many, Obama's 2008 election (and subsequent 2012 re-election) represented a watershed moment whereby American society had extricated arguably one of the largest monkeys on its back since the inception of the country — namely, a publicly supported and elected non-white male who not only represented the "face" of American society worldwide, but who also penetrated into the previously unknown pantheon of *presidential power.*

Equally as fascinating has been the numerous conversations and interactions brokered and fostered on account of this manuscript. I am pleased to share that my six minority archetype rubrics and six White prototype rubrics are shared and employed by educational practitioners at public and private high schools, as well as colleges and universities across the country. I have also been personally recruited and solicited to conduct hundreds of trainings for educators, health practitioners, public and private sector employees and law enforcement officials using this nuanced analytical approach towards mainstream movies.

And perhaps that is precisely the point! While not everyone concedes the efficacy of the rubric, logic and data provided in this manuscript, it is readily apparent in my travels that most of us agree that the movies mean *something* to our society. As with all things human, a range of interest and interaction exists, but for those who do go to the movies, they intimately know the magic and the mystery of the moving image and its worth. Fine. It is only prudent for us to ask what all this means for race in a society largely free from overt acts of racism.

RACISM 2.0

In the ten years since the release of the first edition, racism as we knew it is indeed extinct. It is currently downright unbecoming to appear in public as not having tolerance or to harbor disdain for diversity. Most of us are now more sensitive to the idea that people of different races should be respected in our new age. Yet, Racism 2.0 refers to the stubborn persistence of negative, disparaging narratives of old that are more refined and stylized and thus less obvious and overtly offensive in appearance. Present discrimination is much more subtle, suave and sophisticated in appearance and thereby more difficult to detect, let alone gain consensus upon.

The crux of this concept is that the mere absence of obvious markers of racism (e.g., harrowing, hooded Ku Klux Klansmen burning crosses with nooses in their hands), does not mean that the *narratives* undergirding the obvious markers are any more absent. Such racially problematic thought patterns have been updated (i.e., 2.0) to increase capacity and efficiency while minimizing cost and waste, much like our quieter, faster, sleeker and cleaner high-speed trains in contrast to the loud, lumbering and pollutive locomotives of old.

While American society has made significant social improvements specifically around the topic of race over the years, current data suggest that there may still remain a smidgen of room for improvement. Many Americans and several pockets of America still observe "poor habits" from the past — whether consciously or unconsciously — that perpetuate class, gender and racial discrimination amongst other Americans. Such discrimination is implied generally by statistical data, but seldom acknowledged directly amongst individuals who have been raised by their parents not to "see the color of another's skin" but to see "the content of one's character" instead. Within these pages, we aim to tackle this issue very directly.

For, there was indeed a time when America *and* Hollywood were racist. It is now time to explore whether our present day mainstream Hollywood movies are free from racism or whether under the principles of Racism 2.0, the same sequel is being sold at a theater near you. Another way to frame the inquiry is to ask more directly, if Hollywood's first ground-breaking feature length movie, **The Birth of a Nation** (released in 1915), and Hollywood's first talking film ever created, **The Jazz Singer** (released in 1927), could be considered "racist," since they both featured White actors in blackface, then when exactly did Hollywood stop being racist? Feel free to pick a year, any year actually, between 1927 and 2017.

Although the United States of America is still predominately White, it has grown more diverse at a breath-taking pace in recent decades. Whether Hollywood will reflect America's newfound diversity remains to be seen. As it stands, American mainstream movies are seen and enjoyed by diverse audiences not just in America, but all over the world. There is no debating that mainstream movies are time-consuming, multi-million dollar projects that require the coordinated effort of many different companies, agencies and individuals. Due to the size, scale and cost of creating mainstream movies, everything you see onscreen has a function and a reason for its placement. The purpose of *You Mean, There's RACE in My Movie?* is to stimulate a broader discussion about the significance of race within contemporary mainstream movies[6] and their impact on mainstream society. Regardless of whether you are an aspiring academic or an avid moviegoer, all audiences are welcome to participate in this dynamic discussion. If you are looking for a place to analyze and discuss racial images that you may or may not have seen in *your* movie, then consider yourself seated in the right theater.

PREVIEWS

Book Format

Everything that you are about to read is the result of pure passion and enthusiasm for one of the greatest forms of modern entertainment: movies! The text is segmented into three acts to pay homage to the typical structure of a Hollywood movie. With each turning page, we invite you to star as our fearless and intelligently inquisitive *Protagonist* in this dramatic, action-filled adventure.

In *Act One: Introduction,* we orient you to our ongoing dialogue about race and the movies by exploring threshold concepts that provide the foundation for our discussion. In particular, we outline our method for classifying mainstream movies, since a shared understanding of mainstream movies and their qualities will provide context and structure to our dialogue. In *Act Two: Conflict & Climax,* we define and analyze Hollywood's most common and consistent image patterns for both minority and White characters, exploring a variety of contemporary mainstream movie examples. Lastly, in *Act Three: Resolution,* we explore the power of mainstream movies and examine how racial imagery produced by Hollywood plays a significant role in our lives, even for the most casual of movie fans. Along the way, look for vocabulary words that will root our discussion in consistently definable terms[7] to avoid the ambiguity that often plagues conversations about race.

Book Function

Mainstream movies are a shared social experience of significant value. They are important tools used both to inform and influence cultural identity. We apply our racial analysis exclusively to *mainstream movies* (as opposed to independent films or "made-for-TV" movies) because they have consistently demonstrated the greatest potential for societal and cultural impact. The formulaic nature of mainstream movies is driven by the ever-pressing need to consistently reach a mass audience. When a Hollywood studio takes a risk by investing hundreds of millions of dollars into a single movie project, it also seeks to minimize that risk by going with "what works" to improve the movie's chance of becoming profitable. It is, after all, the entertainment *business*. This formulaic nature of mainstream movies is part of the underlying reason why Hollywood relies on a consistent pattern of racial imagery.

During a movie, viewers must somehow process the various racial images they see, whether consciously or unconsciously. The concepts within this book will enable and empower readers to identify minority character patterns beyond a context of loosely organized and isolated examples. Many viewers are misled because they only look for blatantly obvious caricatures that are indisputably offensive. Readers will learn the subtle, yet significant ways in which movies communicate messages about race.

At the conclusion of this book, you will find that although Hollywood is a White-dominated industry, it consistently produces lucrative mainstream movies designed to appeal "universally" to racially diverse audiences around the world. Nevertheless, Hollywood mainstream movies routinely present a limited view of minorities, in stark contrast to the broadly developed spectrum of White characters. Given Hollywood's extensive reach and economic impact, the consistently marginalized minority images in mainstream movies reflect and reinforce messages of racial imbalance worldwide. Moreover, your firm understanding of Hollywood's racial patterns will liberate you from having to "see every movie" in order to competently discuss race in the movies.

Book Features

This book is designed to allow you, *the Protagonist*, the opportunity to proceed at your own pace. To ensure that our message is communicated in a clear and transparent fashion, we provide numerous checkpoints throughout the text, primarily to build concrete bridges of shared logic and common understanding. As you journey through the text, the following "popout" boxes will be there to enhance your experience:

The Bottom Line
summation of an important theme, usually marking the end of an *Act*

CUT!
an alternative perspective to our alternative perspective

But It's Just A Movie, Right?
interesting threads about the power of movie images

Lights! Camera! Interaction!
an invitation to engage further via *The Pupil's Army Pages* at ***www.theracedoc.com***

Total Anecdotal
anecdotes, facts & trivia about assorted news and events related to a point of discussion

What Do You Think?
intriguing discussion questions posed to you, *the Protagonist* (or humble Reader)

IT'S SHOWTIME!

In accordance with a subject matter that speaks so much to an individual's identity, many discussions about race in movies often take on a personal, emotional quality.[8] Many legitimate arguments and insights are frequently obscured by their emotional presentation, which can distract listeners from accepting or understanding an otherwise solid supporting point.

So how is this book any different?

As paradoxical as it may sound, **You Mean, There's RACE in My Movie?** does not discuss anything "new." The discussion of race in the movies is as old as the movie industry itself, for many of the racial patterns that we address have endured throughout Hollywood's history, largely changing in form, but not in substance. These patterns have been recognized by different names and have taken on different faces over the years,[9] but just like the spokes of a wheel, they all point to a central theme of minority marginalization and White glamorization.

Further, we submit to you that **You Mean, There's RACE in My Movie?** represents an *open work*, meaning that this text is not presented as the "final word" on race in your movies. Rather, our aim is to jumpstart direct, forthcoming and substantive discussions on trends and strands about race in *our movies*. Thus, to make our analysis as transparent as possible, we support our observations and analysis of mainstream movies by relying primarily upon publicly available *mainstream sources* of information. In accordance with our *open work* format, at **www.theracedoc.com**, readers can find even more up-to-date information related to the themes developed within this manuscript. The more you interact, the more developed the analysis will become.

The advantage of discussing race within the context of mainstream movies is twofold: 1) we all are assured of interacting with the same medium and have access to the same images and data; and 2) we avoid the use of uniquely personal and "non-debatable" anecdotes that while individually valuable, often cloud an emotionally charged topic such as race. With mainstream movies as our common denominator, we can focus our potentially fractious conversation on a subject that virtually everyone can access, experience and enjoy.

Lastly, we would be remiss not to mention that within the ten years of the first edition's release, Obama's two terms ended and a new presidential term began with Donald John Trump's election as the forty-fifth President of the United States of America in November of 2016. Many are concerned about what Trump's election will mean for the "racial landscape" in view of several campaign promises and specific rhetoric shared on the campaign trail. Trump's first month in office, punctuated by the issuance of numerous Executive Orders, only served to raise additional questions as to where society will be on racial matters ten years hence. Ah, then. Perhaps this second edition is relevant if only for the fact that the big picture is still unclear. After all, if a picture is worth 1,000 words, then we must endeavor to explore how many words a *moving picture* is worth when it comes to race . . .

-*Dr. Frederick W. Gooding, Jr.*
*AKA, "**The Race Doctor**"*
2017

PLEASE NOTE

We employ the terms "minorities" and "non-whites" not as a static descriptive term assigned to a subset of people, but more so as a term indicative of how various racial groups are regarded (and relegated) by Hollywood. Our aim here is not to (ironically) continue any existing patterns of marginalization, but rather to analyze and thoroughly understand the existing paradigms as we push to create new ones.

CHAPTER 1:
WHAT IS A MAINSTREAM MOVIE?

The symbol for America is the movie industry . . . . You go anywhere in the world, even places that are hostile to us, and you can make friends by referring to movies or actors.

Dan Glickman, President & CEO, Motion Picture Association of America[1]

CHAPTER 1:
WHAT IS A MAINSTREAM MOVIE?

What's new at the movie theater? Even though different people make **mainstream movies** at different times in different locations, they are nonetheless created using similar styles, patterns and formulas. Many mainstream movies are deliberately formulaic for the simple reason that venturing too far from "what people like" may cost **major movie studios** dearly at the box office. While most moviegoers evaluate movies based on their entertainment value and cinematic style, the studios evaluate movies based on their gross box office ticket sales. Such results are not only carefully monitored on a weekly basis, but they are used as "evidence" to support or deny the creation of future movie projects. Mainstream movies are consciously created works that, above all, are designed to make money – lots of it.

So we ask you, *the Protagonist*, to act as if you were a high-ranking, upper-crust Hollywood executive for the next few sentences. You are entrusted with the power to decide on the financing of a new movie project, so what do you do? Do you take a risk and invest in unknown actors with an unconventional storyline, or do you go with better-known actors and a familiar storyline proven to be financially successfully in the past? This is your last sentence to be an executive, so be honest: how hard is it to make this decision? Remember, *your job and possibly your career are riding on it.*

FORMULA FOR SUCCESS

"Mainstream producers are essentially in the recycling business," says famed movie critic Roger Ebert. "Part of the blame goes to the screenplay workshops they've all taken, which train them to reassemble the successful parts of old hits." Nationally known film critic Leonard Maltin also chimes in, "surely there are people out there with bright, original ideas that we aren't seeing. The decision-makers are playing it safe. It's easier for them to justify

---

mainstream movie

a movie designed, produced and marketed with the purpose of reaching the greatest possible audience

major movie studios

the corporate conglomerates responsible for the majority of mainstream film distribution

going down a familiar path or doing something seemingly surefire. That protects their jobs."[2]

These comments support the notion that many mainstream movies share common patterns, themes and motifs, despite having different characters, genres and titles. Since there are only so many truly original storylines out in general circulation (boy meets girl, boy loses girl, boy gets girl back, etc.), movie studios purposely draw upon broad themes to better appeal to wide audiences. Movie studios look to maximize their profits while minimizing their risk, often operating under a business philosophy best described as "same, but different." Movie studios ideally want the same positive features that distinguish a movie as a commercial success, while simultaneously differentiating their product from so many other movies following the same formula.

This formulaic process and philosophy helps explain why movie studios pay significant sums of money to remake movies that have already been made before. Remakes allow studios to create new audiences while connecting with pre-existing and established ones. The rationale is that if the movie was successful before, then it can be successful again, with the *same* story, but *different* actors. This formulaic philosophy also engineers Hollywood's star system of highly recognizable actors.[3] Regardless of the content of a particular movie, an **A-list actor's** name can create instant recognition with audiences familiar with that actor's body of work.[4] Hollywood's mainstream movie formula contains broad themes and general storylines that are familiar and expected – if not outright desired – by movie audiences.

So how do minorities factor into Hollywood's winning formula?

Despite the isolated gains and individual successes of several minority actors (e.g., Will Smith, Halle Berry, etc.), minorities as a whole remain marginalized in mainstream movies. The performance of virtually every minority character is dictated by six consistent minority character patterns known as the **archetypes**, that are explored at length in *Act Two: Conflict & Climax* (can the protagonist withstand the suspense???). The following are the six archetypes:

A-list actor

an actor deemed über-important within mainstream society and worthy of constant attention due to their ability to consistently draw a large following

archetype

benign, but reoccurring character patterns that within the aggregate contribute towards larger patterns of marginalization

---

MINORITY ARCHETYPES

1. THE ANGEL
2. THE BACKGROUND FIGURE
3. THE COMIC RELIEF
4. THE MENACE TO SOCIETY
5. THE PHYSICAL WONDER
6. THE UTOPIC REVERSAL

Unfortunately, the limited and frequently compromised roles that minorities occupy in mainstream movies are an integral part of Hollywood's formula for success. Making Hollywood movies is a *business*, not a *service*. Movie-making is as risky as it is lucrative. Sure, movies entertain audiences, but the movie studios that produce them are *for-profit* businesses, not *non-profit* organizations dedicated to the fine arts. There are no scientific formulas that can accurately predict a movie's success, nor are there regulations that dictate what types of movies should be made. As much as movie studios count upon the patronage of minority moviegoers to contribute to a movie's financial success at the box office, Hollywood is under no obligation to employ minority actors in high-profile roles within its movies.

Another important, but often overlooked detail in the movie-making process is that the images within a movie are *controlled* images. Let us not overlook that a movie's financial failure bears consequences and that employees in Hollywood lose jobs too. A mainstream movie production can easily involve hundreds of different individuals who all help to create the controlled images moviegoers ultimately see. The success or failure of a movie may significantly impact the next available working opportunity – period.

When investing hundreds of millions of dollars with no guarantee of a return, movie studios wish to minimize their risk to whatever extent possible. As it is, movie critics scratch their heads year in and year out about the good movie that fizzles while the mercilessly criticized movie becomes the runaway summer hit. When a movie hits and hits big, all studios take note, trying to decipher the successful formula in hopes of duplicating such a large success for themselves. The studios eschew "reinventing the wheel" each and every time they make a movie and instead rely on time-tested movie-making formulas and patterns. What this means for mainstream movie audiences is the recycling of similar characters and storylines rehashed in different settings with different names, much like the continuously-evolving James Bond character that has been played by six different actors over the last fifty-plus years.[5] The fact that so many mainstream movies driven by majority-White casts traditionally dominate the mainstream box office means that minority actors face a severe limitation of prominent employment opportunities.

The ironic cycle that results from a studio's attempt to protect its profit margins is that the more liberal its spending becomes on a movie, the more conservative it becomes in protecting its investment, and the more formulaic the movie becomes in turn. This business model frames Hollywood's reluctance to depart from standard formulaic conventions when producing a movie

> **WHAT DO YOU THINK?**
> To illustrate how thematic elements are repeated or recycled in mainstream movies, consider the following list of sequels, remakes and spinoffs:
>
> - *SpongeBob Movie* (cartoon)
> - *Warcraft* (video game)
> - *The Help* (best-selling novel)
> - *Baywatch* (2017 remake based upon 1989 TV show)
> - *King Kong* (2005 remake of 1933 film)
> - *The Honeymooners* (2005 remake of 1955 TV show)
> - *Pirates of the Caribbean: Dead Men Tell No Tales* (#5)
> - *The Fate of the Furious* (#8)
> - *X-Men: Apocalypse* (#9)
> - *Batman v. Superman* (2016 release was 10th Superman movie since 1948)
> - *Spectre* (2015 James Bond release was 23rd movie in franchise since 1962)
>
> This list illustrates how much movie studios are attracted to stories with "built-in value" that eliminate the need to expend additional resources to create an "unproven" product. Movies like *Deep Impact* and *Armageddon* demonstrate how the studios can minimize risks and maximize profits by recycling proven ideas. These two movies, although produced separately, contained similar storylines and were released in the same year (1998). Both were financially successful, each grossing over $140 million at the box office.
>
> *How many sequels, remakes and spinoffs can you think of that were released in movie theaters just in the past year?*

CHAPTER 1: WHAT IS A MAINSTREAM MOVIE?   13

greatest possible audience

the ideal number of willing consumers that purchase or view a particular mainstream movie

with the **greatest possible audience** (and the greatest possible revenues) in mind. The more mainstream a movie is, the more likely it is to follow typical formulaic conventions. These formulaic conventions dictate that on any given Friday night at your local movie theater, White actors will most likely be showcased as the primary characters in most – if not all – of the movies that are playing. Formulaic conventions also dictate that *if and when* a minority actor appears in a mainstream movie, their role will likely be marginalized in relation to other White characters.

As this multi-billion dollar industry continues to expand its worldwide audience, influence and marketshare,[6] it is important to note the formulaic portrayal of minority images and minority archetypes. Mainstream movies continue to generate revenues for movie studios years after their theatrical release in an exhibition window that outlasts most other forms of modern media. Not only are movies widely available for sale and rental on DVD and VHS, but they can also be seen on pay-per-view networks, premium cable channels, free-broadcast network television, via satellite, cable television, and a litany of ancillary markets, such as airlines, hotels and libraries. Movie studios are keenly aware of the long shelf life of their most popular movies, and exploit this advantage in the open market with repackaged and re-released "classics," complete with commemorative decorations (e.g., 25th Anniversary Collector's Edition), bonus interviews and "never-seen-before" footage that otherwise was resurrected from the cutting floor.

This remarkable ability of movie studios to market and profit from a movie in multiple markets diminishes the movie studios' risk of return on investment and increases the movie's earning potential. It is not uncommon for some movies to outperform their box office earnings through ancillary markets such as DVD rentals and sales.[7] Mainstream movies, by their very design, are meant to be distributed to the greatest possible audience, both in the short-term and well into the future. This widespread distribution only heightens the importance of analyzing how race is portrayed in mainstream movies, especially when these pre-existing movie-making formulas do not include significant minority exposure.

MAINSTREAM-LINED APPROACH

Before we evaluate the formulaic minority archetype patterns that pervade mainstream movies, we now turn our attention to the factors that, when added together, satisfy the threshold definition of a "mainstream movie." Fifth century philosopher St. Augustine once said, "What, then, is time? If no one asks me, I know what it is. If I wish to explain it to him who asks me, I do not know."[8] Defining a mainstream movie is similar to St. Augustine's age-old dilemma: most people know a mainstream movie when they see it, but they are unable to provide a precise definition for one when asked. For the purposes of our analysis, we will provide you with our definition of mainstream movies so that we can all be on the same frame . . . er, page.

Perhaps more interesting is *why* we felt compelled to construct our own working definition of mainstream movies in the first place. Despite the term's popular usage, it is important to pin down what specifically makes the term relevant to the discussion of race in the movies. Mainstream movies have a significant influence and impact on mainstream society, both economically and culturally. If movie studios must continuously reach mainstream audiences, then we must identify the formulaic factors required to create and distribute these mainstream movies.

By standardizing the definition of mainstream movies, we begin to de-mystify the process through which Hollywood consistently produces and proliferates its products. For example, the same "chronologically-correct" **Mission: Impossible — Rogue Nation** (#5 in series) movie will be shown to audiences across the country without any significant alterations to its visual imagery. Notwithstanding the slight editing of movies broadcast in specific markets (e.g., scenes "deleted" from free-broadcast airings, the removal of profanity and nudity from airline versions, etc.), the same Ethan Hunt will serve as the movie's central character and will shoot the same gun at precisely the same time in the movie, no matter where or how many times the movie is shown to American mainstream audiences. There is a wide range of movies available for public consumption, so defining mainstream movies will ensure that we are all analyzing the same subset of movies.

 **CUT!**
Why do you limit your focus to mainstream movies only? If you included independent or foreign films in your criteria, perhaps you would see more roles that break the disparaging patterns that you describe. Mainstream movies impact society on scale unparalleled by any other medium. Thus, products designed to reach the greatest possible audience must be analyzed for the greatest possible impact.

More importantly, we define mainstream movies to better isolate and define the minority archetypes. The more "mainstream" a movie is, the more likely it is to employ minority archetypes that marginalize minority participation in a formulaic manner. The mainstream movie factors demonstrate that if a movie is in fact mainstream, not only does that virtually guarantee marginalized depictions of minorities (if they are depicted at all), but it also ensures that an expensive and dedicated effort will be made to distribute the movie's imagery to as wide an audience as possible.

We have identified six primary factors that make a movie mainstream. Please note that all six factors listed below need not be present for a movie to be classified as a mainstream movie:

MAINSTREAM MOVIE FACTORS

1. FULL-LENGTH RELEASE
2. WIDESPREAD DISTRIBUTION
3. PRODUCTION/MARKETING COSTS
4. LARGE BOX OFFICE SALES
5. A-LIST TALENT
6. MAINSTREAM MEDIA EXPOSURE

THE MAINSTREAM MOVIE FACTORS
1. FULL-LENGTH, FIRST-RUN, THEATRICAL RELEASE

A typical full-length feature, or "**first-run**," movie typically ranges from ninety minutes to three hours in length. A first-run movie is first exhibited to the public in a movie theater after a heavy promotion schedule. Such a movie is typically released either on a Wednesday or a Friday in movie theater chains across the country, for which moviegoers must pay admission for the viewing privilege. Theatrical exhibition is the traditional market for the initial presentation of feature motion pictures, and is a major method of enhancing the value of the movie's ancillary markets (e.g., DVD sales, television rights, toys, games, apparel, novelty items, etc.), in addition to the box office take itself.

first-run movie

a feature typically ninety minutes to three hours in length that is first exhibited to the public in national and regional movie theater chains

The broad exposure a movie receives from its theatrical release is intended to maximize viewership and the studio's immediate return on its investment. The theatrical release criteria effectively eliminates movies produced for television, any movies released straight to video, any movie shorts, and the vast majority of documentaries.

2. WIDESPREAD DISTRIBUTION WITHIN THE U.S.

Given that there are an estimated 6,000 theaters in the United States,[9] a movie that penetrates at least 1,000 of those theaters will qualify as being nationally distributed in the United States. A "special" movie with a limited engagement in specific major metropolitan areas, such as Los Angeles and New York, falls outside of our definition of a mainstream movie.

To understand why widespread distribution is important, follow this simple math for two mainstream movies released on the same weekend.

Suppose that Movie A is released in 500 theaters and Movie B is released in 3,000 theaters, with each theater having a capacity for 200 people. If both movies sold out for one show in each of these theaters, Movie A would be seen by 100,000 people (*200 x 500*) while Movie B would be seen by 600,000 people (*200 x 3,000*). Even if Movie B only sells half of its tickets for one show, it would still be seen by 300,000 people (*200 x 1,500*), which is three times as many people as Movie A's sold out performances of 100,000.

Some basic math demonstrates that it is simply harder for a movie with a more limited release to be seen by the greatest possible audience nationwide. Movies containing images and themes that defy traditional mainstream formulas typically enjoy smaller audiences. Conversely, movies that enjoy widespread distribution not only reach the greatest possible audience, but they stand the best chance of exerting societal influence. It is therefore significant that most Hollywood movies circulated widely throughout the world primarily feature majority-White casts with only a sprinkling of minority characters. For consider that for individuals living and operating within largely homogenous, racially isolated communities: 1) they have more limited interactions with "real-life" minorities in person, which means that 2) these larger-than-life movie images become all the more magnified and multiplied in their importance and influence.

> **TOTAL ANECDOTAL**
> "Black movies" typically have not fared well at the box office, due in part to limited distribution. For example, consider **Kingdom Come**, containing easily identifiable Black talent such as LL Cool J, Jada Pinkett Smith, Whoopi Goldberg and Vivica Fox. **Kingdom Come** opened on 1,100 screens, while **Josie and the Pussycats**, starring White actress Tara Reid, opened on more than double that number (2,500 theaters) on the same opening weekend in 2001. Despite the handicap, **Kingdom Come** outperformed **Josie and the Pussycats** by a count of $7.5 million to $4.5 million during opening weekend, thereby suggesting that a larger distribution and release deal may have improved its box office take considerably.[1a]

The movie industry represents a uniquely lucrative business wherein the worldwide ticket sales of a single movie alone can exceed hundreds of millions of dollars. In a few exceptional cases, such revenues can approach $2.8 billion dollars (e.g., *Avatar*)![10] The generation of such large sums of money can only be possible with widespread distribution. Close to 1.32 billion movie tickets were sold domestically in 2015.[11] After factoring in the number of movie rentals and sales for home viewing, it is safe to say that a significant number of Americans, whether members of a minority group or not, watched a Hollywood movie at some point in time in recent years. Hollywood executives are well aware of these large numbers, especially since they stand to profit from them.

3. SIGNIFICANT PRODUCTION & MARKETING COSTS

Big movies are big business. Any movie studio that wants **blockbuster** revenues has to pay the cost of doing business. The average cost of producing and marketing a movie is roughly $200 million dollars.[12] This high financial bar sends a loud and clear message that not everyone can afford to show and tell their story on the mainstream stage. The careful attention that studio

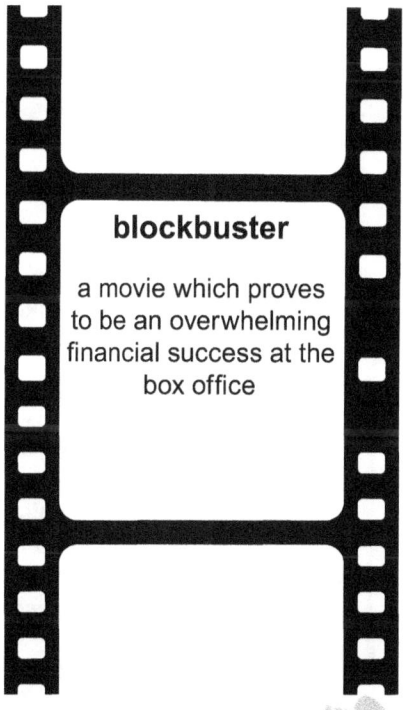

blockbuster

a movie which proves to be an overwhelming financial success at the box office

> **TOTAL ANECDOTAL**
> The pressure to use a large marketing budget continues to grow. With the average cast receiving a total of $27 million, films that cost $130 million or more need to make at least $50 million at the box office on the first weekend to have a shot at eventually becoming profitable. That's how a mainstream movie like *Charlie's Angels: Full Throttle* can have a "disappointing" $37.6 million opening weekend with a budget of $120 million.[1b]

executives pay to high-priced movie budgets presupposes the premeditative aspect of creating mainstream movies. The moviegoer ultimately sees the result of a multi-million dollar investment and the collaboration of thousands of highly-skilled people, many of whom have a financial stake in the success of the movie. Thus, if a movie does not prominently feature minorities, it is presumptuous to simply label the movie's creators as racist. Rather, it is more accurate to state that the lack of minority presence in the movie was *not* unintentional.

Since a mainstream movie can literally cost hundreds of millions of dollars to produce, studio executives are under considerable pressure to distribute their company's movies to the greatest possible audience to increase the prospects of: 1) recouping investment costs and 2) making the greatest possible profit on the movie. A large advertising budget does not guarantee large revenues, but it does spur widespread awareness and greater exposure. For instance, a simple trip to the lobby of your neighborhood cinema multiplex will show that some movie advertising campaigns begin several months in advance of the actual release date.[13]

Movie ads freely emphasize that a movie stars so-and-so, or was produced by so-and-so, or is from the creators of so-and-so, or that the movie is based upon a book by so-and-so. This is all done to breed familiarity and comfort between the potential viewer and the movie. Given the rising financial pressures for a movie to perform well early in its box office release, movie studios seek instant rapport with their potential audiences. By creating sufficient awareness and buzz, studios bank on the hope that the maximum amount of people know about the movie before it ever arrives in theaters.

Typically, in our free market economy, products that can appeal to mass audiences have the best chance of becoming financially successful. This principle is ironic in that the *best* products do not always make the most money. From a purely critical aspect, some of the greatest movies of our time still languish in relative obscurity, only to be whispered about in local coffeehouses. After all, how effective would it be to for local news outlets, newspapers and online blogs to debate a movie for which no one ever saw the trailer, never saw the billboard ad, never saw its television commercial or never heard its radio ad? Such a conversation would be fragmented at best. Mainstream exposure allows for such a "common denominator" to be created.

> **TOTAL ANECDOTAL**
> The DVD *marketing budget* for *Ice Age* was an eye-popping $85 million, an amount that exceeds the entire production budget for many mainstream movies.[1c]

When national media outlets discuss the "greatest movies," such discussions typically revolve around movies that were publicized and distributed through various cost-intensive mainstream outlets in the first

>  **WHAT DO YOU THINK?**
>
> The following is an excerpt from a *Bozeman Daily Chronicle* article entitled: "Report: Paleontologist 'Fudged' Discovery to Promote Movie" by Walt Williams on May 12, 2005:[1d]
>
> Museum of the Rockies paleontologist Jack Horner 'fudged' information about a dinosaur discovery four years ago to promote the third *Jurassic Park* film, National Public Radio reported Wednesday.
>
> In 2001, Horner announced his team in eastern Montana had discovered what may be the largest Tyrannosaurus Rex skeleton ever found. The discovery was used to promote *Jurassic Park III*, which came out that year. Horner has served as a science advisor for all three "Jurassic Park" films.
>
> In a story about marketing films, NPR [National Public Radio] reported that Horner had agreed to change the date of the discovery so news of the finding would break closer to the movie's release.
>
> 'We decided that we could alter discovery dates, at least for the press, for the opening of the movie,' Horner told NPR. Universal Studios, which produced *Jurassic Park III*, sponsors some of Horner's research and came up with the idea.
>
> Was Horner's delay an innocent public relations stunt just to market the movie? Or was Horner's discovery an example of public manipulation for private gain? What do you think?

place. Most major movie studios in Hollywood that can afford such exorbitant investments were founded, owned and operated by Whites. Although an obvious factor for this phenomena is that the American population is still predominately White, the increased presence of minorities within the Hollywood studio system in recent years has done little to fundamentally alter deeply rooted patterns of marginalization of minority characters.

4. LARGE BOX OFFICE SALES

Gross box office receipts are an effective tool to assess the preferences of the viewing audience. Top grossing mainstream movies now routinely make hundreds of millions of dollars at the box office, sometimes within a single weekend (e.g., *Star Wars: The Force Awakens*)! Generally speaking, if moviegoers like or dislike a movie, box office data makes the audience's tastes tangible to the extent that such data quantifies and approximates the total size of the audience.

Audience size is important to the mainstream definition, but it also serves as a financial indicator of which types of movies that studios should continue to make. If a movie is poorly received by the public, then such rejection will be evident by poor box office results. Conversely, large box office receipts indicate that the movie has been seen by a larger audience than a movie with significantly lesser sales.

Using box office receipts as a common indicator of exposure, we can infer that a movie that grossed $41.7 million at the box office was seen by

> **TOTAL ANECDOTAL**
> With a total production cost exceeding $135 million for the movie *Pearl Harbor*, the total amount of money spent on production and promotion of the movie roughly equaled the amount of damage caused in the actual attack.[1e]

CHAPTER 1: WHAT IS A MAINSTREAM MOVIE? 19

> **TOTAL ANECDOTAL**
>
> In Hollywood, there is a metric called the *Ulmer Scale*, which is one of the movie industry's premier methods of tracking, measuring and ranking the star power of 1,800 actors and directors worldwide. Polling more than 100 leading dealmakers from Hollywood and more than a dozen key international territories, the scale uses a 100-point ranking system to measure bankability, the key component of star power. **Bankability** is the degree to which an actor or director's name alone can raise 100% financing up-front for a movie. Often, this is the most critical factor in determining whether an actor or director is hired for a project. The Ulmer Scale tracks bankability exclusively for three movie budget levels: art house, mid-range, and studio-level features. For more information, go to **www.ulmerscale.com**.

more people than the movie that grossed $1.7 million at the box office. If a movie makes upwards of $150 million, although it is not proof that everyone who saw the movie *liked* the movie, it is evidence enough to suggest that a significant segment of the population was aware of the movie. A movie that achieves such significant financial success will accordingly attract significant mainstream media attention and coverage.

5. EMPLOYMENT OF A-LIST TALENT

A-list movie stars are powerful marketing tools. They breed a sense of familiarity and bring about expectations about the type and quality of movie. With some A-list starts commanding up-front fees upwards of $20 million, the studios that employ them are essentially forced to use A-list stars exclusively for mainstream productions. Otherwise, the studios may not be able to recoup their investment on an actor's premium salary if the underlying movie is not widely distributed and marketed on a large scale.

The high visibility of A-list actors only increases the overall profile of a movie. A-list actors are paid significant sums of money because their image represents something larger to the public than a mere name. By casting that A-list star, the studio hopes to improve the movie's prospects of success by offering an additional inducement to see the movie, even if such an enticement is not based upon any of the movie's structural qualities (e.g., plot, cinematography, etc.), but rather based purely upon personal admiration for an individual actor. Thus, it is important to note that A-list actors must be *developed* and given the opportunity to show that they can generate attention and revenues for the projects in which they participate.

The caliber and number of mainstream, minority, A-list actors varies depending upon who is answering the question. What is indisputable is that this number pales in comparison to the larger, more established number of A-list White actors. The paucity of A-list minority actors signals to what degree movie studios have financial confidence in potential moviegoers' abilities to make a "personal" connection with the movie's primary talent. After all, A-list stars are not born; *they are created*. Consequently, casting becomes a business decision that affects the overall frequency of minority imagery in mainstream movies.

> **TOTAL ANECDOTAL**
>
> Speaking to the ingredients of a financially successful movie, Jere Hausfater, president of worldwide distribution and acquisitions for *Intermedia Films* says: "Having a **bankable** actor, or actors, is probably the most important factor. Every year, the importance (of the star) becomes greater and greater in the presales business, with the director right behind. Unfortunately, really good material alone won't do it. To presell and come up with the proper marketing hook in order to launch the picture, the actor is the critical component. I'm not trying to downplay the concept. It really is the total package, but in listing the priorities, it is much more difficult without having a star."[1f]

6. HEAVY INTERACTION WITH MAINSTREAM OUTLETS

Millions of people watch and discuss mainstream movies every day. Mainstream exposure requires the use of mass media (e.g., television, newspapers, etc.) and massive financial resources for widespread distribution. After all, with a population of roughly 318 million, it takes considerable effort to convince a massive audience to pay money to see a movie in the theater, given the wide range of entertainment options that presently exists. Such marketing efforts must be intensely coordinated, consistent and pervasive. The principal vehicle for distributing such information is the mainstream media.

Mainstream media consists of a dizzying array of information channels, structured and designed to reach the greatest possible audience through established nationwide marketing and distribution networks. There are television shows, newspapers, magazines and radio programs accessed by vast numbers of people throughout the country, thereby serving as a means of sharing information, centralizing thought and organizing loose societal networks.

The beauty of this structured information source, or **mainstream pipeline**, is that it brokers relationships among millions of disparate Americans across the country so that they can all have a shared experience. Although many Americans come from varying backgrounds and from different regions of the country, they can all share the same information communicated through mainstream media. Granted, not all movies injected into the mainstream pipeline attain universal acceptance. However, if a movie gains significant mainstream exposure, then its potential for fiscal and social success only increases. Once information about a mainstream movie is aggressively disseminated through principal media outlets, the movie and the imagery within it only grow in their potential to influence mainstream society.

Movies publicized heavily through mainstream outlets also stand a better chance of becoming profitable at the box office. For instance, movies in the ***Spider-Man*** or ***Harry Potter*** series were so heavily publicized that it would be difficult to encounter an American who has *not* heard about their theatrical release. As further indication of the movie's

> **bankability**
>
> the degree to which an actor or director's name alone can raise 100% financing up-front for a movie

> **mainstream pipeline**
>
> the assortment of major media outlets reaching the widest possible audience due to nationwide marketing and distribution networks

> **TOTAL ANECDOTAL**
> National promotional tie-ins allow major corporations to maximize their advertising dollars by promoting their products in conjunction with mainstream movies through mainstream outlets. McDonald's (***Minions***), the United States Postal Service (***The Amazing Spider-Man 2***) and Burger King (***Transformers: Revenge of the Fallen***) are all corporate entities with an established national presence that have access to mainstream outlets. The additional exposure to consumers loyal to large, established corporations augments the marketing impact of a movie. The additional attention a movie receives within corporate America also helps to "legitimize" a movie in the eyes of a consumer that already has loyal ties to the corporate sponsor, thereby solidifying the movie's influential capacity within mainstream society.

> **TOTAL ANECDOTAL**
>
> Movie studios go to great lengths to publicize their movies. In 2005, *Sony Pictures* settled a class-action lawsuit in which they were accused of using a fake movie critic in advertisements featuring several of their movies.[1g]

infusion within **mainstream culture**, *Spider-Man 2* was involved in a minor "scandal" when baseball fans vociferously objected to ads for the movie being placed on bases during Major League Baseball games.[14] Perhaps the most striking but overlooked aspect of this scandal is not the eventual failure of the proposed marketing gimmick, but rather the initial agreement amongst Major League Baseball executives. Apparently, the *Spider-Man 2* ad campaign was originally approved and regarded as compatible with the values of "our nation's pastime."

SPECIAL FEATURES

On average, a movie will exhibit four of the six mainstream factors to achieve mainstream status. There are additional "bonus" factors that may also indicate that a movie is mainstream. These factors are not absolutes, but the presence of these indicators will shore up any doubts about a movie's mainstream status:

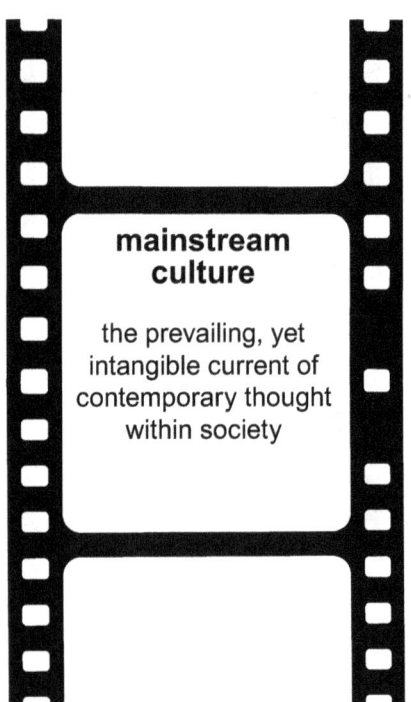

mainstream culture

the prevailing, yet intangible current of contemporary thought within society

MAINSTREAM MOVIE BONUS FACTORS

1. SPINOFF
2. SPUNOFF
3. PROMOTIONAL TIE-INS
4. PARAPHERNALIA
5. THEME PARK RIDES
6. LONG LEAD TIME
7. ACADEMY AWARD NOMINATION/WIN

✦ Spinoff ✦

A spinoff occurs when the movie itself is adapted from an already famous book, television show or comic book. Book spinoff examples include bestsellers like *The Blind Side* and *The Da Vinci Code*, penned by Michael Lewis and Dan Brown respectively, or the *Harry Potter* series composed by J.K. Rowling. Television show spinoff examples include *Avatar: The Last Airbender, Star Trek Beyond, 21 Jump Street, The Man from U.N.C.L.E., Transformers: The Last Knight* and *Jackass. The Flintstones* is a spinoff from a television cartoon, while *Hulk, Iron Man, Captain America, X-Men, Deadpool, Teenage Mutant Ninja Turtles, Batman, Spider-Man, Wolverine* and *Superman* are all comic book characters that came alive on the big screen.

> **TOTAL ANECDOTAL**
>
> In addition to the more traditional sources for spinoffs, ***Resident Evil: The Final Chapter, The Angry Birds Movie, Need for Speed, Prince of Persia: The Sands of Time, Tekken, Max Payne, Hitman: Agent 47,*** and ***Assassin's Creed*** are all examples of mainstream movies adapted from video games.

YOU MEAN, THERE'S RACE IN MY MOVIE?

⚜ Spunoff ⚜

A "spunoff" occurs when an "independent" project related to a mainstream movie is created *after* the movie's release. For example, look at the creation of the television shows styled after the movies ***Psycho*** *(Bates Motel)*, ***Clueless, Limitless*** and ***My Big Fat Greek Wedding***. These spunoffs indicate mainstream acceptance since the companies that produce them believe they can increase their chances for success by offering a product that can easily tap into a proven idea with a proven market. Another spunoff example comes in the form of the *Bubba Gump Shrimp Co.* global restaurant chain, an idea directly grafted from the Academy Award winning blockbuster movie, ***Forrest Gump***.

Mainstream movies may also be spunoff from other mainstream movies as well. These movies qualify as spunoffs since they are not necessarily sequels, but represent stand-alone franchises. Examples include ***Puss in Boots 2*** (2018 release) spunoff from the ***Shrek*** franchise or ***Magneto*** and ***Wolverine*** as spunoff from the ***X-Men*** franchise.

⚜ Promotional Tie-ins ⚜

As mentioned earlier, national promotional tie-ins bolster a movie's marketing efforts since the studio and the corporate partner can promote each other's product either independently or jointly. Examples range from ***Minions*** or ***The Lion King*** toys included in ***McDonald's*** Happy Meals, to ***Curious George*** stickers placed on bananas at grocery stores, to movie advertisements on the back of *Chuck E. Cheese* tokens, to Jeep commercials featuring exclusive footage from the movie ***Sahara***, with a gentle reminder to see the *Jeep* in the movie itself![15]

The promotional tie-ins also illustrate how corporate partners must be involved early on in the movie-making process. For instance, executives from both 20th Century Fox Film Corp. and *7-Eleven* strategized well in advance of ***The Simpsons Movie*** premiere to "convert" twelve *7-Eleven* stores into *Kwik-E-Marts*, the fictional convenience store that – up until that point – only existed in the animated world of Springfield.[16]

⚜ Paraphernalia ⚜

If a movie is popular with the paying public, then studios will maximize the movie's popularity by keeping the movie alive in the minds of moviegoers for as long as possible. One tangible way

---

BUT IT'S JUST A MOVIE, RIGHT?

Did you know that the ***Lord of the Rings*** (LOTR) movie franchise had a traveling museum exhibition? **LOTR: The Exhibition** was showcased as recently as October 6, 2005, through January 3, 2006, at the Indiana State Museum. A "teacher's guide" was available for those who wished to supplement their class fieldtrips, assisting those who also saw the movie as a vehicle for learning. Note how this movie-centered exhibit continued to tour several years after the theatrical release.

More telling is that the LOTR exhibit was developed and presented by the Museum of New Zealand in partnership with New Line Cinema and was subsidized through the support of the New Zealand government![1h]

Similarly, a $5 million **Star Wars: Where Science Meets Imagination** exhibit opened in October 2005 at the Boston Museum of Science. Ioannis Miaoulis, the museum's president and director, expressed concern that "U.S. schools were failing to produce enough future engineers to meet competition from Asia, putting pressure on museums like his to play a more influential role."[1i] Miaoulis' statement intimates that the Star Wars exhibit could help inspire future engineers. *But it's just a movie, right?*

to keep movie images or characters fresh for past, repeat and future movie patrons is through lucrative licensing deals. For instance, the *Star Wars* or *Finding Dory* franchises can be found on everything from bedsheets to coffee mugs it seems,[17] further solidifying a movie's place in the daily consciousness of American consumers. Naturally, such products would be made available to the greatest possible audience via its widespread distribution through nationally recognized stores and outlets.

❖ Theme Park Rides ❖

The creation of a theme park ride solely scripted around a recently released movie indicates that the movie referenced is "mainstream," and that "a significant" amount of people are familiar with the movie. For instance, in Disney's billion-dollar blockbuster *Pirates of the Caribbean: Dead Man's Chest*, several ties made between the original 1967 theme park ride and the 2006 movie include the recreation of the bayou swamp in movie scenes featuring soothsayer Tia Dalma (Naomie Harris), and the new installation of movie characters in the actual ride itself (whose debut was coordinated with the movie's wide release).[18]

The creation of movie-themed amusement park rides modeled after movie themes and characters only undergirds the ability of large Hollywood conglomerates to cross-promote their products across their own range of mainstream outlets. Examples include *Back to the Future, E.T., Terminator 2, Men in Black, Shrek 2, Jaws, Curious George, Twister* and *The Mummy Returns*, all of which have appeared at the Universal Studios theme park. Additionally, Paramount Pictures' Kings Island Park has featured *The Italian Job* stunt car ride while Metro Goldwyn Mayer (MGM) studios has showcased the *Indiana Jones* stunt show.

❖ Long Lead Time ❖

The ability to begin promoting on a national scale several months before a movie's scheduled release not only signals a healthy marketing budget, but also signals studio faith in a movie to successfully penetrate the mainstream and recoup investment costs. The extended length of time studios use to market movies is significant because it virtually guarantees repeated exposure to movie ads prior to the theatrical release.

The promotional lead time for some major studio projects can extend years in advance of the scheduled release date. For example, the Associated Press reported how trailers shown before *Ice Age 2*, released in theaters on March 31, 2006, featured previews for *The Simpsons Movie*. The release date

---

BUT IT'S JUST A MOVIE, RIGHT?

The force is particularly strong with this one! As of May 25, 2007, the United States Postal Service (USPS) commemorates the *Star Wars* franchise with its very own stamp collection. In preparation for the unveiling, postal authorities authorized altering approximately 400 mailboxes to make them externally appear like R2-D2, a robot droid made famous from the movie series.

This promotional action is significant because the sale of stamps represents a vital source of the agency's annual revenue. Presumably, the greater the mainstream appeal, the larger the demand and the higher the sales. Thus, *Star Wars* was chosen in part because of its ubiquitous nature within mainstream culture. A similar promotional tie-in based around an independent film simply would not make as much business (dollars and) sense.

Perhaps more significant is the fact that a stamp series modeled after a movie even exists at all! Commemorative stamps are selected via a vigorous selection process conducted by the Citizens' Stamp Advisory Committee, whose "primary goal is to select subjects of broad national interest for recommendation to the Postmaster General that are both interesting and educational."[1j]

Star Wars, although originally released in 1977 as a movie, is no longer "just a movie." It is far, far and away so much more . . .

for *The Simpsons Movie* was set for July 27, 2007, which at the time was more than a year away![19]

⚜ ACADEMY AWARD NOMINATION/WIN ⚜

The Academy Awards are regarded as the most prestigious awards in the movie business. In an industry of so many people, only a select few are rewarded with an Oscar, an exclusivity that only adds to their austerity and value. Sponsored by the Academy of Motion Picture Arts and Sciences, this yearly televised event has taken on international proportions, commanding top dollar for those wishing to advertise during the ceremony's internationally televised broadcast. Many relatively obscure or independent films crossed over into the mainstream after being nominated in a highly visible "glamour" category such as Best Picture, Best Director, or Best Supporting Actor/Actress. Examples of this Oscar crossover phenomena include *Monster's Ball* and *Monster*.

> **TOTAL ANECDOTAL**
> Did you know that Oscar ads garnered $2 million for 30-second ads with viewership of 43.5 million in 2014? In comparison, ads for one of the highest-watched television programs annually, the Superbowl, cost about $5 million apiece.[1k]

The Academy Awards are so celebrated that movie studios often benefit financially from the increased attention movies receive during Oscar season. This added financial gain and mainstream attention, usually referred to as the "Oscar bounce," usually occurs after a movie receives an Oscar nomination.[20] Movie studios are well aware of the tangential benefits of Oscar nominations and launch extended and expensive lobbying campaigns during the Academy Award voting season, routinely placing full-page ads in industry trade magazines like *Variety* and *The Hollywood Reporter*. Additionally, specific marketing strategies used by studios are designed to capitalize on Oscar success (e.g., a "Winner of Best Picture" label printed on a DVD box cover).

> **BUT IT'S JUST A MOVIE, RIGHT?**
> Did you hear what South African icon Nelson Mandela said when congratulating actress Charlize Theron on becoming the country's first Oscar winner (Best Actress, *Monster*)?
>
> "Theron has proved that we as a nation can produce the best in the world," he said in a statement. "South Africa has done it again, the Nobel prize for peace, Nobel for literature and now an Oscar for best actress."
>
> "She has put South Africa on the map," he told reporters. "Even those who were ignorant of South Africa, having seen her, they must know now that there is a country like South Africa."
>
> This statement demonstrates the international spread and influence of the Academy Awards. More telling is how Mandela equates an Academy Award with that of a Nobel Peace Prize, indicating that they both have positive effects for international recognition of his country.[1l]

DON'T GET TOO ANIMATED

In classifying mainstream movies, an important issue is whether or not animated movies will fall under our racial analysis. Definitely. There are several animated movies released each year that both satisfy the mainstream definition and contain minority archetypes. It is easy to see how animation might be considered "immune" to this racial discussion. In reality, it is not immune. If anything, the world of animation only reinforces Hollywood's consciousness of race, especially since animation is *entirely* premeditated!

Despite the fact that so many animated movies rely on animals, monsters and other creatures of the imagination, these characters are not exempt from the real-life human influence of race. After all, *real* people are still responsible for creating these animated movies and voicing their characters.

Whether an animated character is overtly represented as a minority (e.g., Frozone in *The Incredibles*) or a minority actor merely supplies the character's voice (e.g., Eddie Murphy as Donkey in *Shrek*), animated movies are nonetheless susceptible to the minority archetypes and overarching patterns of minority marginalization. Yet, the practice of transferring human racial patterns onto an animated screen is not a new concept. Did you know that the jive-talking, jazz-singing black crows in Disney's 1941 cartoon classic *Dumbo* were knowingly used to represent Black people?[21] (Get it? *Jim Crow...*)

Since animation, by its very nature, requires a great deal of planning and foresight, *everything* onscreen is consciously created. This means that minority participation in animated movies is often an even more calculated decision than live-action movies. Any animated movie finalized for sale on the open market is the result of purposed and concerted efforts from a dedicated team of adults, and should not be hurriedly disregarded as mere child's play.

For instance, take **Sinbad: Legend of the Seven Seas,** which features a Black character named Kale. Although voiced by Black actor Dennis Haysbert, the muscle-bound Kale appears bare-chested in every scene (including snowy conditions). Similarly, Disney's **Lilo & Stitch** features the voice of Black actor Ving Rhames as the hulking welfare officer, Cobra Bubbles. Disney's **Brother Bear** utilizes Black actor Michael Clarke Duncan's voice for the larger-than-life bear character named Tug. So what's in an animated image you ask?

LIGHTS! CAMERA! INTERACTION!

In *Star Wars I: The Phantom Menace*, although there were several "diverse" animated characters, director George Lucas drew criticism for the character Watto, "the blue-skinned Toydarian who owns Anakin, claiming the character's nose, accent, and greedy nature reflect caricatures traditionally associated with Jews and Arabs."[1m]

Some critics also felt that characters Nute Gunray and Rune Haako of the nefarious Trade Federation similarly incorporated offensive Asian caricatures.

However, there was no animated character more embroiled in controversy than Jar Jar Binks, who became indebted for life (uh, slave?) to Qui-Gon Jinn (Liam Neeson), bumbles clumsily about, and speaks in a broken dialect with lines such as, "That's why you no liking us meesuh thinks." Black actor Ahmed Best provided the voice.

Check out *Star Wars I: The Phantom Menace* and tell us what you think!

Each of these animated characters are in supporting roles and their identities are largely defined by their imposing physical presence. All three of these characters are voiced by Black actors. Given the paucity of other Black characters and voices in **Sinbad, Lilo & Stitch** and **Brother Bear**, the similarities surrounding these three roles only heighten the subtle pattern that noted Black film historian Donald Bogle would term as the "Black Buck" (which fits within the Physical Wonder archetype classification; see *Chapter 8: Physical Wonder*). The significance of the Black Buck character pattern is that it was freely employed in Hollywood's earlier days (before the prevalence of political correctness) and many dark-skinned Black men were typecast as rude, raving and ravishing physical brutes with scant intellectual capabilities. *While these more recent iterations are less patently offensive than their more flagrantly disparaging predecessors, these "modern" animated images still share many of the same characteristics deemed offensive in past renditions.* Whether appearing "overtly" as a minority in a human form or "ambiguously" in creature form, portrayals of animated minority characters (or the use of minority voices behind these characters) illustrate that Hollywood's formulaic conventions about race nonetheless persist. Far from being a relic of the past, consider how all of the Black Buck/Physical Wonder examples cited in the prior paragraph occurred many generations later in 2002!

The majority of mainstream animated movies are either oriented around White characters or feature characters voiced primarily by Whites, even though the characters themselves may be "raceless" (e.g., **Secret Life of Pets, Monsters University, Finding Dory, Cars 3**, etc.). Animated movies often marginalize minority characters, especially since the frequent use of non-human characters frees Hollywood from the pressures of having to *visually* represent diversity like they do in live-action movies. A vivid example of this marginalized minority presence (as contrasted against White depictions onscreen) comes from the blockbuster animated series **Shrek**. Many will be quick to point out that Black actor Eddie Murphy is one of the top-billed stars and has a significant role in this movie. However, further analysis reveals that not only is he the literal sidekick to the White, er, green ogre lead voiced by Mike Myers, but that his character name – *Donkey* – is merely just a descriptive term for the animal he voices! With a name like Donkey, how much can – or more to the point – how much *should* we expect from such a character? Murphy merely supplies the voice *offscreen* that characterizes Donkey's antics *onscreen*, but Murphy's minority status – despite his status as an A-list actor – causes him to be marginalized. Given Donkey's large bucked

> **TOTAL ANECDOTAL**
> Did you know that it took five years to film the children's movie **Wallace & Gromit in The Curse of the Were-Rabbit**? Since the characters were clay animation figures, the crew only captured enough footage for three seconds worth of footage every day! These painstaking efforts only underscore the amount of premeditated, conscious planning involved in creating a movie for a mainstream audience.[1n]

teeth, his excessively loud voice, and his exaggerated mannerisms, Murphy's character is literally and figuratively the movie's *jackass*.[22]

These examples draw us to the conclusion that minority marginalization is not just limited to "real" humans on movie screens. Racial hierarchy is also communicated through the rank, order and importance of the human voices behind "raceless" animated characters. Finding the archetypal structure within a consciously created medium such as animation suggests that Hollywood's attitude towards race may be a bit more sketchy than previously believed.

INDEPENDENT FILMS

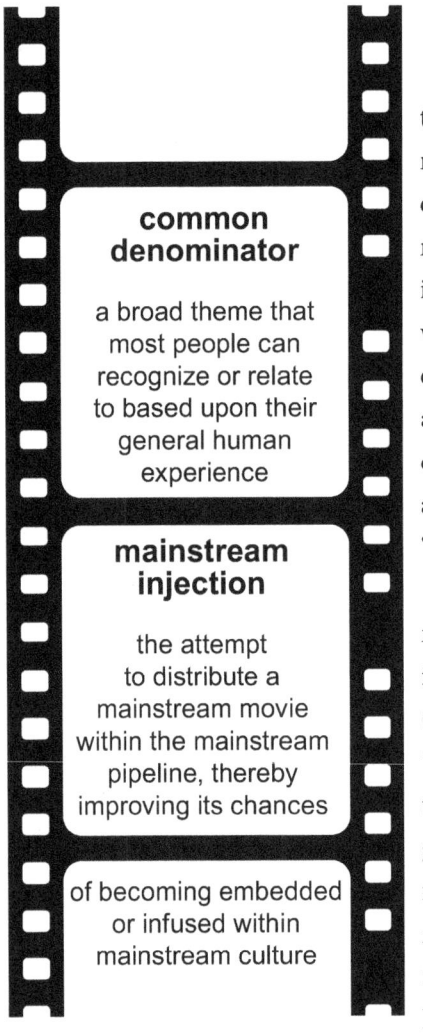

common denominator

a broad theme that most people can recognize or relate to based upon their general human experience

mainstream injection

the attempt to distribute a mainstream movie within the mainstream pipeline, thereby improving its chances of becoming embedded or infused within mainstream culture

Mainstream movies are typically studio-driven projects because they have the resources to invest in features commonly taken for granted in mainstream movies (e.g., A-list actors, computer graphics, explosions, etc.). In order to serve the greatest number of people equally, such movie productions must be distilled down to a **common denominator**. Generally speaking, independent movies that are not intended for **mainstream injection**, or widespread dissemination, are liberated to explore themes and issues outside of the familiar patterns of mainstream entertainment. Independent films are freer to manipulate the traditional storytelling patterns of introduction, conflict and resolution. While some independent movies attain mainstream acceptance, they rarely have enough marketing muscle to become mainstream "independently."

We will only analyze independent films if and when they become mainstream. For instance, there are scores of movies that start off as smaller, independent releases and then subsequently acquire mainstream status (e.g., ***Bend It Like Beckham***, ***The Blair Witch Project***, ***Lost in Translation***, ***The Passion of the Christ***, etc.). Once this mainstream transition occurs, then the "independent" movie grows in its ability to affect and influence the greatest possible audience. We focus on mainstream movies because of their formulaic nature and widespread influence. Most mainstream movies are more formulaic than independent films, because they *have to be* formulaic in order to reach a broader audience. In contrast, many independent films have more targeted audiences in mind and are not governed by the same economic pressures that plague mainstream movies. Although independent filmmakers are also prone to utilize traditional and formulaic representations of minorities, their increased "artistic freedom" often accounts for alternative imagery that challenges mainstream conventions. However, just because an independent film challenges *mainstream* conventions does not mean that it challenges *minority* conventions.

FOREIGN FILMS

We acknowledge that many members of the American mainstream audience enjoy foreign films. However, similar to independent releases, our standard classification of mainstream movie does not automatically apply to foreign releases unless these movies successfully cross over into the mainstream pipeline here in America.

MAINSTREAM'S UNIVERSAL APPEAL

Since successful mainstream movies enjoy such high levels of international distribution, their worldwide exposure places a higher premium on the quality of the racial images that they contain. Foreign impressions of America are undoubtedly influenced by mainstream movie images, especially when so few members of international audiences have the opportunity to visit America for themselves. For millions of people around the globe, mainstream Hollywood movies are more than just a source of entertainment; they "open the window to the world about America,"²³ a window through which to learn about American life and culture.

The most successful movies abroad are typically the most formulaic movies. If not initially released on a worldwide scale, mainstream movies that eventually perform well abroad are those that usually perform well within the United States market first, having employed the six mainstream movie factors crucial to the movie's widespread distribution and acceptance. Consequently, since many major studios freely employ minority archetypes as part of their successful formula, the movies that are most formulaic and most likely to feature images of marginalized minority characters are those movies that receive significant exposure abroad.

Many minority actors encounter difficulty landing leading roles in mainstream movies partly because American studio executives do not wish to jeopardize losing members of the greatest possible audience – whether domestically or abroad. The reluctance of studio executives to widely market movies featuring minority characters in the same "universal" manner that they promote White-dominated movies indicates that race plays a stronger role in the movie-making process than perhaps what is publicly discussed.

Movies have become so expensive to market and distribute that an enterprising studio will seek assurance beforehand that it can recoup its money

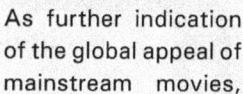

TOTAL ANECDOTAL

As further indication of the global appeal of mainstream movies, Hollywood's massive box office take practically doubles in foreign markets. According to **Motion Picture Association of America** (MPAA) President Dan Glickman: "Our movies earned $8 billion in the domestic market [in 2005], but $15 billion in the international market."¹ᵒ

According to *The Hollywood Reporter* article "International Markets Have Long Been Crucial to Film Biz," over 83% of the top movies that made over $100 million in the overseas box office exceeded their domestic revenues in 2004.¹ᵖ

In fact, many a Hollywood movie has performed modestly or poorly domestically, only to make double or triple of its domestic take abroad. For instance, the 2016 release *X-Men: Apocalypse* "only" made $155M domestically — arguably a total that is difficult to label a disappointment in normal-land, but in Hollywood-land, it was indeed disappointing seeing how the budget was estimated to be $178M, which means the movie lost money. However, the box office take overseas came in nicely at $388M, which was more than what the previous two *X-Men* films made in American box offices combined!¹ᑫ

Un/Fortunately, this total box office haul all but ensures yet another sequel is ever in play...

> **greenlight**
>
> process whereby an idea for a movie project receives authorization for filming by a major movie studio, matched with financial backing

> **faux presence**
>
> whereby the marketing campaign misleadingly suggests that a minority character has a more prominent role (or more screen time) than actually depicted

from the increasingly important international audience. For this reason, a minority-themed movie with a low-profile cast may encounter additional difficulty getting **greenlighted** in the first place.²⁴ The overseas market is vitally important, since international sales will often outperform domestic sales two or three times over, either increasing the margin for a successful film, or salvaging a movie that would otherwise be considered a financial failure domestically.²⁵ Movies with minority protagonists, such as ***Drumline, Soul Food, How Stella Got Her Groove Back,*** and ***Two Can Play That Game***, all grossed less than $2 million overseas. However, they were released only in Britain, the Caribbean, and a handful of Latin American countries, steeply diminishing any chances for large international box office receipts.

Most studios do not push minority-themed movies abroad because they argue that large markets like Germany and Japan do not have large African or Caribbean populations. Such an argument contradicts Hollywood's strategy to penetrate and even dominate foreign markets that contain few White persons, such as China and India. Further, failing to contest this rationale suggests the studios perpetuate a self-fulfilling prophecy of diminished returns for minority-themed movies. Since the studios *believe* these movies will not perform well at the box office, these movies end up with smaller budgets, which ultimately truncates the number of their "mainstream" factors and resulting financial revenue. Poor or tepid box office returns thereby "prove" Hollywood's belief that these movies will not sell abroad.

Many mainstream movies featuring predominantly White casts are domestically and internationally marketed as "universal films," meaning that they are appropriate for all audiences or all particular members of a sub-market (e.g., women, teens, etc.). Conversely, movies featuring predominantly minority casts are usually marketed *domestically* towards minorities only, which suggests that those stories are somehow not as universally appealing. This targeted "minority marketing" is particularly evident with dramas centered around minority characters, although somewhat less so with comedies and action adventures. Comedies and action adventure stories tend to retain more of a universal appeal since there is less "work" required of the viewer to identify personally with the central characters in order to appreciate the story's development. This emotional distancing contrasts with the intimate or "personal" connection that must take place between the audience and the characters in a drama or a "serious" romance.

The **faux presence** of minorities in many mainstream movies provides a more favorable picture of diversity and inclusion than what is actually the case. Under the "you-can-have-your-cake-and-eat-it-too" philosophy, Hollywood studios often deliberately pander to minority audiences by highlighting certain racial imagery during the marketing of a movie. For instance, trailers for the movie **Pearl Harbor** intimated that Black actor Cuba Gooding, Jr., played a much larger role in the movie than he actually did.[26] Such dual marketing approaches also reinforce marginalization of minority actors, for if they occupied significant roles, then they most likely would be prominently featured in the original trailer.

Movie studios, in efforts to maximize their profits, promote movies containing themes and characters with which they believe foreign audiences will readily connect. Consequently, concerns that the experiences of minorities in America are not representative enough of the American experience, or are not "universal" enough in their aesthetic appeal, dampens the incentive for the studios to create movies with largely minority casts. Ultimately, a circular logic surfaces whereby few studios are willing to invest into the full marketing potential of mainstream movies that prominently feature minority actors, and as a result Hollywood continues to doubt that movies starring predominately minority characters are internationally (and domestically) lucrative.

Many people the world over love American mainstream movies, partly because their formulaic approach breeds familiarity and comfort. The minority imagery in these movies falls within familiar and formulaic character patterns. These minority character patterns, or archetypes, both reflect and reinforce messages of racial imbalance structured upon a racial hierarchy, with minorities on the outside, marginalized from any central activity. So the question is, in analyzing Hollywood's complete body of work, what messages about race are communicated by minority images, if and when they appear?

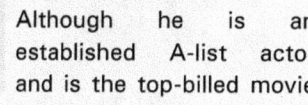

WHAT DO YOU THINK?
Although he is an established A-list actor and is the top-billed movie star in the thriller **Collateral**, Tom Cruise allowed the movie studio DreamWorks SKG to drop his face from some Collateral posters. Cruise granted the studio permission to do so only in some select urban areas as part of a promotional strategy to better highlight Black co-star Jamie Foxx' involvement in the movie during the summer of 2004.[1r]

If studio executives plan to show the same movie that "universally" appeals to both urban and general audiences alike, then why deliberately split the marketing campaign? How is the movie studio using race to sell its product? Are the movie studio's actions an implicit acknowledgment of the notion that if urban audiences do not see a character that they can "identify" with, that they are not going to patronize it? If so, is this marketing approach unique to urban audiences or does it work in reverse for general, majority-white, mainstream audiences?

Additionally, does this marketing strategy suggest a power imbalance wherein Cruise effectively controls the amount of exposure for Foxx? If so, can you think of an example of a minority actor controlling a White actor's image in the same manner? ***Further still, have you heard of a minority actor controlling their own image this way?***

CHAPTER 1: WHAT IS A MAINSTREAM MOVIE?

CHAPTER 2:
THE CAST OF CARICATURES

 *I made more than 30 movies, most of them commercial action films: good guy, got a problem, learning martial arts, come back, revenge, kill the bad guy. Lot of that. I want to find movies to make that are different.*

Jet Li, actor[1]

CHAPTER 2:
THE CAST OF CARICATURES

We will study Hollywood's minority archetypes in terms of **Hollywood's Racial Makeup**, the five primary racial classifications that Hollywood consistently provides us viewers through its movies: Asian, Black, Latino, White and Other.[2] Please note that "Other" is not an official racial categorization inasmuch as it is a catchall term that accounts for Hollywood's sheer dearth of Native Americans, Middle Easterners and "other" ethnic groups that are rarely cast in mainstream movies (e.g., Asian ethnic groups that are not Chinese, Japanese or Korean). Thus, characters placed within the Other category typically are literally (and figuratively) depicted as drastically different, foreign or simply as something "other" than the mainstream status quo.

FOR HUE? FOR WHAT?

In analyzing race in mainstream movies, it is critical to understand that race and ethnicity are not synonymous concepts. We define **race** as a general group affiliation based largely upon *tangibly observable* characteristics or physical constructs, such as skin color or hair type. We define **ethnicity** as a specific group affiliation based upon particular *cultural* ties, speech patterns or mannerisms. In essence, race is a broad categorization, whereas ethnic classifications are more specific in nature, and multiple ethnicities can be part of a larger racial grouping.

For instance, English, French, Italian and German are all examples of *ethnic* classifications under the White *racial* category. Many social scientists increasingly consider race as a sociological construct rather than a biological fact. Nevertheless, in the world of mainstream movies, these constructs are very real. Movie studios in Hollywood routinely use racial constructs to communicate messages, tell stories and help sell movies. Racial caricatures and clichés are just two methods available by which information is communicated

---

Hollywood's Racial Makeup

refers to the racial categories most consistently portrayed by Hollywood onscreen: Asian, Black, Latino, Other and White

race

general group affiliation based upon physically observable characteristics or physical constructs, such as skin color or hair type

ethnicity

specific group affiliation based upon particular cultural ties, often related to a shared country of origin

stereotype

a negative classification based upon specific conduct or characteristics ascribed to a particular racial group

CUT!

Wasn't **Memoirs of a Geisha** *a sign of progress? Wasn't that a mainstream movie featuring primarily Asian actors?* With respect to a well-financed mainstream movie featuring primarily Asian characters and actors, this is definitely a landmark movie.

The movie, budgeted at $85 million, grossed $57 million at the box office. While certainly notable that a movie of this profile and expense was made, it is also sobering to see how it sparked controversy – possibly out of racial insensitivity – over the decision to use Chinese actors to play Japanese characters.[2a]

Not only was the movie not set in the United States (i.e., depicting Asian actors as part and parcel of American mainstream society), but the movie was a financial failure since it did not break even at the box office.

Lastly, note that this movie is a spinoff from a best-selling book, not an original screenplay. The studio executives likely felt that the "risk" of a mainstream drama with an Asian-led cast would be offset by the "built-in" audience familiar with the book.

simply and quickly. For example, a Black character with an oversized winter coat, baggy pants, gold chains and a baseball hat on backwards is presumed to be "from the 'hood," eliminating the need to use dialogue or significant screen time to establish this idea. Many directors choose imagery that they believe will assist the audience in quickly identifying characters and their tendencies, even if it requires using race as a visible clue itself.

RACIAL MAKEUP, PLEASE

The following discussion teases out a few more details about Hollywood's Racial Makeup, or the five primary racial categories most consistently employed in mainstream movies. We readily acknowledge that more than five "categories" exist in Hollywood. However, in working with the material that Hollywood has provided us to date, we extrapolated the most common and consistent racial representations into five overarching categories for quick reference and further study. We now explain each category in turn.

ASIAN

"Asian" is a widely used racial classification. Here, the use of the word Asian primarily refers to Chinese, Japanese and Korean characters and actors. Unfortunately, very few mainstream movies overtly make ethnic distinctions (e.g., Japanese vs. Korean vs. Indian vs. Indonesian) within this racial category.[3] Given the small number of mainstream movie parts afforded to Asian actors, their limited appearances often register as **stereotypes**, or the scene *requires* the use of Asian characters.

From Charlie Chan to Bruce Lee, Asian stereotypes have ranged from physical comedy to hardcore martial artists. Rarely do we see an Asian character with a complex and developed role in a mainstream movie. Virtually all of the better-known Asian male leads presently headline martial arts movies. Most Asian actresses either fulfill sexualized roles, or serve as love interests for White males.

A **racial requirement** occurs where a minority actor fulfills a specific role, that – generally speaking – cannot be played by a person of any other race. Take an example from ***Inspector Gadget***, which lists a character in the credits by the name of "Running Japanese Tourist."[4] Here, being Japanese is an obvious racial requirement for this stereotypical role. Additional examples include characters like "Heavy Black Woman" (Sharon Wilkins) from ***Bad Boys II***, "Samoan Boyfriend" in ***Guess Who***

(Nicholaus Iamaleava) and "Mexican Janitor" (Jesus Perez) in *The Day After Tomorrow*. Movies such as *The Last Samurai* or *Pearl Harbor* are also manifestations of the racial requirement where the setting requires Asian characters. These movies could not have been made without Asian actors, even though the vast majority of those depicted were not prominently featured (although Whites have a history of playing non-White characters).

To demonstrate the overall scarcity with which Asians appear in mainstream movies, consider a study of the "Top 250 Films of 2002" that found that the majority of female characters in mainstream movies were White (73%), followed by Black (15%), Latino (4%), Asian (3%), and other worldly characters (3%) in 2002. This means that moviegoers were just as likely to see an Asian female as they were to see someone or something from another planet![5]

racial requirement

where a minority actor fulfills a specific role, often stereotypical in nature, that is not deemed to be a universal character playable by a person of any other race, let alone a White actor

BLACK

The Black image in cinema has endured a long and arduous history. Black imagery has ranged from *The Jazz Singer*, Hollywood's first talking picture released in the late 1920s featuring a White performer in blackface, to blaxploitation movies in the 1970s, where Blacks represented themselves in stereotypical roles.

Traditionally, Black images were either replete with stereotypes or irrelevant to the overall storyline. Black actors, especially when sharing the screen with White actors, were routinely relegated to unflattering and disparaging roles. This negative history spawns the common "the Black guy got killed first" refrain within the Black community, which still receives fuel from movies such as *Scream 2* (Jada Pinkett Smith and Omar Epps are disposed of in the opening scene), *Crimson Tide* (the Black cook is the first person to die onboard the submarine, *before combat is even initiated*), and *Kill Bill: Vol. 1* (Vivica Fox's character is violently impaled in front of her daughter

WHAT DO YOU THINK?

There have been recent attempts in Hollywood to feature Black characters as protagonists in mainstream movies. However, a closer look reveals that such attempts have come where the Black actor or director contributed funding either personally or through their production company. Following the name of each Black actor/director is the name of the production company that they themselves own:

Actor/Director	Production Company
Will Smith	Overbrook Entertainment
	MOVIE: I, Robot; Hitch
Denzel Washington	Muddy Lane Entertainment
	MOVIE: Antwone Fisher
Wesley Snipes	Amen Ra Films
	MOVIE: Blade
Ice Cube	Cube Vision
	MOVIE: Friday; Are We There Yet?
Queen Latifah	Flavor Unit Entertainment
	MOVIE: The Cookout; Beauty Shop
Spike Lee	40 Acres & Mule Filmworks
	MOVIE: Malcolm X; Inside Man
Tyler Perry	The Tyler Perry Company, Inc.
	MOVIE: Diary of a Mad Black Woman
Laurence Fishburne	Cinema Gypsy
	MOVIE: Akeelah and the Bee

Without the ability to finance their own opportunities, what are the chances of these movies being greenlighted at major studios? Does the rise of Black production lessen the need for major studios to produce movies with Black characters? What responsibility (if any) do movie studios have to produce movies reflecting the experiences and lifestyles of the audience that pays to see them?

CHAPTER 2: THE CAST OF CARICATURES

at the movie's beginning). With the last example, note how the "early exit" of Black characters also pertains to females and not just the Black "guy."

"BLACK MOVIES"

Since the mid-1990s, there have been a spate of movies providing new alternatives to traditionally stereotypical Black characters. Such alternative movies include dramas like ***The Best Man***, ***Waiting to Exhale***, ***The Wood***, ***The Brothers***, ***Kingdom Come*** and ***The Preacher's Wife***, as well as romantic comedies like ***Brown Sugar***, ***How Stella Got Her Groove Back***, ***Love & Basketball***, ***Love Jones***, and ***Two Can Play That Game***. Although many of these movies contain universal themes, they are commonly branded as "Black movies" by Hollywood insiders, mass media and moviegoers because of their predominately Black casts.

These movies, while exhibiting some of the characteristics associated with mainstream movies, are not marketed widely to all general audiences. When a movie is tagged with the "Black movie" moniker, the presumption implicit in that label is that the movie is not acceptable for general consumption. The tacit message is that the movie will contain images and themes *only relevant* to Blacks, as opposed to containing universal themes that are *merely depicted* by Blacks. Not surprisingly, many of these movies do not fare well at the box office (at least in comparison to mainstream movies) because the public *at large* does not patronize them, or they suffer from limited releases and limited marketing budgets. Until these movies are viewed as commercially viable – both nationally and abroad – it is unlikely that Hollywood will increase its efforts to make these movies more "universally" appealing.

BETTING ON BLACK (ARTISTS)

Oftentimes when casting a Black character in a mainstream movie, studios will lean on the talents of an established Black music artist or comedian. This reduces their overall risk since many of these rappers and comedians have already demonstrated that their name can generate mainstream attention and capital. These Black

> **WHAT DO YOU THINK?**
> *Knowing that hip hop and rap music have at times represented alternative viewpoints than mainstream expression, what do you make of the following rap lyrics?*
>
> "BURN HOLLYWOOD BURN," Public Enemy, 1992[2b]
>
> [BIG DADDY KANE]
> As I walk the streets of Hollywood Boulevard
> Thinkin' how hard it was to those that starred
> In the movies portrayin' the roles
> Of butlers and maids, slaves and hoes
> Many intelligent Black men seemed to look uncivilized
> When on the screen
> Like I guess I figure you to play some jigaboo
> On the plantation, what else can a nigger do
> And Black women in this profession
> As for playin' a lawyer, out of the question
> For what they play Aunt Jemima is the perfect term
> Even if now she got a perm
> So let's make our own movies like Spike Lee
> 'Cause the roles being offered don't strike me
> There's nothing that the Black man could use to earn
> Burn, Hollywood, burn
>
> "WHY?" Jadakiss, 2004[2c]
>
> Why Halle have to let a White man pop her to get a Oscar?
> Why Denzel have to be crooked before he took it?

celebrities already have a built-in, financially proven audience that can help the studio recoup its initial investment, and draw an audience that might not have otherwise patronized a certain movie (e.g., Erykah Badu and Biz Markie in *Cider House Rules*). Unfortunately, Hollywood's increasing reliance on Black rappers and comedians has come at the expense of "classically trained" Black actors, who already face a disadvantage landing parts in mainstream movies. Consider the career of actor-turned-rapper-turned-actor Mos Def. A classically trained actor, Mos Def did not gain any traction in Hollywood until *after* he achieved commercial success as a rap artist.

Take a look at a sample listing of Black musicians (notably rappers) who have crossed over to the big screen:

> Will Smith (*Independence Day*; *Men in Black*; *I, Robot*; *Hitch*)
> Ice Cube (*xXx: State of the Union*, *Barbershop*, *Are We There Yet?*)
> Queen Latifah (*Bringing Down the House*, *Chicago*, *Taxi*)
> Beyoncé (*Austin Powers: Goldmember*; *The Pink Panther*)
> LL Cool J (*Deep Blue*, *The Last Holiday*, *S.W.A.T.*)
> Mos Def [AKA Yasiin Bey] (*The Italian Job*, *Monster's Ball*, *16 Blocks*)
> Whitney Houston (*The Bodyguard*, *The Preacher's Wife*)
> Snoop Dogg (*Starsky & Hutch*, *Training Day*)
> DMX (*Romeo Must Die*, *Cradle 2 the Grave*)
> 50 Cent (*Get Rich or Die Tryin'*, *Home of the Brave*)
> Ludacris (*Crash*, *Hustle & Flow*, *Fast & Furious* franchise)
> André Benjamin (*Be Cool*, *Four Brothers*, *Idlewild*)
> Alicia Keys (*Smokin' Aces*)
> Nelly (*The Longest Yard*)
> Lil' Kim (*You Got Served*)
> Tyrese (*Fast & Furious* franchise)

Some Black comedians include:

> Eddie Murphy (*The Nutty Professor*, *Shrek* series)
> Chris Rock (*Madagascar* series, *Bad Company*, *Lethal Weapon 4*)
> Chris Tucker (*Rush Hour*, *The Fifth Element*, *Friday*)
> Martin Lawrence (*Big Momma's House* series, *Bad Boys* series)
> Cedric the Entertainer (*The Honeymooners*; *Be Cool*)
> Steve Harvey (*Johnson Family Vacation*)
> Eddie Griffin (*Deuce Bigalow*, *Male Gigolo*; *Armageddon*) and
> Mo'Nique (*Soul Plane*, *Precious*) [won Academy Award]

CUT!
Why wouldn't you celebrate the fact that more Blacks are receiving breakthrough roles than ever before, led partly by the hip-hop generation? While this trend is undoubtedly positive for some hip-hop stars trying to advance their careers, it unfortunately undercuts the honest efforts of "pure" actors, both those that are established and those who are still trying to break into Hollywood. This also illustrates Hollywood's unwillingness to develop young minority talent.

"When you look at the appeal of someone like Ice Cube, it's across all borders," says Rory Bruer, distribution chief for Sony Pictures, which distributed *Are We There Yet*. "Kids follow him from music to video to movies."[2d]

LIGHTS! CAMERA! INTERACTION!
Find out how many mainstream movies starring Black actors are released around February (Black History Month) in comparison to the rest of the year. Be sure to contrast this with the number of releases during the summer months – traditionally one of the best periods for box office blockbusters.

CHAPTER 2: THE CAST OF CARICATURES

Although at first glance it may appear that movie studios are being progressive by employing cutting-edge Black musicians (who can sell ancillary products like movie soundtracks) and comedians, this decision is actually based on an effort to lessen the risk and pressure of developing new Black talent. From the perspective of the movie studio, there is no need to make the expensive investment to "discover" new Black *commercially bankable* talent when they can rely on established Black talent that is already relatively established. The resulting effect is that very few "unproven" Black actors ever receive the chance to see how much bankability they have. Recall how many small and critically panned movies A-list actors like Tom Cruise or Tom Hanks had to make before they became the stars we know today. Given the larger amount of screen roles available to White actors, young White actors have more opportunities to "break into" the business.

LATINO

Despite being the largest minority population in the United States, major roles for Latino actors are still hard to come by. There are certainly some well-known Latino actors floating around Hollywood, even if their original names are not. Historically, some Latinos were pressured by studio executives to change their names as they became stars. Among those who complied with Hollywood's request was Rita Hayworth (born as Margarita Carmen Cansino), who also dyed her hair and underwent electrolysis to look more "White." Others refused, including Ricardo Montalban, who declined to change his name to "Ricky Martin." But as the stereotype of Latinos as "dark, dumb and violent" increased, so did threats of boycotts of U.S. films by Latin-American countries. Even President Woodrow Wilson implored Hollywood to "please be a little kinder to the Mexicans" after many Latin American countries banned films that portrayed disparaging images of Latinos.[6]

The precarious nature of Latino actors obtaining work in Hollywood as *distinctly Latino characters* is encapsulated in this line in the "Latinos in Entertainment" article from *The Hollywood Reporter*: "Latino directors sometimes have to de-Latinize their movies in order to appeal to bankable stars and, thus, the studios." In the same article, Jessy Terrero, a Dominican American director, complains that MGM studios cut three male Latino roles that he created for **Soul Plane**: "It's not easy. Everybody wants a Latin project. But when you pitch it to the studio, they wonder who they're going to put on the poster . . . [A]s much as everyone wants to tap into the Latin market, nobody wants to take that chance."[7]

TOTAL ANECDOTAL

Latinos spent $1.5 billion at the box office in 2002 according to MPAA, a number expected to double by 2012 according to Nielsen Cinema Audience Reports. In major markets such as Los Angeles and New York, Latinos make up 55% of opening weekend audiences.[2e]

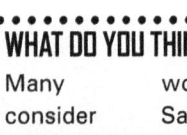

WHAT DO YOU THINK?

Many would consider Salma Hayek as a Latina actress that has "made it," and that her success would insulate her from any race-related problems. Yet, she states that she still has to "persuade people that my accent won't be a problem, but is an asset. Everyone's afraid of doing something a bit risky. Everyone wants a $200 million hit and anything they think might get in the way of that kind of success is considered a liability." Hayek further adds, "at the beginning [my career] was hard. People were like, 'who is this Mexican jumping bean?'"[2f]

38 YOU MEAN, THERE'S RACE IN MY MOVIE?

OTHER

"Other" refers to the racial category of those minorities that do not fit within one of the previously described categories, but whose employment in Hollywood is so infrequent, that it is difficult to substantially maintain the construction of an individually separate category. Many actors of Native American, East Indian, and Middle Eastern descent appear in this classification. We also reserve this classification for those characters (and actors) that occupy racially ambiguous roles onscreen. Yet in this text, we focus primarily on Native Americans and Middle Easterners, as they constitute a major proportion of such minor appearances.

NATIVE AMERICAN

Native Americans have experienced a tumultuous history on the silver screen. In many of the early Westerns, Native Americans were depicted as bloodthirsty, bow-and-arrow wielding savages that would terrorize (White) "Americans" with impunity. This "traditional" image has since become less politically correct, although Native Americans have yet to fully escape the looming shadow of early stereotypical portrayals (e.g., see the savage Native American "witch doctor" in *The Missing*, released in 2002). Even rarer is the depiction of a Native American that does not dispense sage advice in broken English, as seen in the Disney animated movie **Pocahontas**, which also contains a descriptive song entitled "Savages."[8] Although the historical "Injun-on-the-warpath" depiction has been all but discarded of late, the list of contemporary Hollywood mainstream movies that center around contemporary Native American life (outside of any southwestern or forest setting) is nonetheless a very short list.

Although no Native American has won an Academy Award for Best Actor/Actress or Best Supporting Actor/Actress, Native Americans were nonetheless indirectly part of a very controversial moment within Oscar history. In 1973, when Marlon Brando won the Best Actor Academy Award for his role in *The Godfather*, he sent Sacheen Littlefeather (also known as Maria Cruz) to accept the award on his behalf. Littlefeather was an actress pretending to be an Apache and stated that Brando would not personally appear due to poor treatment of Native Americans by Hollywood. Littlefeather's speech was not well received by the attending audience.[9]

> **WHAT DO YOU THINK?**
> Further supporting the notion that minority characters are showcased as something "Other" than conventional mainstream, consider *Night at the Museum*, featuring Larry Daley (Ben Stiller) as an exasperated museum guard who must contend with exhibits that come to life at night.
>
> In addition to taming a rather attitudinal T-Rex fossil, and an assortment of warring wax figurines, Attila the Hun (Patrick Gallagher) serves as a chief nemesis of Daley. As a historical figure, Attila the Hun's racial heritage is often disputed, but he would likely be described as "Eurasian" in contemporary terms. Gallagher, who was born in Canada, was likely cast because of his racial "ambiguity" and "versatility" (e.g., he was once credited as "Hispanic Cop" in an episode of the television show Dark Angel).
>
> Regardless of Attila the Hun's true racial heritage, the movie clearly attempts to portray Attila the Hun as an "Other-worldly" minority character. He speaks in a patently indecipherable "foreign" tongue, a gibberish language which Gallagher "created" himself.[2g] Along with this unintelligible dialect, the movie cements Attila the Hun's minority status by surrounding him with several "distinctly" Asian henchmen:
>
> - HUN #1: Randy Lee
> - HUN #2: Darryl Quon
> - HUN #3: Gerald Wong
> - HUN #4: Paul Chih-Ping Cheng
>
> Additionally, Attila and his Huns are clad in exotic (and bulky) battle gear that serve to distance them from Daley's "normal" dress and heighten the contrast between "Other" and mainstream normalcy. The combination of the aforementioned factors place Attila the Hun squarely on the periphery as an "Other" character, and as such, the movie's creators proceeded to marginalize the minority character from mainstream conventions.

> **TOTAL ANECDOTAL**
> Did you know that Latin pop music star Ricky Martin has pledged to combat negative Middle Eastern images in the movies? Martin states, "I have been a victim of stereotypes. I come from Latin America and to some countries, we are considered 'losers,' drug traffickers, and that is not fair because that is generalizing."[2h]

MIDDLE EASTERN

Characters of Middle Eastern descent appear infrequently in mainstream movies. Middle Eastern characters commonly fulfill background roles, often for comedic effect or in foreign settings that warrant a racial requirement. An emphasis is usually placed on the character's "foreignness" – especially in movies set in America – often denoted by a heavy accent, which in many instances serves as comedic fodder. Ironically, while "foreignness" is emphasized, such characters in actuality reinforce the highly-valued Protestant work ethic emblematic of an ideal "American" melting pot tradition. Such American values of "hard work," thrift and independent enterprise are demonstrated through their consistent portrayal as store owners and cab drivers (e.g., **Crash** and **Bad Boys II** – incidentally, the convenience store clerks in these two movies are played by the same actor, Shaun Toub).

Animated features are not immune. Take the Disney movie **Aladdin** which, as an animated feature, played to massive audiences of children. The movie's opening song, "Arabian Nights," begins its depiction of Arab culture with a decidedly racist tone. The lyrics of the offending stanza state:[10]

> *Oh I come from a land-From a faraway place-Where the caravan camels roam.*
> *Where they cut off your ear-If they don't like your face. It's barbaric, but hey, it's home.*

Movies that feature an abundance of Middle Eastern characters often showcase leading actors that are not Middle Eastern. **Three Kings**, starring George Clooney, Mark Wahlberg and Ice Cube, is set in Iraq during the first Gulf War. The movie contains an array of Iraqi characters; some help the protagonists, others attempt to hinder them, but none of them are leading characters. Another noteworthy item from this item is the appearance of actor Cliff Curtis, who plays the role of an Iraqi named Amir Abdullah. This character has some of the most significant dialogue and screen time of any of the Iraqi characters. Nevertheless, Curtis is of Maori descent, the native ethnic group that first inhabited New Zealand. His racially "ambiguous" appearance has allowed him to portray a variety of racial/ethnic characters in mainstream movies, ranging from Middle Eastern (**The Insider**) to Latino (**Blow, Runaway Jury, Training Day**).

> **WHAT DO YOU THINK?**
>
> To illustrate the limited nature of mainstream opportunities available to minorities in Hollywood, let alone statistically small groups of minorities, consider the career trajectory of Indian actress Parminder Nagra and White actress Keira Knightley who co-starred in the 2002 international crossover, **Bend It Like Beckham**.
>
> Nagra, the central protagonist in **Bend It Like Beckham**, has since landed a recurring role on the television series ER. Knightley has since landed starring roles in mainstream movies like the **Pirates of the Caribbean** series, King Arthur and **Pride & Prejudice** (where she received a Best Actress Academy Award nomination). *What accounts for the difference in career trajectories? Is race a possible factor?*

WHITE

White characters represent the overwhelming majority of mainstream movie roles. The enveloping presence of White characters means that they constitute the "default" racial group through which most onscreen activity takes place. While minority characters highlight, juxtapose and contrast some aspect of the human experience, such experiences are typically seen and interpreted through White characters. Undoubtedly, minority characters are not the only ones depicted in unflattering roles. Many White characters have been portrayed as buffoons and villains. However, negative portrayals of White characters are typically balanced by the fact that the most developed **character arcs** belong to White characters.

Even though many White actors come from diverse ethnic backgrounds (e.g., Sean Connery is British, Nicole Kidman is Australian), the fact that they are cast and marketed as White characters is what is most important for our racial categorizations. This shared aesthetic allows those actors who play White characters the privilege of occupying a wider array of roles due to the large amount of **racial capital** available to them. This is a luxury that other racial groups do not have.

In view of the larger and more complex range of characters that Hollywood employs for White actors, White characters are generally "free" from the marginalizing effects that limit minority characters. If anything, many White characters routinely fulfill positive character patterns in mainstream movies. We explore some of these common White character patterns, or Prototypes, in *Chapter 10: White Balancing Act*.

> **character arc**
> the charting of the emotional or psychological change that occurs within a character as they progress through a story

> **racial capital**
> the amount of power (economic, political or social) ascribed collectively to a particular racial group

MINORITY REPORTS

To add more context to our current discussion about the frequency of racial groups in mainstream movies, we will now analyze some statistical data. Such data will further illuminate to what degree race is literally in your movies. As of 2002, White persons (not of Hispanic/Latino origin), accounted for 69.1% of the U.S. population.[11] This ratio is mirrored by the statistics profiling movie admissions according to race (see "Percentage of U.S. Movie Admissions/Population According to Race" chart on pg. 42).

According to *President Emeritus* Jack Valenti, the former head of the Motion Picture Association of America (MPAA), "[the] Hispanic population is the heaviest in moviegoing with a per capita viewing of 9.9 films per year and represents 15% of admissions."[12] He also noted that the Black population

> **TOTAL ANECDOTAL**
> The fully widespread presence of Whites in Hollywood is also evidenced through the occurrence of "paint-downs" in Hollywood. A paint down occurs when a White stunt double is made up in order to pass as the minority actor they are replacing.[2i]

viewed 7.6 films per capita the previous year and comprised 11% of admissions, while the White population saw 8.1 films per capita per year with 68% of admissions.[13] The correlation between population and movie admission statistics is illustrated in the following chart:

PERCENTAGE OF U.S. MOVIE ADMISSIONS/POPULATION ACCORDING TO RACE

	Native American	Asian/Other	Black	Latino	White
Movie Admissions, 2015 (1.32 Billion)	N/A (less than 6%)	9%	11%	23%	56%
U.S. Population, 2015 (318 Million)	1.5%	8%	12%	17%	62%

Source: U.S. Census, MPAA[2j]

In order to measure race within the movie industry, we pieced together data provided by the main movie industry trade unions within Hollywood for statistics they keep about their own members. Some data, while accurately reported, is nonetheless dated due to the union itself not having publicly provided recently updated information. The lack of race-related statistics communicates a distinct message about the priority Hollywood places on diversity. The unions are not necessarily transparent in their reporting, possibly due to the embarrassing nature of the paltry, and at times, dismal statistics. Nonetheless, the main service unions' voluntary attempts to collect racial data remains the best source for these statistics. Given their influence and importance to those who wish to work as actors, writers or directors, the main service unions are a good place to start our analysis of the racial make-up of Hollywood behind the scenes:

RACIAL REPRESENTATION IN HOLLYWOOD'S MAIN SERVICE UNIONS

RACE	U.S. Population, 2015	Screen Actors Guild, 2008	Directors Guild of America, 2014	Writers Guild of America, West, 2012
White	62%	72.5%	87.6%	91.2%
Black	12%	13.3%	13.4%	4%
Latino	17%	6.4%	for all	2.4%
Asian/Other	8%	3.8%	minorities	2.2%
Native American	1.5%	.3%	combined	.2%

Source: U.S. Census, SAG-AFTRA, DGA, WGA[2k]

SCREEN ACTORS GUILD

Most mainstream movies prominently feature White actors, which is borne out by the latest statistics available from the Screen Actors Guild-American Federation of Television and Radio Artists (SAG-AFTRA). SAG-AFTRA is the dominant national union for actors in major theatrical and television works, containing nearly 160,000 members.[14] As of 2008, Blacks accounted for 13.3% of all theatrical and television roles (excluding animation, which likely shows heavy White participation), Latinos accounted for 6.4%, Asian/Pacific Islanders accounted for 3.8%, and Native Americans a paltry .3% of all roles.[15] Overall, minority presence increased from 24.2% in 2002 to 27.5% for all theatrical and television roles in 2008.

In comparison to their percentage of the U.S. population, every minority group was under-represented across all theatrical and television roles in 2008. This means that 72.5% of the remaining roles went to Whites, which means that Whites were over-represented in relation to their percentage of the U.S. population (62% of U.S. population vs. 72.5% of SAG roles). It is understandable that if 62% of the country consists of non-Hispanic Whites, then many roles are going to be occupied by White actors. Yet, these numbers represent a marked *increase* for minority involvement overall in comparison to even more disparate ratios from years past. Whites thus landed acting roles at a three-to-one ratio in comparison to *all minority roles*, which means the ratio of Whites to each particular racial group is even higher.

The fact that Latinos actors are grossly underrepresented (6.4% of SAG roles vs. 17% of U.S. population in 2008) is especially troubling in light of their status as the fastest growing racial group in America. This is even more concerning when considering that Latinos account for the majority of residents in Los Angeles, the home of the entertainment industry! Black roles in 2008 were actually overrepresented, since they only accounted for 12% of the U.S. population, versus 13.3% of SAG roles. This 1.3% "overage" could be touted as an "encouraging sign" (along with the 50% surge for Native Americans, up from their .2% allotment in 2002). Despite this seemingly encouraging statistic, there are two main problems with touting these increases as significant signs of racial progress in Hollywood:

1) Quantity vs. Quality

The available statistics measure, in limited fashion, the existing quantity of minority roles, but according to SAG itself, such statistics only "track the quantity, not quality, of role."[16] If the increasing amount of roles mostly results in marginalized depictions of minority characters, then such

CUT!
Shouldn't Blacks be encouraged by the latest statistics since they were actually overrepresented in theatrical and television roles in relation to their percentage of the population? This statistical "progress" may be somewhat misleading. This figure only measures the quantity — not the quality — of the roles. Furthermore, the available statistics do not distinguish whether the Black actors were used in mainstream movies, independent movies or television roles. While the overall percentage of Black theatrical and television roles may have increased, there is not enough data to conclusively determine whether the percentage of Black mainstream movie roles actually increased.

roles may be more harmful than helpful, regardless of a statistical increase. By focusing exclusively on quantity, the ultimate substance of these roles is never fully questioned, even though this aspect is vitally important to the discussion of race in mainstream movies.

Closer inspection also reveals that when a significant number of Blacks *do appear*, they frequently appear in "Black movies." This means that minorities are likely to appear at an ever lower ratio in "mainstream" movies than what the available percentages suggest, especially when depicted in movies featuring predominately White characters. Nonetheless, Hollywood is quick to tout any statistical increase – no matter how small – as "progress" without a critical analysis of what criteria constitutes progress (See "Lights! Camera! Interaction!" pg. 46).

2) Recycling Diversity

Of those minorities featured in leading roles, Hollywood tends to recycle a select group of "proven" actors. This conservative trend obscures data about the true spread of minority participation in Hollywood. For example, ***Independence Day, Wild Wild West, Men in Black, Bad Boys II*** and ***I, Robot*** were all mainstream, commercially successful movies that grossed at least $100 million at the box office. All five movies also count separately under the category of "mainstream movies featuring at least one minority lead." It just so happens that they all share the same minority lead, Will Smith. This is no "fault" of Will Smith, yet compare the repeated use of A-lister Will Smith in major mainstream movies to the liberal casting of relatively unknown non-A-list Whites in prominent roles (e.g., ***Superman Returns, Batman Begins, Casino Royale).***

To illustrate the ubiquitous nature of White starring roles, consider the following list: ***War of the Worlds, Charlie and the Chocolate Factory, Batman Begins, Harry Potter and the Goblet of Fire***, and ***Wedding Crashers.*** Not only did all of these movies gross over $200 million at the box office, but they each showcase a different leading White actor, underscoring the point that diversity in Hollywood may not be as widespread as it appears, but rather illusorily represented by just a few minority actors.

LIGHTS! CAMERA! INTERACTION!

Make a list of minority A-list movie actors. Make sure that you screen out well-known B-list actors that enjoy merely a modicum of notoriety and recognition. A-list actors consistently star in movies, and occupy central roles in their movies. In contrast, B-list actors, while familiar, nonetheless occupy more peripheral roles. Specifically focus on A-list names that command instant recognition within mainstream media.

As an informal litmus test, go to your local supermarket check-out counter and ask yourself: how many times and how recently have you seen any of these minority actors on a magazine cover (tabloid or commercial) in contrast to mainstream A-list White talent?

Speaking of White talent in Hollywood, Charlie Kaufman and his imaginary brother were both nominated for Best Adapted Screenplay at the 2003 Academy Awards for ***Adaptation***.[21] Find out whether any minorities have ever been nominated for Best Adapted Screenplay as well. Is it possible that an imaginary White person has received more nominations than any real minority ever in the same category?!

Directors Guild of America

A director serves as the onset "author" of the movie, charged with communicating a broad vision to a variety of different players on a movie's production team. Above all, the director is under pressure to produce a profit-worthy product that is both on time and under budget. A director's perspective undoubtedly influences the images that moviegoers ultimately see on the big screen.

The Directors Guild of America (DGA), which has over 16,000 members, is the official guild representing directors in the movies, television and radio.[17] With respect to minority participation in 1996 and 1997, the two years before the DGA study, "DGA minority film directors went from 6.9% of total days worked in 1996 to 6.4%, and saw their actual days worked drop." Such a decline is particularly alarming because the total number of days worked by all DGA film directors increased, from 45,955 in 1996 to 48,659 in 1997.[18] The DGA's latest statistics are from 2014, representing the total films released by major studios directed by Caucasians or Minorities. Also note that in parsing out the total number of films minority directors worked, this statistic does not detail *the exact percentages of minority directors.*

For example, if all of the DGA directors worked for a total of 1,000 days, then Asian directors, by comprising 1.5% of the total directors, would have worked for a total of fifteen of those days. What this statistic does *not* reveal is whether there were fifteen *different* Asian directors working on fifteen different days, or whether there were only three Asian directors who worked all fifteen of the days. Suppose that, of these three directors, one Asian director worked a television sitcom, another directed a cable television movie, and the remaining director worked a mainstream movie. It is possible that the percentage of Asian directors directing *mainstream movies* is even smaller than the statistic initially suggests, further masking the lacking diversity for mainstream directors.

BUT IT'S JUST A MOVIE, RIGHT?

For an illustration of how many Native Americans are acutely aware of the dearth of their images within mainstream movies, see the article "Apaches Praise 'The Missing' for Accuracy."[2m] The article emphasizes the Apaches' appreciation of **The Missing** employing accurate language translations. A few scenes contain characters conversing in an authentic Apache dialect entitled Chiricahua.

The praise from Apache tribal members strongly suggest that this movie transcends the screen in its importance. Most of the movie's dialogue was in English. Yet, due to the relative absence of Native Americans within mainstream culture overall, the language (even if only a small quantity) adopts a larger political meaning that Native Americans do in fact matter.

Writers Guild of America

The Writers Guild of America, West (WGAW), complete with over 8,375 members (as of 2012), is the official union for writers within the movie industry west of the Mississippi.[19] The screenwriters are the individuals responsible for writing the screenplays that are ultimately interpreted by actors, directors and producers alike. Screenwriters are essential to Hollywood's movie-making process since they directly affect the images that moviegoers see, from choice of dialogue, to time and setting. Naturally, the personal perspectives of writers influence their use of racial imagery.

Older statistics available from the WGA show that from 1991 to 1997, minority employment in both television and feature film increased by 66%.[20] However, despite overall gains in employment for minority writers, White writers still accounted for more than 94% of all movie-writing jobs, down from 99% in 1982.[21] In spite of the recent growth of minority participation, the total percentage of minority writers (6%) still falls well-short of the previously mentioned population and movie attendance ratios.

In addition, some minority writers find that they are largely limited to working in a narrow range of minority-themed genres. Undoubtedly, race matters at the writing stages of a movie project. Still, writers often face dilemmas of having to "code" characters for race since the default standard for any character is White unless otherwise stated (e.g., Latino cop, Black judge). The "burden" of writing "quality" roles does not rest solely with minority writers. *All* writers must use this coding if they want a character of a specific race that is not White. The dilemma may be explained in the following manner: a Native American writer pens a screenplay about space travel taking for granted that the protagonist looks like her. However, if a studio executive reads the screenplay (typically in the absence of the writer), he will probably assume the protagonist is White. This means the writer must code the screenplay if she wants the protagonist to be Native American – be it through language or other cultural markers. However, in so doing, defining the character as Native American unwittingly suggests race "inherently" affects the character and/or character development.

LIGHTS! CAMERA! INTERACTION!

In skimming a newspaper and discovering a headline such as "Blacks, Latinos Make Movie Gains," it is conceivable that the reader may walk away from the newspaper with a more favorable impression than what reality suggests.

For instance, the aforementioned article reported that Blacks and Latinos experienced a 1 and 1.2 percent gain in acting roles from the year before respectively.[2n] While the headline is technically true, it obscures the fact that such a minimal increase may actually translate into an overall loss – not gain – for these minority groups in mainstream movies, especially when factoring in practical considerations such as the quality of a role and the quantity of television-only performers.

In analyzing the gains touted in the above paragraph, conduct your own research and tell us: How many mainstream movies released this year prominently or exclusively feature minority characters? Would you classify such representations as an increase or decrease from the year before? *Why or why not?*

The Industry Picture

The foregoing statistics demonstrate that the movie-making industry is dominated by Whites in the three vital areas of movie production (e.g., acting, writing, and directing). Further, these statistics do not factor in the plethora of employees that work "behind the scenes" as studio executives, makeup artists, set designers, etc., many of whom are White as well.[22] These trade unions should not be mistakenly singled out individually as promoting "anti-diversity" agendas, despite their disparate numbers. All three unions have documented efforts to increase diversity awareness, with SAG-AFTRA in particular sponsoring initiatives dating back for over three-quarters of a century.[23] However, in analyzing Hollywood as a collective entity, the available statistics cumulatively paint a picture of limited minority participation. These statistics do not incorporate other vital positions within the industry, such as production, financing and marketing.

Despite the growing number of a few highly-placed minority executives in Hollywood, many high-powered executives – who are used to working in racially isolated, homogenous communities – might find themselves more receptive to existing tried-and-true racial casting formulas in order to satisfy their "risk-averse" studio employers' objective for maximum profits. Furthermore, minority involvement does not automatically ensure fair and balanced images, or the absence of stereotypes and archetypes. Even minority-produced works can recreate many of the same patterns espoused by the mainstream. Unfortunately, some minority writers, directors and producers, perhaps overwhelmed by the seemingly irreversible status of familiar racial patterns, are led to believe that making movies containing racial stereotypes is the surest way to mainstream acceptance and financial success.

LIGHTS! CAMERA! INTERACTION!
Try finding specific, recent, accurate and reliable data or statistics about minority participation in Hollywood. As a starting point, we recommend surfing through the websites of the three main movie trade unions (SAG, DGA and WGA). How easy or difficult was your search? Log on and tell us what you find at *www.theracedoc.com!*

Now that we have taken an overarching look at race in the movie-making industry, we will proceed to explore the six minority archetypes over the course of the next few chapters. We have analyzed the *quantity* of minority roles in Hollywood, so we will take a closer look at the *quality* of minority imagery as we feed you, *the Protagonist* more clues to the thrilling question *"You Mean, There's RACE in My Movie?"* Regardless of the actual number of minority roles, the next Act will substantively illustrate how virtually any minority character you see in your movie will exhibit behaviors from at least one of six character patterns.

The Bottom Line #1: White Screens, Dark Theaters

Although Hollywood consistently produces lucrative mainstream movies designed to appeal universally to large, broad audiences of all races, it remains a White-dominated industry.

ACT TWO

ACT 2: Conflict & Climax

CHAPTER 3:
THE COLOR SCENE

 *I'd rather play a maid and make $700 a week than be a maid for $7.*

Hattie McDaniel, first minority to win an Oscar[1]

CHAPTER 3:
THE COLOR SCENE

We continue by looking at how diversity in Hollywood is reflected through racial imagery on the big screen. With the increasing acceptance of non-White characters and actors, Hollywood is more diverse now than it has ever been before. Moviegoers can point to a variety of big-name minority actors as proof that Hollywood has expanded its historically close-knit circle. Race, as a topic unto itself, is infrequently featured as a central theme in mainstream movies. When race *is* part of a movie's overall theme, it is usually in the form of indisputably obvious – if not downright anachronistic – discrimination (e.g., the overtly evil images of the murderous racists in ***A Time to Kill, Mississippi Burning, Rosewood***, etc.), or it is set against the backdrop of humor and parody (e.g., ***Get Hard, Bringing Down the House, White Chicks***, etc.).

Recognizing the full complexity of race presents a different challenge for Hollywood since it is less common for mainstream movies to incorporate or address more subtle and covert racial matters, which are more common than overt acts of discrimination in everyday society (see "Racism 2.0 on p.4). Presenting nuanced racism in a way that does not scare audience members away from the box office is precisely what made the Academy Award-winning movie ***Crash*** a heralded "breakthrough" in Hollywood. Yet, it is important to note that ***Crash*** is an unusual "indie-crossover." ***Crash*** was not a major studio production and had a modest $6.5 million budget, though it employed a fair number of well-known Hollywood talent. The movie received extensive mainstream press coverage and considerable Oscar buzz, winning three out of six Academy Award nominations, including Best Motion Picture of the Year.

NOW PLAYING: SAME, BUT DIFFERENT

While it appears at face value that Hollywood continues to add diversity to its movies, minority characters, on the whole, do not enjoy the same amount of freedom and range as White characters. Analyzed in the aggregate, many minority images actually perpetuate character patterns rooted in historical stereotypes that have been modified over time. In Hollywood's earlier days, it was common – if not expected – for minorities to fulfill roles that ranged from the servile and pandering to the violent and oversexed. The studios freely employed stereotypical roles for minority characters that in today's age would appear patently discriminatory and racist.

Nowadays Hollywood operates in an age where such blatant displays of discrimination and racism are publicly frowned upon. These images do not appear as frequently as they did in the past, yet many minorities are still marginalized. How can this be despite the fact that so many signs point to progress? Many of Hollywood's historically offensive stereotypes have now been replaced by a new set of marginalizing character patterns, which we refer to as archetypes. As mentioned briefly in *Chapter 1: What is a Mainstream Movie?*, virtually *all* minority characters fulfill one of the six primary archetypes for minority roles in mainstream movies:

MINORITY ARCHETPYES

1. THE ANGEL
2. THE BACKGROUND FIGURE
3. THE COMIC RELIEF
4. THE MENACE TO SOCIETY
5. THE PHYSICAL WONDER
6. THE UTOPIC REVERSAL

STEREOTYPE VS. ARCHETYPE

While stereotypes are typically derogatory in nature and are specific in their application, archetypes are more neutral in nature and more general in their application. For example, Hattie McDaniel won an Academy Award for her performance as "Mammy" in **Gone with the Wind**. McDaniel's role was stereotypical in its depiction of a dutiful Black woman whose sole purpose and function was to serve the domestic needs of Whites. At that time, the mammy figure was a popular stereotype that served as a stalwart caretaker for White families, virtually replacing White mothers and their child-rearing duties. The mammy stereotype also reaffirmed hierarchical social roles forced upon Blacks as far back as the era of enslavement centuries earlier.

Let us contrast this negative mammy stereotype against that of a "neutral" archetype. A prime example is the role of Judge Julius Alexander Randolph, portrayed by J.A. Preston, in the thrilling drama **A Few Good Men**. Being a judge would largely be considered an overall positive characterization, and at the very least could hardly be regarded as a stereotype. If anything, given Hollywood's history of negative portrayals of Black characters over the years, the sight of a Black actor occupying such an esteemed social position would appear to be a sure sign of progress. Unlike negative stereotypes that depict Blacks as criminals and thieves, the Black judge in *A Few Good Men* presents mainstream audiences with an explicit alternative. The role defies historical conventions of old Hollywood cinema.

However, when collectively analyzing the judge from *A Few Good Men* alongside other Black judges found in mainstream movies (e.g., ***Intolerable Cruelty***, ***The Devil's Advocate***), we can see an archetypal pattern start to emerge. Although such characters arguably make a positive *impression*, they nonetheless fail to significantly revise stereotypical limitations concerning positive *impact*. All of the Black judges mentioned above are limited in their dialogue, screen time and overall importance to the story's development, thereby demonstrating a subtle, yet consistent limitation to this archetypal role.

Although the casting of Black actors as judges in movies is now considered "acceptable," in reality Blacks only constitute 3.9% of all lawyers nationally and 8.8% of all judicial positions.[2] Frequent images of Blacks and other minorities in these positions distorts perceptions about social equality. Ultimately, these judge roles are *not* a true reflection of society. As a result, we can only surmise that such roles are an effort by Hollywood to "add diversity." Nevertheless, this "diversity" is not applied across the board since minorities less frequently fulfill the prominent allotted to White characters. Archetypical roles deceptively present neutral (and positive) minority images while reinforcing traditional onscreen limitations based upon race.

Marginalization resulting from the use of the archetypes is more difficult to detect than the patently offensive stereotypes of the past. At first blush, many of these new minority roles appear to defy traditional stereotypes based upon their individual portrayals. However, closer analysis reveals that many of the devices and thematic elements employed by past stereotypes still plague many of today's minority characters. When discussing race in mainstream movies, rather than focus on individual *stereotypes* that foster racial *discrimination,* it is best to analyze *archetypes* that collectively fuel minority *marginalization*. Instead

CUT!
So are you saying that Hollywood is not free to create an unflattering minority character? Are you saying that every time a minority appears that they must be valiant and brave?

Of course not. Unflattering characters are part of basic storytelling. Yet, the low frequency of minority participation, combined with the high frequency of minorities in minor and unflattering roles, places a greater degree of negative attention on such characters (see the **premium of proportion** definition on p. 58). Not only do few minority roles stray beyond formulaic stereotypes and archetypes, but complex minority characters of any real "depth" are also hard to come by.

OK, but what about the fact that not all White people are depicted in glamorous roles?

White actors have a wider variety of roles to choose from and have played just about every role possible. Other racial groups have not had the same range of roles, and oftentimes, when they are afforded those roles, such movies are not targeted for mainstream audiences.

Additionally, unflattering White roles are balanced out by the overwhelming number of heroic and leading roles occupied by White characters (see **Chapter 10: White Balancing Act**).

of seeing the old stereotypes of the past, the Hollywood Audience of today is more likely to find minority characters with roles that are marginalized in relation to the more prominently featured White characters.

THE HARM THEORY

Minority roles in mainstream movies typically fall victim to **Hollywood's Acting Rule for Minorities**, succinctly referred to as the HARM theory. The HARM theory essentially holds that if and when a minority character appears in a mainstream movie, this character will be compromised in some way, shape or form, often in relation to the White lead counterpart. According to the HARM theory, a typical minority character in a mainstream movie will be confined to at least one of six archetypes.

In *Chapters 4* through *Chapter 9*, we explore the concrete ways in which these minority archetypes are consistently employed, using varied examples from a wide range of mainstream movies. With the sustained analysis of examples from different years and different genres, Hollywood itself will proceed to illustrate the pervasive pattern of marginalization that limits the majority of all minority images onscreen. What follows are brief descriptions of the six minority archetypes:

❖ ANGEL ❖

usually found in a servile position or functioning as a sidekick, this character serves as a source of spiritual strength, guidance and support to the central characters

❖ BACKGROUND FIGURE ❖

inconsequential to the overall storyline, this character has limited dialogue (if any) and does not help to advance the plot, thereby serving as mere "window dressing" to reinforce a visual — albeit illusory — message of diversity

❖ COMIC RELIEF ❖

this character's culture serves as the fodder for most of the jokes; typical conduct includes boisterous and improper grammar, exaggerated motions and facial expressions, and intense emotion, often in stark contrast to standardized, White, middle-class behavior

Hollywood's Acting Rule for Minorities

if and when a minority character appears in a mainstream movie, their character will be compromised in some way, shape or form

CUT!

You can't possibly be saying that movie studios purposely try to marginalize minority groups in the movies, can you? Couldn't it just be random coincidence? Too much money is at stake in order to chalk up the final images that we see on the big screen as mere coincidence. Although it is highly unlikely that Hollywood has any formal plan to consistently generate marginalized images of minorities, the resulting effect is still the same when different studios with different movies provide essentially the same formulaic result.

Further, the consistency and the duration of the discernible minority archetype patterns discussed in **Chapters 4 through Chapter 9** speak strongly against "mere coincidence" in all instances.

◆ MENACE TO SOCIETY ◆

this character is portrayed as possessing a value system that poses a threat to civil "normalcy," either through violence (or potential violence) and/or moral corruption

◆ PHYSICAL WONDER ◆

this character is regarded for their physical or sexual prowess, typically at the sacrifice of intellectual or emotional capacities

◆ UTOPIC REVERSAL ◆

occupying a high social position or position of authority (e.g., police chief, judge, etc.), this character's "authority" is usually undermined, thereby rendering their authority as mostly symbolic in nature

CUT!
Hey wait! What you are saying is not always true! I saw a minority character that did not fit cleanly within your six main analytical categories! There may be occasional mainstream minority characters that deviate from the **HARM Theory**. However, virtually all mainstream minority characters overwhelmingly support and validate the theory. Although there are limited exceptions to every rule, the exceptions do not disprove the rule. Feel free to log on to **www.theracedoc.com** and take the *Exceptional Exception Challenge* today!

The minority archetypes provide the best available means of consistently assessing the quality of minority roles within mainstream movies. The power of recognizing the archetypal pattern stems from the fact that seemingly isolated roles and minority depictions are now connected. The inclusive archetype categories enable moviegoers to characterize virtually all non-White roles within these six character patterns. We must also add that the archetypes are equally applicable to minorities found in background roles and leading roles alike.

The minority archetype patterns are remarkably consistent. The archetypes, in aggregate, demonstrate that minority roles largely fulfill hierarchical notions of power and privilege based upon race, with Whites positioned at the top of the pecking order. Though the presentation of negatively stereotypical roles reserved for minorities has changed over time, the overall pattern of marginalization has remained the same. Again, the key is to focus on the overall quantity *and quality* of mainstream minority roles. Although the six general minority patterns are applicable to *all* minorities, each minority group is cast within the archetype patterns in similar, yet distinct ways.

TOTAL ANECDOTAL
Did you hear that Jamie Foxx had to police the *Miami Vice* movie set for racist pranks?

Foxx insisted that two crew members be dismissed after they approached Foxx' stand-in, David Brown, with nooses, "suggesting that he and Foxx were heading for a Ku Klux Klan-style lynching." The crew members approached Brown under the auspices of playing a joke.

Publicists for the movie confirmed the incident but refused to provide a further comment.[3a]

BUT LESS IS MORE

Many minorities fulfill a wide range of roles, much like their White counterparts, albeit at a lower rate given their more less frequent appearances. In the purest sense, there is nothing dramatically unique or offensive about minority actors occupying small or insignificant roles in Hollywood movies. However, since the overwhelming majority of background, supporting and primary characters in mainstream movies are White, if and when a minority character appears onscreen, this character usually draws more attention than that of a similarly situated White character.

Minority characters, especially those in leading roles or highly visible supporting roles, typically attract increased attention since these roles have historically been reserved for White actors. Not only are these characters typically isolated from other minority characters, but they are often depicted as largely insulated from White characters as well. This "paradox" suggests that while minorities are depicted as operating comfortably with Whites, they are not fully involved within the private White sphere towards the middle/end of the movie, where most of the "important" action and "heavy-lifting" takes place. The continued isolation and insulation of minority characters in mainstream movies over time has had the cumulative effect of communicating that somehow, irrespective of the storyline and associated themes, minority characters are simply not as integral to the movies as their White counterparts.

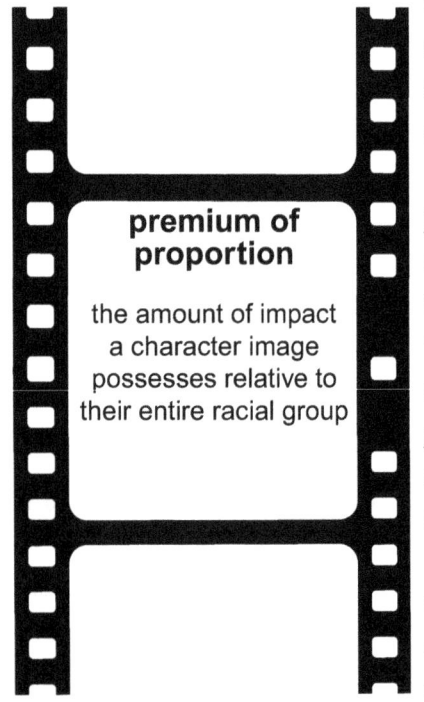

premium of proportion

the amount of impact a character image possesses relative to their entire racial group

Take, for example, a typical "corporate office" scene where a White janitor may only appear onscreen for a few seconds. Although this qualifies as a bit role for a White actor, the character's brief appearance is balanced by the fact that the primary characters, protagonists and heroes are all most likely White. In contrast, if the only *minority* character to appear in a mainstream movie is the janitor, such racial isolation unwittingly places an increased *premium* on this image. The isolation of this minority character, even if they are not serving as the protagonist, essentially makes the character's race that much more relevant.

If a minority is isolated in a role that is depicted unfavorably in an otherwise White-dominated movie, such an unfavorable image in effect disparages the "entire" racial group to which that minority belongs. According to the **premium of proportion** theory, a heightened emphasis, or premium, is placed upon limited minority images, resulting in a disproportionate amplification of the character's traits, especially if there are no other available minority images onscreen to provide any additional depth or balance.

The premium of proportion is based upon the amount of racial capital, that a racial group has available to "spend" on the portrayal of its image. Typically speaking, the larger the presence of the racial group, the more racial capital it has at its disposal. The larger the amount of disposable racial capital, the more that the racial group can "afford" to make expenditures that do not necessarily add to positive racial imagery without threatening the overall favorable position of the racial group. The higher the amount of racial capital endowed to a racial group, the lower the premium of proportion will be for imagery associated with that racial group.

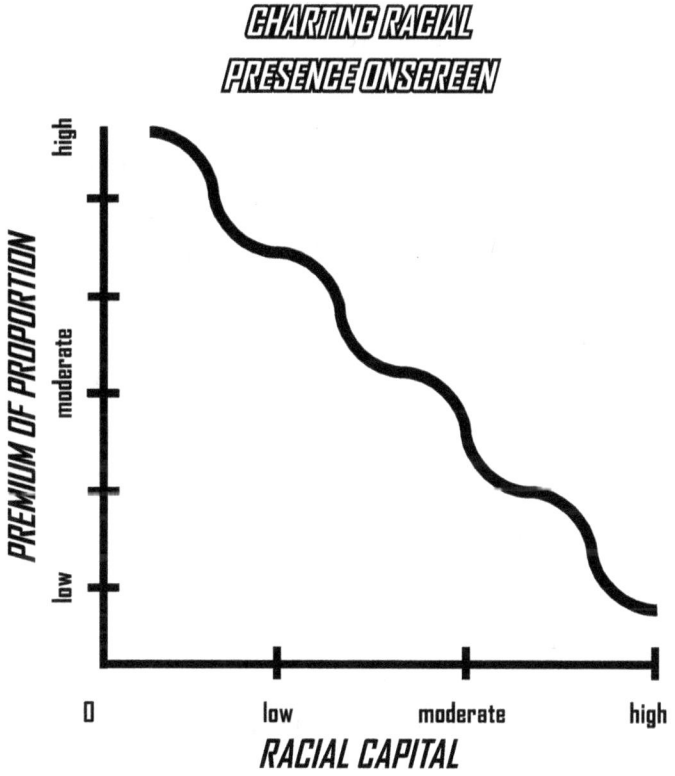

This graph helps illustrate the inverse relationship between **Premium of Proportion** and **Racial Capital**. The smaller the **Racial Capital** (the racial group's collective onscreen presence), the greater the **Premium of Proportion** (the attention placed upon individual onscreen images as reflective of the larger racial group).

Please note that the premium of proportion is not limited to a case-by-case application basis for individual movies. The **Premium of Proportion** is often best applied when analyzing the aggregate number of roles available in the industry as a whole.

As an illustration, imagine that you have $100 to spend on a single meal at a restaurant. Spending $7 on dessert does not worry you too much since, notwithstanding taxes and gratuity, you still have more than enough money left over for appetizers, a main course and drinks. Now, if you have only $10 to spend on a meal at the same restaurant, spending $7 on dessert may not sound as appetizing any more. If you are truly hungry for a substantive meal, you will want the full $7 to be applied towards your entrée rather than a dainty cup full of berries and cream, given your smaller amount of total capital. Since the proportional leverage of your buying power is substantially decreased, an increased premium is placed on the available dollars presently at your disposal. Hence, the relative importance of each dollar increases, along with your decision on how to spend it.

Dominance by Whites in nearly all facets of mainstream movie production accounts for an incredibly high amount of racial capital, both onscreen and off, which considerably subdues the overall impact of any isolated or negative White images. Whites as a group can "afford" wasteful or negative imagery without sustaining significant damage to their overall image, because at the end of the movie, such imagery is controlled and balanced by redeeming protagonists that are most likely White as well. In contrast, isolated minority images can become representative of an entire race's culture. Such representation can be intentional (e.g., the "Japanese tourist" is meant to represent "all" Asian/Japanese people). Often, critics will defend the latest iteration of an adult-themed rated-R, comedic mainstream movie by stating that "no one is safe from satire" or that the movie "makes fun of everybody."[3] These assessments are actually thinly veiled defenses of the unchallenged ability of Whites to lampoon minority races. Generally speaking, a negative depiction of a White character does not hurt the entire group's "bottom line" as much as a minority character whose group is depicted onscreen with less frequency, but in a consistently disparaging light.

WHITE BEAUTY STANDARD

Through consistent marginalization, minority characters are continuously slotted as secondary options behind more financially-attractive White leads considered popular enough to carry a story. When assembling mainstream movie projects, the studios freely dictate what minority imagery will be most appropriate for their needs; minority actors by and large do not dictate what type of imagery is most appropriate for the studios.

Due to the imbalance of racial capital in Hollywood, when minorities are cast in more prominent roles, movie studios can easily demand that selected minority talent conform to a crafted image of what minority representation should look and sound like. Studios use their massive leveraging power to use whomever they want, however they want. This imbalanced power dynamic presents a major dilemma to minority actors that choose to dissent with a particular characterization of one solitary movie role. Consequently, movie studios seek to "minimize their risks" by deciding to showcase only those minorities that will be most appealing or non-threatening to majority White audiences (unless the role calls for it).

Nowhere do we see this bait-and-switch technique better than when minority actresses take center stage. From Jessica Alba to Lucy Liu to Halle Berry, those minority actresses that are considered "beautiful" by Hollywood standards are those who more closely approach the **White Beauty Standard,** the "ideal" paradigm by which most White women are measured. In other words, movie studios are free to employ a "bait-and-switch" technique, whereby studios lure diverse audiences to see a minority that is asked to play an anglicized role or accentuate their anglicized features. Consider Asian actress Lucy Liu's role as Alex Munday in *Charlie's Angels: Full Throttle* where her father, Mr. Munday, is played by White actor John Cleese. Faced with an open choice on who to cast as Alex Munday's father, the movie's creators chose a White man. The imagery onscreen suggests that Alex Munday, with a White father, is somehow closer in association to White standards, values and culture than she initially appears to be.

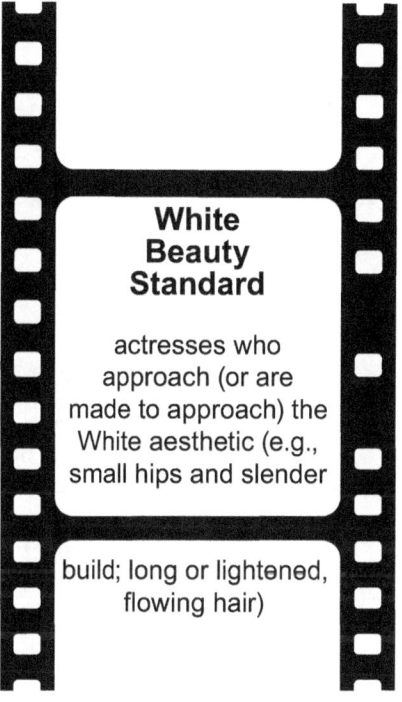

White Beauty Standard

actresses who approach (or are made to approach) the White aesthetic (e.g., small hips and slender build; long or lightened, flowing hair)

For an example of the bait-and-switch strategy, consider *The Wedding Planner,* starring Puerto Rican actress Jennifer Lopez. Lopez plays the role of an Italian woman, Mary Fiore, who falls in love with a likeable White male, Steve Edison (Matthew McConaughey). This is an example of the movie studio having its cake and eating it too. By casting Lopez as a White woman, the movie studio was able to promote a prototypical love story with mainstream appeal based upon a standard "White male plus White female" formula, thus appealing to the majority White audience. Additionally, the movie studio was able to leverage Lopez' appeal with minority audience markets, all without ever having to take on the "full risk" that accompanies greenlighting a movie featuring primarily minorities. The issue is not so much that the movie would have to feature primarily minorities, but that casting Lopez as a Puerto Rican would cause other casting "concerns." Lopez' father in the movie

WHAT DO YOU THINK?
Did you see *Vanity Fair's* "2017 Hollywood Issue?"[3b] The eleven actresses were Natalie Portman, Emma Stone, Amy Adams, Lupita Nyong'o, Ruth Negga, sisters Dakota Fanning and Elle Fanning, Dakota Johnson, Greta Gerwig, Aja Naomi King and Janelle Monáe. *How many of the eleven actresses are minorities? Have the minority actresses appeared in as many movies as their White counterparts? Of these minorities, how many fit the White Beauty Standard?*

CHAPTER 3: THE COLOR SCENE 61

would likely have to be Latino, as well as replacing her other Italian suitor with a Latino male. Suddenly, the movie might take on an "interracial" romance angle, one that might undermine the conventional "White male plus White female" formula.

The White Beauty Standard directly impacts which minorities get cast and can even result in White actors being cast in minority roles! In *The Mask of Zorro* and *The Legend of Zorro*, Welsh actress Catherine Zeta-Jones plays a Latina character, Elena de la Vega. In this instance, the movie studio decided to cast a known White actress for a Latina role that fulfilled the aesthetic requirements they were looking for, rather than take the time to locate a Latina actress that fit the bill. As another example of the White Beauty Standard's deceptively strong influence, even the critically-acclaimed and purportedly racially progressive movie *Crash* employed Italian-American actress Jennifer Esposito to play Ria, the Latina detective!

WHAT DO YOU THINK?

Now that Halle Berry has won an Oscar for Best Actress, does her A-list status cast her personal appearance in a new light? How does her mixed racial heritage (her mother is White, her father is Black) and her mainstream acceptance inform traditional notions of "Black beauty"? More importantly, as a Black A-list actress, do her roles now transcend "racial politics"?

One mainstream role that Berry accepted in her "post-Oscar era" was that of Storm in the *X-Men* series. Consider that Berry agreed to participate in the second X-Men sequel only after she was promised a larger role in the third sequel. Apparently, Halle was miffed that she had significantly less screen time than Hugh Jackman, Rebecca Romijn, and Famke Janssen.[3c] Berry's perspective appears supported by the fact that at least two spinoff movies received greenlights (*Wolverine, Magneto*) based upon characters other than hers – arguably played by actors with less celebrity status (at the time) than Berry.

Furthermore, despite the Oscar and the newfound fame that accompanied it, Halle Berry still feels regularly confronted with her racial status. Said Berry, "there's so much more subtle, insidious ways that racism occurs here in Hollywood. I don't care what anyone says – they may think it doesn't exist, but it's usually those who aren't black who think that."[3d]

If the perennially publicly popular Halle Berry is affected by race, than what does these casting decisions say about the impact race may have on lesser-known minority actresses?

APPROACHING WHITENESS

Many actors approach the White Beauty Standard, but never fully reach it, giving rise to the **asymptote** phenomenon. The term asymptote traditionally describes a mathematical phenomena wherein a function approaches a value, moving closer to the value in perpetuity, yet never reaches that value. Actors that qualify as asymptotes are those actors who most closely resemble the White Beauty Standard, but cannot reproduce the paradigm completely since they are not White. The asymptote allows Hollywood to establish an illusory comfort level with diversity by accentuating and promoting minority images that ironically do not reflect "typical" racial features and appearances.

Within mainstream culture, the White Beauty Standard establishes the paradigm for beauty by which all other beauty standards are measured against. The White Beauty Standard, especially for women, is exemplified by its overwhelming presence throughout mainstream media – from the covers and content pages of female fashion magazines to most female leads in television shows and movies. Minorities are generally promoted, rewarded and recognized for their beauty based upon their ability – or the studio's ability – to express their physical appearance *in accordance with the mainstream White Beauty Standard*.

The asymptote is to be contrasted with the appearance of **"across-the-street" minorities**, those minority actors where little ambiguity exists as to their racial identity based upon their physical appearance. For instance, there is no disputing that actresses Regina King and Angela Bassett are "Black." Cameron Diaz, on the other hand, as a tall, blue-eyed blond, presents a different issue. Despite her Latina surname, courtesy of her Cuban American father, Diaz appears "White" and typically plays White female characters onscreen.[4]

Consider the movie *Guess Who* featuring Zoë Saldaña and Ashton Kutcher as the soon-to-be-married Black and White couple of Theresa Jones and Simon Green. Theresa Jones is African-American, but Saldaña is actually Latina (she is from the Dominican Republic). Meanwhile, Theresa Jones' Afro-toting Black sister Keisha is more "distinctly ethnic," played by an African-American actress, Kellee Stewart. Not only is Keisha's hair noticeably different from Theresa's, but

> **asymptote**
>
> a non-White actor whose physical attributes approach the White Beauty Standard or allow the actor to portray White characters

> **across-the-street minorities**
>
> a character whereby little ambiguity exists as to their racial identity or minority status based upon their physical appearance

> **WHAT DO YOU THINK?**
>
> In the 1967 original, *Guess Who's Coming to Dinner*, the interracial couple consisted of Sidney Poitier as Dr. John Wade Prentice, the older and exceptionally accomplished medical professional, and Katharine Houghton as Joanna "Joey" Drayton, the young and vibrant daughter of a liberal household.
>
> Ashton Kutcher and Zoë Saldaña star in the 2005 remake *Guess Who*, and reverse the Black male/White woman dynamic featured in the original. The original movie possessed a more "serious" social message (with virtually no intimacy between the two characters), while the remake features a much more intimate and balanced interracial couple in terms of age and social status.
>
> Since *Guess Who* was a remake, why did the studio decide to depart from the original screenplay and switch the races of the two lead characters? What was the underlying rationale for this fundamental character change? Guess Who grossed a respectable $67 million in domestic box offices. Would the movie have fared as well, better or worse had the Black male/White female dynamic in the remake been preserved? How many movies have you seen with a Black male/White female relationship? ***Would you market the movie the same way to both Black and White audiences? Why or why not?***

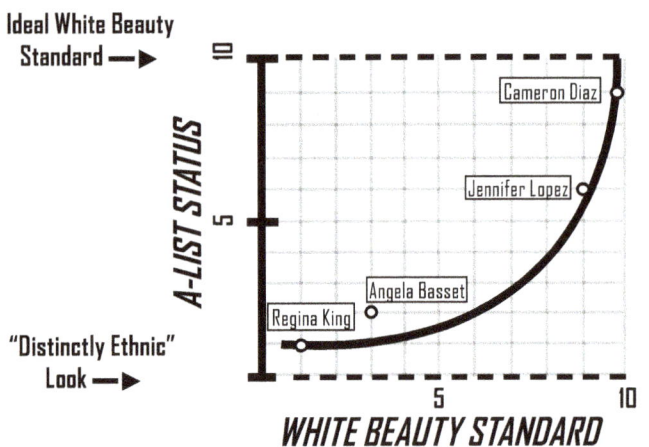

CHARTING ASYMPTOTES

The adjacent **Charting Asymptotes** graph helps illustrate the asymptote concept. If you were to take popular minority actresses in Hollywood and rate them on a scale of 1 to 10, with 1 representing the "distinctly ethnic" look and 10 representing the ideal **White Beauty Standard**, a pattern would emerge.

When a minority actress enjoys significant dialogue and/or screen time in mainstream movies, her "ethnic" qualities are often de-emphasized in order to make her more palatable to majority White audiences. This strategy is especially acute in movies with predominately White casts.

Actresses "approach" the White Beauty Standard in primarily one of two ways: passively through deliberate Hollywood marketing, or actively by personally taking affirmative steps to alter or "improve" her individual beauty or marketability. Sometimes both factors can be at play. Also, some "asymptotes" approach the **White Beauty Standard** by birth and do not have to significantly "alter" their appearance. Lastly, the counsel and advice of additional cogs in the Hollywood machine (e.g., managers, acting coaches, stylists, etc.) can affect an actress' public look as well.

Minority actresses who most closely approximate the White Beauty Standard typically have the best chances of being prominently featured in mainstream movies. Compare the career trajectories of all four actresses listed in the chart to see how race factors into their studio casting decisions.

Is it a denial of racial heritage that Jennifer Lopez and Cameron Diaz are offered and accept roles in which they are not allowed to be "their racial selves" onscreen? Or is it merely sound business practice for by both to maximize their crossover appeal to mainstream audiences? How much of does their fair-complexioned appearance factor into their marketability?

In contrast, how many prominent, dark-complexioned mainstream movie actresses do you know? What is the crossover appeal for "distinctly-ethnic" leading actresses?

Keisha appears more animated and more expressive with more "attitude." Would Keisha's "more ethnic" appearance and mannerisms have translated just as well with mainstream audiences in an interracial romance? Or would casting Stewart opposite Kutcher rather than Saldaña contravene Hollywood's aesthetic ideal?

Minority actresses who are naturally fair in complexion are not to be faulted for "looking White." Hollywood studios consistently limit high-profile, "glamorous" mainstream movie roles to those actresses who best approximate

> **WHAT DO YOU THINK?**
> In profiling some of the better-known actresses in Hollywood, what do make of the fact that many of them have culturally mixed backgrounds with European (White) influences? What does this pattern say about Hollywood's reliance on asymptotes? ***What are the prospects for minority actresses devoid of multi-ethnic backgrounds or "exotic" looks?*** Each actress' name is listed in bold, followed by their background.
>
> - **Halle Berry** - of African American and White American descent
> - **Cameron Diaz** - of Cuban, English and German descent
> - **Jennifer Lopez** - of Puerto Rican descent (maternal grandparents are European)
> - **Salma Hayek** - of Mexican and Lebanese descent
> - **Jessica Alba** - of Mexican, French and Danish descent
> - **Rosario Dawson** - of Puerto Rican, Cuban, African American, Irish and Native American descent
> - **Eva Mendes** - of Cuban and White American descent
> - **Kelly Hu** - of Chinese, Hawaiian and English descent
> - **Sophie Okonedo** - of Nigerian, European and Jewish descent
> - **Devon Aoki** - of German, English and Japanese descent
>
> Source: Internet Movie Database.

the White Beauty Standard. In some cases, individual actresses undergo personal changes in their external appearance which help them approach the White Beauty Standard (e.g., lightening of the hair or eyes). Such personal changes often precede a growing interest in mainstream popularity. Compare early pictures of Jessica Alba, Beyoncé, Queen Latifah, and Jennifer Lopez to their present-day photographs, observing the changes in their appearance (e.g., Jennifer Lopez as the dark-haired Mexican Terri Flores in ***Anaconda*** versus her role as the light-haired Italian Charlie Cantilini in ***Monster-in-Law***).

In many cases for minority actresses, studios will cast someone who is closer to the White Beauty Standard than an across-the-street minority, perhaps to minimize the risks associated with not casting a White woman instead. Also note that asymptotes are often used for more prominent roles or roles that call for aesthetic beauty, while across-the-street minorities are often used for bit parts (e.g., the black judge in ***Austin Powers: Goldmember***), comedic effect (e.g., Sharon Wilkins role as "Woman" in ***I, Robot*** and "Heavy Black Woman" in ***Bad Boys II***), or to reinforce racial status and/or affiliation (e.g., Jennifer Lopez' distinctly Latina mother in ***Maid in Manhattan***). In this sense, asymptotes become tangible symbols for studios to exploit while in search of the greatest possible audience. Studios use asymptotes to attract White moviegoers that might otherwise feel that they could not identify with someone who looked different from them.

For instance, consider Don Cheadle and Sophie Okonedo starring as Paul and Tatiana Rusesabagina in **Hotel Rwanda**. Visually speaking, the decision to cast Cheadle as Paul Rusesabagina was effective since Cheadle resembles the real Rusesabagina with respect to complexion and stature. But what about Okonedo's resemblance to Tatiana Rusesabagina? A visual comparison would reveal that Okonedo, who is of Nigerian, European and Jewish descent, is significantly lighter in complexion and smaller in build, and unlike Rusesabagina, her hair is straightened. Regardless of Okonedo's acting skill, her selection fits within the larger pattern of the White Beauty Standard, suggesting that casting an actress resembling the real Tatiana Rusesabagina would (in the studio's eyes) curtail the movie's commercial and mainstream appeal. Studios employ asymptotes because such images require less of a **connective switch** with mainstream audiences than it would for an-across-the-street minority.

> **connective switch**
>
> the ability of a viewer to adopt the perspective of a character in order to form an emotional connection with that character

> **masking**
>
> whereby an actor is able to hide their racial identity on or offscreen and blend in with the White majority through a superficial change (e.g., lightening of hair, change of surname)

Since asymptotes foster a low need for a connective switch, they are also effective because they help studios achieve mainstream penetration, as demonstrated by the financial success of **Spy Kids**. The **Spy Kids** trilogy is an example of a "successful" mainstream crossover featuring mostly minority characters since this action-adventure series for families collectively grossed over $300 million at the box office. Written and directed by Robert Rodriguez, it featured a largely Latino cast where the central family shared a "racialized" surname in the Cortez family (yet, none of the actors who portray the four central Latino family characters is "fully" Latino[5]).

Also note how all the central characters, despite their "minority" status, are endowed with fair complexions. If the starring children were darker in appearance and did not closely approach the White Beauty Standard, do you think the movie still would have maintained its mainstream appeal? The marketing campaign did not portray **Spy Kids** as a "Latino" movie and was widely marketed to a broad audience, perhaps as an attempt by the movie studio to preserve the movie's broader appeal amongst a majority White, ticket-paying audience. Certainly, on one hand, the non-mention of race in the **Spy Kids** marketing campaign possibly suggests that "race doesn't matter," and that mainstream society is in fact tolerant and accepting. On the other hand, the non-mention of race in the **Spy Kids** marketing campaign raises a more difficult question: would mainstream society have been just as accepting of the movie if the characters were distinctly portrayed as racial minorities? In this case, the non-mention of race may have worked to the studio's advantage wherein many moviegoers might have assumed that the cast comprised White actors – a construction that would not have been quite so easily formed had *Spy Kids* starred a "distinctly ethnic" Black or Asian family.

WHAT'S IN A NAME?

Actors have often changed their names as a means to insulate themselves from negative expectations or to increase their mainstream appeal. There are also a significant number of people working in Hollywood who disguise their ethnic visibility in order to increase their public marketability. There are several historical examples of Italian American stars (Sophia Loren, born Sofia Villani Scicolone), Bolivian American (Raquel Welch, born Jo Raquel Tejada) stars and Jewish American stars (Kirk Douglas, born Issur Danielovich Demsky) who have changed their names before launching themselves in the public eye. With the simple stroke of a pen, these actors were not so much members of Italian, Latino and Jewish ethnic subgroups inasmuch as they were now part of a larger White racial group, or at the very least, ambiguously neutral.

Such actor transformations are made possible through **masking**, whereby an actor attempts to hide or blur their racial identity and more successfully blend in with the White mainstream majority. Currently, the masking technique is illustrated by the Sheen family. Ramon Estevez changed his name to Martin Sheen (***Apocalypse Now***), to avoid being typecast in ethnic roles. Martin Sheen's son, Charlie Sheen (***Wall Street***), decided to follow suit and use his father's stage name. Martin Sheen's other son, Emilio Estevez (***The Breakfast Club, St. Elmo's Fire***), decided to keep their original surname. With a simple name change, both Martin and Charlie Sheen were perhaps better positioned to play blanket, likeable White characters given their physical appearance. Judging by his movie career, Emilio did not enjoy the same broad mainstream appeal, even in spite of his seemingly "White" aesthetic. Although there are a myriad of factors that determined why the career trajectories of Charlie Sheen and Emilio Estevez took on entirely different paths, it is prudent to consider whether Estevez' "racialized" surname was at least one of the factors that affected his ability to land roles.

> **TOTAL ANECDOTAL**
>
> Consider Indian-American actor Kal Penn's comments on casting:
>
> "Our hope for a film like [***Harold & Kumar Go to White Castle***] is that producers can see that if they cast colorblind and just cast the best actor, it's more interesting for an audience to watch. It's not the same old thing they've seen, and it'll still make money at the end of the day. A good movie is a good movie, and the audience isn't as dumb as they think."[3e]
>
> In the same article, Penn states that it is "weird and absurd" that he started receiving more auditions only after changing his approach and divided his original name, Kalpen Modi, into Kal Penn. The implication from Penn's experience is that the more "ethnically neutral" his name, the more appealing or useful he became to the movie makers.

Some movie stars, like Vin Diesel (*The Fast and Furious, xXx*), are intensely sensitive about discussing their racial heritage (which ironically fueled his 1994 short film *Multi-facial*, about a struggling actor who is rejected for part after part because he does not look "Black/White/Jewish" enough). Vin Diesel's aura of racial ambiguity allows for him to play a "wider" range of mainstream roles. In discussing these individual examples, we do not suggest that these individuals are ashamed of their heritage, but rather that because of the historically marginalized imagery associated with their "original" racial heritage, many actors must devise alternative strategies for increasing their appeal with the mainstream White audience.

> **TOTAL ANECDOTAL**
>
> This name-changing phenomena is nothing new. At Hollywood's inception, many Jewish actors were careful to keep their ethnic identity separated from the public eye, due to fears of arousing anti-Semitism.[3f] The conventional wisdom was that by appearing "less ethnic," public appeal for an actor would improve, and consequently, the movie studio would be able to market the movie to a wider audience. Of particular irony is that so many Jewish actors opted for "stage-names" in spite of the strong Jewish presence that helped create Hollywood.
>
> This significant Jewish presence in Hollywood may have also contributed towards positive onscreen images for many Jewish actors, or at least, contributed towards the absence of many negative Jewish images. Film scholar Patricia Erens states that despite "their small numbers in the United States, Jews have enjoyed an advantage unequaled by any other group in America — a virtual control over their own self-image on the [movie] screen."[3g] Despite the significant presence of Jews in the movie industry and despite the increasing tolerance of our society, this name-changing trend continues today (e.g., Winona Horowitz, better known as Winona Ryder or Milena Markovna Kunis, better known as Mila Kunis, or Katherine Litwack, better known as Kat Dennings or Allison Brie Schermerhorn, better known as Allison Brie).

It is not surprising that some minority actors will attempt to leverage the best career move for themselves, even if it means consciously changing their appearance or identity to improve their appeal to the mainstream. Efforts by minority actors to establish their "Americanness" often encourages an acknowledgment of a simplified heritage, free of ties to anything but America. However, the resulting invisibility of the minority actor's "original" race is what becomes problematic. Ultimately, the message communicated to aspiring actors is that minority marginalization is simply more marketable.

CHAPTER 4:
THE ANGEL

What's remarkable about Mr. [Morgan] Freeman these days is how reliably he delivers whenever he's plugged into a film as a symbol of wisdom and integrity.

Joe Morgenstern, movie reviewer, *Wall Street Journal*[1]

CHAPTER 4:
THE ANGEL

Now it is time to look specifically at racial patterns within mainstream movies. Each of the following six chapters will introduce an archetype and then provide examples of the archetype as manifested in different minority characters. The examples serve as an illustration of a larger pattern and are not highlighted to limit an archetype to those particular movies. The HARM theory and the archetype pattern stretch beyond these few examples, and you will undoubtedly think of other examples as you begin to recognize the pattern for yourself.[2] We provide examples for each of our minority group classifications in order to demonstrate that Hollywood's formulaic pattern of marginalization applies widely to *all* minority groups. Although each example primarily focuses on one archetype at a time, please note that it is entirely possible for a minority character to exhibit traits from more than one archetype simultaneously or within the same movie.

TOUCHED BY AN ANGEL

We begin with not only one of the most recognizable archetypes, but one of the most enduring as well. Usually found in a servile position or functioning as a sidekick, the Angel serves as a source of spiritual strength, guidance and support to the central characters, who are most often White. Frequently, despite the smaller amount of privilege and screen time that they command relative to the protagonist, this character occupies a "teacher" type role, imparting insightful perspectives and life lessons. Angel characters can range in their approach by either proactively pursuing their responsibility to provide help to the White protagonist, or by adopting a more passive stance whereby they are actively solicited by the White character for assistance. It is not uncommon for some Angel archetypes to literally possess a spiritual quality in addition to their figurative function as an Angel figure.

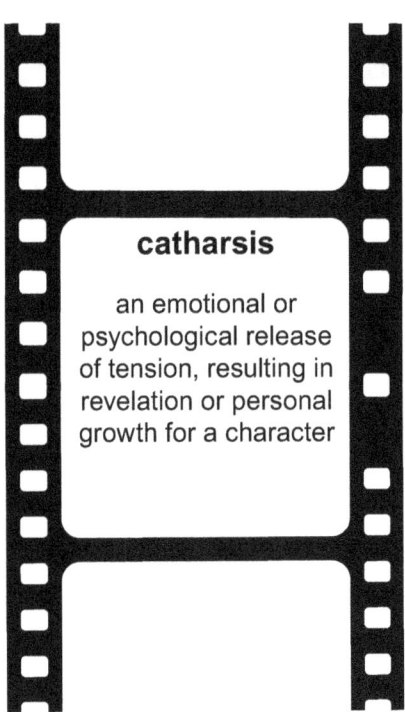

catharsis

an emotional or psychological release of tension, resulting in revelation or personal growth for a character

The characters that fit within this archetype are denoted by how much assistance they provide to the protagonist. This archetype is instrumental in facilitating an emotional **catharsis** for the central White character. Such catharsis is often necessary for the White character to transcend to a higher level of understanding, receive an increase in status, or step closer towards accomplishing their goal. Ironically, the Angel, with all of their wisdom and insight, experiences a more limited character arc than the protagonist and rarely endures significant personal growth. Their "catharsis" happens only insofar as their ability to facilitate a metamorphosis for the protagonist.

The Angel is virtually devoid of any external relationships outside of the White character(s), effectively communicating to the audience that the protagonist is the Angel's sole responsibility onscreen. In fact, Angel figures often prove their use and loyalty to White characters by facilitating the romantic interests of White protagonists – literally by using their bodies as physical conduits to channel emotions of which they themselves do not necessarily partake (e.g., Whoopi Goldberg in **Ghost**, Jennifer Lopez in **Shall We Dance**, Alanna Ubach in **Meet the Fockers**, Queen Latifah in **Bringing Down the House**, Will Smith in **Hitch**, etc.).

Essentially, Angels are important only to the degree that they influence the central character, who is then empowered to right the wrongs at the end of the day. Although the Angel archetype seems important in its function, this character pattern ultimately marginalizes the minority image, since Angel figures remain on the periphery of true onscreen participation. The actions and dialogue of the Angel archetype primarily serve as a catalyst for the White protagonist to take the decisive action that will determine the movie's ultimate trajectory. Due to the enduring presence of the Angel archetype within Hollywood's history, we must adequately contextualize how this archetype has been framed differently for different characters within Hollywood's Racial Makeup.

The Angel figure for Asian characters is such a recurring character, that his presence is almost cliché: the wise old martial arts master who is able to dispense centuries-old wisdom in short sentences punctuated by broken English, all while sitting comfortably in some variation of the lotus position amidst some serene background. When this wise master is killed off early on in the movie – a common plot device – the memory of his teachings nonetheless guide and instruct our protagonist towards the movie's conclusion. This "wise master" variation was popularized by the 1970s hit television show *Kung Fu*, and was later reprised in the 1980s by Mr. Miyagi's (Pat Morita) instructions to, "Wax on, wax off," in *The Karate Kid* series.

Blacks have fulfilled the Angel role in a variety of different ways over Hollywood's history. From Bill "Bojangles" Robinson in **Rebecca of Sunnybrook Farm** to Morgan Freeman in **Million Dollar Baby**, many a Black character has proved their worth and mettle by offering aid and assistance to White characters. Such a concept dates back to America's earlier history when it was customary for Whites to expect Blacks to wait on and service them in recognition of the social and economic hierarchy in place. Times have now changed and many legitimate challenges have been made to existing social barriers that were once thought insurmountable. Consequently, it is currently politically incorrect to have a Black actress play the role of a "mammy." The mammy was a stereotypical figure, usually depicted as obese and unattractive, and hearkened back to an age when Blacks were enslaved and treated as inferior.

Nowadays, rather than depict a mammy, it is nonetheless perfectly normal to see an isolated, middle-class Black female character as having no other purpose outside of providing spiritual guidance and valued assistance to a primary White character (e.g., see Gloria Foster's role as the Oracle in the **Matrix** series). Thus, although external and outward markers denoting lower socio-economic status for Blacks are different, the character's purpose essentially remains the same. In fact, the pattern of Black Angel figures has become so commonplace that we can see this archetype fulfilled by Blacks even when headlining their own mainstream movie! Denzel Washington, for example, despite heading the bill for **Man on Fire**, is essentially a Black protagonist whose character arc revolves around providing protection and rescuing a young, central White character played by Dakota Fanning (see the "Archetypes at Work" profile on pg. 78).

Latino actors have also fulfilled the Angel archetype by providing assistance to White protagonists. Movies like **Shall We Dance** and **Take the Lead** feature Latino dancers who – largely through physical assistance – help other characters get in touch with their emotional side. For instance, in **Shall We Dance**, Jennifer Lopez is Paulina, a dancer who assists an upper-middle class White lawyer named John Clark, played by Richard Gere. In **Take the Lead**, Antonio Banderas as Pierre Dulaine helps the proverbial "problem-kids-from-the-inner-city" through dance instruction. Latino characters that espouse about the ameliorative nature of dance are a derivation of the "Latin Lover" stereotype that exaggerates personality qualities such as sensuality, passion and romance.

With respect to characters that fall within the Other category, Native Americans rarely appear in mainstream movies, but when they do, they often qualify as Angels. This character is frequently presented as the shaman, or wise medicine man, who is recognizable by his emphasis on spiritualism, holistic healing, and his strong connection to the ways of nature. His spiritualism is often contrasted with the "skepticism" of "modern" medicine or an alternate religion. The shaman's method of imparting knowledge is an example of **one-way culture sharing**, where one racial group's cultural resources are exploited without reciprocation. Since the mainstream movie market industry is dominated by Whites, it is not uncommon to see minority perspectives onscreen as envisioned and articulated by Whites offscreen. This often leads to one-way culture sharing – where culture of a traditionally marginalized minority is seen largely through the dominant group's perspective.

By way of example, consider *Bulletproof Monk,* where the title serves as a prime contrast between East and West cultures (i.e., "bulletproof" is associated with Western violence, while "monk" connotes the staid philosophy of the East). In *Bulletproof Monk*, the "natural" style of the Monk with No Name (Chow Yun-Fat) is contrasted against a gung-ho "American" attitude towards action and violence, exemplified by Kar (Seann William Scott). The one-way culture sharing dynamic then flows from the monk/martial artist in the direction of the "American," who learns to control his aggression whilst enduring an emotional catharsis.

one-way culture sharing

where one racial group's cultural "resources" are exploited chiefly to benefit a White character without a reciprocal exchange

HOT TICKET ITEMS

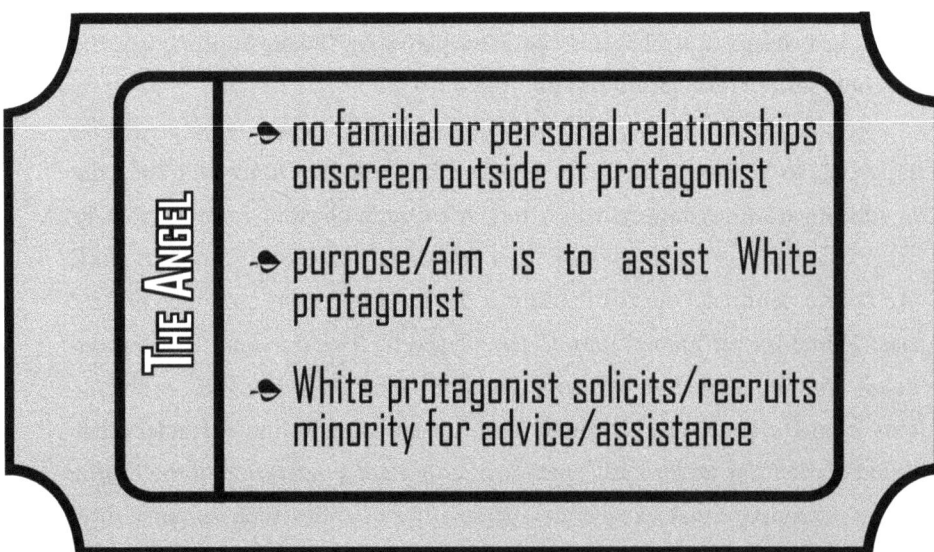

The Angel
- no familial or personal relationships onscreen outside of protagonist
- purpose/aim is to assist White protagonist
- White protagonist solicits/recruits minority for advice/assistance

ARCHETYPE EXPLORED
ANGEL: Asian Examples

1) Bulletproof Monk (2003)

» actor/character: Chow Yun-Fat as Monk With No Name

» analysis: Chow Yun-Fat is a nameless (yes, nameless!) Tibetan monk who has spent his lifetime protecting a sacred ancient scroll. In his search for an heir apparent, the monk stumbles upon "the one," a young White man by the name of Kar (Sean William Scott). Despite Kar's reluctance, the monk fulfills the Angel role by becoming his mentor, imparting wisdom and martial arts techniques along the way. Kar ultimately gains a true understanding of his unique powers and supplants the nameless (yes, nameless!) monk as the new protector of the sacred scroll.

» bonus: Note the transitions that Kar and the Monk With No Name both undergo. Kar transforms from a "gifted but misdirected" pick-pocket thief into a leader of other nameless monks and a guardian of sacred scrolls. Conversely, the Monk With No Name literally transfers all of his knowledge, energy and life force to Kar. During the process of transferring the sacred scroll inscriptions to Kar, the Monk With No Name ages significantly, and the movie concludes with him having changed into a decrepit old man. The Monk With No Name ultimately hobbles off into obscurity, but only after informing Kar and his romantic interest (Jaime King as Jade) that they are "inseparable."

LIGHTS! CAMERA! INTERACTION!
See if you can think of a mainstream movie where a peripheral White character provides a central minority character with a relic or artifact of White culture. In these cases, did the White cultural artifact play a vital role in the minority character accomplishing their objective? Did the minority character experience a catharsis as a result of the White character's assistance?

Go to *www.theracedoc.com* and let us know what you find!

2) Seven Years In Tibet (1997)

» actor/character: Jamyang Jamtsho Wangchuk as the Dalai Lama (at fourteen years old)

» analysis: Heinrich Harrer (Brad Pitt) is an Austrian mountaineer running away from troubles at home who finds himself atop the Himalayas during World War II. There, in the holy city of Lhasa, Heinrich befriends the Dalai Lama, and his life changes forever. The Dalai Lama serves as Harrer's Angel figure, inspiring hope and self-awareness in Harrer, and offering him a chance at redemption from his sordid and selfish past.

CHAPTER 4: THE ANGEL   75

> **WHAT DO YOU THINK?**
>
>
>
> *San Andreas,* (2015) a disaster movie focused on large, destructive Californian earthquakes, stars Dwyane "The Rock" Johnson, Carla Gugino and Paul Giamatti. The movie also features Korean actor Will Yun Lee, who plays Dr. Kim Park, the "best friend" and research partner of Paul Giamatti's Dr. Lawrence character.
>
> Early in the movie (as in *early*), early celebration of the "predictive model" Drs. Park and Lawrence were testing for earthquakes was cut short while the Hoover Dam research cite started crumbling quickly in the wake of an unannounced 7.1 quake.
>
> Since Dr. Park was inside the dam, he had to first surface, and then cross the top of the dam to get to solid ground. Dr. Lawrence was already outside and on top of the dam when the earthquake started, and was urging Dr. Park to hurry to safety.
>
> Whilst en route, Dr. Park spots a white blonde girl (complete with pink sweater) cowering and crying in a corner of the terrace. He stops to pick her up and carries her with him to safety.
>
> The ground crumbles beneath Dr. Park's feet prompting him to throw the girl to Dr. Lawrence right at the safety border. Dr. Park is immobilized due to a large stake that has pierced his foot.
>
> Dr. Park's last words are "No! Close your eyes!" directed toward the white girl so that she does not have to witness his fantastic and terrifying death as Hoover Dam disintegrates.
>
> *Do you see the Angel Figure? Did this scene have to unfold this way?*

» key scene: When Harrer leaves the Dalai Lama at the movie's conclusion, the Dalai Lama removes a white sash from around his neck and gives it to Harrer. After securing the sash around Harrer's neck, the Dalai Lama and Harrer's heads softly and intimately touch, while the Dalai Lama dispenses some parting words of wisdom.

3) Kill Bill: Vol. 1 (2003)

» actor/character: Sonny Chiba as Hattori Hanzo

» analysis: The Angel is revealed through the relationship between The Bride (Uma Thurman) and her sage Japanese mentor, Hattori Hanzo. Hanzo not only bestows words of wisdom on Thurman's character, but he also comes out of retirement to provide her with a new sword and some more timely insights.

» bonus: Notice the one-way culture sharing that takes place between Hanzo and The Bride. When Hanzo bequeaths his ultra-sharp sword to The Bride, a tangible product of "Asian culture" flows directly from the minority character to the White character, all for the White character's benefit. At no point do we see the opposite dynamic occur, wherein a White character assists an Asian character.

ANGEL: Black Examples

1) The Matrix (1999)

» actor/character: Laurence Fishburne as Morpheus; Gloria Foster as Oracle

» analysis: Morpheus fulfills the role of the Angel, his sole purpose in life being to aid "the One." The One is Neo (Keanu Reeves). In addition to Morpheus, Gloria Foster's role as the Oracle also qualifies as an Angel. Her function was to help Neo understand his latent ability to fulfill the prophecy and save the world.

2) The Green Mile (1999)

» actor/character: Michael Clarke Duncan as John Coffey

» analysis: Tom Hanks stars as Paul Edgecomb, a firm but fair death row prison guard who realizes that taking lives has taken a toll on his own life. Enter the Angel, John Coffey, a big, Black, slow-witted inmate whose gentle-giant behavior reinvigorates new life in Edgecomb – literally. Coffey has a special gift for healing and his mysterious powers cure Edgecomb of his nagging problems.

» **bonus**: Despite Coffey's assistance to Edgecomb and Edgecomb's boss, Warden Hal Moores (played by James Cromwell), Edgecomb returns the favor by executing him (so much for *quid pro quo*). While Coffey's life is cut short, the movie ends by suggesting that Edgecomb may just live forever. Michael Clarke Duncan received a Best Supporting Oscar nomination for his depiction of John Coffey – a man incarcerated and executed for a crime that he did not commit!

3) The Legend of Bagger Vance (2000)

» **actor/character**: Will Smith as Bagger Vance
» **analysis**: Rannulph Junuh (Matt Damon) is a small-town war hero with a gift for golf who finds himself in a tournament with two golf greats. Here's the problem: he has lost his swing. Enter the Angel, the "legendary" Bagger Vance, a mysterious caddy who offers to help Junuh find his "authentic swing." Bagger Vance helps Junuh master the game of golf, which in turn helps Junuh master the game of love and the game of life. Bagger Vance, his services fully rendered, walks off into the sunset, never to be heard from again.
» **bonus**: Although Junuh is the central protagonist, the movie title, ***The Legend of Bagger Vance,*** implies that Vance is actually the lead character. Other examples wherein the leading minority character serves as an Angel archetype, thereby subverting their lead role to another White character, include ***Big Momma's House 2***, ***Man on Fire*** and ***Hitch***.

ANGEL: LATINO EXAMPLES

1) Spanglish (2004)

» **actor/character**: Paz Vega as Flor Moreno
» **analysis**: The Angel archetype is fulfilled by the Mexican immigrant, Flor Moreno. Moreno accepts a job working as a housekeeper for well-off, yet dysfunctional family in Brentwood, California. Although Moreno cannot speak English all that well initially, she overcomes this barrier to prove her worth to a family that does not seem to appreciate the

ANGEL ARCHETYPE AT WORK

PROFILE: *Man on Fire* (2004)

Denzel Washington plays John W. Creasy, an ex-marine and a recovering drunk who has nothing left to do with his life. He lands work providing protective transportation for a young White girl named Pita (Dakota Fanning), who has a White mother and a Latino step-father (Lisa and Samuel, played respectively by Radha Mitchell and Marc Anthony). Samuel's role as a father figure is questionable and Creasy essentially becomes the child's surrogate father, helping her with homework and training her for swim meets. Creasy's status as a surrogate father is confirmed by Sister Anna, one of Pita's Catholic school teachers, who upon hearing Creasy's explanation for the absence of Pita's parents intones, **"Today, you are her father."** After Pita is kidnapped as part of an insurance scam hatched by Samuel, Creasy stops at nothing to avenge her loss. After receiving the directive, **"You kill 'em all,"** from Pita's mother, Creasy proceeds to cut a murderous swath through the corrupted ranks of the Mexico City police and government to uncover the truth about Pita's whereabouts.

Creasy has no family of his own, but he hunts for Pita as if she were truly his own child. At the end of the movie, Creasy gives his own life in exchange for the girl's safe passage back to her mother. Although Denzel Washington occupies the central role in this mainstream movie, complete with heroic and adventurous character traits, the character is still a reprise of the Angel archetype. While Creasy's relationship with Pita is not as stereotypical as Bojangles and Shirley Temple's, over the years, the historically negative stereotype has given way to a more complex archetype that nonetheless continues the pattern of marginalization.

On a separate but related note of minority marginalization, be sure to observe the negative portrayal of Latino males throughout the movie. Samuel turns out to be a scheming father who is willing to ransom his own daughter for money to pay for debts inherited from his father. Samuel ultimately commits suicide to "atone" for his wrongdoings. The fact that Latino pop star Marc Anthony fulfills this role fits in line with the minority musician crossover theme (highlighted with the high prevalence of Black rappers used as actors on pg. 37).

Aside from Samuel, corrupt Latino "authority" figures and other criminals involved in the kidnapping ring are prevalent throughout the movie. The brutal method in which Creasy responds to these Menace to Society characters (i.e., chopping off fingers, inserting explosives in the rectal area, etc.) reinforces this negative portrayal.

personal sacrifices she endures in the process. She does, however, attract the attention of the patriarch John Clasky (Adam Sandler), who in turn rediscovers passion in his life.

» key scene: Since Moreno's dignity would not allow her to experience love in imperfect conditions, she ultimately decides against consummating her magical connection with Clasky after having a "magical" private dinner alone in his restaurant. Nonetheless, Moreno's actions still help Clasky rekindle his sense of romance, offering him a chance to redeem his relationship with his disenchanted wife Deborah (Téa Leoni).

2) Shall We Dance (2004)

» actor/character: Jennifer Lopez as Paulina
» analysis: The Angel is represented by Paulina, who serves as a dance instructor for a fatigued businessman, John Clark (Richard Gere). Although the two share a climactic "steamy" tango scene (much like Adam Sandler and Paz Vega's characters share a climactic scene in *Spanglish*), no additional intimacy takes place between the two. Instead, Paulina's dance moves inspire Clark to rekindle the flames of passion with his disenchanted wife (Susan Sarandon as Beverly), which also sounds a lot like *Spanglish*.
» key scene: Toward the movie's end, Clark makes a grand entrance at Paulina's farewell party with his wife, Beverly. Paulina repeats the movie's title and allows Clark the opportunity to show his wife and all others in attendance just how much he has learned and grown. This scene signals the end of Clark's relationship with Paulina (she leaves the country to "resume" her dance career). Meanwhile, at the end of the movie, Clark and his wife are subsequently depicted dancing merrily together, as final confirmation that after a "temporary" setback, their love is here to stay.
» bonus: *Shall We Dance* is an example of a movie where the White character uses the minority female body for catharsis. Since Clark learned how to rekindle the romantic spark missing in his life through the aid of Paulina, we see a conduit theme where the body of the minority actress is used as a tool for White catharsis. Additional examples where the body of a minority character is specifically used as a cathartic tool include *Ghost, Bringing Down the House* and *Hitch*. In *Ghost*, Oda

Mae Brown (Whoopi Goldberg) literally allows for the ghost of Sam Wheat (Patrick Swayze) to occupy her body during a séance so that he and Molly Jensen (Demi Moore) could communicate. Charlene Morton (Queen Latifah) in **Bringing Down the House** delivers a "hands on" crash course to Peter Sanderson (Steve Martin) on how to aggressively make love to a woman, highlighted by her telling him to "grab these" in making reference to her own breasts. In **Hitch**, Alex "Hitch" Hitchens (Will Smith) teaches Albert (Kevin James) about the ways of courtship by instructing Albert to attempt to kiss him ("show me the magic"). Albert ultimately feels the magic, but the trick ends up on Hitch when Albert goes all the way and kisses Hitch on the mouth.

3) The Incredibles (2004)

» **actor/character:** Mirage as voiced by Elizabeth Peña
» **analysis:** The Angel in this animated feature is represented by Mirage, the cream-colored seductive accomplice who works for Syndrome (Jason Lee) at his island headquarters. Unable to blindly assist the nefarious Syndrome in his plot to hurt the Incredibles family, Mirage provides key help that enables the family to escape Syndrome's lair and "save the day."
» **bonus:** The character Frozone, voiced by Samuel L. Jackson, also qualifies as an Angel. Frozone's character is largely defined by his ability to assist the Incredibles during the movie's climax.

ANGEL: OTHER EXAMPLES

1) Windtalkers (2002)

» **actor/character:** Adam Beach as Private Ben Yahzee; Roger Willie as Private Charles Whitehorse
» **analysis:** Decorated Marine Sergeant Joe Enders' (Nicolas Cage) mission is to protect Privates Ben Yahzee and Charles Whitehorse, two Navajo Marines who use their native language as an unbreakable code that the Japanese cannot decipher during World War II. Enders is initially frustrated by the assignment, but Yahzee is resilient in reaching out to Enders and is not dissuaded by Enders' gruff exterior. In the midst of

---

WHAT DO YOU THINK?

Avatar (2009) features Latina actress Michelle Rodriguez as Trudy Chacon, a military pilot who changes her allegiance to that of the native Na'vi by movie's end. In the climactic battle of the Tree of Souls, she purposely engaged the larger Resources Development Association (RDA) mother warship just long enough for the white male protagonist (Jake Sully) to escape and continue the revolution unharmed before falling to her death.

Avatar also features East Indian actor Dileep Rao as Dr. Max Patel, a scientist from the RDA facilities who risks his welfare to team up with Trudy Chacon to help Jake Sully and Dr. Grace Augustine escape confinement.

Do you see the Angel Figure in either/both of these examples?

battle, Enders not only comes to admire the codetalkers, but he also reaches an understanding of his own personal issues and overcomes the enemy within himself.

2) The Terminal (2004)

» **actor/character:** Kumar Pallana as Gupta Rajan
» **analysis:** Gupta is an elderly Indian immigrant who works as a janitor in the airport terminal where the protagonist, Viktor Navorski (Tom Hanks), is stranded after political turmoil in his native country invalidates his travel documents. Viktor's dilemma is that he must leave the airport to complete an unstated "mission" for his late father. Despite Gupta's initial surliness, he becomes an entertaining and insightful ally to Viktor while Viktor struggles to pass the interminable time. Gupta not only provides companionship and romantic assistance to Viktor, but he also makes a key sacrifice that allows Viktor to leave the airport and fulfill his pledge to his father.
» **key scene:** The elderly Gupta has a troubling past: he is a violent fugitive who stabbed a man decades ago and fled his native India. Gupta's illegal refuge in the United States, coupled with his thick accent, help to reinforce his foreignness. Viktor is foreign as well, but his unyielding kindness helps endear him to the audience – not to mention that he is portrayed by the well-known White American actor, Tom Hanks. Gupta's abrasive attitude initially has the opposite effect and presents him as the "ugly" foreigner. Yet, Gupta proves his worth to the audience in time. In true form to the Angel archetype, Gupta's redemption comes as the result of sacrificing himself on behalf of the protagonist. Gupta gets arrested when he goes out on the tarmac to disrupt an incoming plane, which ultimately means he will be deported and forced to face up to his past crime. In so doing, he gives Viktor enough time to leave the terminal so that Viktor can carry out his deceased father's last wishes. What is this lofty mission?! Viktor goes to a jazz club to collect one last missing signature on a picture of legendary jazz artists . . . . This is a clear example of an Angel sacrificing everything within his power in order to allow the White protagonist to complete his emotional catharsis, even if it means not getting away with murder.
» **bonus:** Viktor and Amelia Warren (Catherine Zeta-Jones) enjoy a dinner

catered by Gupta and two other Angel figures (Mulroy, played by Chi McBride, and Enrique Cruz played by Diego Luna). Gupta, dressed in "traditional" garb, entertains Viktor and Amelia while they wait for their food to arrive. Gupta begins playing an instrument in the background and then leaves the scene. When he returns, Gupta juggles hoops before leaving to balance a series of spinning plates, all for the amusement of Viktor, Amelia and the viewing audience.

» **double bonus:** Kumar Pallana can also be found in ***The Royal Tenenbaums*** as Pagoda. In this movie, he serves as an Angel figure, primarily as the servant to Royal (Gene Hackman). Pagoda – like Gupta – also has a history of stabbing someone, and even goes so far as to stab Royal himself!

3) Avatar (2009)

» **actor/character:** Wes Studi as Eytukan; Zoe Saldana as Neytiri
» **analysis:** The central Angel figure is represented by Native American actor Wes Studi (Cherokee), who lends the voice to the Computer Generated Image character of Eytukan. Eytukan was the clan leader of the Omaticaya and also father of Neytiri who decided to take a young White boy, Jake Sully (Sam Worthington), into his family. Through his instruction, Neytiri was to train Jake in the lifestyle and ways of the Na'vi — the fictional Indigenous people of the fictional planet Pandora. This order essentially saved Jake's life by agreeing to take in "an outsider" or a human temporarily using the body of a Na'vi for espionage purposes, and bestow him loyalty, wisdom and familial support so that Jake can be successful in both the Native and White worlds. As another example of one-way culture sharing, Neytiri gives Jake advice and guidance on how to dominate/conquer/connect his mind to the bird/dragon-like predator (i.e., *leonopteryx*) called the Toruk by the people. Although Zoe Saldana's ethnic heritage is Afro-Latina, her human image was never seen onscreen and she voiced a character indigenous to the planet of Pandora that White settlers wanted to clear out of the way in order to make use of the planet's valuable resources. Theoretically this movie displays heavy interaction between both the Na'vi and White "worlds," but notice how interaction is actually limited to White characters, since most of the dialogue and all intimacy is filtered through Jake's "crossover" character.

- » **bonus**: A very similar storyline is at work in ***The Last Samurai***, wherein the leading Japanese Samurai warrior, Katsumoto (Ken Watanabe), essentially adopts a White American, Nathan Algren (Tom Cruise), into his clan. Katsumoto, through one-way culture sharing, provides so much tutoring and attention to Algren that upon the movie's conclusion, *Algren* proves to be the last samurai warrior worthy of honor – more so than any of the *native* Japanese samurai! This is similar to how Jake, who has not been a true Na'vi all of his life, is more Na'vi than all other Na'vi, becoming only the sixth Toruk Makto (conqueror of fierce bird/dragon respected and feared by Na'vi) in four generations Na'vi history with the great-grandfather of Eytukan being the fifth.
- » **bonus quote**: As proof of the minority Angel Figure bestowing and giving all that they have to assist the protagonist, who is most often White, upon induction into the Omaticaya clan, Eytukan says to Jake: "You are now a son of the Omaticaya. You are part of The People." If the Whites in this movie had adopted a similarly inclusive stance, perhaps there is no conflict and no movie is made.

The Angel Figure archetype is often endowed with admirable qualities: strength, empathy, caring and resourcefulness. These qualities are not inherently disparaging by any stretch of the imagination. However, when such attributes are present solely to provide a White character with help or support, these attributes adopt a more hollow meaning. Ultimately, in spite of the many ways in which the Angel is presented, this minority archetype is limited to a role of service to a White character. Even though it appears that this character is "involved" in the movie's storyline, the Angel's only purpose is to assist the central White characters in fulfilling *their own* purpose.

CHAPTER 5:
THE BACKGROUND FIGURE

*We're furniture.
We're isolated from the main
action and dependent
on the white characters.
We really could be rented
and moved around.*

Anne-Marie Johnson, Chair, Ethnic Employment Opportunity Committee, Screen Actors Guild[1]

CHAPTER 5:
THE BACKGROUND FIGURE

Look! On the ground! By the curb! Near the drain! It's the minority Background Figure! Sheltered from the intense glare of the open spotlight is this silent crusader for "diversity," methodically and meticulously placed to remind movie audiences that race is not lost upon Hollywood studios. The Background Figure's presence is inconsequential to the overall storyline. This character has limited dialogue, if he or she speaks at all, and does not advance the plot, thereby serving as mere "window dressing" to reinforce a visual – albeit illusory – message of diversity. This archetype is deceptive because this character can make multiple, yet fleeting appearances and may even deliver limited dialogue. Although the moviegoer subconsciously notes that a minority is onscreen, the Background Figure has no ultimate impact on advancing the plot.

(BACK)GROUND ZERO

Background Figures typically crop up in movies where the context calls for a "cross-section of society" (e.g., movies set in major cities, disaster movies, juries in courtroom dramas, etc.), or where they will have peripheral or tangential relationships to the White protagonists (e.g., casual friends, coworkers, etc.) that have little overall bearing on the plot. For example, most mainstream filmmakers feel compelled to employ minority Background Figures for movies set in New York City. Without them, the movie runs the risk of omitting non-White characters in a film set in a city that is an icon of diversity, thereby lessening the "reality" of the setting. Prudent movie studios include Background Figures in their movies to maintain their ability to appeal to the wider White audience, while avoiding any backlash from minority audience members that might otherwise feel left out. Background Figures serve merely as visual teasers for the viewer. Technically speaking,

ugly American

minorities that display "undesirable" characteristics to serve as a contrast with the "normal" American protagonist

their roles could be deleted entirely without sacrificing any significant effect on the advancement of the movie's plot.

Background figures frequently fall victim to unceremonious and incidental deaths, underscoring their marginalized value onscreen. Another variation on the Background Figure is the **ugly American** role, where the "foreign" minority character is juxtaposed against "normal" American (typically White American) behavior. These minority characters appear briefly, and are usually depicted in service positions such as taxi cab drivers and convenience store owners/clerks. The ugly American is presumably an American citizen, but this character's race and limited command of the English language is often emphasized for comedic effect.

Prominent minority characters are typically depicted in social isolation from other minorities (i.e., devoid of onscreen familial relationships, lacking romantic counterparts, etc.). However, as Background Figures, minority characters may see a significant increase in their numbers. Often, minority actors are utilized in order to satisfy a racial requirement, meaning that the movie *requires* characters of a certain race to maintain a level of authenticity (e.g., Asian actors en masse portraying Japanese warriors in *The Last Samurai* or Japanese citizens in *Lost in Translation*). Background figures fulfilling the racial requirement construct are frequently depicted in collective groups and share one discernible but "foreign" identity. Background Figures not only apply in "foreign" abroad settings, but also apply to domestically "foreign" settings for White characters (e.g., Bruce Willis interacting with Blacks in Harlem in *Die Hard: With a Vengeance*; Ethan Hawke in the presence of Latinos and Blacks in the run-down streets of Los Angeles in *Training Day*).

WHAT DO YOU THINK?

In *Kill Bill: Vol. 1*, there are a significant amount of Asian actors featured in the movie. However, they largely serve as sacrificial fodder for Uma Thurman's character (The Bride) as she hacks out a bloody path on her road to revenge the attempt on her life by Bill, a White male. The Bride kills in the order of a hundred different Asian characters, culminating in a "villain's death" for Lucy Liu, who gets sliced through the head. The continuous slayings administered by a White lead illustrates the low racial capital for Asians in this movie. Ironically, despite the large number of Asians present, their individual identity is unimportant and their repeated killings desensitize the audience to the value of these Asian characters. The message is that these Asian characters are expendable, only present so as to serve as a cathartic slaughter for the White protagonist. ***Can you think of a mainstream movie where an Asian lead wantonly kills White characters just to settle a score with another Asian character?***

HOT TICKET ITEMS

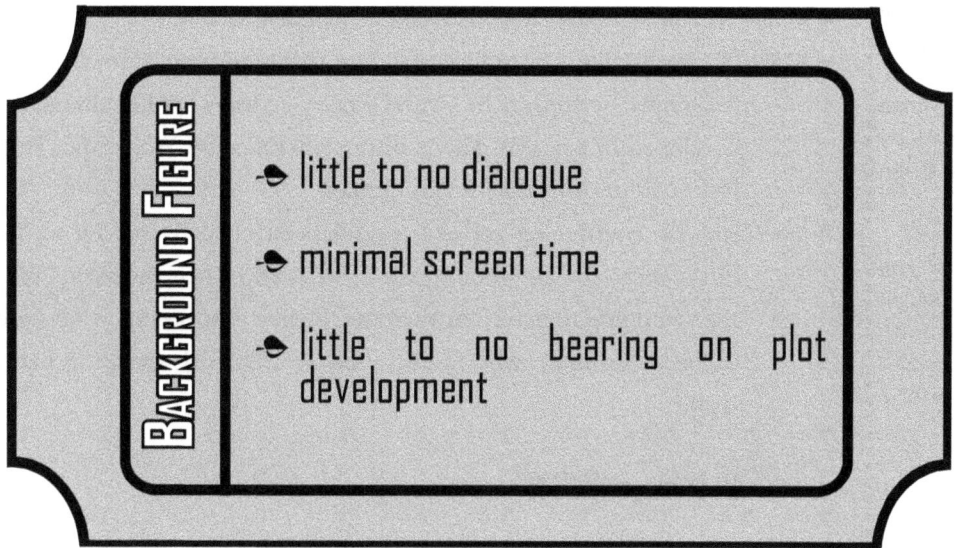

BACKGROUND FIGURE
- little to no dialogue
- minimal screen time
- little to no bearing on plot development

ARCHETYPE EXPLORED
BACKGROUND FIGURE: Asian Examples

1) Pearl Harbor (2001)

» **actor/character:** Nameless Japanese soldiers
» **analysis:** Fitting into the racial requirement subset of Background Figures, the Asian characters here are "required" as part of the scenery for this story about Japan's infamous attack on Pearl Harbor. None of the Asian actors receive top-billing and the central protagonists are White Americans.
» **bonus:** This movie establishes the racial requirement role for many Asian pilots who are seen during combat scenes, but are never fully humanized through close-up angles and dialogue. For those Asian characters that do have dialogue, they largely consist of high-ranking officers who speak only in Japanese with English subtitles, thereby reinforcing their "otherness" to the viewing audience.

> **WHAT DO YOU THINK?**
> In *Jurassic World* (2015), there is a significant amount of diverse actors featured in the movie. One of the more notables was Hamada as played by Japanese American actor Brian Tee.
>
> Hamada was the leader of the Asset Containment Unit (ACU), or a glorified group of security guards posted on the island in case of emergency with a wayward dinosaur (or two).
>
> *Does Hamada's character fit the Background Figure profile? If so, how so? If not, why not?*

2) X2: X-Men United (2003)

» **actor/character:** Kelly Hu as Yuriko Oyama/Deathstrike
» **analysis:** Deathstrike is introduced as a non-thinking, programmable brute. Although she appears in several scenes, no aspect of her character is developed in any way. She is ultimately killed by Wolverine (Hugh Jackman) towards the movie's climax.
» **key scene:** The emotionless and expressionless Yuriko delivers only one line in the entire movie (around the 25:41 mark) when she asks, "What are you doing in here?" At the time, Yuriko is speaking to Mystique (Rebecca Romijn), who is disguised as a Spanish-speaking Latino janitor.

3) Chicago (2002)

» **actor/character:** Lucy Liu as Kitty Baxter
» **analysis:** Kitty appears onscreen at roughly the 1:04:32 mark for a vignette that lasts a little more than two minutes. Kitty was a fascinating new client for Billy Flynn (Richard Gere) who was wanted for the triple murder of her husband and his two lovers. Billy abruptly loses interest in Kitty when Roxie Hart (Renée Zellweger) passes out under the belief that she is pregnant.

BACKGROUND FIGURE: BLACK EXAMPLES

1) Lara Croft Tomb Raider: The Cradle of Life (2003)

» **actor/character:** Djimon Hounsou as Kosa; numerous and nameless Masai warriors
» **analysis:** The Kenyan Masai warriors are nameless characters who silently smile and provide an exotic background for the action and dialogue of Laura Croft (Angelina Jolie). Limited speaking parts are limited to one particular warrior: Kosa.
» **bonus:** Kosa also fulfills an Angelic function by escorting Croft to the African tribe that knows the exact location of the Cradle of Life. Kosa helps Croft in a variety of other ways as well. He assembles Croft's supplies before their rendezvous in Africa and he translates

her dialogue with the tribal chief. Kosa also hatches an impromptu strategy to assist Croft when she is pressured to reveal the Cradle's location to the villains.

BACKGROUND FIGURE ARCHETYPE AT WORK

PROFILE: *Harry Potter and the Sorcerer's Stone (2001)*

The "Quidditch" scene from **Harry Potter and the Sorcerer's Stone** is a perfect illustration of Background Figures at work. The Harry Potter franchise is a worldwide phenomenon of epic proportions. This much-anticipated book-into-movie adaptation yielded a whopping $976 million at the worldwide box office.[5b] All of the central protagonists are White, and the remainder of the top-billed characters are also White, so there are few chances to see non-White characters in the movie. The Quidditch scene serves as a perfect opportunity to add in an ensemble of Background Figures for a number of reasons.

Quidditch is a friendly game played by Harry Potter (Daniel Radcliffe and his classmates. Quidditch is important to the discussion of Background Figures because the game serves as the movie's opportunity to add in "diversity" where it might not otherwise "fit." In this scene, Harry Potter zooms around on his broom, frantically trying to prove his worth to his other classmates. Several of the players in the game flying around in the background are non-White characters, none of whom are prominently featured in the movie after the Quidditch scene.

Inserting Background Figures in an action sequence like the Quidditch game gives the impression that non-White characters are involved in the story or have an influence on the direction of the plot. This is a clever illusion, given the fast pace and the visibility of the Background Figures during the scene. However, in order to experience the vicarious thrill of winning the Quidditch competition, all audience members must make the connective switch to identify with Harry Potter, the White protagonist. The Background Figures are peripheral and merely serve as obstacles and facilitators for Harry Potter's cathartic heroism. While Harry Potter's celebrated victory propels him through the rest of the movie, the other Background Figures are swept to the sidelines for the rest of the movie.

Quidditch is no longer a fictional movie game. Go to ***www.theracedoc.com*** to find out how!

> **TOTAL ANECDOTAL**
>
> Leonardo DiCaprio, Jennifer Connelly and Djimon Hounsou all star in **Blood Diamond** (2006), a movie that depicts the contentious fight for control of diamond mines during a period of civil war in Sierra Leone.
>
> In order to illustrate the horrors of such bloody conflict, the movie's creators employed several teenage and children amputees as Background Figures. Numbering twenty-seven in total, these amputees were real victims of tribal warfare and were pulled from local hospitals to appear as extras.
>
> According to *The New York Post*, Warner Bros. promised these orphaned African amputees prosthetic limbs after shooting finished in June of 2006.
>
> After several months of waiting, the amputees were allegedly told by Warner Bros., "You will have to wait for December, when the movie comes out, so we can get some publicity out of it."[5a]
>
> A local African charity entitled Eastern Cape stepped in and provided the **Blood Diamond** amputees prosthetic limbs and stated that if Warner Bros. does produce the promised money, that such funds will be used to outfit twenty-seven other amputees.

2) The Rainmaker (1997)

» actor/character: Danny Glover as Judge Tyrone Kipler
» analysis: Judge Tyrone Kipler presides in this legal drama featuring lead characters Rudy Baylor (Matt Damon) and Deck Shifflet (Danny DeVito). Despite being a well-known star, Glover's judge character has limited dialogue and his screen time is adjourned rather quickly. Not surprisingly, the role went uncredited. Now was that Glover's decision or the studio's decision? You be the judge.
» bonus: Notice how Judge Kipler occupies a subtle Angel archetype role. As a former civil rights lawyer with a reputation for being tough on insurance companies, this newly-made judge is both patient and sympathetic with Rudy Baylor, the fledgling and outmanned novice who is arguing his first case.

3) Intolerable Cruelty (2003)

» actor/character: Isabell O'Connor as Judge Marva Munson
» analysis: Judge Marva Munson is a divorce judge who has little dialogue outside of a few token lines she delivers from the bench. Her impact is minimal and she is only relevant insofar as it relates to the two lead characters, Miles Massey (George Clooney) and Marylin Rexroth (Catherine Zeta-Jones).
» bonus: Note that O'Connor has played a judge in at least three other movies throughout her career: **Family Business** (1989), **With or Without You** (1998) and **Here on Earth** (2000).

BACKGROUND FIGURE: Latino Examples

1) Star Wars II: Attack of the Clones (2002)

» actor/character: Jimmy Smits as Bail Organa
» analysis: While Bail Organa arguably plays an important role to the overall storyline, most of his "heroic" action takes place offscreen and in the past (he and his wife raised the infant Princess Leia in seclusion). The brevity of his scenes and dialogue denote him as a Background Figure, and his role as a caretaker also presents him as an Angel figure.

» **bonus:** The brief and limited role of Bail Organa is played by the well-known Latino actor, Jimmy Smits. This role underscores the extent of minority marginalization, wherein the talents of a well-known minority actor are expended purely for a limited, non-cameo role. Nonetheless, the message to the average moviegoer is that "diversity" has been briefly achieved – albeit in limited fashion. Further emphasizing the limited impact of Bail Organa is the fact that this *character* is rather short-lived. In **Star Wars IV: A New Hope**, Lord Vader decides to "test" the Death Star on the Alderaan system (i.e., "blow up" the planet) where Bail Organa resides.

emasculation

the process whereby the male identity of a minority character is overtly compromised or challenged in the face of conventional gender roles

2) Maid In Manhattan (2002)

» **actor/character:** Marilyn Torres as Barb; Priscilla Lopez as Veronica Ventura
» **analysis:** Even though *Maid in Manhattan* features a Latina lead (Jennifer Lopez as Marisa Ventura), the movie still contains Latina Background

> **WHAT DO YOU THINK?**
> Low racial capital for Latino Background Figures is exemplified by **Man On Fire**, where Denzel Washington stars as John W. Creasy, a bodyguard who cuts a violent and murderous swath – in graphic fashion – through Mexico City to find the people responsible for kidnapping his employer's daughter (Dakota Fanning as Pita).
>
> For an example of this violence towards these Latinos, consider how Creasy "interrogates" one of the criminals for information about Pita's whereabouts. With the criminal's hands taped to the steering wheel of a car, Creasy proceeds to lop off his extended fingers one-by-one until he overcomes his reluctance to divulge secret information. Creasy dispenses and disposes of the criminal by pushing the car off a cliff when his interrogation is concluded.
>
> In another instance, Creasy has bounded Fuentes (Jesús Ochoa) to the trunk of a car under a freeway overpass. This Latino male is the President of La Hermandad, an underground and corrupt organization of Mexican police officers. Creasy, in another effort to obtain more information about the kidnapped girl's whereabouts, explains that he has lodged an explosive discharge inside of the President's rectal area. The "anal discharge" is further emasculation of the President, who is already exposed wearing only his boxer undergarments – replete with hairy back – in broad daylight. Creasy threatens to detonate it if the President does not offer up any information. Alas, Creasy obtains his information . . . and detonates the device anyway!
>
> *Can you recall a mainstream movie where Whites were depicted with such severely low racial capital in relation to a more powerful minority group? More specifically, can you recall a Latino character methodically chopping off the fingers of White characters or inserting explosive discharges into the rear ends of White characters, with their resulting deaths serving as a mere afterthought?* Supporting the implication that the lives of White characters are valued more highly than those of more marginalized minority characters, Creasy himself dies in the course of rescuing and reuniting the central White characters. The movie ends with the White mother and daughter alive.

WHAT DO YOU THINK?

Poseidon (2006) tells the story of a dedicated group of survivors who seek to escape a large cruise ship overturned by a giant wave before it sinks.

Predictably, the original group is whittled down to a select few who ultimately prevail. Although the movie features at least three minority characters with dialogue, only one lives past the movie's halfway point (Latina actress Mía Maestro as Elena). Black actor Andre Braugher appears as Captain Michael Bradford, but "incorrectly" instructs his crew to seal all passengers in the ship's glass ballroom, which eventually collapses under the intense water pressure, drowning everyone inside. Elena dies shortly after the halfway point, which means that all minority characters are dead well before the movie's climax and conclusion.

The third minority character is a Latino waiter who qualifies as a Background Figure with minimal screen time and dialogue (Freddy Rodríguez as Marco Valentin). He also fulfills the Angel archetype by providing crucial directions to the survival group with his intimate knowledge of the ship's layout. As an indicator of his only value to the White characters, the central protagonist (Josh Lucas as Dylan Johns) refers to Valentin as an inanimate object ("Hey, Map!").

Unfortunately for Valentin, he did not prove himself to be indispensable. While trying to escape from an elevator shaft, Valentin finds himself holding on to Richard Nelson's (Richard Dreyfuss) legs who in turn is clinging to Dylan Johns' arms. Johns is outside of the shaft, frantically trying to pull both to safety before the elevator above Nelson and Valentin falls. After some effort, Johns instructs Nelson to "Shake him off!" Nelson literally shakes off Valentin – the same Valentin who provided crucial assistance to the group only moments before – and sends him plummeting to a grisly fate at the wrong end of the elevator shaft.

To what degree is the manner in which Valentine dies indicative of the marginal status of minority Background Figures in Hollywood? Would the impact of the scene been the same had Nelson shaken off a young, clean-cut White male? Can you recall seeing a "disaster movie" where no White characters survived to the end of the movie?

It should also be noted that Richard Nelson contemplates suicide at the beginning of the movie. ***Does this make it any more "ironic" that he should survive until the movie's end? What does it say about the elevated status of the White characters that the actions of Johns and Nelson are considered "heroic" instead of "murderous"?***

Figures. Look for Marilyn Torres as Barb, one of Marisa's maid co-workers. Although Marisa and Barb are both Latina, Barb is much more "ethnic" (e.g., Spanish accent, darker skin and hair, etc.). Barb has no impact on the plot, but her distinctly "ethnic" appearance serves as a contrast to the upwardly mobile Marisa, whose appearance fits the asymptote model. Marisa's mother, Veronica, is also marked by distinctly "ethnic" characteristics, particularly her "cultural conservatism." Veronica's "backward thinking" casts her as somewhat of a villain. Marisa rebels, ultimately achieving financial success and finding romance with an influential White male (Ralph Fiennes as Christopher Marshall). Her "success" only further distances her from the "ethnic" trappings of Background Figures Barb and Veronica.

» **bonus**: Notice the racial diversity of the characters found in the hotel's working staff in contrast to the predominantly White cast of characters in the more affluent settings and positions of authority (e.g., White hotel guest, Christopher Marshall's White political advisors, the White attendees at the socialite gala event, etc.).

3) The Mask of Zorro (1998)

» **actor/character**: Mexican slaves
» **analysis**: Falling under the racial requirement heading, pay close attention to the climax featuring the enslaved Mexican prisoners locked in cages. As petty offenders and peasants commissioned for slave labor in a secret gold mine, these minority characters are frantically desperate for the heroism

of Zorro (Antonio Banderas) and his faithful love, Elena Montero (Catherine Zeta-Jones). Zorro succeeds releasing them just before the entire mine is detonated. These Latino characters are quintessential Background Figures since a heavy visual emphasis is placed on their collective identity (i.e., a throng of slaves) and not on any one particular character.

» **key scene**: With possibly the exception of one child that Elena clutches and another child that Zorro carries away from the decimated mine, notice how few camera shots focus on the faces of the slaves in the moments leading up to the explosion. While the slaves can be heard clamoring for freedom in the background, many visual shots of the enslaved prisoners are limited primarily to their limbs and legs. The resulting visual effect is that the heroic efforts of the movie's protagonists remain the primary focus, not the emotions of the freed slaves.

» **bonus**: Indicative of the dearth of opportunities provided to Latino actors in mainstream movies, notice how, despite the movie's setting, that all the three leading roles were depicted by *European* actors. Anthony Hopkins (Don Diego de la Vega) and Catherine Zeta-Jones are from the United Kingdom, while Antonio Banderas is from Spain. The use of European actors posing as Latino figures only heightens the paucity of mainstream movies that freely feature Latino actors from South, Central or North America as "themselves" within heroic mainstream movie roles. Contrast this to the "distinctly ethnic" Mexican slaves.

BACKGROUND FIGURE: OTHER EXAMPLES

1) Old School (2003)

» **actor/character**: Sarah Shahi as Erica
» **analysis**: Even if you saw **Old School**, you might not recall seeing a Persian-Spanish actress in the movie. The aforementioned actress is Sarah Shahi, who probably had more screen time when she was a Dallas Cowboys cheerleader than she has in this movie. Shahi plays Erica, a friend of Frank Ricard's (Will Ferrell) wife, Nicole (Ellen Pompeo). Given the degrees of separation from Shahi's character to Ferrell's protagonist, it is easy to see how her character serves as a Background Figure.

» **bonus**: The racial "ambiguity" of Shahi's character sets her up as an "acceptable" associate of a White character. In this case, the "ambiguity" refers to the *audience's* racial categorization of Erica's character as opposed to Shahi's true racial and ethnic heritage. What registers with the audience is that Nicole has a friend "of color," aesthetically distinct enough to be distinguished as non-White, but innocuous enough to remain in the background.

2) Snow Dogs (2002)

» **actor/character**: Graham Greene as Peter Yellowbear
» **analysis**: Graham Greene, a Native American actor, plays Peter Yellowbear in this comedy set in Alaska. Mr. Yellowbear makes two brief cameo appearances during the movie, and demonstrates the utmost thrift and economy with his speech. With a name like Peter Yellowbear, can we really expect him to be anything else but a Background Figure?
» **bonus**: Further underscoring how race can be used for comedic effect, the movie's storyline revolves around the fact that Dr. Ted Brooks (played by Black actor Cuba Gooding, Jr.) is actually an adopted child with an Alaskan mother. He visits Alaska for the reading of her will and, with the help of his female "Eskimo" friend Barb (played by Philippine actress Joanna Bacalso), he discovers his true identity. Brooks ultimately learns that his father is actually an old and crusty, cantankerous and uncouth, old and curmudgeonly White mountain man named James "Thunder Jack" Johnson (James Coburn).

WHAT DO YOU THINK?
In *Suicide Squad* (2016), we have another example of an ensemble cast featuring a significant amount of diverse actors featured in the movie. Interestingly enough, the first member of the squad to be killed was Slipknot, played by First Nations Saulteaux actor Adam Beach.

In determining Slipknot's status as a Background Figure, compare and contrast the quantity & quality of dialogue and screen time to his other squad members.

Why do you think Slipknot was chosen to die first? Was it random?

3) Deja Vu (2006)

» **actor/character**: Nadia Shazana as Trauma Nurse
» **analysis**: This actress of East Indian heritage plays a Trauma Nurse who renders aid to Alcohol, Tobacco and Firearms agent Doug Carlin (Denzel Washington). Carlin briefly appears unexpectedly in a hospital bed after having traveled back in time to avert a terrorist plot. Shazana's character likewise appears unexpectedly and briefly.
» **bonus**: As a possible view into the formulaic categorization of minority talent, notice how Shazana also played a nurse several times on the television shows *Inconceivable*, *The Shield* and *ER* before her debut on the silver screen.

The Background Figure archetype, although not terribly significant in terms of storyline impact or dialogue, is nonetheless important for Hollywood. Even though current statistics show that Whites are overrepresented in movie roles relative to their percentage of the population, few mainstream movies completely exclude minority characters. Many moviegoers may see or hear a minority character for a few moments onscreen and walk away with a more favorable impression of minority participation than what is truly offered by Hollywood. Background Figures demonstrate that Hollywood studios are in fact making efforts to include "diversity," albeit in a manner that limits sustained and active participation by minority characters. Background Figures represent a low-risk, low-cost investment in a superficial display of visual diversity that allows studios to channel the majority of a mainstream movie's plot development through central White characters.

CHAPTER 6:
THE COMIC RELIEF

On The Lion King, *we did everything to have a racial balance among the voice talent and the singers . . . . But then we had complaints that it was racist because Whoopi Goldberg and Cheech Marin were hyenas. But they were just playing themselves. It was the same way they act in live-action movies.*

Tom Schumacher, President, Walt Disney Feature Animation[1]

CHAPTER 6:
THE COMIC RELIEF

Some minority roles in mainstream movies are included strictly for comic relief. The minority character's culture serves as fodder for humorous material. Typical conduct includes boisterous and improper grammar, exaggerated motions and facial expressions, and intense emotion in stark contrast to standardized, White, middle-class behavior. Such conduct, especially when gratuitously displayed by minorities, smacks of the minstrel performances that first graced the silver screen in early Hollywood cinema.

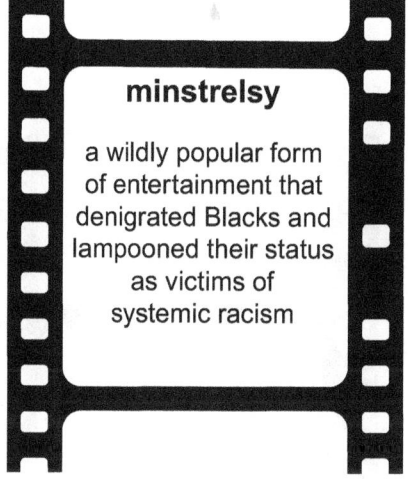

minstrelsy

a wildly popular form of entertainment that denigrated Blacks and lampooned their status as victims of systemic racism

COMIC DEBRIEF

In an atmosphere marked by political acrimony and social tension, **minstrelsy** had a vital unifying function for White Americans at the turn of the twentieth century. Minstrel shows made light of slavery and the political issues surrounding emancipation. Images of happy-go-lucky plantation slaves distorted public perception of the actual human suffering wrought by the institution of American slavery. Much like court jesters during medieval times, antebellum minstrels and their absurd antics served not only to entertain, but also to reassure their patrons of their own superiority during a period of social and economic uncertainty. By defining Blackness so absurdly, antebellum minstrels constructed

TOTAL ANECDOTAL

Past **minstrel** imagery was often exaggerated by "blackface" depictions (from both White and Black actors alike), where burnt cork and water was applied to paint the face a dark Black color, after which red or White lips were painted on top.

This type of imagery has long since been deemed highly offensive to the image of Black people in this country. However, did you notice that as recent as 2001, Ben Stiller appeared in blackface in two separate scenes in the hit comedy ***Zoolander***? Did you notice that Johnny Knoxville and Sean William Scott also appear in blackface in the 2005 hit ***The Dukes of Hazzard***?[6a]

Contemporary depictions of blackface share a storied history. Al Jolson was the star entertainer in ***The Jazz Singer***, the revolutionary 1927 movie commonly referred to as the first talking picture with sound. Al Jolson was a Jewish entertainer who gained stardom performing songs in blackface. However, Al Jolson was not the only actor to use blackface. Many stars, including *Judy Garland, Mickey Rooney, Bing Crosby and Shirley Temple*, also used blackface in their performances.[6b]

a cultural image to which all Whites could feel superior, whether they be immigrant or native-born, urban or rural, working class or well-to-do. Minstrelsy helped foster White social and political unity at the expense of Blacks and other minorities.[2]

Despite the popular use of minorities in the past, contemporary mainstream movies refrain from depicting minorities in "minstrel" performances since that would be considered politically incorrect. Nonetheless, most movies starring well-known minority comedians draw much of their comedic elements from absurd mannerisms reminiscent of the minstrel shows of old. Yet, contemporary minstrel performances are not exclusive to well-known minority comedians. Modern minstrels can be portrayed by stars and bit players alike, even those who are not "comedians" by trade.

In making the link between minstrel shows of old and contemporary mainstream movies, the continued use of culture as fodder for humor remains a consistent trend. In addition to the almost-cliched recurring comic relief characters for minorities (e.g., the ignorant Japanese tourist, the fat Black woman, the minority sidekick with a high-pitched voice), exaggerated mannerisms and frequent slapstick humor involving minorities make today's performances quite similar to the minstrel performances of old. The character's behavior is "isolated," thereby creating a **contra-juxtaposition** tension (e.g., the lone Black character operating in a predominantly White context) which consequently highlights any "wrong" or negative conduct of the minority character by relative comparison. A fertile source for such contra-juxtaposition tensions are "Buddy-cop movies" (e.g., ***Beverly Hills Cop, Lethal Weapon*** series, ***Taxi, Bad Company, Men in Black, Rising Sun***, etc.), whereby a minority is paired with a White law enforcement official in pursuit of a common goal, albeit with two markedly different approaches. It is not uncommon for the White "officer" to perform the "heavy-lifting" required to advance the plot and solve the overarching crime, while the minority "officer" helps when given direct action or "accidentally" helps through unintended bumbling.

"Comic Relief" differs from "standard" comedic conventions. For example, it is rare to see minority leads in mainstream romantic comedies, most likely because the audience must identify with romantic comedy characters. On the other hand, Comic Relief figures are intended to be "laughed at." For instance, in order to achieve an objective, the minority character may purposely play upon cultural stereotypes to manipulate others. ***Rush Hour 2*** provides a prime example when James Carter (Chris Tucker) purposely

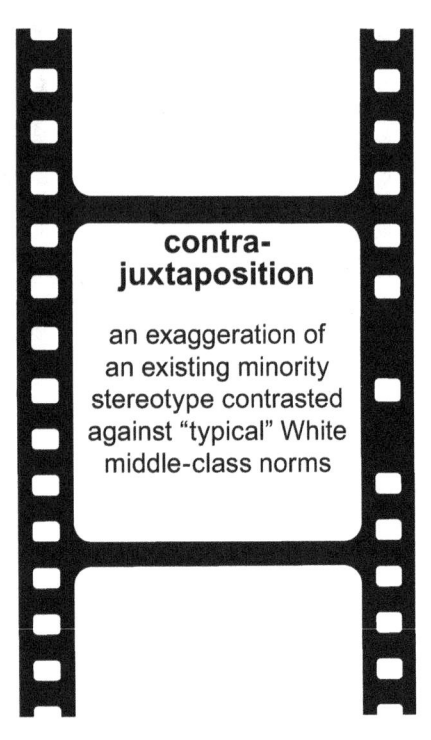

contra-juxtaposition

an exaggeration of an existing minority stereotype contrasted against "typical" White middle-class norms

provides a distraction by (loudly) claiming discrimination to "free" Chief Inspector Lee (Jackie Chan) to investigate a shady casino. The self-inflicted race card can also appear more subtly, such as when a minority character – without prompting – makes "race" a direct issue, usually for the purposes of setting up a punchline in the movie. **Lethal Weapon 4** demonstrates the self-inflicted race card when Detective Lee Butters (Chris Rock) accuses Leo Getz (Joe Pesci) of harboring racist assumptions when Getz mistakes Butters for a criminal in the backseat of a police car. While Butters plays the race card to "defend his dignity," in reality it provides the moviemakers an opportunity to insert racially-themed humor that otherwise might not be funny if such lines were delivered by a non-minority actor.

Common Comic Relief traits to look for include:

- "Permanency" of character traits or flat character arc (e.g., the "you-can-take-the-person-out-of-the-ghetto-but-you-can't-take-the-ghetto-out-of-the-person" dynamic)

- Exaggerated actions, gestures or mannerisms

- Excessive, loud, "inappropriate" or profane language

- Contra-juxtaposition against White characters

- The self-inflicted race card

HOT TICKET ITEMS

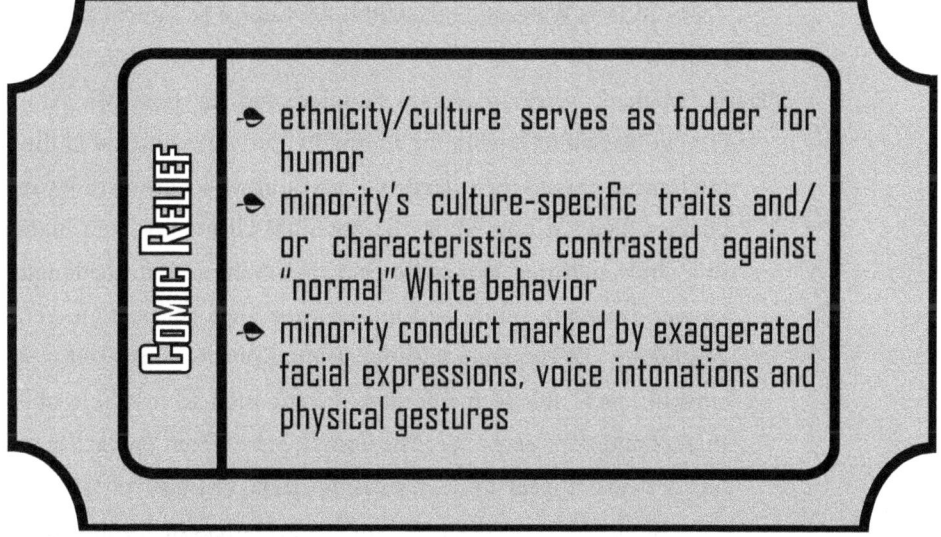

ARCHETYPE EXPLORED

COMIC RELIEF: Asian Examples

1) Austin Powers: Goldmember (2002)

» actor/character: Carrie Ann Inaba as Fook Yu; Diane Mizota as Fook Mi

» analysis: In the beginning of the movie, Austin Powers (Mike Myers) is "busy" partying with "twin" Asian darlings, Fook Yu and Fook Mi, draped on his arms. After Austin asks for their names, he replies, "Fook Mi! That was fast!" punctuated by a gratuitous smile. Notice how culture serves for fodder on several levels: the stereotype of the sexually seductive Asian females, the implied sexual innuendo at the expense of butchered "Asian language," and the implicit reference to all Asians looking alike (i.e., the identically dressed "twins").

» bonus: You may recognize the name Carrie Ann Inaba; as of the time of print, she was a host on ABC's hit television show, "Dancing with the Stars." Compare her command of the English language on the television show to her "accent" in the movie.

2) Click (2006)

» actor/character: Michael Yama as Watsushita Head Executive; Mio Takada as Watsushita Executive #1; Eiji Inoue as Watsushita Executive #2; Toshi Toda as Watsushita Executive #3; George K. Eguchi as Ancient Executive

» analysis: Michael Newman (Adam Sandler) and his boss Mr. Ammer (David Hasselhoff), work for an architecture firm and are at dinner attempting to land their next "big" account with a group of Japanese businessmen. At one point, the potential clients are seen huddled in a circle engaging in a conference. Normally, due to the language barrier, Newman would be shut out from the conversation. Yet, by employing the language selection feature on his "universal remote control," he is able to manipulate the situation so that he is able to understand their exchange. The humor comes from the fact that the businessmen appear to be discussing trivial critiques of the project while simultaneously discussing off-topic matters such going to eat at

Burger King. Later, when all parties reconvene, Newman proposes to the Japanese businessmen exactly what they want (based upon what he heard), which is punctuated by a "F—k yeah!" (in English, mind you) by the Ancient Executive.

3) Lost In Translation (2003)

- » **actor/character**: Diamond Yukai as Commercial Director; Nao Asuka as the Premium Fantasy Woman
- » **analysis**: Japanese culture and the Japanese way of life are juxtaposed against an average White (American) male's standard of living as reflected by Bob Harris (Bill Murray).[3] Several comedic scenes develop as Bob attempts to negotiate life abroad in Japan. In one instance, the Commercial Director attempts to explain how he wants Bob to deliver his lines in a commercial. Another instance is when the Premium Fantasy Woman appears outside of Bob's room and attempts to communicate her function as an escort.
- » **bonus**: In 2004, director Sofia Coppola won an Oscar for Best Writing (Screenplay Written Directly for the Screen) for this movie.
- » **note**: Even though Bill Murray is a comedian, his culture is not the fodder for humor, and these "nameless" Japanese characters only further relegate them to "Other" status.

COMIC RELIEF: BLACK EXAMPLES

1) The 40 Year Old Virgin (2005)

- » **actor/character**: Romany Malco as Jay
- » **analysis**: Jay is the fellow electronic store associate of Andy Stitzer (Steve Carell) who endeavors to assist Andy in losing his virginity. The profane and oversexed Jay dispenses advice to Andy in humoristic fashion while adopting Andy's cause as his own: "Yo' d—k [slang term for penis] is my d—k! I'm getting you some p—y [slang term for female vagina]!"
- » **bonus**: For another example of a minority character "safely" playing the race card without prompting or pressure from Whites, consider the racial barbs lobbied by the "East Indian" characters Haziz (Shelley Malil) and Mooj (Gerry Bednob). While observing Jay and another Black Smart

WHAT DO YOU THINK?
In *The Hangover Part II* (2011), Taiwanese-American actor Mason Lee plays Theodore "Teddy" Srisai.

In keeping with the movie's title, the central white protagonists embark upon a "mystery hunt" to retrace their steps from their (drunken) misadventures the night before. Dr. Stuart Price's (Ed Helms) wedding is taking place in a matter of hours and quick work must be made to piece everything back together.

One of the final pieces of the puzzle was the discovery of Stu's future brother-in-law, Teddy, who somehow went missing, but was found inside an ice machine with his finger missing. Apparently, after an unsuccessful round of the "knife game" the evening prior, he went to get ice to preserve his finger, the power went out and he was stuck.

For our purposes, go back and check out the character's reactions to the lost finger (that cannot grow back!) The three white protagonists were relieved if anything, and the mutilation of Teddy's finger and subsequent circumstances were a mere punchline. Plus, Teddy shrugs the whole matter off and does not emote over what some might deem to be a major loss.

Further, this finger loss emasculates Stu's father-in-law who Stu saw as an antagonizing character who always assumed the worst about him and his friends. During the rehearsal dinner, the father-in-law publicly praised Teddy after masterfully playing the cello: "Thank you Teddy! Hands of a brilliant musician, and one day a great surgeon." Teddy will now have to "finger" something else out.

Tech Customer (Kevin Hart) argue publicly in the store, Haziz remarks to Mooj, "Today's forecast? Dark and cloudy, and chance of drive-by."

2) Shrek 2 (2004)

» **actor/character:** Donkey as voiced by Eddie Murphy

» **analysis:** Donkey (yes, that is his name) fulfills the role of the Comic Relief in this wildly successful animated movie. Donkey, who is figuratively and literally a jackass, proves to be the butt of numerous jokes, and his ignorance serves as a source of ongoing humor. Not surprisingly, Donkey's character traits fit the mold of most live action comedic inserts. Given that Eddie Murphy is the only "Black" voice in the movie (at least the only prominent Black voice), his voice is "isolated" and stands out even more in the context of his exaggerated actions. Despite the protestations of other characters, Donkey never reaches a catharsis or learns the errors of his ways. This state of "permanency" is a reflection of his flat character arc and further serves to illustrate his limited utility.

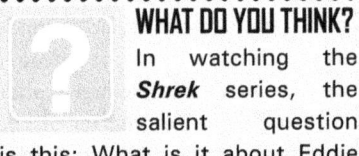

WHAT DO YOU THINK? In watching the **Shrek** series, the salient question is this: What is it about Eddie Murphy's Donkey character that makes him humorous? Since Mike Myers is also a comedian, what do you think would happen if we switched Myers to Donkey's role and Murphy to Shrek's role? Would it be the same? Why or why not? *How much does "culture" factor into the humor associated with the Donkey character?*

» **bonus:** Note the annoyingly elevated level of Donkey's voice and his exaggerated features — Donkey's large White teeth are reminiscent of the wide grinning that typified early minstrel figures. Although Donkey is clearly an animal and there are no explicit references linking him to a racial identity, Donkey is nevertheless voiced by Eddie Murphy — a well-known Black male comedian — which serves as an implicit reference to his racial status.

3) Me, Myself & Irene (2000)

» **actor/character:** The Baileygates as played by Anthony Anderson, Mongo Brownlee and Jerod Mixon

» **analysis:** One of the ongoing comedic bits throughout the movie is that Jim Carrey's White character (Officer Charlie Baileygates/Hank Evans) has three Black children that he somehow believes he has fathered with his White wife. The Baileygates manifest most of the "urban" mannerisms pop culture has come to associate with young Black men (i.e., baggy pants, foul language, etc.). The three are also "unusually" endowed with genius-level intelligence. The comedy, of course, ensues due to the "clash" between the implicitly extreme identities, with the

COMIC RELIEF ARCHETYPE AT WORK

PROFILE: Soul Plane (2004)

In a contemporary mainstream movie replete with racially stereotypical imagery like **Soul Plane**, how important is it to have participation from the group being stereotyped? In this case, Black culture served as the primary fodder for most of the "humor" throughout this movie. Although co-written by a Black screenwriter, Chuck Wilson, **Soul Plane** was also co-written by a White screenwriter, Bo Zenga, directed by a Latino, Jessy Terrero, and produced primarily by White employees.

The plot outline for **Soul Plane** is that in response to a humiliating experience on a "regular" commercial flight, the victim-turned-airline founder attempts to create the "first full-service carrier designed to cater to the urban traveler."[6c] Virtually all of the movie's humor is premised on the blurring of the socioeconomic class and racial lines. The descriptive adjective "Black-owned" contains the unspoken adjectives "poorly managed, unrefined, inexperienced and Black-owned airline."

In marketing this movie, it simply would not be enough to state that the airline is owned by "Americans." By focusing on the "Blackness" that characterizes **Soul Plane**, the marketing hook is that the inexperienced, ignorant, party-minded Black people operating the plane will do so in a manner that is comical, in contrast to the "normal" airline procedure to which everyone is accustomed. The "last-minute passenger additions" mentioned in the plot outline refers to the "standard" White family of four (two adults, one teenage daughter and one son) who serve as the surrogate eyes through which the audience can measure the airline's shortcomings. In contrast, there are no clearly identifiable Black family units of the same size and structure.

What responsibility do the actors have in "controlling" images like these? Additionally, what responsibility do corporate actors have in promoting images like these, given their growing presence as corporate partners in mainstream movies? Major corporate sponsors, such as **Cadillac, Foot Locker,** the **99¢ Only Stores** and **Roscoe's House of Chicken' n Waffles**, are clearly visible during the movie, lending mainstream support to these images. Plus, as an example of how corporate branding is used to promote a mainstream movie, the DVD press releases for **Soul Plane** were distributed in authentic **Popeyes Chicken & Biscuits** boxes. As a movie tie-in, **Popeyes** chicken was "served" on the plane (without any plates, utensils or napkins).

former touching on common stereotypes and the latter reminiscent of the Utopic Reversal archetype (see *Chapter 9: The Utopic Reversal*). Also note how the obesity of the three Baileygates children "distances" them from the audience as "others" and adds to their comedic value.

» key scene: During a cookout when the kids are young, one of Charlie's colleagues approaches him at the grill and tries to bring to Charlie's attention that he is not the father of his three Black triplets. The colleague, in growing frustration over Charlie's denial ("the kids have a 'year-round tan'") suddenly exclaims: "C'mon Charlie — those kids' d—ks [slang term for penis] are bigger than those sausages!" The mere notion that nubile genitalia would be the subject of a "joke" raises the salient question of whether different humor applies to different racial groupings. Given the trend towards minority marginalization and the constructed perspective of Blacks as "Other," the movie's creators may have felt "safe" in making such a joke, because these characters are essentially defined by race, not age. Such "age-inappropriate" humor only "succeeds" because it relies on traditional racial stereotypes.

» bonus: Even though this is a slapstick comedy, the Baileygates "permanency" is still the crux of their comedic value. Their "urban" identity is implicitly represented as a genetic character trait, especially in light of their (surrogate) father's suburban household. By "contrasting" their intelligence with their "urban" identity, the implicit gag is that such intelligence found in urban Black males like these would be otherwise highly uncommon in the "real world." Charlie Baileygates observes the behavior of his three children with the curiosity of a passerby, further reinforcing the audience's perspective as an observer of the Baileygates children, not as an identifier with them. Although there may be three Baileygates children, they are still as "isolated" as any other minority comedic inserts.

LIGHTS! CAMERA! INTERACTION!

Notoriously unapologetic D.L. "King of Comedy" Hughley has made onstage apologies about his participation in the movie **Soul Plane**. He tells Mark de la Viña of the San Jose Mercury News that, "I have always had a level of dignity in what I do, but that is the one thing that I'm just ashamed of. I didn't believe in it at all. I did it out of a momentary lapse of sanity, and it was embarrassing."[6d]

Hughley's candid disclosure may come from the fact that he is a comedian by profession, and is perhaps more comfortable in "laughing at" himself. Yet, how many other minority actors do you think have harbored similar thoughts over roles they have accepted? Have you seen any minority character roles that ventured beyond the bounds of comedy and struck you as embarrassing? Log on and tell us what you think at ***www.theracedoc.com!***

COMIC RELIEF: Latino Examples

1) The Lion King (1994)

» **actor/character:** Cheech Marin as Banzai
» **analysis:** Cheech Marin lend his voice to the conniving hyena, Banzai, who provides delight and merriment to audiences with his carousing and buffoonery.
» **bonus:** See the quote from Tom Schumacher (one of the producers of *The Lion King*) at the opening of this chapter in reference to Marin and Whoopi Goldberg, who voiced Banzai's companion, Shenzi.

2) Meet the Fockers (2004)

» **actor/character:** Ray Santiago as Jorge Villalobos; Alanna Ubach as Isabel Villalobos
» **analysis:** The comedic subplot revolves around Jack Byrnes' (Robert De Niro) suspicion that Greg Focker (Ben Stiller) fathered an illegitimate child by the name of Jorge Villalobos. Jack's suspicions are fueled by the idea that Jorge's mother, Isabel, used to serve as the Fockers' housekeeper and cook. In addition to helping around the house, Isabel used to help Greg "practice" and explore his sexuality when he was younger — a fact that was openly referenced by the Fockers at the dinner table. Here, questions of sexuality and paternity are used as comedic elements for these Latino characters, both of whom are passive "participants" in the storyline driven by White characters.
» **key scene:** The open exploitation of Isabel's sexuality is punctuated by her acknowledgment of getting a "boob job" after Greg notices her new look. Jack's grandson, Little Jack (Spencer and Bradley Pickren), also takes note of Isabel's busty figure and proceeds to stick his tongue out and make a milking motion with both of his hands. All of the adults laugh as Isabel reflects the same milking motion back to Little Jack. This is essentially a continuation of the sexual exploitation of Isabel.

3) Doctor Dolittle (1998)

» **actor/character:** John Leguizamo as Rat #2
» **analysis:** John Leguizamo plays a wise-talking rat in this comedy about talking animals. Actually, he is listed in the credits as "Rat #2." Sadly,

the American Humane Association only monitors cruelty towards animals, not actors. Rats!

» bonus: If you are feeling adventurous, compare Rat #2's performance to Ronnie Rizzat as voiced by Snoop Dogg in *Malibu's Most Wanted*. For the *truly* adventurous, compare Eddie Murphy's performance to that of Rex Harrison in the 1967 original, *Doctor Dolittle*.

COMIC RELIEF: Other Examples

1) Wedding Crashers (2005)

» actor/character: Unnamed members of a wedding party
» analysis: During a visual montage without dialogue, the two White male protagonists, Jeremy Gray (Vince Vaughn) and John Beckwith (Owen Wilson), "incorrectly" crash a wedding party that consists of persons who appear to be of eastern Indian descent. The scene was part of a montage illustrating the habitual passage of time.
» bonus: Would the premise of two divorce lawyers crashing weddings to "score babes" still receive a greenlight by a major Hollywood studio if the two leads were anything other than White? Perhaps. Yet, on the official *Wedding Crashers* website, a "Crasher Kit" is featured containing helpful accessories and tactics on how to successfully crash weddings. Among them is a Name Tag Marker, "where to really blend in you need a culturally appropriate name tag."[4] This Crasher Kit prop suggests that only a White person with masking abilities could merely change their name (and not their physical appearance) on a name tag and possibly "become" Jewish, Italian, German or French (see "What's in a Name," pg. 67). An across-the-street minority may possibly encounter more difficulty blending in despite publicly sporting a name tag suggesting that their presence is "appropriate."

2) The Scorpion King (2002)

» actor/character: Grant Heslov as Arpid
» analysis: Arpid is a Middle Eastern trickster (i.e., thief) who proves to be a fearful but faithful sidekick to the eventual Scorpion King (Dwayne "The Rock" Johnson). With punchlines like, "it is not the size of the hump, but the degree of motion in the camel," told in a distinctive

falsetto, Arpid's character is intended to provide contrasting levity to the "serious" action.

» bonus: This is an example of how culture can serve as fodder for humor even in the absence of a White protagonist. In addition to Arpid, pay close attention to the storylines and "jokes" involving the character Balthazar (Black actor Michael Clarke Duncan) as well.

3) Spider-Man 2 (2004)

» actor/character: Aasif Mandvi as Mr. Aziz
» analysis: Mr. Aziz is the owner of the pizza shop at which Peter Parker (Tobey Maguire) works. Aziz has a distinct accent and partly serves to continue the comedic tone of the opening sequence of the movie.
» bonus: Aziz chastises Peter Parker for his work ethic and proceeds to fire him, thereby adding to the hero's initial woes. To call Aziz an antagonist would be a stretch, but his actions against Parker – even if fully justifiable – serve to alienate Aziz from the audience, further reinforcing his "foreign" identity as an "Other." This is a classic example of the "ugly American" (see pg. 86).
» note: Although set in the exceedingly diverse metropolis of New York, there are no prominent minority characters, and those that do appear could be classified as Background Figures. When you observe a minority character in this movie, notice how their attitude and dialogue are used to convey humor, illustrate "ignorance" of Spider-Man's powers, passively facilitate and observe Spider-Man (or Peter Parker)'s heroism, and – as in the case of Mr. Aziz – establish benchmarks from which the average (White) protagonist will rise above in reaching their anticipated hero status.

Comic Relief characters often retain and exhibit many elements of stereotypical roles recycled from a seemingly bygone era in Hollywood. However, the sting of such stereotypical conduct is diffused or blunted under the auspices of humor, parody and burlesque. With the ironic result of minorities often paying to see humor marketed through mainstream movies at their culture's expense. Minorities are certainly not above satire. However, their historically low levels of racial capital in Hollywood call into question whether minorities are still being left out of the joke.

WHAT DO YOU THINK?
The Ridiculous 6 is a 2015 western comedy starring well-known actors Adam Sandler, Terry Crews, Danny Trejo, Taylor Lautner, Blake Shelton and others. It is a "made for Netflix" movie, thereby making it difficult to gauge its total intake, but it did have a $60M budget and at the time of its release in late 2015, it was the most streamed film in the company's history.

Controversy arose when discovered by the public shortly before the movie's release that in the name of "humor," some Native American characters were not depicted favorably. For example, some character names included "Beaver Breath," "Smoking Fox" and "Wears No Bra." Jewish actor Rob Schneider plays a Mexican character named Ramon.

Do you find Schneider's cross-casting funny? How about the female Native American character's names? Who has the power to decide "what's funny?"

Speaking of power, see what you can do to discover what happened when Native American actors confronted the producer on set...

CHAPTER 6: THE COMIC RELIEF

CHAPTER 7:
THE MENACE TO SOCIETY

 *I still turn down a lot more roles than I accept. A lot of scripts still call for you to play the street hood or the sidekick. It can be discouraging.*

Don Cheadle, actor[1]

CHAPTER 7:
THE MENACE TO SOCIETY

The Menace to Society archetype is a character who possesses a value system that poses a threat to civil "normalcy," either through violence (or potential violence) or through moral corruption. The mood of this minority character can range from seemingly innocuous to outright menacing and applies to both genders. Although the Menace to Society archetype encompasses a broad spectrum that ranges from arch-villain to social threat, it is common for most minority characters fulfilling this archetype to play "low-level" threats to other characters (as opposed to a James Bond nemesis who pines for world domination).

Menace to Society archetypes will also reflect stereotypical fears expressed about minorities in other mainstream media (e.g., television shows, nightly news, newspapers, etc.). Some common Menace to Society archetypes include drug dealers, street thugs, prisoners, terrorists, gang members and obnoxious "socialites."

During Hollywood's earlier years, Blacks once portrayed most of the Menace to Society roles. Latinos, who still have relatively little racial capital within Hollywood, have begun to be placed in more Menace to Society roles that were once filled almost exclusively by Black actors. Meanwhile, Native Americans have been primarily slotted as untamed "savages" throughout their history in mainstream movies.

Part of this traditionally violent typecasting for Native Americans is perhaps explained by an overall trend towards violence in Westerns and other period piece movies. However, unlike the cowboys and soldiers in these Western movies, the Native American characters tend to be portrayed as having a singular group identity rather than as unique individuals that represent a subset of a particular group (e.g., violent cowboys as a subset of benevolent and heroic White settlers and pioneers).

Common Menace to Society characteristics and trends include:

- Minority characters in urban dramas, cop movies or drug-themed movies
- Typically portrayed by minority males
- Physically imposing presence; sometimes partially clothed to reveal imposing physique
- Character is purveyor of unorganized, aggressive or "random" violence (including the threat of personal, physical violence)
- Minority character(s) contrasted against more "civil" White protagonist(s)
- The use of rappers and/or hip-hop artists

THE PHANTOM MENACE

Despite the high number of new movies released each year, there are only so many variations on the theme of good versus evil. These movies frequently feature a character that is easily recognizable as "the bad guy" to allow for a compelling contrast with the hero. The more evil and nasty the villain, the more valorous our hero. Over the years, Hollywood has furnished many imposing and treacherous villains that have excited the imaginations of viewers long after the movie has ended. We venture that scarcely a soul alive has resisted the temptation to imitate the imminently imposing Darth Vader's breathing apparatus at some point. Clearly, some imagery in mainstream movies is *supposed* to appear negative and threatening. Minorities do not possess a monopoly over negative movie characters. Nonetheless, in mainstream movies, it appears that minority characters have a sizeable share of the market with respect to anti-social imagery, which is ultimately left unbalanced by the infrequent number of roles featuring minority characters in heroic situations.

When the Menace to Society archetype is expressly portrayed as having the capacity for violence, this violence is traditionally treated as "unexplained" and "intrinsic" as opposed to the reasoned (yet, socially unacceptable) response to a particular issue or incident. The result is that threatening minority characters are most often depicted as capable of "random," and spontaneous yet individualized acts of violence. If such violent actions are explained, they are done so only on the most basic of terms (e.g., minority criminal motivated by money, minority thug directed by henchman).

Still, this "natural" predilection of minority characters towards violence contrasts sharply with the "rational" approach to violence displayed by evil White characters. Many superhero villains fulfill this pattern, whereby when stricken with an unfortunate condition or set of circumstances early in life, they project and displace their unresolved feelings on the public at large. Despite the eventual condemnation that results from the villain's efforts, in most cases the actions of the villain are *justified* and *explained*, often by the villain himself!

Many White actors have had the opportunity to play esteemed "villains," characters that measure up to be equal or superior to the hero, a stark contrast to the proverbial minority thug. Notable examples range from the civilized calm of the evil leader Henri Ducard (Liam Neeson) in **Batman Begins**, to the intellectually terrifying Hannibal Lecter in **The Silence of the Lambs** (for which Anthony Hopkins claimed Best Actor Academy Award honors in 1991). Memorable examples of threatening White characters in mainstream movies often revolve around grandiose and well-financed plans to achieve overarching aims, such as destroying all of humanity or taking over the world.

The Menace to Society archetype is especially damaging because the threat of violence by minority characters is usually depicted as more "realistic" to the audience. For instance, a threatening drug dealer is a more realistic threat to society than an egomaniac aiming lasers at the moon in order to change the Earth's weather and control the world. Ultimately, as intimidating a presence as Darth Vader is, very few people fear his merciless and unsuspecting wrath lurking for them around the next corner.

PROTECTIVE STEREOTYPE

Aside from glamorized and burlesqued White villains, White characters also fulfill non-archvillain bit roles that call for anti-social and threatening behavior. Ironically, such roles can fulfill **protective stereotype** patterns that help – rather than hurt – the bottom line of White racial capital. Protective stereotypes portray exceedingly exaggerated images of racial hatred that most White people no longer openly condone. Such imagery serves a "protective" function in that it helps audience members – particularly White audience members – distance themselves from conduct that would be considered abnormal and devoutly anti-social according to mainstream

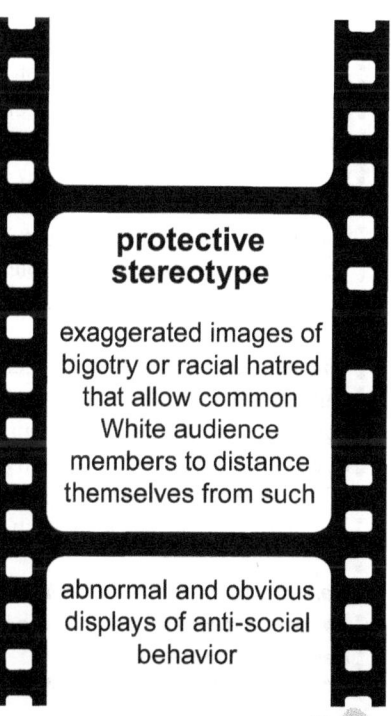

protective stereotype

exaggerated images of bigotry or racial hatred that allow common White audience members to distance themselves from such

abnormal and obvious displays of anti-social behavior

standards. Protective stereotypes are effective because, for example, a rabid Ku Klux Klan member in white sheets frothing at the mouth and spewing racial epithets can be simplified as the face of racism, although many minorities in contemporary times experience discrimination in much more subtle and institutional ways in today's society.[2]

WHAT DO YOU THINK?

A quick survey of how mainstream movies have treated White and minority characters within prison settings helps illustrate the contrast between the two groups. Typically, prison is not a desirable location and is reserved for those who perform highly undesirable acts within our society. Minority characters are frequently depicted in jail without much explanation as to the circumstances that brought them there (nor the circumstances that could lead to their eventual exoneration and departure). On the other hand, the Hollywood Audience is often informed about the circumstances surrounding jail time for White characters. Minority characters in prison are usually portrayed in a permanent state of being, especially since they are so often used as background figures that "add authenticity" to the setting. White characters are much more complex – since they are often the protagonists – and enjoy a more fluid association with prison, whereby their status is imminently more transitive. This theme is known as the **plasticity of white criminality**.

Take for example ***The Shawshank Redemption*** featuring White actor Tim Robbins as Andy Dufresne, and Black actor Morgan Freeman as Ellis Boyd "Red" Redding. Although Red actually "narrates" the story, the movie revolves around Dufresne's unjust imprisonment and his justifiable escape. Red's actions are only relevant as they relate to Dufresne – Red is already a long-standing inmate at the time of Dufresne's incarceration, and he serves out the remainder of his sentence after Dufresne has escaped. Red is released from prison after serving his time to the system, and his difficulty in readjusting to society is a reflection of his "permanency" as an "inmate," in spite of being a . . . ahem . . . free man. Meanwhile, Dufresne beats the system and his ingenious method of escape only adds to his complexity and further illustrates that the system cannot control or contain his will.

White characters are not always innocent, nor do they always escape prison, as is the case with Paul Crewe (Adam Sandler) in the 2005 remake of ***The Longest Yard***. Crewe never leaves prison, but the movie still revolves around his ability to master his environment. Much like Dufresne in ***The Shawshank Redemption***, Crewe's time in prison is marked by his interaction with prominent prison officials (e.g., the warden), his access to a cross-section of inmates, and his ability to manipulate his "confines" to cathartic effect. Once again, the story "starts" with the incarceration of the White character, and the minority characters are strewn across the background to set the scene and serve the central White character (in fulfillment of the Angel archetype, Chris Rock plays a supporting character literally named Caretaker). Even though Crewe does not escape by movie's end, he ultimately "overcomes" prison by controlling it instead of allowing it to control him, punctuated by a victory over the prison guards in the football game.

The Hurricane, starring Denzel Washington as Rubin Hurricane Carter, is an example of a movie where the imprisoned minority character is the central protagonist and gains his freedom by the end of the movie. Note, however, that Carter's freedom is obtained primarily through the beneficence and advocacy of White characters, in stark contrast to the self-driven protagonists like Crewe and Dufresne. The Hurricane is based on true events, which further suggests that such a story involving minority characters is only "palatable" to the Hollywood Audience when the movie is the subject of "fact," rather than the subject of fiction.

Can you think of other movies where White and minority characters received different treatment with respect to an explanation for their presence in prison, a justifiable reason for their shortened stints in prison, and their early departures therefrom?

Not only do protective stereotypes help the audience recognize symbolic evil and feel better about themselves as "objective" observers, but the audience is also part of the moral victory in condemning such overtly racist behavior. When the characters depicting these protective stereotypes are punished or thwarted by the protagonist (who is often White as well), White moviegoers receive a moral, cathartic release in seeing other valiant Whites mete out such justice. Despite being the "victim," the minority is often just a foil for the protagonist, and as a result the experience is not nearly as cathartic for the minority viewer.

Consider the racist White murderers in **A Time to Kill**. Although these Whites are portrayed in a negative light, such imagery is trumped by the benevolence and heroism of the White protagonists Jake Tyler Brigance (Matthew McConaughey) and Ellen Roark (Sandra Bullock). Samuel L. Jackson plays Carl Lee Hailey, the father of a ten-year-old Black girl that is raped and murdered. Yet, his emotional and mental state are secondary to the quick thinking and heroism developed in the White legal team that "saves" the victim from an unjust fate.

Another protective stereotype can be found in the 1997 movie **Amistad**, starring Anthony Hopkins, Morgan Freeman and Djimon Hounsou. The callous White slave traders are neutralized by the articulate, compassionate and caring John Quincy Adams (Anthony Hopkins), who saves the day with his powerful, intellectually moving legal argument. The story of the slaves' rebellion and freedom is largely told through the eyes of the beneficent Whites, who by movie's end restore the audience's faith that not all Whites are savage and cruel like the blood-thirsty slave traders, even in a time in history when slavery was alive and well and moreover accepted by many "God-fearing" Whites.

Due to their abundance of racial capital in Hollywood, Whites have more effectively framed and limited negative, Menace to Society-type imagery through the rather consistent use of protective stereotypes and cathartic character arcs. Conversely, due to low levels of minority racial capital in Hollywood, there is a paucity of balancing or corresponding redemptive imagery with which to contrast menacing minority characters. In accordance with the premium of proportion theory, the resulting effect of these recurring Menace to Society archetypes is that their anti-social behaviors usually serve to define "all" disparate members of that racial group.

HOT TICKET ITEMS

MENACE TO SOCIETY
- objectifies criminal element, has criminal tendencies, has interaction with the criminal justice system
- character threatens White status quo by violating or disregarding social norms
- marked by intimidating presence and aggressive actions

ARCHETYPE EXPLORED
MENACE TO SOCIETY: Asian Examples

1) Lethal Weapon 4 (1998)

» actor/character: The evil henchman Wah Sing Ku as played by Jet Li

2) Rush Hour 2 (2001)

» actor/character: The evil henchman Ricky Tan as played by John Lone

3) Die Another Day (2002)

» actor/character: The evil henchman Zao as played by Rick Yune

» analysis [for all three Asian examples]: Notice how the Menace to Society pattern has reappeared numerous times through various representations of Asian mafias and crime syndicates. Contrast this recurring pattern against the general lack of Asian protagonists in mainstream movies.

» **bonus**: The Asian Menace to Society archetype is exemplified by Jet Li in ***Unleashed***. In this movie, Danny (Li) is literally raised as a ruthless killing animal by his White master, Bart (Bob Hoskins). To continue the metaphor, Danny literally wears a special collar that, when removed, releases Danny's "killer" martial arts skills. There is a scene where Danny literally eats food out of a can as if he were a dog, which further casts him as an animal rather than a human. The movie was released in the United States as ***Unleashed***, but the title used abroad was ***Danny the Dog***.

MENACE TO SOCIETY: BLACK EXAMPLES

1) Traffic (2000)

» **actor/character**: Russell G. Jones as Mark
» **analysis**: When "girl next door" Caroline Wakefield (Erika Christensen) has sexual intercourse with her Black drug dealer, Mark from the inner city, this represents the low-point of her journey into the world of drugs. This sex scene with a sexualized Black male, who is depicted as aggressive, confrontational and partially clothed, contrasts sharply with the sex scene she shares with her White, fully-clothed, preppie colleague earlier in the movie (who incidentally introduced her to drugs).

2) Monster's Ball (2001)

» **actor/character**: Sean "Diddy" Combs as Lawrence Musgrove
» **analysis**: Lawrence Musgrove is seen only as a death row inmate, without any explanation as to how or why he arrived in that position. Musgrove's onscreen execution only confirms his permanent, criminal state for the viewing audience.
» **bonus**: Notice how this small role was fulfilled by a well-known rap mogul in Sean "Diddy" Combs.

3) Changing Lanes (2002)

» **actor/character**: Samuel L. Jackson as Doyle Gipson
» **analysis**: Doyle Gipson is an alcoholic (uh-oh) insurance salesman who gets

into a car accident with an ambitious young White lawyer, Gavin Banek (Ben Affleck). The accident causes Gipson to miss a child custody hearing (uh-oh, again) while Banek races off to *conduct* a court hearing, leaving Gipson stranded and vowing vengeance (with reservation, we must uh-oh thrice).

» bonus: As confirmation of his Menace to Society status, observe the contrasting methods Gipson employs to exert power over Banek. During the remainder of the day, Gipson threatens Banek with physical violence, while Banek fights back with political and institutional power plays that make life difficult for Gipson. The very nature of the contrasting power struggles underlie the movie filmmakers' thoughts about the "innate" capacity of both characters to handle conflict. Also notice the difference in social stressors that each character faces: Gipson loses custody of his children, engages in fisticuffs, discovers that he is bankrupt, gets arrested at his children's school and even gets scolded by his Alcoholics Anonymous buddy. Gipson is burdened by a disheveled life while Banek is burdened by disheveled papers pertaining to a multi-million dollar trust! At the end of the movie, Banek agrees to live and work with a corrupt law firm, making pro bono cases a high priority without renouncing the salary due him as a newly minted partner in the firm.

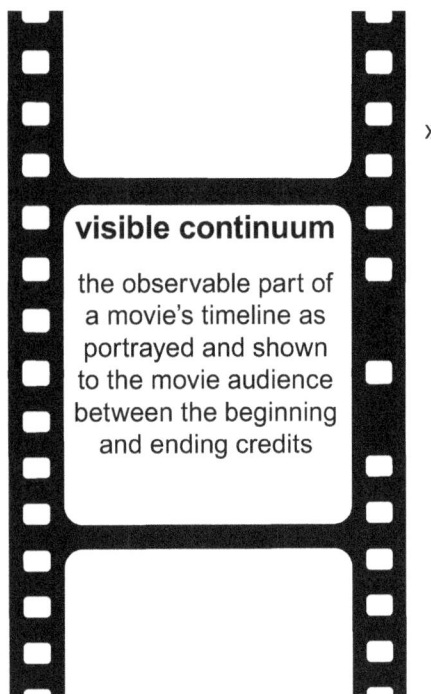

visible continuum

the observable part of a movie's timeline as portrayed and shown to the movie audience between the beginning and ending credits

MENACE TO SOCIETY: Latino Examples

1) Training Day (2001)

» actor/character: Assorted Latino gang members
» analysis: The Menace to Society pattern is fulfilled by the Mexican gang lords who are entrusted by Detective Alonzo Harris (Denzel Washington) to kill Jake Hoyt (Ethan Hawke). Compare their urban violence to that of the corrupt – but no less nefarious – "Three Wise Men" played by Tom Berenger, Harris Yulin and Raymond Barry. The gang members presented an immediate and visceral threat while the *White* wise men are presumed to be "wise" and well-connected to political power and influence. Contrast Alonzo Harris' "King Kong" demeanor amongst unnamed Menace to Society figures to his "intimidated" and contrite behavior in the setting with the wise men.

LIGHTS! CAMERA! INTERACTION!

Compare and contrast the permanent and plastic states of minorities and Whites in prison scenes from the following movies. "Permanency" means that the actor, for the length of the **visible continuum**, is always depicted in jail, or their perpetual presence in jail is assumed without any qualifying explanations. "Plastic" means that more context is provided for the character's presence in prison, which does not last for the duration of the movie's visible continuum — the white character's criminal state is much more flexible and pliable. Further, temporary status often applies to characters who, while technically are "guilty" enough to warrant jailing, provide audiences with enough circumstantial evidence to call the intentional anti-social nature of the crime into dispute. Jail often "holds back" Whites from completing their catharsis.

Compare the following examples:

MINORITY CHARACTERS

Monster's Ball - the unexplained death row status of Black character Lawrence Musgrove (Sean "Diddy" Combs)

Austin Powers: Goldmember - the permanent state of Black Prisoner #2 (Tommy "Tiny" Lister)

Con Air - the permanent state of Black characters Nathan 'Diamond Dog' Jones (Ving Rhames), Joe 'Pinball' Parker (Dave Chappelle), Mike 'Baby-O' O'Dell (Mykelti Williamson) and Ajax (Mongo Brownlee); Latino characters Johnny 'Johnny-23' Baca (Danny Trejo), Ramon 'Sally-Can't Dance' Martinez (Renoly Santiago), Francisco Cindino (Jesse Borrego); and Native American character, Smoke (Don Charles McGovern)

The Green Mile - permanent state of Black character John Coffey (Michael Clarke Duncan) and Arlen Bitterbuck (Native American actor Graham Greene)

NOTE: although Coffey is temporarily "released" from prison, it is only for the purpose of fulfilling an **Angel Figure** function in healing the White jail warden's wife — Coffey's permanent criminal state is confirmed when he is executed for a crime he did not commit, despite the movie audience's knowledge of his innocence.

WHITE CHARACTERS

The Butterfly Effect - the permanent state of the Latino criminal Carlos (Kevin Durand) versus protagonist Evan Treborn (Ashton Kutcher) and his temporary jailing

Meet the Fockers - temporary jailing for White protagonists Jack Byrnes and Greg Focker (Robert De Niro and Dustin Hoffman respectively)

The Fugitive - justified escape of innocent White protagonist Dr. Richard Kimble (Harrison Ford)

Bedazzled - temporary jailing for White protagonist Elliot Richards (Brendan Fraser), in contrast to the permanent status of Black actor Gabriel Casseus as Elliot's Cellmate/Angel

» **key scene:** The movie begins by showing Officer Jake Hoyt arising in his calm, suburban setting for his first day of work (i.e., *his* training day). This establishes the thematic foundation for the ensuing contrast between his "civil" home life and the chaos of the city streets.

MENACE TO SOCIETY ARCHETYPE AT WORK

PROFILE: *The Missing* (2003)

The Missing is a Western drama set in nineteenth century New Mexico. As such, the movie predictably employs Native Americans to fulfill racial requirements based upon the time and the setting. This movie, like so many others featuring Native Americans, actually contains multiple stereotypical references. The main antagonist is El Brujo (also known as Pesh-Chidin), portrayed by Native American actor Eric Schweig. Despite the Spanish moniker ("El Brujo" translates to "witch doctor"), he is a Native American outlaw who makes a living by kidnapping young girls and selling them as prostitutes in México. Although El Brujo kidnaps girls of all races, the story revolves around the kidnapping of a young White girl (Lilly Gilkeson as played by Evan Rachel Wood).

Aside from his blatant moral misstep into prostitution, El Brujo also has a nasty mean streak and shows an unwillingness to let anyone stand in the way of his plans. Within moments of El Brujo's first appearance onscreen, he succeeds in humiliating several captive girls and kills a harmless White photographer. El Brujo deposes of a photographer by blowing a "lethal dust" into his eyes, showing evidence of a combination of the shaman and savage stereotypes. His capacity for violence is immediately evident, both in his treatment of the young women and his ability to kill without regard for pity.

One of the more significant scenes in the movie revolves around this contrast between the "modern" medicine and religion of Whites and the spiritual ways of the Native Americans. El Brujo casts a spell on Maggie Gilkeson (Cate Blanchett), a medicine woman who has an open disdain for Native Americans. Nevertheless, the spell subjects her to a feverish illness that she cannot explain. She is cured in a culminating scene in which Samuel Jones (Tommy Lee Jones) and Kayitah (Jay Tavare) break the fever with an "anti-spell," while Maggie's daughter, Dot (Jenna Boyd), recites verses from the Bible. While it remains a mystery as to which one plays the most significant role in breaking the spell, the juxtaposition between White religion and Native American spirituality is a central part of the overall story.

El Brujo, as a Menace to Society, ends up dead by the movie's conclusion. Native American benevolence is only useful insofar as it relates to helping White characters, limiting any potential cathartic effect for any other Native American characters.

» **bonus:** In fulfilling the Menace to Society archetype, note the emphasis on "realism" and the strong association between onscreen and offscreen criminality. Suspect Entertainment, an entrepreneurial venture that employs Latino "gangstas" in Hollywood (many of whom are really ex-cons), provided many of the extras for the Menace to Society characters in this movie.[4] Pre-production buzz for the movie also talked at length about director Antoine Fuqua using "real gangstas" from the Los Angeles neighborhoods where the movie was filmed in an effort to add "realism."

» **double bonus:** Further underscoring the limited amount of roles for "classically trained" Latino actors, also note that Smiley, the Latino "gangsta" ringleader with the most amount of power, screen time and dialogue, is not even played by a Latino actor. He is played by Cliff Curtis, who hails from New Zealand. Much like *The Mask of Zorro*, the "prominent" Latino character is played by a non-Latino asymptote, while the Background Figures used for the supporting roles are cast as "distinctly ethnic" in their aesthetic and function.

2) Proof of Life (2000)

» **actor/character:** Assorted anti-government guerillas
» **analysis:** Menace to Society figures are provided by the anti-government guerillas who kidnap the husband of protagonist Alice Bowman (Meg Ryan) for ransom in the Republic of Tecala, a fictional South American country.
» **bonus:** Notice how many Menace to Society archetypes overlap with Background Figure archetypes.

3) The Butterfly Effect (2004)

» **actor/character:** Kevin Durand as Carlos
» **analysis:** Protagonist Evan Treborn (Ashton Kutcher), who has the ability to manipulate time, finds himself in jail during one of the movie's story threads. Treborn is initially startled to find that his cellmate is a physically imposing, religious, Latino convict named Carlos. The focus immediately turns to Treborn's "errant" placement within the correctional facility and his (justified) efforts to get out of jail. While Evan is able to manipulate time as his "Get-Out-of-Jail-Scot-Free

WHAT DO YOU THINK?
As proof that animated movies are not immune from **The HARM Theory**, take a closer look at ***Despicable Me 2*** (2013) to see if you see any **Menace to Society** archetypes. Perhaps you need only look to the principal antagonist Eduardo "El Macho" Perez as voiced by Latino actor Benjamin Bratt. Not only did he desire world domination (a no-no in children's animated movies), but he wanted to do so by using the highly potent PX-41 mutagen to transform the likeable and harmless yellow minions into aggressive, purple minions complete with misshapen teeth and wild hair (a definite no-no when so many children came to the theater to see the likeable and harmless yellow minions).

If unsure that Eduardo/El Macho was a Latino character, in the movie, his cover was serving as owner of the Salsa & Salsa restaurant and we wears a Mexican wrestler "luchadora" mask (and ill-fitting leotard) as part of his El Macho alter ego.

Additionally, Eduardo's son Antonio Perez (voiced by Colombian actor Moises Arias) may have shown hints of following in his father's morally corrupt footsteps when he woos the protagonist Gru's (Steve Carrell) daughter, only to "cheat" on her by later showing interest in another girl (if twelve year olds can have relationships and "cheat" upon one another, that is).

LIGHTS! CAMERA! INTERACTION!

It is conventional wisdom in "mainstream movie morality" that he who endeavors to harm a character played by a mainstream actress must pay the price for doing so. This common movie convention raises an interesting point of discussion about minority characters harming White women and how these minorities are ultimately deposed (sexuality thwarted), in contrast to White men who impose their will upon minority females and go largely unpunished (sexuality facilitated). Consider the following movies from both sides of the issue:

Minority male threatens/harms White woman

- ***Casino Royale*** (Isaach De Bankolé as Steven Obanno) - This classically trained, award-winning actor plays a "warlord" who threatens to machete off the arm of the villain's White "girlfriend." Bond ultimately deposes him by choking him to death.
- ***Crash*** (Larenz Tate as Peter Waters) - Waters' carjacking threatens Jean Cabot (Sandra Bullock) and forces her to change locks on the house, etc. Waters ends up getting shot and killed by a White police officer (Ryan Phillipe).
- ***Gothika*** (Charles S. Dutton as Dr. Douglas Grey) - Dr. Grey is killed in villainous fashion by a White ghost that possesses his wife Miranda (Halle Berry). Dr. Grey imprisoned and sexually abused several White women.
- ***Man on Fire*** (various Latino criminals; Marc Anthony as Samuel) - Mexicans involved in a plot to kidnap Pita (Dakota Fanning) are maimed and killed by Creasy (Denzel Washington). Samuel commits suicide out of guilt for his involvement.
- ***The Missing*** (Eric Schweig as El Brujo) - El Brujo is killed by Maggie Gilkeson (Cate Blanchett) for kidnapping her daughters for re-sale.
- ***Sin City*** (Benicio Del Toro as Detective Lieutenant Jackie "Boy" Rafferty) - Rafferty has a history of domestically abusing his old flame Shellie (Brittany Murphy). As a result, he ends up getting his hand sliced off, sustains a shuriken in his arse, shoots himself in the head, gets his neck sliced open, has his head fully severed for "bartering purposes," and lastly, has his decapitated head stuffed with explosives and detonated to help Dwight McCarthy (Clive Owen) kill Manute (Michael Clarke Duncan).

White male threatens/harms minority woman

- ***Alexander*** (Colin Farrell as Alexander; Rosario Dawson as Roxane) - Alexander accosts Roxane and strips her naked, forcing himself upon her until she sexually acquiesces. Alexander also chokes Roxane in a later scene.
- ***Crash*** (Matt Dillon as Officer John Ryan; Thandie Newton as Christine Thayer) - Officer Ryan sexually assaults Thayer during a traffic stop (after caught performing fellatio on her husband). Ryan later becomes the hero of the movie by saving Thayer's life after a car accident. By standard movie conventions, Thayer's husband, Cameron (Terrence Howard), is the most likely character to avenge this assault, but instead is emasculated by Officer Ryan and only "vindicates" himself by directing a verbal tirade at would-be carjacker Anthony (played by the rapper Ludacris).
- ***Payback*** (Mel Gibson as Porter; Lucy Liu as Pearl) - Val Resnick (Gregg Henry) batters Pearl repeatedly (including striking her with a phone) as a part of their ongoing S&M "relationship." Resnick is later killed by Porter — but Porter's motivation was personal revenge, not personal honor for Pearl. Later, after a stalemate standoff between Pearl, Porter and evil Asian henchmen, evil White henchmen interrupt the scene by knocking Porter out and taking him away. Pearl yells out, "Hey, who are you? What are you doing? Hey! Fat boy! Yeah, I'm talking to you." Fatboy punches her out of the picture before he hauls off. Moments later, Pearl wipes blood from her lip and sucks her finger with pleasure. This is her final scene.
- ***Sin City*** (Clive Owen as Dwight McCarthy; Rosario Dawson as Gail) - McCarthy strikes Gail in an effort to "knock sense" into her. This blow to the face marks the turning point where she becomes his romantic interest on his path to heroism.
- ***X-Men 2*** (Hugh Jackman as Wolverine; Kelly Hu as Deathstrike) - Wolverine kills Deathstrike as a necessary step before reaching the main villain.

Card," Carlos, the lone Latino character with a speaking part in this movie, remains frozen in time as a criminal.

» **bonus**: If the name Kevin Durand does not "sound" like a Latino surname to you, do not be alarmed. Kevin Durand, who plays the Latino character Carlos, is actually a White Canadian.

MENACE TO SOCIETY: Other Examples

1) Rules of Engagement (2000)

» **actor/character**: Assorted Yemeni "protesters"
» **analysis**: The movie revolves around a court-martial case of Colonel Terry L. Childers (Samuel L. Jackson), after he has issued an open-fire order on Yemeni civilians storming the United States embassy. Yet, during the course of the trial, it is Childers good friend and counsel, Colonel Hayes 'Hodge' Hodges (Tommy Lee Jones), who helps show the court that Childers' actions were completely justified. In defense of Childers' actions, Hodges exposes and underscores the high proportion of angry and *armed* Yemeni adults (including women and children) who were attacking the United States Embassy out of an *unexplained* hatred.
» **key scene**: At the 1:37:13 mark, the audience sees a Little Girl (Jihane Kortobi) firing a gun in the direction of the U.S. embassy, establishing that Menace to Society archetypes are by no means limited to adults. A key issue in the court-martial trial was whether Childers' orders to "waste the mother f—ers" and open fire on the unruly crowd followed established "rules of engagement." Although Childers' orders resulted in the death of eighty-three Yemeni and a hundred more critically wounded, he was not found guilty of murder since his directive to open fire was essentially an act of self-defense.
» **bonus**: Notice the Utopic Reversal (see *Chapter 9: Utopic Reversal*) for Colonel Childers. Although Childers is eventually vindicated (although found not guilty on charges of murder and conduct not becoming an officer, he was nonetheless found guilty of breach of peace), his actions, mental state and temperament were scrutinized, criticized and questioned throughout the course of the entire movie. For instance, to underscore the gravity of the political fallout from Childers' "mistake," National Security Advisor Bill Sokal (Bruce Greenwood) scoffed that

because of his "hot-headed miscalculation, we're in danger of losing our embassies in Saudi, Jordan and Egypt. We're in danger of losing our presence with every moderate in the region." Childers' Utopic Reversal role is heightened by his juxtaposition against his buddy Colonel Hodges, who serves as the movie's emotional center. **Rules of Engagement** focuses on the emotional and intellectual battle that Colonel Hodges faces in accepting such a difficult case (e.g., disputing with family members whether this "move" is well-advised or not), rather than focusing on the emotional and intellectual battle that Colonel Childers faces as the actual "victim" of trumped up charges. Hodges is depicted interacting with his supportive family, managing the emotional state of Childers, traveling abroad to investigate the case in Yemen, and battling wits with the sharp and young opposing counsel (Guy Pearce as Major Mark Biggs). Meanwhile, Childers' character is socially isolated throughout the movie, with most of his dialogue limited to exchanges with Hodges.

2) The Siege (1998)

» **actor/character**: Ahmed Ben Larby as Sheik Achmed Bin Talal
» **analysis**: Sheik Achmed Bin Talal is an identifiable threat to New York city and is subsequently held in custody as a suspected terrorist. The Sheik's imprisonment sparks more terrorist attacks in response, prompting the government to declare martial law for the public good. As a result, the audience sees the effects of martial law "hit home" through the eyes of Agent Frank Haddad (Tony Shalhoub), partner of lead detective, Anthony Hubbard (Denzel Washington). Hubbard witnesses the anguish felt by his partner who, in working to protect America, sees his teenage son carted off and imprisoned without cause in the name of security. Whether justified or not, the message communicated throughout the whole movie is that Middle Eastern males are perceived to be a constant threat to civil society.
» **bonus**: Tony Shalhoub has also played a role as a "foreign" Menace to Society. Look for him in the **Men in Black** series as Jack Jeebs, the seedy alien whose head can grow back after it has been shot off.

TOTAL ANECDOTAL

Apocalypto (2006), directed by Mel Gibson, is unique in that it is a mainstream movie produced by a major studio featuring almost exclusively Native American and Latino actors.

Despite the lack of prominent Whites in the movie itself, high levels of White racial capital nonetheless affect the movie's look and feel. Consider this quote from production designer Tom Sanders: "We had an archeologist, Dr. Richard Hansen, onboard . . . It was really fun to say, 'Is there any proof they didn't do this?' When he said, 'There is no proof they didn't do that,' that gives you some license to play."[7a]

Based upon recommendations by a White archaeologist, White filmmakers fashioned an image of what they believed "ancient native culture" should look like.

However, according to *The New York Times,* not all movie patrons saw the "license to play" as playing fair. Some Native American activists objected to the movie's imagery, stating that "scenes of scary-looking Mayas with bone piercings and scarred faces hurling spears and sacrificing humans promote stereotypes about their culture."[7b]

3) True Lies (1994)

- » **actor/character:** Art Malik as Salim Abu Aziz
- » **analysis:** The scheming arch-nemesis, Salim Abu Aziz, is portrayed as a Middle Eastern man, although his original heritage in the movie is not disclosed. What *is* disclosed is that Aziz is the leader of a radical Islamic terrorist faction that is smuggling stolen nuclear warheads into the United States, handily qualifying Aziz as a Menace to Society.
- » **bonus:** Salim has a seductive Asian female, Juno Skinner (Tia Carrere), to serve as his accomplice. Nevertheless, he "punishes" her more for her failings than he does his actual enemies, punctuated by open displays of female battery (note the correlation to minority female battery in the "Light! Camera! Interaction!" popout on pg. 120).

The Menace to Society archetype establishes an important aspect of minority marginalization, whereby many minority characters appear static in their opposition to "benevolent" mainstream society and their threat to civil "normalcy." Within the universe of mainstream movies, such threats are often defined in terms of the threat they pose to *White* characters, which is ultimately what makes them such a menace. In this respect, the exclusion of Menace to Society figures from full participation in mainstream society is justified, and in some cases required for the security of the common good, further underscoring subtle messages of racial difference.

CHAPTER 8:
THE PHYSICAL WONDER

I wasn't going to be a prostitute on film. I couldn't do that because it is such a stereotype about Black women and sexuality.

Actress *Angela Bassett* on turning down the lead role in **Monster's Ball**[1]

CHAPTER 8:
THE PHYSICAL WONDER

The Physical Wonder archetype consists of minority characters who are primarily regarded for their physical or sexual prowess, typically at the expense of their emotions or intellectual capacity. Their ability to affect the storyline's development is stunted inasmuch their intellect and emotions remain undeveloped and unexplored.

Often, the Physical Wonder's physical presence or ability is explicitly referred to or acknowledged by other characters (e.g., "Hey, big guy . . . "). This character can display uncanny athletic ability or highly-coordinated physical skills, such as martial arts, proficiency in a sport or dancing. The characteristics of the Physical Wonder archetype restrict the audience's ability to identify with this character. In view of the identification process, the continued emphasis on physical skill limits audience interest to a skin deep, physical assessment of the character's overall worth.

The Physical Wonder archetype can also be manifested in minority roles featuring overtly or highly sexualized characters, often depicted as scantily clad, bare-chested or nude. This is not to say that White characters never appear in sexualized roles or roles that call for nudity. However, sexualized depictions of minority characters are far more salient in light of the premium of proportion theory, which dictates that there are more images of White characters to balance – if not outweigh – such sexual imagery. Further, White sexuality is frequently glamorized, cherished and treasured, in contrast to minority sexuality that is often exploited, seen as excessive, or regarded as animalistic.

PHYSICAL BLUNDER

The most common stereotype for Asian characters is the martial artist, which is a variation of the Physical Wonder archetype. This character

WHAT DO YOU THINK?

In fulfilling the **Physical Wonder** archetype, the following movies feature well-known minority actresses in roles where they are strippers, prostitutes, or involved in scenes containing nudity. We list the sexual profession of the character (e.g., an exotic dancer or stripper) and the extent of nudity. In many of the movies listed, the sexualized character signified a "breakout" role where their movie career "turned the corner," or helped elevate the profile of the actress within mainstream circles:

- Jessica Alba (Latina)
  Sin City (2005) - stripper; breakout role
- Devon Aoki (Asian)
  Sin City (2005) - prostitute
- Halle Berry (Black)
  The Last Boy Scout (1991) - stripper (completely naked)
  Jungle Fever (1991) - prostitute/drug addict
  Monster's Ball (2001) - nudity/sexually explicit scene; breakout role
  Swordfish (2001) - nudity (breasts)
- Rosario Dawson (Black)
  Sin City (2005) - prostitute
  Rent (2005) - stripper/drug addict
  Alexander (2004) - nudity (completely naked)
  He Got Game (1998) - nudity (breasts)
- Shannon Elizabeth Fadal (Syrian/Lebanese/Cherokee Indian)
  American Pie (1999) - nudity/sexually-themed masturbation scene (breasts); breakout role
- Vivica Fox (Black)
  Independence Day (1996) - stripper
- Salma Hayek (Latina)
  Desperado (1995) - nudity/sexually explicit scene; breakout role
  Dogma (1999) - stripper/deity
  From Dusk Till Dawn (2001) - stripper/vampire
- Taraji P. Henson (Black)
  Hustle & Flow (2005) - prostitute; breakout role
- Lucy Liu (Asian)
  Payback (1999) - prostitute/dominatrix; breakout role
- Eva Mendes (Latina)
  Training Day (2001) - nudity (completely naked); breakout role
- Sophie Okonedo (Black)
  Dirty Pretty Things (2002) - prostitute

Contrast this list against White leads playing prostitutes and strippers. For example, consider the message of transition and redemption for Julia Roberts' character in *Pretty Woman*. Also consider that the storylines in *Pretty Woman, Striptease,* and *Showgirls* allow audiences to learn about and empathize with the protagonists, even though they revolve around White females playing prostitutes and strippers. The "plight" of these White characters are explained and they manage to "transcend" their temporary state of being. In contrast, all of the minority prostitutes and strippers are presented in their circumstances without explanation (e.g., in *Independence Day*, Vivica Fox was depicted as a stripper without a reason as to why). Coincidentally, Cameron Diaz and Jennifer Lopez, two well-known minority actresses that qualify as asymptotes, are not listed above.

Ultimately, what do the above roles say about racial coding for minority actresses in Hollywood? Are such "sacrifices" simply part and parcel of a minority actress' career?

has limited dialogue but is unlimited on action, typically relying on their own physical abilities as their sole source of offense and defense, oftentimes eschewing "advanced" weaponry like guns. For instance, in **Rush Hour**, Detective James Carter (Chris Tucker) chides Chief Inspector Lee (Jackie Chan) for not using a gun, the traditional weapon of choice for good ol' American action movies. A similar scene takes place during the culminating scene of **Lethal Weapon 4**, when Wah Sing Ku (Jet Li) opts for a hand-to-hand battle royal with the protagonists (Mel Gibson and Danny Glover) — again, despite the ample presence of guns.

Many will be quick to counter that actors like Jackie Chan and Jet Li are martial artists who turned into actors. While this may be true, this does not eliminate the pervading archetype. If anything, this argument only further underscores the concept of the Physical Wonder. A closer look also reveals that previous martial arts experience is not a prerequisite for Asian Physical Wonders. Chinese-American actress Lucy Liu, born in New York and an actress by trade, plays the leader of a Japanese gang in **Kill Bill: Vol. 1**, a gang in which every member seems capable of performing martial arts, including Liu. Again, note the "foreign" emphasis (i.e., Japanese) for the American-born actress.

Despite our familiarity with the stereotypical martial artist role, the stereotype has further implications besides a close association between Asians and choreographed hand-to-hand combat. The martial artist reinforces the "un-American" and "Other" status of Asians in America. Though the martial artist is a stereotyped role in and of itself, the emphasis on Asians as "un"-Americans is a current that runs throughout most roles portrayed by Asians in Hollywood movies.

The fact that Asian male Physical Wonder characters (especially lead characters) tend to be *under*-sexualized in comparison to action-oriented characters of other races is another detail that should not be overlooked. These men are seldom presented as sexually appealing and rarely "get the girl" in the end, a common convention for most action movies. The lack of developed and explored feelings for Asian Physical Wonders helps concretize their status as "fighting machines," in stark contrast to how the audience is encouraged to identify with the typical well-balanced, White male action lead, who often has a romantic side story, thereby further idealizing him as a hero. *Red flag:* do not be surprised if the Asian Physical Wonder's Background Figure mentor (i.e., master, uncle, etc.) is killed off early on in the movie, for this is a standard story starter for the martial artist.

BUT IT'S JUST A MOVIE, RIGHT?

The emasculation of minority males – Black males in particular – is a historically documented method employed by the White majority to keep Blacks and other minorities "in their place" dating back to the era of enslavement. This emasculation strategy even pervaded White vernacular during the *Jim Crow Era*, when it was common for a White man to address another Black man as "boy." In light of the paucity of "Alpha-male," heroic protagonist roles for minority males, this emasculation continues when minority males are cast in roles portraying gay characters, female characters, cross dressers, effusively effeminate characters, characters that imply homosexual behavior or characters that are sexually assaulted. These roles are often played for comedic effect. Examples include:

- Dwayne "The Rock" Johnson, **Be Cool** (homosexual)
- Ving Rhames, **Pulp Fiction** (sexually assaulted) **Chuck & Larry** (homosexual)
- Will Smith, **Six Degrees of Separation** (homosexual); **Bad Boys II** (homosexual innuendo; "humorous" solicitation of sex with Black youth)
- Tracy Morgan, **The Longest Yard** (homosexual; effeminate, shown kissing another man)
- Michael Clarke Duncan, **The Scorpion King** (cross-dressing); **School for Scoundrels** (cross-dressing)
- Eddie Murphy, **The Nutty Professor** (plays female characters); **The Nutty Professor II: The Klumps** (plays female characters)
- Martin Lawrence, **Big Momma's House 1 & 2** (plays female character); **Bad Boys II** (homosexual innuendo)
- Chris Tucker, **The Fifth Element** (effeminate)
- Wesley Snipes, **To Wong Foo Thanks For Everything, Julie Newmar** (cross-dressing)
- Tyler Perry, **Diary of a Mad Black Woman** (plays a female character); **Madea's Family Reunion** (plays a female character)
- Shawn Wayans, **White Chicks** (plays a female character); **Scary Movie** (implied homosexual behavior)
- John Leguizamo, **To Wong Foo Thanks For Everything**, **Julie Newmar** (cross-dressing)
- Marlon Wayans, **White Chicks** (plays a female character)
- Luiz Guzman, **Anger Management** (effeminate)
- Miguel A. Núñez, Jr., **Juwanna Man** (cross-dressing)

Undoubtedly, White male actors have played similar roles, but are the percentages of high-profile White actors who do similar in proportion? Is the end effect the same?

NOTE: we are not condemning homosexual behavior as an outright form of emasculation. However, mainstream Hollywood often depicts, utilizes and regards homosexuality as a form of emasculation, especially since the overwhelming majority of male protagonists have heterosexual interests as written in the script.

Black Physical Wonder characters are frequently marked by their hulking physical stature or their hyper-sexuality. These archetypes take root in the Black Buck and Jezebel stereotypes that were prominent in Hollywood's early years.[2] With the focus placed on the Physical Wonder as a physical specimen, neither the audience nor the protagonists are concerned with this character's feelings or general sense of well-being, but more so with what utility their physical prowess offers to the storyline. Many roles portrayed by Michael Clarke Duncan (***Armageddon, The Green Mile***), Tom "Tiny" Lister (***Friday, Austin Powers: Goldmember***) and Ving Rhames (***Pulp Fiction, Con Air***) are noted for this archetype since their hulking, physically imposing builds are necessary for the character's identity construction.

For many Latino roles, the Physical Wonder is represented by characters who "appreciate" the finer points of love, passion and sensuality. The Physical Wonder archetype for Latinos borrows heavily from the "Latin Lover" stereotype. Although Italian Rudolph Valentino is widely acknowledged as the first "Latin lover," the craze was actually started by Antonio Moreno, a Spaniard who cultivated the idea of Hispanic men as sensuous and romantic. This character evolved over the century, through such notable practitioners as Ramon Novarro, Cesar Romero, Ricardo Montalban and Antonio Banderas. Female stars like Lupe Velez and Dolores Del Rio helped reshape Latinas (initially portrayed as "loose") into cultivated sirens, an image taken to dizzying heights in the talking-picture era by Rita Hayworth also known as Margarita Cansino.[3]

While early movies relegated many Latino men with accents to supporting roles, accents in women were often considered marketable assets with exploitable assets. This trend continues today with the growing number of Latina actresses starkly contrasting the dearth of mainstream roles for Latino males. In may ways, the absence of Latino males is another form of emasculation, especially given the sexual exploitation of Latinas that takes place in many mainstream movies. Additionally, there is a high volume of movies whereby Latina actresses are paired with White male leads (e.g., ***Sahara, After the Sunset, Maid in Manhattan***) and virtually no mainstream movies where they are paired with high-profile Latino male protagonists.

Furthermore, the Latino Physical Wonder character's emphasis on sensuality is frequently merged with a tangible physical skill, such as salsa dancing, as an extension of this character's ability to love or to manifest it within the White protagonist.

HOT TICKET ITEMS

PHYSICAL WONDER
- primarily valued for physical prowess
- explicit acknowledgement of physical stature, talent or skill set
- overly sexualized; often bare-chested, scantily clad or nude

ARCHETYPE EXPLORED

PHYSICAL WONDER: Asian Examples

1) Romeo Must Die (2000)

» actor/character: Jet Li as Han Sing
» analysis: Han Sing displays fearsome martial arts skills, but few emotions.
» bonus: Notice the implied – but not overtly consummated – romance between the lead characters played by Jet Li and Aaliyah.

2) Ocean's Twelve (2001)

» actor/character: Shaobo Qin as "The Amazing" Yen
» analysis: Yen is a contortionist (i.e., Physical Wonder) who helps carry out the planned heist. Yen is shown only to be valuable to the team for his ability to bend and contort his body like a human pretzel.
» key scene: One of the movie's gags consists of Yen being placed in luggage that ends up getting lost by the airline (leave it to Hollywood to still be thinking inside the box). Also, his English skills are limited, thereby adding a Comic Relief element to his character.

» **bonus**: Shaobo Qin is a classically trained *performer*, not an actor. As of the time of filming, Qin was a member of the internationally known and critically acclaimed *Peking Acrobats*.[4] Unsurprisingly, since Yen's true value onscreen comes from his physical abilities and not his emotional capacities, his speaking lines are markedly limited.

» **double bonus**: To this point, when the sequel ***Ocean's Thirteen*** premiered in Cannes, France, a Hong Kong reporter asked director Steven Soderbergh why Shaobo Qin's character is "made to seem like a 'clown' and why a joke is made of him only speaking in Chinese." "I think we're an equal opportunity offender," Soderbergh replied. "The joke is that everyone can understand him. It's like Chewbacca. He talks and everyone acts like they know what he's saying. I think if you get the point where you have to explain comedy you're in trouble. But I'm really sorry."[5] Notice how Soderbergh analogizes Shaobo Qin's character to that of an otherworldly character (Chewbacca is an alien in the ***Star Wars*** universe). Also note how Soderbergh, in stating that he did not have to explain the joke up until that point, implicitly defends his creative process, whereby such imagery was created in an environment that supported *his* perspective and was not scrutinized or screened for its offensive impact beforehand. Despite Soderbergh's response, which essentially admits to non-consideration of Asian sensitivities, the direct question posed by the Chinese reporter reinforces the international reach and importance of mainstream Hollywood. The reporter's question also serves as a simple reminder that unflattering minority imagery does not go unnoticed, be it domestically or abroad.

3) Sideways (2004)

» **actor/character**: Sandra Oh as Stephanie

» **analysis**: Stephanie fulfills the Physical Wonder archetype from the perspective of being utilized as a sex object for a White male. Stephanie is sexualized in her very first scene, stating that she needs to be spanked, going so far as to spank herself lightly as she walks away from lead characters Miles and Jack (Paul Giamatti and Thomas Haden Church respectively). She "goes all the way" with Jack on the very first date, punctuated by load moans that can be heard by the guests in the other room.

WHAT DO YOU THINK? *Rogue One* (2016), although set in the future, or at least a long, long time ago in a galaxy far, far away, employs one of the oldest non-white character archetypes: the Asian male martial artist.

Rogue One's contribution to this seemingly never-ending trope comes by way of Chirrut Îmwe (Donnie Yen), a blind warrior who can nonetheless see his feet and hands hit their targets with impressive martial arts skill and (blind?) faith in the force, of course.

Chirrut is paired with Baze (Jiang Wen) and both Chinese actors bring to life "minority" characters who not only serve as **Angel Figures** in providing direct assistance to the white female protagonist Jyn (Felicity Jones) by helping her make contact with Saw Gerrera (Forest Whitaker, who also saved Jyn's life earlier by serving as her caretaker once her parents were killed, thereby fulfilling the **Angel Figure** as well).

Despite the fact that Chirrut cannot see himself, the question we must ask is *how many times have we seen an Asian male using his body as an instrument of martial arts expertise?*

> **key scene:** Later, Miles unwittingly barges in on Jack and Stephanie while they are engaged in intercourse. Instead of stopping or having the audience see Stephanie rush to cover herself in an attempt to be modest, a "focused" Jack continues his activity and merely barks at Miles, "Not now! Not now!" Stephanie's value is perhaps best summed up by Jack when he states, ". . . She smells different, she tastes different, she f—ks different . . . she f—ks like an animal."

> **bonus:** Notice the differences between Stephanie's *sexual* relationship with Jack and Miles' *emotional* romance with Maya (Virginia Madsen). The Miles-Maya romance is teased out over the course of the entire movie. Meanwhile, Jack's tryst with Stephanie ends abruptly when she discovers that he is engaged. The last scene in the movie shows Miles knocking on Maya's door in hopes of sparking a long-lasting relationship. Meanwhile, Stephanie's last appearance in the movie is when she forcefully breaks Jack's nose. Further underscoring the temporary physical value of Stephanie's character, Jack is later shown marrying his fiancée.

PHYSICAL WONDER: BLACK EXAMPLES

1) Swordfish (2001)

> **actor/character:** Halle Berry as Ginger Knowles
> **analysis:** Halle Berry bears her breasts on the big screen for the first time (before the release of her famously graphic sex scene with Billy Bob Thornton in **Monster's Ball**) in one of the most gratuitous nude scenes in movie history. Sadly, it was a flop . . . uh, the movie, that is.
> **key scene:** During the movie's climax, Gabriel Shear (John Travolta) forces Stanley Jobson's (Hugh Jackman) hand and pressures him to hack into a bank's computer system and transfer billions of dollars to his account. Shear creates incentive for Jobson to do his bidding by threatening to kill his "friendly" starlet, Ginger Knowles (Halle Berry). His instructions to his henchmen? "String her up." Shear's henchmen then grab hold of Knowles and literally start to hang her from a rafter in the building. As she proceeds to gag and choke, Jobson frantically works to successfully hack the bank's system while Shear counts down the sixty second time period he estimates it will take for Knowles to die if Jobson does not succeed.

TOTAL ANECDOTAL

Consider this in analyzing whether an actor's onscreen image affects their offscreen persona: the very next year after claiming Best Actress honors at the 76th Academy Awards for her performance in **Monster's Ball** (which contains the famously graphic sex scene between herself and Billy Bob Thornton), Halle presented the award for Best Actor. The winner, Adrien Brody (for **The Pianist**), went on stage and swept her in his arms, and planted a sustained mouth-to-mouth kiss on Berry.

Not only was Berry unaware of Brody's prior plans, but the two were not publicly involved in any romantic way. The only relevant subplot was that she was married at the time to a known celebrity – musician Eric Benet – who was watching from the audience. Even though the sweeping kiss took her by surprise, Brody thought he was well within his rights: "Well, if you ever have an excuse to do something like that, that's it," said Brody. "I took my shot."[8a]

Do you think that Halle Berry's **Physical Wonder** role had any impact on how Adrien Brody interpreted Berry's sexuality and the boundaries thereof? Would the effect have been similar had a minority actor like Wesley Snipes swept a married White actress like Catherine Zeta-Jones off her feet, while her celebrity husband in Michael Douglas looked on from the distance?

PHYSICAL WONDER ARCHETYPE AT WORK

PROFILE: *Payback* (1999)

Payback features Chinese-American actress Lucy Liu as Pearl. Porter (Mel Gibson) is shot and left for dead in a plot hatched by both his former crime partner Val (Gregg Henry) and wife, Lynn (Deborah Kara Unger). This was one of Liu's "breakout" roles that helped her gain mainstream exposure. Perhaps it is telling that her scenes are marked by her fixation on sexuality, all the way from her attire (or lack thereof) to the degree and type of sexual excitement that she enjoys (S&M). Payback presents a quintessential example of the sexual and physical exploitation of the female **Physical Wonder** archetype.

Liu is hardly the first actress in a mainstream movie to appear scantily clad. However, as a rare mainstream role for an Asian female, it is telling that Liu's sexuality is taken for granted. Instead of being depicted as a love interest capable of human emotion, Liu's scenes are marked by a callous and desensitized response to pain.

Pearl is a call girl dominatrix and Val is a frequent client. During Pearl's introductory scene, her sexual aggression is so overwhelming that Val strikes her forcefully across her face with a rotary phone (Val: "I'm on the f—king phone!"). In a later scene, Val once again delivers a blow to Pearl's face – this time using his fist – that literally knocks her off her feet. Pearl appears to derive a devilish pleasure out of delivering and receiving physical blows, and she arguably delivers as much punishment as she receives. This nonchalance over female battery – both by Pearl and the surrounding male characters – is played to comedic effect, which reinforces Pearl's role as a one-dimensional physical object.

In Pearl's final scene with Val, she delivers a fearsome head-high roundhouse kick, an implicit stereotypical reference to the "natural" disposition for Asian characters towards martial arts. A more explicit reference to Pearl's own "racialized" character occurs when she stands over a prostrate Val and says, "Me love you long time," before twisting her black, knee-high patent leather boots in Val's scrotum. The "me love you long time" phrase is a classic stereotypical reference to the broken English promise of the Asian female concubine (made all the more ironic since Liu was born in New York and speaks perfect English). To punctuate the scene further, if you listen closely to the radio in the background, Dean Martin can be heard crooning "Ain't That a Kick in the Head."

» bonus: Given the particular history of Blacks in this country who met untimely and illegal deaths at the hands of lynching, it is curious that this manner of death was chosen. The imagery of a Black character hanging by her neck seems to be a play on a historical association with this image, especially in light of how infrequently this form of coercion is used in movies (i.e., as opposed to the common "gun-to-the-head" threat). The fact that this scene was written, discussed, rehearsed, filmed, screened and included in the movie's final version indicates that the scene's potential for racial "insensitivity" was not outweighed by the "cinematic effect" of such imagery.

2) Dodgeball: A True Underdog Story (2004)

» actor/character: Jamal Duff as Me'Shell Jones

» analysis: You will not have to look to hard to find Jamal Duff, a former football player who plays Me'Shell Jones, the large, scowling opponent on the purple team.

» bonus: "Me'Shell" is awfully close to "Michelle." Bonus points are awarded to those of you who recognized the Black male emasculation.

3) Planet of the Apes (2001)

» actor/character: Michael Clarke Duncan as Colonel Attar

» analysis: The Physical Wonder archetype crosses over into the Animal Kingdom with the biggest, darkest ape *literally* portrayed by one of the biggest and darkest Black males in Hollywood. Although Attar is a high-ranking ape soldier with a fair number of scenes and speaking lines, his presence still pales in comparison to the diminutive and lighter-skinned General Thade (as played by White actor Tim Roth), who is the authority in charge of the whole army of apes.

» bonus: Given that it was nearly impossible to discern facial features of the actors due to the elaborate make-up jobs in creating the ape costumes, it begs the question, why distinguish the apes in tone and complexion? Many

WHAT DO YOU THINK?

Furthering the notion that minority female sexuality is often gratuitously exploited by White characters, consider the following example from **The Last King of Scotland**. The protagonist, Dr. Nicholas Garrigan (played by White actor James McAvoy), is a Scot who has just recently arrived in Uganda after graduating from medical school. He beds an African woman he meets on the bus a mere five and a half minutes into the movie. In fact, their brief tryst takes place before the movie's title is shown during the opening credits!

This sexual interlude is not meant to begin a romantic storyline, but more so symbolizes how Garrigan has thrust himself into completely new surroundings as a White man in Uganda in search of adventure and fun (as evidenced by his spinning the globe and picking the first place on the map to travel to after graduating from medical school). As such, this sexual conquest is essentially indicative of his ability to easily adapt to his surroundings and "master" the culture.

Dr. Garrigan ultimately goes on to have a more involved relationship with another woman, who just so happens to be one of the wives of Uganda's ruler, General Idi Amin Dada (Forest Whitaker). This follows the prototypical pattern of White male sexual conquest and thwarted minority male sexuality, since the relationship essentially amounts to an emasculation of Amin (i.e., another man sleeping with his wife). In spite of the "tragic" circumstances taking place in the movie, the sexual conquests of the minority females essentially serve as symbolic checkpoints for the White male protagonist's story arc.

of the apes with high-profiles (e.g., General of Army, Senator Sandar, "lead mate" Ari) are lighter in complexion than the lower-ranking apes.

PHYSICAL WONDER: Latino Examples

1) Con Air (1997)

» actor/character: Danny Trejo as Johnny 'Johnny-23' Baca
» analysis: As with many movies involving the criminal justice system, be on the lookout for big, beefy Black and Latino males. In particular, pay close attention to Johnny 'Johnny-23' Baca.
» bonus: The movie contains various instances of comic relief in an otherwise "serious" action movie. Observe how virtually all of the lines delivered by Joe "Pinball" Parker (played by Black comedian Dave Chappelle) rely upon racial barbs and stereotypes for punchlines.

2) Sin City (2005)

» actor/character: Jessica Alba as Nancy Callahan
» analysis: Nancy Callahan provides little dialogue but plenty of midriff as she twirls around as a stripper.
» bonus: The "non-racialized" name (i.e., Nancy Callahan) indicates the movie studio's attempt to frame Alba as an asymptote for this role.
» double bonus: Notice the Utopic Reversal of Detective Lieutenant Jackie "Boy" Rafferty played by Latino actor Benicio Del Toro. Rafferty is a corrupt cop who physically batters women, openly solicits prostitutes and suffers the indignity of becoming physically maimed in multiple ways. His head becomes tangible bounty that mercenaries and female prostitutes from Sin City literally toss around and fight over as they use it to leverage power in an ongoing turf dispute. Compare Rafferty's position of "authority" to Officer John Hartigan's (Bruce Willis) opening scene. The stoic and unflinchingly honest Hartigan delivers a monologue wherein he walks the audience through his thoughts, while he braves evil and his own physical limitations to save the life of an eleven-year-old kidnapping victim. Meanwhile, in its final scene, Rafferty's head is used by Dwight McCarthy (Clive Owen) to house an explosive discharge (via the mouth). The explosive (and the head) are detonated by McCarthy in heroic fashion.

3) Dogma (1999)

» **actor/character:** Salma Hayek as Serendipity
» **analysis:** Salma Hayek busts onto the screen in this movie as a stripper.
» **bonus:** Take care not to confuse this role with Hayek's role in *From Dusk Till Dawn*, where she also plays a stripper. In *From Dusk Till Dawn*, Hayek plays Santanico Pandemonium, a stripper and a vampire. In *Dogma*, she plays a stripper and a deity named Serendipity... *How's that* for serendipity.

PHYSICAL WONDER: Other Examples

1) Pocahontas (1995)

» **actor/character:** Pocahontas as voiced by Irene Bedard (Judy Kuhn provides the singing voice)
» **analysis:** The romantic attraction between Captain John Smith (voiced by Mel Gibson) and Pocahontas furthers the trend of the "White male/exotic minority female" dynamic. Without this dynamic in mind, one questions whether a Hollywood studio would greenlight an animated movie of this budget and scale featuring two minority leads as the love interests. Interestingly enough, Disney took some liberties in order to facilitate the romance — namely, Pocahontas' physical appearance approximates that of the White Beauty Standard with her small waist and large bust, as opposed to the more "common" appearance of her fellow female tribal members.
» **bonus:** To see to what extent Disney producers amplified the mainstream sexual appeal of her character, look for a picture of the 1616 engraving of Pocahontas by Simon van de Passe. His is the only reproducible likeness created of Pocahontas during her lifetime.
» **key scene:** Not only does Pocahontas help avert a bloody battle between the settlers and the Native Americans, but she also fulfills the Angel figure archetype by "sacrificing" herself for her love, John Smith, thereby sparing his life. During the movie's climactic scene, just as her father Chief Powhatan (voiced by Russell Means) is about to deliver Smith a fatal blow, she lunges forward on top of Smith's body exclaiming: "If you kill him, you'll have to kill me too."

2) The Longest Yard (2005)

- » **actor/character:** Dalip Singh as Turley
- » **analysis:** The 7'2", 400-pound Dalip Singh plays Turley, an inmate that's small on brains but big on brawn. His minimalist dialogue is delivered in an unwavering monotone. To emphasize Turley's status as an "Other," English subtitles are provided for Turley's (minimal) dialogue, even though he is speaking in English! Did we mention that he was 7'2" and weighs 400 pounds?!
- » **bonus:** There are several other Physical Wonder archetypes visible on the prison grounds, many of which feature Black males without their shirts or only partially covered (see the early scenes featuring former NFL receiver Michael Irvin as Deacon Moss and actor Terry Crews as Cheeseburger Eddy). Yet, one Physical Wonder is especially reminiscent of "dynamic, dark and dumb" character types reserved for minority actors in early American cinema. Switowski, played by Bob Sapp, is a hulking, towering mass with limited mental capacities. He talks and behaves like a child, peppering his speech with phraseology like, "Will you teach me to football?" and "I brokeded [sic] your toy." Switowski (a Black male outfitted with a Polish surname, probably as a joke) is constantly provided direction by a smarter and more diminutive White male, Paul Crewe (Adam Sandler), even though Switowski clearly has the physical advantage (which is the traditional "political leverage" used in the prison yard). Moreover, what makes Sapp's casting as the proverbial powerful-but-impotent-childlike Negro all the more telling is that in reality, Sapp is an intimidating mixed-martial arts specialist who has competed admirably in Japan. Evidently, his skill set in the ring did not translate into a more "serious" depiction outside of it.
- » **double bonus:** Perhaps as a joke, at approximately the 1:23:50 mark, ESPN television personality Chris Berman (playing himself) makes the play call of, "Look at that little Megget run!" Not only is he referencing the speedy running back character Megget (the rapper Nelly) blazing down the field, but this line is also a reference to a famous incident wherein the famous television commentator, Howard Cosell, made the call of, "Look at that little monkey run!" during a 1983 Monday Night Football game. Cosell was making reference to Alvin Garrett, a Black wide receiver for the Washington Redskins.

3) The Mummy (1999)

- **actor/character**: Arnold Vosloo as High Priest Imhotep
- **analysis**: The anti-hero High Priest Imhotep is the evil Egyptian mummy that terrifies all within his path. Notice that Imhotep is bare-chested throughout many of his scenes.
- **bonus**: Interestingly enough, even though this character is played by Arnold Vosloo, a native of the Republic of South Africa, he represents a "Middle Eastern" character onscreen. Although the actor is White, the character still represents an ancient Egyptian who menaces (White) characters with his imposing stature and other-worldly aggression.

The Physical Wonder archetype encompasses a broad range of minority characters. With respect to minority males, the Physical Wonder archetype places an emphasis on the brute strength, size or speed of the character, as if he were a specimen to be marveled. With respect to female minority characters, the Physical Wonder includes characters who are regarded for their sexual prowess, with a negligible focus on their romantic capabilities or interests. For both sexes, the Physical Wonder archetype speaks to characters endowed with special physical talents or skills, which typically explains or justifies the minority character's utility to the plot or involvement with the central characters.

CHAPTER 8: THE PHYSICAL WONDER

CHAPTER 8:
THE MYOPIC REVIEWER

It's been very difficult for me to find any role that can give me some satisfaction. Hollywood destroyed my dreams a long time ago.

Ricardo Montalban, actor[1]

CHAPTER 9:
THE UTOPIC REVERSAL

The Utopic Reversal minority character pattern is relatively new in this recent age of diversity. Usually found occupying a high social position (e.g., police chief, judge, etc.), this character is in actuality a *pseudo*-authority figure. Their power and authority are undermined, usurped or called into question (either explicitly or implicitly) in relation to other White characters, thereby rendering their authority or position as mostly symbolic in nature.

REVERSAL OF FORTUNE

Utopic Reversal roles serve as a protective "insurance" from those who bemoan menial roles for minority characters. Few could argue that there is anything inherently negative or stereotypical about seeing a minority character as a police chief or judge. If anything, most people would consider this a surefire sign of progress. Nevertheless, the onscreen privileges accorded Utopic Reversals are minimal, which only reinforces the marginalized status of minority characters in Hollywood. The roles themselves are not necessarily negative, but it is the character's interaction with other characters that informs the audience of the true worth of the Utopic Reversal's position. A general example would be that of a Black police chief who, in his brief time onscreen, gives orders that are summarily ignored or deliberately disobeyed by the White maverick cop in order to save the day.

This archetype distorts the perception of "progress" within the industry since studio executives can point to these "high-ranking" characters as "evidence" of increasing racial equity and equality in the movie business. However, a full analysis reveals that these characters either have power in name only or that they are largely unable to get others to respect the privileges associated with their position. Thus, it is not uncommon for a Utopic Reversal to have their privileges marginalized or subordinated by a White character.

Black characters account for the preponderance of Utopic Reversal figures in mainstream movies, which is perhaps reflective of the long-standing social and political struggles between Blacks and Whites in this country. As it is, Latinos, Asians, Native Americans and people of Middle Eastern origin make infrequent appearances in mainstream movies, and when they do appear, it is rare to see them occupy a position of power, except as it relates to their own ethnic group. Additionally, these authority figures are frequently associated with crime or some warring faction (against Whites) that must be deposed.

Asians only occupy only 2.5% of all theatrical and television roles (see "Minority Reports," *Chapter 2: The Cast of Caricatures*). Aside from isolated crime bosses, there are scant examples of Asian characters depicted in positions of power. While Asian male martial artists can also be considered authority figures in some instances, it is important to note that their "authority" is limited to the realm of the Physical Wonder. Whereas a Black police chief or judge with limited powers is almost cliché, the low level of racial capital enjoyed by Asian characters translates into few depictions as authority figures in the first place.

Due to an overall dearth of significantly powerful minority characters in mainstream movies, the opportunities for "Other" minorities to play high-ranking positions are even fewer. Virtually all of the examples that we compiled for this category could also be considered Background Figures, since many Utopic Reversals fitting in the Other racial category simply do not have enough dialogue or screen time to be truly representative of the Utopic Reversal archetype.

Yet, there are some movies that prominently feature minority actors in positions of authority that appear to complicate the Utopic Reversal archetype with their overwhelmingly positive portrayals. **Hidden Figures, Cesar Chavez, Concussion, The Last King in Scotland, Red Tails, The Soloist, Ray, Hotel Rwanda, The Pursuit of Happyness, Coach Carter, Ali, Lean on Me, The Hurricane, Malcolm X, Stand and Deliver, What's Love Got To Do with It, La Bamba, Selena, Frida, The Great Debaters, Pride** and **Talk to Me** are all examples of mainstream movies that prominently feature a minority character as the central protagonist. These "biopic" movies feature top-billed minority leads in dramatic roles without the support of White co-stars. However, the significant thread that unites all of the aforementioned movies is that they are all based upon *extraordinary* life stories of *real-life* minorities. As such, the degree of "fantasy" required for mainstream White audiences to enjoy these movies is "minimal."

HOT TICKET ITEMS

UTOPIC REVERSAL
- occupies a high-ranking position, usually in isolation from other minorities
- authority or power is not fully exercised or recognized onscreen
- rarely depicted in informal, personal or romantic settings

ARCHETYPE EXPLORED

UTOPIC REVERSAL: Asian Examples

1) Red Corner (1997)

» **actor/character:** Corrupt Chinese government

» **analysis:** American Jack Moore (Richard Gere) is a business executive in China who is wrongly accused of murder after a one-night stand (the accusations are always wrong, aren't they???). Moore must fight through the political "Red tape" as he battles to prove his innocence in the face of corrupt Chinese generals, judges and jilted businessmen. Moore's lawyer Shen Yuelin (Ling Bai), risks exile when she takes on his case in the search for earnest justice. Moore ultimately vindicates himself and exposes a far-reaching chain of corruption throughout the Chinese government.

» **bonus:** The Chinese-born, Hollywood-based, Ling Bai risked exile in real life. The movie was partly filmed in China, without permission from the Chinese government, and Ling Bai still faces scrutiny in her homeland for her controversial role as the "free-thinking" lawyer. Wow, don't you hate when you paint yourself into a ***Red Corner***?!

 **WHAT DO YOU THINK?** As proof that animated movies are not immune from **The HARM Theory**, take a closer look at *Kung Fu Panda* (2008).

The central protagonist is Po, a large, rotund, panda whose voice is provided by White male actor Jack Black. One of Po's friends and ancillary character with limited screen time and dialogue is Monkey, an agile baboon whose voice is provided by Chinese male actor, Jackie Chan.

If the characters are animated and appearance is not paramount, why not switch the roles of Jack Black and Jackie Chan? After all, the movie is set in China and Chan truly is a martial artist expert, no? Consider whether placing Chan in a glorified Background Figure role also creates a Utopic Reversal in real life?!

2) The Last Samurai (2003)

- » **actor/character**: Masato Harada as Omura; Shichinosuke Nakamura as Emperor Meiji; Ken Watanabe as Katsumoto
- » **analysis**: Take your pick here. First, there is Omura, the villainous politician hell-bent on extinguishing the samurai. Then there is Emperor Meiji, the young, soft-spoken and ineffectual leader whose indecision allows Omura's army to crush the samurai. Lastly, there is Katsumoto, the *second*-to-last samurai. Despite his many years as a skilled samurai, Katsumoto is unable to survive the penultimate battle, leaving White American Nathan Algren (Tom Cruise) to fulfill the movie's namesake and right any remaining wrongs (i.e., depose Omura). Well, live by the sword, die by the sordid.
- » **bonus**: Notice the almost-literal emasculation of the Asian male onscreen since Algren ends up living with the wife of the man he killed!

3) Rising Sun (1993)

- » **actor/character**: Stan Egi as Ishihara
- » **analysis**: Over the course of the murder investigation led by Capt. John Connor (Sean Connery) and Lt. Web Smith (Wesley Snipes), Ishihara reveals himself to be a high-ranking but corrupt Japanese corporate official. Specifically, Ishihara covers up the murder (of a White woman) so that a major business deal can proceed unhindered.
- » **bonus**: Cary-Hiroyuki Tagawa plays Eddie Sakamura, a flamboyant, affluent playboy accused of the murder. Given the infrequency that Asian males play this type of role in mainstream movies, it is interesting to note Sakamura's depiction. While a "playboy" is not exactly a high-ranking social position, it is nonetheless rare to see an Asian male "living it up" according to mainstream standards (e.g., fast cars and women) independent of any crime syndicate. Sakamura is eventually proven innocent, yet his character is initially portrayed as sleazy and untrustworthy and does not survive until the end of the movie.

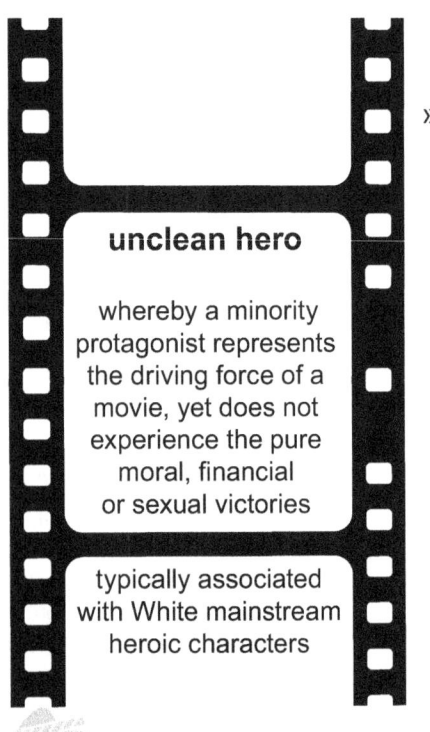

unclean hero

whereby a minority protagonist represents the driving force of a movie, yet does not experience the pure moral, financial or sexual victories

typically associated with White mainstream heroic characters

CUT!
What about Denzel Washington and his roles in mainstream movies? Do his characters accurately fit the description of the described archetypes? We acknowledge that Denzel Washington has portrayed characters that contain much more complexity than many of the typical roles allotted to minorities over the course of his distinguished career. Nonetheless, one of the most celebrated minority actors in Hollywood's history is still not immune to the HARM theory.

While many of Denzel Washington's characters do not fit neatly within the proscribed archetypes, many of his characters follow archetypal themes, albeit in a more subtle manner. In any particular movie, Washington's character will often experience a heroic story arc, yet he is frequently portrayed as an unclean hero. Although his character is the clear driving force of the movie, this character does not experience the pure moral, financial and romantic (or sexual) victories frequently enjoyed by leading White male characters played by fellow A-list stars like Mel Gibson, Harrison Ford and Tom Hanks.

For example, consider Washington's role as Lt. Cmdr. Hunter in **Crimson Tide**, wherein the story revolves around a power struggle between Hunter and Capt. Ramsey (Gene Hackman) over an unconfirmed order to launch a nuclear warhead into enemy territory. During the climactic confrontation over the nuclear submarine's correct mission orders, Capt. Ramsey punches Lt. Cmdr. Hunter twice without any retaliation by Hunter. Ramsey thus visually asserts himself as the dominant force while Hunter sits by passively, waiting for the final transmission of the submarine's true orders that will vindicate him. Although Washington's character is ultimately proven correct, Ramsey is technically the antagonist and violates protocol in his effort to remain dominant. Even when Hunter should be vindicated or held up as a hero (i.e., for preventing World War III), at the movie's conclusion he is informed by the administrative judge that they were both wrong! A "split decision" results whereby Capt. Ramsey retires with his dignity intact and in parting, lends his blessing along with his gracious recommendation that Lt. Cmdr. Hunter be considered for future command. Muddling Hunter's moral "victory" even further is the movie's final scene whereby an unnamed naval cadet salutes a pristine Capt. Ramsey in his white naval uniform as he walks "off into the sunset," with his faithful canine companion accompanying him.

Or, consider **John Q**, where Washington portrays a sympathetic character who uses any means necessary to secure a heart transplant for his son. The movie's final scene nonetheless provides the lasting image of John Quincy Archibald (Washington) handcuffed in the backseat of a police car, being carted off to await his imminent sentencing and jail time for his kidnapping and false imprisonment conviction, three months after his "triumph."

Although some of Denzel Washington's roles complicate the standard archetypal patterns for minority characters, this does not mean that the patterns themselves are broken. Consider the following examples where despite Washington's complex character traits, his roles still satisfy the **HARM Theory** of minority characters slotted in archetypal roles:

- *Training Day* - he satisfies the **Menace to Society** archetype as a rogue police detective
- *Remember the Titans* - he fulfills the **Angel** archetype as coach of an interracial football team
- *Man On Fire* - he satisfies the **Angel** archetype as the bodyguard and rescuer of a kidnapped White girl
- *The Bone Collector* - he serves as an **Angel** archetype in helping his "attractive" partner (Angelina Jolie) catch the killer, despite his quadriplegic state (essentially a form of emasculation with no romance at end)
- *Out of Time* - he fulfills the **Utopic Reversal** archetype as an ethically dubious police chief
- *Crimson Tide* - he fulfills the **Utopic Reversal** archetype as he battles a mutinous crew
- *John Q* - he satisfies the a **Menace to Society** archetype when he holds a hospital emergency room hostage in order to force a heart transplant for his ailing son

If anything, Washington's isolated success as a "unique" minority actor is proof positive of the limiting effects the archetypes have on all minority actors in the movie industry.

CHAPTER 9: THE UTOPIC REVERSAL

UTOPIC REVERSAL: Black Examples

1) Gothika (2003)

» **actor/character:** Charles S. Dutton as Dr. Douglas Grey

» **analysis:** The Utopic Reversal archetype is demonstrated by Dr. Douglas Grey, whose role is a perfect example of the HARM theory at work. Miranda Grey (Halle Berry) is married to Dr. Douglas Grey, a professional psychologist who heads the hospital where she works. Dr. Grey is only alive onscreen for all of five minutes, but it turns out, that he was half of a sinister female kidnapping and raping ring. Dr. Grey is killed by the spirit of one of the victims (a White female), who possesses the body of Miranda to execute the physical act of murder.

» **bonus:** Additionally, Dr. Grey is the victim of an emasculation procedure when Miranda admits to her White colleague Pete Graham (Morton Downey, Jr.), that she wanted to have an affair with him. This admission occurs *before* she learns of Dr. Grey's "wrongdoings," further undercutting his status as a Utopic Reversal.

» **double bonus:** Upon **Gothika's** release in 2003, Halle Berry was "victimized" in real life when she was targeted for a practical joke by MTV's hit show, *Punk'd* (hosted by Ashton Kutcher). Berry was "denied" entrance to the movie theater hosting the premiere. The fact that Berry was "snubbed" at such a crucial moment of her career – albeit staged – reflects the limited influence of Hollywood's *leading Black actress* (at the time). Despite having won her Academy Award over two years prior, **Gothika** was Berry's first top-billed role after **Monster's Ball**. The influence and collaboration required to pull off such a practical joke – which included assistance from **Gothika** producer Joel Silver – speaks to the power imbalance of racial capital *offscreen* and reinforces the familiar theme of minority marginalization. Recall that this was only Kutcher's second season of *Punk'd* and that he had yet to gain prominence as a movie star. This essentially means that the machinations of a young, White male television star (Kutcher) were allowed to "trump" Berry's (potentially) shining moment on the sacred ground of the red carpet, all for a minutes worth of footage for an episode of *his* television show.

> **WHAT DO YOU THINK?**
> Recall, how characters that meet the criteria for Utopic Reversal generally start the movie in a position of power or esteem, but this power is significantly undermined, undercut, usurped by movie's end. In other words, these non-white characters are "put back in their place."
>
> An excellent example containing three different minority characters comes by way of the 2008 hit, **The Dark Knight**.
>
> The Joker (Heath Ledger) threatens to kill Gotham City citizens unless Batman (Christian Bale) reveals his identity. To make good on his promise, he starts by killing Black character Gillian B. Loeb, who turned out to be an ineffective Police Commissioner.
>
> The Joker then kills the Judge presiding over the mob trial (see the movie), who *just happens* to be Latina: Nydia Rodriguez Terracina as Judge Janet Surrillo.
>
> Lastly, Singaporean actor Ng Chin Han plays Lau, a bigtime accountant who turns out to be corrupt. Not only does the mythical Batman from the mythical Gotham City go to the real Hong Kong to "crash through" Lau's office space to bring Lau back to justice in Gotham City, but Lau ends up getting burned alive along with the money he stole earlier.
>
> Do you think these three fates stick out more than any other White deaths? ***How many other minority characters are there? And do they also escape the HARM Theory?***

2) After the Sunset (2004)

» **actor/character**: Don Cheadle as Henri Mooré
» **analysis**: Henri Mooré first appears onscreen as a cultured and scrupulous businessman, an entrepreneurial spirit who has an appreciation for fine linen and multi-syllabic vocabulary words. Yet, as the plot turns, Mooré proves to be a manipulative tycoon who wants Max Burdett (Pierce Brosnan) to steal Napoleon's Number Three Diamond. Towards the movie's climax, moviegoers see that Mooré's early appearance was only an aristocratic veneer, and he ultimately turns "hood," punctuating his abrupt change with harsh invective and by physically slapping Lola Cirillo (Salma Hayek).

3) Bruce Almighty (2003)

» **actor/character**: Morgan Freeman as God
» **analysis**: Even though Morgan Freeman plays God, the role of the most knowledgeable, most powerful and most awesome force in the universe, the plot revolves around the empowerment of Bruce Nolan (Jim Carey). God endows Bruce with his powers in order to teach him several valuable life lessons. Bruce primarily exploits the powers to benefit himself and his love life, even at the expense of others. For instance, the morning after Bruce's "night to remember" with Grace Connelly (Jennifer Aniston), Grace learned during an international news report that hundreds of Japanese citizens were stranded after "unusual lunar activity" caused a freak tidal wave (notice the casual displacement of hundreds of minority Background Figures in exchange for the private pleasure of two White characters). Meanwhile, Freeman's character is relegated to a supporting role, appearing occasionally to offer comedic and angelic support to the White protagonist. Hence, the title of the movie is ***Bruce Almighty***, not ***God Almighty***.
» **key scene**: To add to the irony, the movie introduces Freeman's character dressed in a one-piece janitorial outfit, and the movie closes with a shot of him "disguised" as a homeless man. Some may call that a sign of humility; we call that the sign of a Utopic Reversal.
» **bonus**: Notice the Menace to Society archetypes present with the six Latino "Hood" characters (as they are all so named in the credits).

Initially they attack an unarmed homeless person, then they (with little provocation) set their sights upon Bruce during his "worst day ever." Bruce gets his comeuppance when he confronts them again around the 38:31 mark by emasculating their ring leader (played by Noel Gugliemi). Bruce asks the Hoods to apologize for beating him up earlier, but the ring leader refuses, stating that "the day a monkey comes out of my butt – then you'll get your 'sorry.'" Since Bruce has "the power," not only does he oblige by having a monkey literally rip its way out of the Hood's pants (much to the horror of the other Hoods), but he also wipes his hands of the matter by sending the monkey back where it came from with the line, "Hey, little anal-dwelling, butt monkey – it's time for you to go home little buddy!"

UTOPIC REVERSAL: Latino Examples

1) Collateral (2004)

» actor/character: Emilio Rivera as Paco
» analysis: Paco is the deductive police officer in charge of tracking down Vincent (Tom Cruise) before the hitman can claim another victim. Despite his sense of independence, quick wits and perceptive demeanor typical of successful cops in similar mainstream roles, Paco unfortunately fails to complete his mission and becomes one of Vincent's final victims.
» bonus: Emilio Rivera is one of the six Latino "Hood" characters referenced in the **Bruce Almighty** Black Utopic Reversal example above.

2) The Hunted (2003)

» actor/character: Benicio Del Toro as Aaron Hallam
» analysis: Aaron Hallam is an exceptionally trained assassin from an elite Special Forces squadron who received his tutelage from survivalist guru L.T. Bonham (Tommy Lee Jones). Unfortunately, all of this special training goes to "waste" when Hallam quietly slips over the edge of sanity. The F.B.I. is brought in to bring Hallam and his wildlife-surviving days to an end.
» note: Although Aaron Hallam is not necessarily a "Latino" in this movie, this example is included to illustrate how a well-known, Academy

Award-winning Latino actor in a prominent mainstream role remains limited to portraying an archetypal role.

> ► **NOTE** ◄
> Although **Man on Fire** was previously profiled in **Chapter 4** ("The Angel: Black Examples"), for the following example we selected the movie again to underscore the point that mainstream movies – and characters as well – are not limited to just one archetype classification and may embody several different combinations.

3) Man on Fire (2004)

» **actor/character:** Jesús Ochoa as Fuentes, El Presidente de la Hermandad
» **analysis:** John W. Creasy (Denzel Washington), in his attempt to find out who kidnapped Pita (Dakota Fanning), cuts a murderous swath that winds its way through the Mexican government. More than mere isolated thugs at work, Creasy's investigation reveals that the Mexican police are involved in a cover-up operation. Creasy, in his one-man attempt to enforce justice, follows the trail all the way up to the top, where he finds that the chief of police is also el Presidente de la Hermandad, the secret organization responsible for kidnapping Pita.
» **key scene:** Creasy turns the tables by kidnapping el Presidente. In el Presidente's last scene, he finds himself taped to the hood of a car. He is aesthetically unappealing, with his sweaty, hairy chest exposed, along with his sizeable gut. Unfortunately for el Presidente, he pays the ultimate price for threatening to harm the White protagonist in the movie. El Presidente is the victim of emasculating violence: his boxer undergarments are exposed and Creasy, through elaborate explanation, informs el Presidente that he has an explosive discharge lodged in his rectum. Fuentes' authority as a high-ranking official reaches rock bottom when Creasy is "justified" in taking the law – and Fuentes' life – into his own hands.
» **bonus:** In addition to el Presidente, Samuel (played by famous Latin pop star Marc Anthony), would also be considered a Utopic Reversal. Samuel is a Mexican national married to a White American named Lisa (Radha Mitchell). Samuel and Lisa are Pita's parents, although Samuel's paternity of Pita cannot be presumed. Both Lisa and Pita have a blond-hair and blue-eyed aesthetic, while Samuel is distinctly Latino. Samuel is originally depicted as a man of means, complete with a sizeable mansion and seemingly strong political connections. However, he is eventually shown to be in desperate financial

UTOPIC REVERSAL ARCHETYPE AT WORK
PROFILE: *Bad Boys II* (2003)

In *Bad Boys II*, narcotics cops Mike Lowrey (Will Smith) and Marcus Burnett (Martin Lawrence) must take down a Cuban drug trafficker named Hector Juan Carlos 'Johnny' Tapia (Jordi Mollà). This movie is significant because it is a big-budget mainstream movie distributed by a major studio featuring two minority leads. However, their roles do not escape the long arm of the HARM theory, as the movie's creators use "Black culture" to undermine their authority and present Lowery and Burnett as Utopic Reversals.

One scene indicative of their Utopic Reversal status occurs when a young Black male named Reggie (Dennis Greene) shows up at the Burnett residence to take his daughter out on a date. Reggie presents himself as a well-mannered, well-dressed and well-groomed fifteen-year-old, an image and demeanor that counters the proverbial "hip-hop," anti-social symbology often associated with young Black males. Unfortunately for Reggie, the running gag comes from the fact that this dating scenario is turned on its head, whereby Reggie, the traditional threat to virgin chastity, is actually harmless, while the elder protectors – in this case, Burnett and Lowrey – become the aggressors. What ensues is a lengthy scene in which Burnett and Lowrey badger and berate Reggie.

The two officers freely use foul language (referring to Reggie as "nigga" on more than one occasion), rudely interrogate Reggie about his sexual past and openly drink alcohol in the teenager's presence. The cops also place Reggie through a mock police-search for illicit paraphernalia while reading him his "rights." Further, Burnett openly represents to Reggie that Lowrey is not a police officer but actually an ex-con who "just got out" and is mentally unstable. Lowrey, while pretending to be an ex-con, solicits Reggie:

> *Lowrey*: You ever made love to a man?
> *Reggie*: No.
> *Lowrey*: [leaning in towards Reggie] You want to?

Here, homosexuality is not so much the issue as it seems more so a reference to jail culture. The threat is not appropriate merely because it is "homosexual" in nature, but because Reggie is underaged, the setting is highly inappropriate, the "solicitation" is a sexual threat – which is an effort to emasculate Reggie and threaten his manhood – and Lowrey is an officer of the law.

Furthermore, as part of this intimidation routine, Lowrey cavalierly waves a firearm in the young man's face! Note the sensitive nature of such an act in light of issues about gun violence within the Black community. At a minimum, it is hard to recall many mainstream movies featuring White cops threatening White kids in a similar nature, even to comedic effect!

condition, and it is revealed that he has arranged a scheme to pay off his debts that involves kidnapping his own daughter! Samuel could also be considered a Menace to Society figure – even though he wields no weapons or drugs, he is guilty by his association with the kidnappers. Samuel's initially positive portrayal is usurped by his morally reprehensible actions, and he punctuates his status as a Utopic Reversal by taking his own life to atone for his sins.

» **double bonus**: In **Bad Boys II**, narcotics cops Mike Lowrey (Will Smith) and Marcus Burnett (Martin Lawrence) must take down a Cuban drug trafficker named Hector Juan Carlos 'Johnny' Tapia (Jordi Mollà). Incidentally, these two Black cops are not assigned to investigate White crime lords, but are employed to rid the scourge of other criminally-minded minorities that threaten the status quo. Much like **Man on Fire**, where Denzel Washington's character single-handedly dismantles a corrupt Mexican government, Lowrey and Burnett must take down the Cuban drug cartel. Along the way, the two cops engage in gun battles with Latino drug runners in an effort to rid Miami of ecstasy. They also encounter Haitians and engage in a shoot-out with them as well. After vanquishing the latter, Burnett can be quoted as saying, "I hate f—in' Haitians." In this case we have Latinos playing Menace to Society roles, and we also have Lowrey and Burnett exploiting the racial capital paradigm. Much like Chris Tucker's character in **Rush Hour**, Lowrey and Burnett are not rebuffed for their obvious racial and ethnic antagonisms. Also note the similarities between Lowrey and Burnett's arrival in Cuba and Denzel Washington's actions in **Man on Fire**. In both cases, the racial capital of the Latinos involved is devalued due to an association with some sort of corruption (i.e., drugs, kidnapping, etc.). As a result, the protagonists are allowed to enter the respective countries and act "at will." Thus, low racial capital value and the Menace to Society archetype go hand-in-hand.

UTOPIC REVERSAL: Other Examples

1) Last Holiday (2006)

» **actor/character**: Ranjit Chowdry as Dr. Gupta
» **analysis**: Dr. Gupta fulfills the Utopic Reversal in that not only does he

> **WHAT DO YOU THINK?**
> In *Jurassic World* (2015) East Indian actor Irrfan Khan played the role of Simon Masrani, head of the Masrani Global Corporation. As the new owner of the Jurassic World park, island and thriving business, he initially comes off as very confident proof that his created dinosaurs will behave and avoid the destructive fate that *Jurassic Park* suffered.
>
> Masrani begins his descent from on high by first ignoring Owen Grady's (Chris Pratt) waning about raising the large, new and unknown *Indominus Rex* creation in isolation from other dinosaurs, thereby increasing the possibility it could become more aggressive. Apparently, Masrani was wrong. Second, Masrani, ignored advice from a White "alpha" male (inside joke inside the movie) and refused to kill the *Indominus Rex* but sent out a personalized security team (Asset Containment Unit headed by Japanese male character Hamada) instead. The ACU failed and he was wrong again.
>
> Thirdly, he ignores sound, White advice again. Masrani was depicted earlier in the movie with his helicopter instructor and triumphantly told his trusted operations manager Claire Dearing (Bryce Dallas Howard) that he was to obtain his piloting license in two days. This detail ominously foreshadowed the potential for error. Later, once *Indominous Rex* escaped, Masrani "takes charge" during the clamor to pilot the helicopter and find it — against the suggestion of his worried (White) assistant. Masrani proved that despite his money and status, it takes three strikes to crash, burn, and be out for the remainder of the movie. ***Do you see or disagree?***

provide an incorrect diagnosis of Georgia Byrd's (Queen Latifah) "terminal illness," but he is initially unsuccessful in delivering the news to Byrd. Dr. Gupta is visibly smaller in stature than Byrd and delivers the news to her in a timid and apologetic manner while retreating from her (which also subtly invokes the stereotype of the burly and bellicose Black woman). Further confirming his diminutive status, at a later point, Sean Matthews (LL Cool J) interrupts Dr. Gupta's on-the-job meditation session by physically picking him off the ground and cradling him, bare feet and all. This demonstrative move proves effective for Sean, as he successfully usurps the standard doctor-patient privilege protections in order to obtain information about a woman (i.e., Georgia Byrd) that he has yet to have a date with.

» **key scene:** After Dr. Gupta's initial botched attempt to communicate Byrd's medical condition, the next scene features Dr. Thompson (Dan Ziskie). Dr. Thompson is an older and more senior White doctor (we are left to assume) who is seen sauntering about in his well-lit office, calmly explaining to a more subdued Byrd the extent of her diagnosis. Dr. Gupta is also present in the scene, sitting in a chair on the side, making side remarks about his futile attempts to explain the same diagnosis to her. The contrast between the two doctors sends the subtle message that the White doctor is more competent and commands more respect since he is able to "translate" what Dr. Gupta said.

» **bonus:** As further "proof" that Dr. Gupta is not cut out to be a medical professional, in the movie's culminating scene, he arrives at Byrd's new restaurant and greets both her and Sean while repeating the line, "I quit my job."

2) Sixth Sense (1999)

» **actor/character:** M. Night Shyamalan as Dr. Hill
» **analysis:** Dr. Hill fulfills the Utopic Reversal when he debriefs Lynn Sear (Toni Collette) about her son Cole (Haley Joel Osment) and the results of his medical examination. Test results do not indicate evidence of a seizure, even though in reality Cole had a "stressful" contact with the spiritual world of ghosts. The Utopic Reversal is subtle, but nonetheless present since Dr. Hill's brief scene is set up as an antagonistic role. Lynn grows upset at Dr. Hill when he does not corroborate her version

LIGHTS! CAMERA! INTERACTION!

Take a closer look at minorities who fulfill law enforcement or military personnel roles. Hollywood has a distinctive pattern of slotting minority characters in comedic or ineffective law enforcement/security personnel/military roles. What follows are but a few examples. *Can you think of any others?*

MOVIE	ACTORS	ROLE
Rush Hour series	Jackie Chan	comedic
	Chris Tucker	comedic
Beverly Hills Cop series	Eddie Murphy	comedic
Big Momma's House series	Martin Lawrence	comedic
Lethal Weapon series	Danny Glover	comedic
Agent Cody Banks series	Anthony Anderson	comedic
	Keith David	comedic
Police Academy series	Michael Winslow	comedic
	Bubba Smith	comedic
	Marion Ramsey	comedic
National Security	Martin Lawrence	comedic
Soul Plane	Mo'Nique	comedic
	Loni Love	comedic
The Day After Tomorrow	Kwasi Songui	ineffective
Crash	Keith David	comedic
Armageddon	Keith David	ineffective
Batman Begins	Colin McFarlane	ineffective
I, Robot	Chi McBride	ineffective
Last Action Hero	Frank McRae	comedic
White Chicks	Shawn Wayans	comedic
	Marlon Wayans	comedic
Out of Time	Denzel Washington	ineffective
Training Day	Denzel Washington	ineffective
Collateral	Emilio Rivera	ineffective
Bad Company	Chris Rock	ineffective
The Man	Samuel L. Jackson	comedic
Metro	Eddie Murphy	comedic
Men in Black	Will Smith	comedic
Wild Wild West	Will Smith	comedic
Jumanji	Kevin Hart	comedic
Snakes on a Plane	Samuel L. Jackson	comedic
Rules of Engagement	Samuel L. Jackson	ineffective
Casino Royale	Jeffrey Wright	ineffective
The Hunted	Benicio Del Toro	ineffective
Man on Fire	Jesús Ochoa	ineffective
Traffic	Luis Guzman	ineffective
Sin City	Benicio Del Toro	ineffective
Low Down Dirty Shame	Keenan Ivory Wayans	comedic
Bulletproof	Damon Wayans	comedic
Major Payne	Damon Wayans	comedic
First Kid	Sinbad	comedic
Reno 911!	Cedric Yarbrough	comedic
	Niecy Nash	comedic

CHAPTER 9: THE UTOPIC REVERSAL

of the events that led up to Cole's hospital admission. Although Dr. Hill is calm and rational, his role is perceived as cold and accusatory by Lynn since he wants her to speak to a hospital social worker about some "cuts and bruises" on her son that concern him. Lynn confronts Dr. Hill about the cloud of suspicion he casts on Lynn's parenting skills by demanding from him, "You think I hurt my child? You think I'm a bad mother?" The Utopic Reversal is reinforced by the fact that the audience "knows" Lynn as a faithful and concerned single mother who would not purposely harm or injure her child. The scene is punctuated with Lynn's protest, "What happened to my child today? Something was happening to him, physically happening, something was very wrong!" This underscores the simple construction that Lynn is "right" and Dr. Hill is "wrong."

» bonus: M. Night Shyamalan wrote and directed this incredibly successful blockbuster hit. Yet, in casting himself for a brief cameo, his role actually fulfills the HARM theory as a Background Figure as well, despite his position as director to shape the movie in whatever manner he wished. The fulfillment of the HARM theory may implicitly speak to the unspoken pressures in Hollywood to produce movies in accordance with traditional mainstream formulas. For example, casting himself as the lead actor instead of Bruce Willis may have significantly truncated potential box office sales in view of his (at the time) unknown stature and non-White appearance, in contrast to A-list White talent that typically connects well with mainstream White audiences.

3) Analyze This (1999)

» actor/character: Aasif Mandvi as Dr. Shulman
» analysis: Dr. Shulman fulfills the Utopic Reversal when he attempts to inform insecure mob boss Paul Vitti (Robert De Niro) early in the movie that Vitti's medical examination does not show evidence of heart trouble. Vitti thought previously that he was suffering from "like, eight heart attacks in the last three weeks" and was informed that he was merely having anxiety or panic attacks instead. Vitti not only questions this diagnosis, but he openly questions where Dr. Shulman attended medical school. The fact that Dr. Shulman is "wrong" prompts Vitti to take more desperate measures to cure himself, which leads him to

the movie's "real doctor" and other leading character, Dr. Ben Sobel (White actor Billy Crystal).

» bonus: Dr. Shulman also satisfies the Comic Relief archetype indirectly when used as an outlet for Vitti's pent-up frustration and aggression. Visibly dismayed over Dr. Shulman's "accusation" that he has been having panic attacks (perhaps which Vitti interprets as a slight to his masculinity), one of Vitti's stooges closes the curtain in the examination room while another keeps watch outside to allow Vitti both the privacy and space to "express himself" to Dr. Shulman. The scene was comedic in that it encapsulated the extremely stressed and insecure nature of Vitti's personality. Dr. Shulman appears at roughly the 14:21 mark and is last seen onscreen at roughly the 14:56 mark. The scene ends outside the examination room with a view of the curtain drawn, allowing viewers to see the rustling of medical equipment amid crashing sound effects.

The Utopic Reversal archetype is perhaps the most difficult to detect since it is the most deceptive in its function and appearance. Much like the Angel figure, the *individual* character may not appear to have any overtly negative characteristics. It is only when viewed from a macro-perspective that moviegoers can recognize the limitations of this character. The lasting effect of the Utopic Reversal archetype is similar to that of the Background Figure. These two archetypes have visual effects on viewers, but the characters themselves are very different (i.e., Utopic Reversals have "power" while Background Figures are frequently just "there"). Both types of minority characters are designed to give the viewer the impression that diversity and power are spread evenly amongst the movie's characters, but the authority of these characters is frequently thwarted, undermined or used for comedic effect.

The Utopic Reversal archetype's impact is minimized by limited screen time and dialogue. This character also has limited displays of authority, especially in relation to the character's job title or seemingly high social position. This character's ineffectiveness is often heightened when lower-ranking White characters trump or usurp this character's authority as a matter of due course in fulfilling their objective during the movie (e.g., a White detective defying his Black police chief to solve the case, the White partner does all the "heavy-lifting" or strategizing or most significant work in an otherwise equal Black/White buddy-cop pairing).

I knew there was a great 40 million fans out there who love Spiderman the character and I didn't want to get in the way of them. . . . I had a responsibility to the kids of America who are going to this movie who are going to look up to the character that was up there and say, 'That's my hero.'

Spider-Man Director Sam Raimi[1]

CHAPTER 10:
WHITE BALANCING ACT

In *Chapters 4* through *Chapter 9*, we explored the six common minority archetypes in mainstream movies and how their continued use helps reaffirm and reinforce a larger message of marginalization. However, many discussions about race in mainstream movies ironically ignore White characters, *the most prevalent characters in mainstream movies!* While the archetypes clearly characterize the patterns of minority *marginalization* reinforced by archetypes in the movies, we wish to explore White *glamorization* and how consistently positive White images help paint an overarching picture of power, authority and respect. It is against this backdrop that we analyze White character patterns and themes.

AS GOOD AS IT GETS

White actors, more so than any other racial group, have the distinct privilege of occupying the widest range of roles in Hollywood. White characters have fulfilled roles that embody many or all of the characteristics displayed by minority archetypes. Although minority actors by no means maintain a monopoly over unflattering imagery, their typically limited onscreen presence is defined by one or more of the minority archetypes discussed in *Chapters 4* through *Chapter 9*. The principal difference between archetypal roles for White and minority actors is that marginal roles for White characters do not encompass the full scope and depth of the existing range of White characters. Further, due to the overwhelmingly high rate of frequency with which White characters appear in mainstream movies, negative roles with limited screen time and dialogue do not define the entire spectrum of White characters that appear in a particular movie. Recall the racial capital analogy used in *Chapter 3: The Color Scene* demonstrating the relative purchasing power of $100 versus $10 at a restaurant (pg. 60). This example also illustrates how the proliferation of White imagery means that Whites can "afford" or "withstand the cost" of negative imagery, much easier than a minority group with limited exposure and influence on the mainstream movie screen, thereby blunting any lasting effect from a negative White character. If anything, the large amount of racial capital enjoyed by Whites, coupled with the wide variety of roles depicted by Whites, allow for more individualized associations of negativity (e.g., the lecherous Hannibal Lecter in *The Silence of the Lambs*), rather than blanket generalizations of negativity associated with a larger group (e.g., the menacing Latino gangsters in *Training Day*).

Thus, White roles that could satisfy minority archetype definitions are balanced by the wider range of neutral and positively portrayed White characters. The muted presence of negative imagery is a luxury enjoyed by Whites that other racial groups do not have due to the larger amount of racial capital that they control throughout the movie industry.

WHITE BALANCE

White balance is a technical term in the filmmaking process wherein all colors are properly adjusted on a camera. The camera operator first fixes upon a white object. With the color white serving as a starting point of reference, the camera then calculates the difference between the current color setting of that object and the correct color setting of a white object. Only after establishing a white color paradigm can the camera shift all remaining colors in the spectrum by that difference.

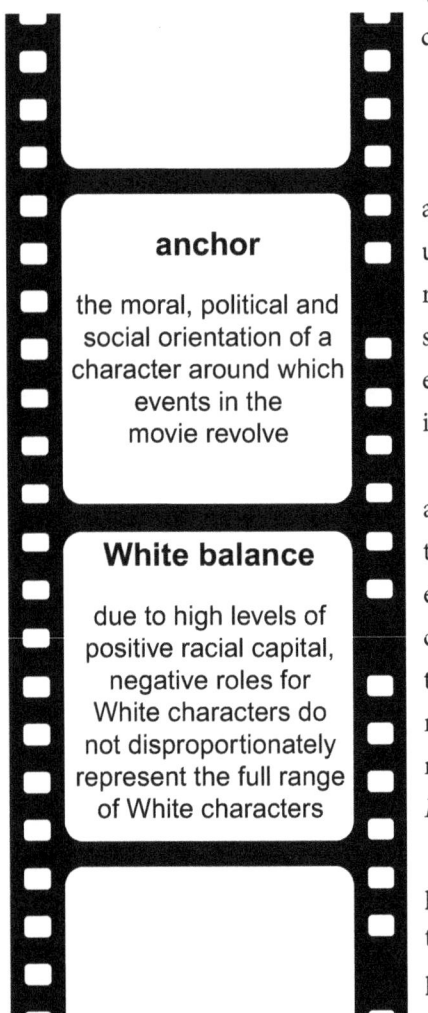

anchor

the moral, political and social orientation of a character around which events in the movie revolve

White balance

due to high levels of positive racial capital, negative roles for White characters do not disproportionately represent the full range of White characters

Similarly, due to the collective amount of positive racial capital amassed by Whites in Hollywood over the years, White characters constitute the "default" race for the vast majority of mainstream movies and serve as emotional **anchors** by which all other characters revolve. By and large, White characters are universally utilized — so much so that when Whites *are not* the focus of a mainstream movie, it is usually specifically noted. For example, movies like **Barbershop** and **Soul Food** are commonly referred to as *Black* movies, or actresses such as Salma Hayek and Eva Mendes are designated as *Latina* actresses, and so on and so forth.[2]

Even though writers of all races may be writing movies with minority protagonists in mind, the race of the protagonists can always be changed by the studio system. Additionally, if a writer truly wants to have minorities as protagonists, then the writer must "racially code" their script or specifically state that the characters are not White – otherwise, presumably the characters are White. This default assumption further "limits" minority characters, for if a character's race is explicitly mentioned, the assumption is that their race has some bearing on their character (e.g., Running Japanese Tourist).

The premium of proportion theory explains why the HARM theory and the minority archetypes magnify the negative effects of marginalized minority images, but this theory is not the only determinant factor at play. Minority roles often pale in scope, depth and complexity in comparison to common White characters. With so many mainstream movies prominently featuring White actors in a wide variety of roles – to say the least of the preponderance of leading roles – movie audiences have been conditioned to believe that White characters are almost exclusively the ones who are able to experience the subtleties of love, the thrills of fantasy, the challenging responsibilities of power and the euphoric satisfaction of saving the world.

This **White balance** process in Hollywood is effectuated by the large number of people working individually without malice that do not necessarily awaken each day with an intent to exclude minorities from Hollywood. This goes far beyond the writers who compose "raceless" scripts; there are also producers, casting agents, directors and studios along the way that exert influence and control over which actors are cast, what they will look like and what they will say. When the efforts of these separately placed individuals are aggregated across the board, the end result is a grainy picture of diversity.

However, this is not to say that Hollywood has never produced movies with minority characters as strong protagonists in "non-White" movies. Undoubtedly, there are themes of love present in Tyler Perry's ***Madea's Family Reunion***, Martin Lawrence saves the day in ***Big Momma's House 2*** and Jamie Foxx is a modern-day swashbuckling hero in ***Miami Vice***. Nonetheless, the universality of "Whiteness" manifests itself with the inability of mainstream filmmakers and studio executives – the majority of whom are White – to envision minority characters and actors squarely outside the reaches of the HARM theory and the minority archetypes. The issue thus becomes whether or not minority characters can experience the same breadth of emotions and opportunities as their White counterparts without being *marginalized* or *compromised*.

THE ARC OF THE CHARACTER

The message conveyed by mainstream movies is that White characters will most likely be able to solve their problems, accomplish their objectives, achieve their goals, or achieve whatever it is they deem important, in spite of the attendant conflict. It is therefore very rare that a mainstream movie will end on a discordant note for a White protagonist, as the mainstream

BUT IT'S JUST A MOVIE, RIGHT?
After reading the initial script for ***The Devil's Own***, Brad Pitt protested, telling the studio the screenplay made him "uneasy" because it was loaded with stereotypes, "full of leprechaun jokes and green beer." The dialogue, he argued, unfairly painted his character as a stereotypical Irish "bad" guy. Pitt explained, "I had this responsibility to represent somewhat these people whose lives have been shattered. It would have been an injustice for Hollywood to produce it." The studio ultimately assented to Pitt's request to modify the script.[10a]

Notice how much "capital" Pitt had to influence change. How many instances do you think occur where minority actors receive unflattering scripts but have them modified due to their "uneasiness" with the role?

Contrast the studio's willingness to accommodate Pitt with that of Angela Bassett's criticism of the leading female role in ***Monster's Ball*** (see pg. 124). In this instance, Bassett declined the role in protest, but rather than modify the role for Bassett, the studio simply replaced her with Halle Berry.

protagonist most always ends up with some sort of positive catharsis, or at least with some redeeming lesson that provides hope for the future.

Conversely, with the vast majority of minority characters limited to the more narrow range of minority archetypes, many minority character are deprived of character arcs, which ultimately leads the audience to care less about these characters. Even if audience members want to care about these characters, there often is not enough emotional context for the audience to do so, since these characters lack many of the characteristics that lead viewers to care about the White characters (e.g., emotionally wrenching familial ties, supernatural abilities to "change the world," etc.).

Case in point, consider **Dodgeball: A True Underdog Story**, starring Vince Vaughn, Christine Taylor and Ben Stiller. Despite the fact that the movie revolves around the three lead characters, there are other significant characters introduced to the audience, namely the makeshift members of the Average Joe's dodgeball team that help Peter La Fleur (Vaughn) prevent the loss of his humble and homely workout gym. In addition to La Fleur and Kate Veatch (Taylor), the remaining members of the victorious dodgeball team are Justin (Justin Long), Gordon (Stephen Root), Owen (Joel Moore), Steve the Pirate (Alan Tudyk) and Dwight (Chris Williams). Notice the character arcs *for the White supporting characters* – all of the above characters listed are White with the exception of Chris Williams who is Black:

- **Justin** – takes on a *leadership role* in rallying the misfit troops to take action to save La Fleur's gym from being bought out by the scheming White Goodman (Ben Stiller) at the movie's beginning; he has a developed romance story (complete with flashback) with Amber (Julie Gonzalo); he *saves the day* by becoming a stellar last-minute replacement for Amber's cheerleading championships taking place at roughly the same time as his dodgeball tournament final; and being unable to catch thrown balls all movie long, he catches a ball at a *pivotal* moment, helping his team salvage a victory in their ultimate quest for the championship
- **Gordon** – has the original brainstorm from his *Obscure Sports Quarterly* magazine to enter into a dodgeball tournament in Las Vegas to win the $50,000 necessary to save La Fleur's gym; he has a heroic moment and saves the team during the semifinals – he gets angry at his "mail order wife" (incidentally,

she is a minority female, Suzy Nakamura) who he spies cavorting with a very friendly fan in the stands and channels that anger against his opponents – even though he was grossly outnumbered before mounting an improbable comeback; lastly, his deft knowledge of the rule book allows for the team to successfully appeal their premature withdrawal from the final (thanks to Chuck Norris)

- **Owen** – although a relatively quiet character, Owen nonetheless cultivates a romance with the opposition's feared female opponent Fran (Missi Pyle) – it is developed to the point where it "distracts" him during the final, leading to his elimination
- **Steve the Pirate** – Steve's character, despite being limited to a few enjoyable lines, undergoes an emotional journey whereby his identity as a "pirate" is questioned; upon the movie's conclusion, this emotional question is answered when he is allowed to "be himself" and be the lovable pirate that his friends know him to be

Contrast these White character arcs with the character arc for Dwight, a Black male with essentially no emotional development and is the lone minority member of the dodgeball team. Dwight has several lines peppered throughout the movie, but he does not have any significant dialogue that reveals any other layer of his personality other than the fact that he is a team player who is willing to help out his team. At the movie's conclusion, he is seen "celebrating" the team's championship victory with two Black female cheerleaders who simultaneously plant peck kisses on each of his cheeks. The cheerleaders were not introduced prior to this scene, nor are they seen afterwards. In other words, there is no "closure" to his story since there was no character arc in the first place. (*Note*: in reference to the trend of the disparaging depictions of Black emasculation noted in *Chapter 8: Physical Wonder*, compare Dwight's milquetoast role with that of the hyper-aggressive *consigliere* of White Goodman, Me'Shell Jones played by Jamal E. Duff).

In the case of **Dodgeball**, even with the bit supporting characters, a pecking order is discernible based upon the amount of emotional investment the audience is asked to make. All of the White characters received enough screen time and dialogue development to the point where their characters changed or progressed over time. With respect to Dwight, Me'Shell Jones, and Gordon's Wife, these characters remain static as two-dimensional figures.

LIGHTS! CAMERA! INTERACTION! Try this at home with the next movie you see. To test out the strength of a character's character arc, ask yourself if at the end of the movie, you are asking yourself, "What happened to so and so?" If so, then the character was probably developed in some way to make you curious about their status at the movie's conclusion. If you do not ask yourself that question, then it may speak to the minimal impact of that character, whereby their absence from the movie's resolution does not interfere with your satisfaction over all principal conflicts having been solved.

Just as Hollywood employs formulaic character arc patterns, mainstream audiences develop formulaic expectations over time. Not only are audiences "conditioned" to expect certain conduct from White characters, audiences are also conditioned *not* to expect as much from minority characters!

MAJORITY RULES

Even with increasing diversity in mainstream movies, minority characters still appear relatively infrequently – especially in leading roles. Therefore, it is easier to identify minority characters and analyze their roles according to the limited spectrum of minority archetypes. With respect to identifying White character patterns within mainstream Hollywood, this proves a more difficult task since the immense amount of racial capital enjoyed by Whites translates into a much more extensive and complex character range. Nevertheless, this is a necessary task, since the minority archetypes are only part of a larger dynamic that better explains the status and portrayal of minorities in the Hollywood universe. A full analysis of minority characters in Hollywood must study the inter-connectedness between Hollywood, minorities *and Whites*, and not just focus on the relationship between Hollywood and minorities. This would be the metaphorical equivalent to learning the phases of the moon by studying only the sun and the moon, as opposed to studying the shared relationship between the sun, moon and planet Earth (Fig. 1).

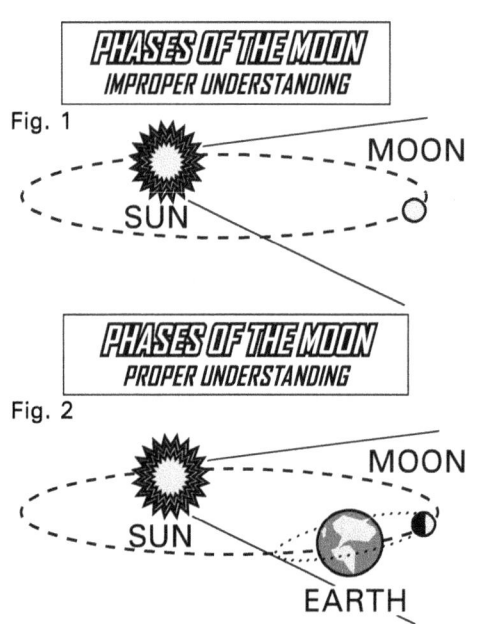

If within our Hollywood "universe," the heat and intensity of the mainstream spotlight represent the sun, planet Earth represents the large body of "universal" White characters and the moon represents the smaller body of minority characters that revolve around these White characters. The phases of the moon represent the formulaic (or cyclical) pattern of minority archetypes. To understand why a half moon appears in the sky roughly every thirty days, one must appreciate that the Earth prevents sunlight from reaching the moon as both the moon and Earth rotate around the sun (Fig. 2). Omitting the Earth from our study of the moon's phases results in only a partial explanation for the moon's "appearance and behavior." Similarly, studying minorities in Hollywood without studying their relationship to the larger body of White characters would test the bounds of lunacy.

The overwhelming presence of Whites within mainstream movies eliminates the need to attempt to list every type of White character, since they have the luxury of playing an unparalleled array of roles. Nonetheless, there are some broader threads by which White characters can be grouped and classified. We have outlined six overarching character patterns, or **prototypes**, that classify the majority of central White characters in mainstream movies:

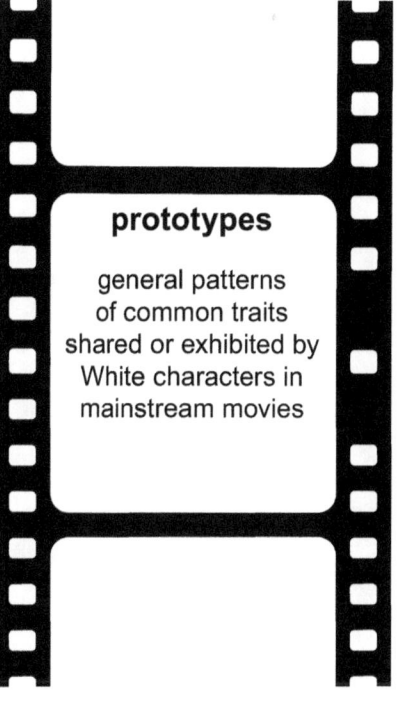

prototypes

general patterns of common traits shared or exhibited by White characters in mainstream movies

WHITE PROTOYPES

1. THE AFFLUENT
2. THE FAMILY-TIED
3. THE HERO
4. THE INTELLECTUAL
5. THE MANIPULATOR
6. THE ROMANTIC

These prototypes prioritize Whites as central characters whereby the thoughts, feelings, sentiments and actions of these White characters become a primary concern for the viewing audience. Moreover, these characters typically serve as emotional anchors for the movies in which they appear, often harnessing and marshaling their stated attributes in order to achieve some measure of cathartic growth or achieve resolution for their individual character arc – even in movies with predominately minority casts! The archetypes restrict the range of expression for minority characters, while the White prototypes serve as open channels that facilitate and inspire a broad range of feeling and emotion.

We define these prototypes by outlining specific character traits, but this list also encompasses prototypical themes that can dominate a movie's storyline. These six prototypes represent the consistent patterns and themes that help depict White characters as vitally important, and at least one prototype can be found in just about every mainstream movie. There is a virtual absence of minority characters exhibiting the same characteristics as these White prototypes, especially in mainstream movies that do not feature "minority worlds." Thus, in studying the extent and range of White prototypes, it is absolutely vital to bear in mind how the premium of proportion further elevates the status of White characters while further relegating minority characters to the margins. Let us now outline each prototype in detail.

PROTOTYPICAL BEHAVIOR
PROTOTYPE #1: THE AFFLUENT

The *Affluent* prototype is present where the plot or a character arc is facilitated by affluence or access to significant capital. This prototype covers a broad span that stretches from the overt "sacrifice" and scheming that White characters willingly engage in with the hoped-for reward of a financial prize (e.g., **Bringing Down the House**) to the unstated and unquestioned source of fantastical opulence (e.g., **Mr. Deeds**). If anything, the Affluent prototype lends credence to the theory that it is easier to create storylines that are lubricated by the presence of capital, since insufficient funds cannot finance high-speed boat chases, swanky dinner parties and exotic poolside arguments. Most representations of prototypical Affluence are depicted through two nuanced means: *Assumed Affluent* and *Financing Fantasy*.

a) Assumed Affluent

This character, while seldom seen working, mentioning or speaking about money, nonetheless has plenty of it at her disposal. While lavish lifestyles of the über-rich are occasionally put on display in mainstream movies, the Assumed Affluent often appears in more subtle ways, such as the deceptively "average" middle class White American. In actuality, their socioeconomic status may be more appropriately classified as upper-middle or upper class. When mainstream movies showcase a "typical" American family, the value of the home, furnishings and possessions displayed onscreen (not to mention their activities) can easily exceed the budget of a real middle class family, yet this lifestyle is projected as standard fare for the average American mainstream family. For instance, the "normal" house used as Greg Heffley's residence in the **Diary of a Wimpy Kid** series is in Canada with an estimated value of over $1 million dollars (3200 sq. ft.).[3]

While status symbols for the extremely poor and extremely rich may be more readily identified, average middle class status symbols, if not for aesthetic purposes alone, generally revolve around White, upper-middle class imagery. Movie studios are well aware of this fact. Practically speaking, if a movie is filmed in the city of Los Angeles, where real estate is always at a premium, an "average" home worth $200,000 elsewhere may not be as large or as aesthetically pleasing for on-location filming the way an "average" $650,000 home might be. Thus, when the assumed affluent are portrayed as "normal" or "average," such imagery "incorrectly" presents a class of people that is simply not representative of average Americans, even though it is depicted as such.

In instances where White characters *are not* affluent, there is often an explanation or exploration of the attendant circumstantial factors, in contrast to minority characters that frequently appear static in their more limited financial condition (this dynamic is akin to minority Menace to Society characters that appear in or around prison culture without much explanation – see "The Phantom Menace" in *Chapter 7: The Menace to Society*). This character often transcends this "temporary" non-affluent state by reaping some financial reward by movie's end, or acquires some skill that elevates this character's status (e.g., **Spider-Man**, **Good Will Hunting**, **Invincible**, **Dodgeball**, **Night at the Museum**).

This is not to say that upper-middle class and other wealthy White characters do not qualify under the heading, Assumed Affluent. While such characters may not be presented as "typical" Americans, their affluence is often still "assumed" and taken for granted without any real need for elaborate explanation. Even when these characters do explicitly mention money, it is often wielded without much concern (e.g., Bruce Wayne in **Batman Returns**) or wantonly used to facilitate plot developments (e.g., the one million dollar deal to sleep with another man's wife in **Indecent Proposal**).

Assuredly, several depictions of minority affluence exist – **The Last Samurai, Hitch,** and **Diary of a Mad Black Woman** are but a few examples of this phenomena. Yet, overall, most minority characters depicted or associated with affluence in mainstream movies are compromised to some extent. For instance, recall Samuel (Marc Anthony) from **Man on Fire**, or consider Nashawn Wade (Kevin Hart) in **Soul Plane**. As an example of how layered a singular movie can be with respect to highlighting differences between both minority archetypes and White prototypes, we return to **Man on Fire** for another telling example. Samuel's apparent opulence condition in **Man on Fire** is a sham, for he is heavily indebted to the point where he agrees to a plan to covertly kidnap his own daughter and steal the ransom money fronted by his insurance for his own personal use. In **Soul Plane,** Nashawn Wade (the airline's founder), receives his seed money from a farcically generous $100 million dollar settlement *awarded to him* after a humiliating experience suffered on a "regular" commercial flight. In both cases, the affluence of these minority characters is called into question. Samuel's affluence – or rather his attempt to maintain such a veneer – turns out to be fraudulent, and while Nashawn Wade's affluence may not be *legally* fraudulent, the "use" of his affluence is regarded as such due to the absurdity of his expenditures.

BUT IT'S JUST A MOVIE, RIGHT? Producers for the hit summer blockbuster *Wedding Crashers* had their honeymoon interrupted when United States Congressman John Salazar (D-Colo) issued complaints about the movie's official website offering printable Purple Heart medals as a part of the online "Crasher Kit." In the movie, lead actors Vince Vaughn and Owen Wilson use the military medals as a gimmick to help them bed down unsuspecting maidens and obtain free drinks.

Following the complaint, New Line Cinema promptly removed the printable Purple Hearts from the website with spokesman Richard Socarides stating: "We understand the sensitivity regarding the medals and did not intend to make light of their significance in any way."[10b]

If anything, consistent imagery of minority characters *disassociated* with affluence have become part of standard Hollywood convention. Minority characters are frequently depicted as isolated and desolate individuals in mainstream movies, thereby increasing their dependence and interaction upon a lone White protagonist (e.g., **Monster's Ball, Nothing to Lose, Take the Lead, Dangerous Minds, A Time to Kill,** and **Hard Ball**). Further, many minority characters have had objects of affluence in their possession, only to have such property damaged, taken away, or unfulfilled due to the character's death. Consider how Detective Mike Lowrey's (Will Smith) Ferrari is shot up in a car chase scene in **Bad Boys II** and the cost of the repair becomes the running gag. At the end of the movie, Detective Marcus Burnett's (Martin Lawrence) bayside pool at his "middle class" estate gives way, and he and Lowrey end up in the bay. Also consider how Roger Murtaugh's (Danny Glover) boat *and* home are destroyed in **Lethal Weapon 4**. His home is also damaged in **Lethal Weapon 2**, wherein a bomb is rigged to explode his toilet while he is using it. Lastly, characters like Samuel (Marc Anthony) in **Man on Fire**, Joe Morton (Dr. Miles Bennett Dyson) in **Terminator 2: Judgment Day**, Eddie Sakamura (Cary-Hiroyuki Tagawa) in **Rising Sun**, and Hector Juan Carlos 'Johnny' Tapia (Jordi Mollà) in **Bad Boys II** are all affluent, but they all end up dead by movie's end.

b) Financing Fantasy

Movie studios will often go to great lengths to create as "real" a world of fantasy as possible for its audience. Whenever mainstream movies utilize "official locations" (such as the United Nations building in *The Interpreter*), film in exotic and remote locations (*Cast Away*), employ accurate models of the oval office (*Air Force One*; *Independence Day*), or make full use of official law enforcement and military equipment (*Saving Private Ryan*; *Die Hard: With a Vengeance*), the message communicated is that exclusive access, money and privilege were marshaled to provide the audience with the most authentic fantasy possible. In the same vein, when "ordinary" characters are depicted using specialized "high-tech" equipment, the demonstrated mastery and use of such expensive tools and instruments quietly communicates not only a knowledge of their existence, but a tangible connection to affluence in obtaining access to the instruments in the first place.

The presence of the Affluent prototype *onscreen* highlights the limitations of the **Minority Cycle of Movie-Making** *offscreen*. When a movie studio itself is financially endowed, it can afford to spend millions of dollars on the creation and destruction of movie sets, costly special effects and elaborate props — all for footage that may appear onscreen for only a few seconds. For instance, there is a particularly long chase scene in **Terminator 3: Rise of the Machines** where the new T-X Terminator (Kristanna Loken) has overtaken a crane in her chase of the truck commandeered by the original T-800 Terminator (Arnold Schwarzenegger). The crane's arm is extended during the chase and rips right into several buildings and utility poles as a consequence. In addition to the subtle message that the destruction of such property is validated by the "importance" of the goals and objectives of the characters, the fantasy is heightened by the fact that most audience members will never experience the "thrill" of such grand scale property destruction in their own lives.

Such large-scale fantasies are rarely seen in movies with minority-driven casts or minority-produced budgets. For example, consider this sample list of "Black movies" that revolve around comedic themes and personal relationships:

- The Best Man
- The Wood
- Kingdom Come
- Brown Sugar
- Love & Basketball
- Boyz n the Hood
- Waiting to Exhale
- The Brothers
- The Preacher's Wife
- How Stella Got Her Groove Back
- Love Jones
- Two Can Play That Game

These movies rarely contain multimillion dollar explosions, extended chase scenes, fluid integration of computer generated images, or other fantastical special effects. Case in point, **Biker Boyz**, which performed rather poorly at the box office in 2003, was headlined as a smorgasbord of well-known minority talent and featured a storyline revolving around biker gangs, a genre that has typically featured White protagonists. What is significant about this project is that not only did the storyline appear to necessitate a higher budget for equipment and stunts (in contrast to the relationship-based movies listed previously), but the director, Reggie Rock Bythewood, publicly complained about how the movie studio pressured him to replace the minorities with White actors for the leading roles by offering to double his budget.[4] With the movie studio committing to greenlight the movie – but at a significantly reduced cost – one could easily argue that the "imagination window" of the viewing audience was adversely affected since the smaller budget restricted the director's ability to employ things like special effects, special stunts and special camera tricks. The ability to finance fantasy is just another factor to consider when analyzing limitations on minority participation within

WHAT DO YOU THINK?

Perhaps the principle of white male prison plasticity (p. 117) has applicability here. For it appears that not all of our protagonists have at their disposal, the privilege of property destruction to protect them.

In the 2008 "superhero" film *Hancock* (starring Black male actor Will Smith), Smith's character Hancock was viewed by the public as a destructive menace and court subpoenas were issued to hold Hancock accountable. The byproduct was for Hancock to "turn himself in" and rehabilitate his public image by going to jail, courtesy of the idea of Hancock's friend Ray (Jason Bateman).

How many White protagonists do you recall having to "pay" for any property destruction incurred while on their hero's journey?

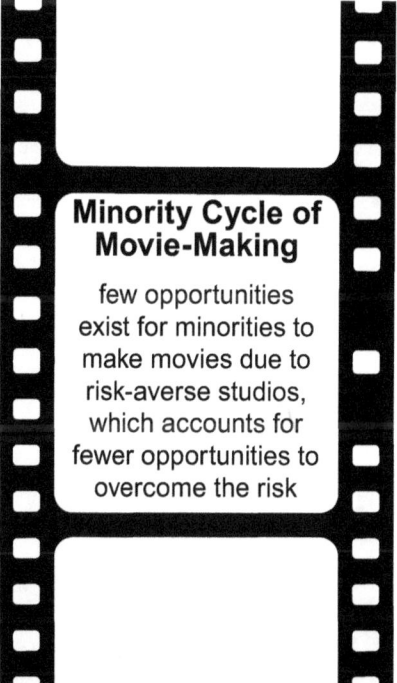

Minority Cycle of Movie-Making

few opportunities exist for minorities to make movies due to risk-averse studios, which accounts for fewer opportunities to overcome the risk

mainstream movies since, over time, the cumulative message from such symbols of affluence is that White characters are afforded facile access to unchartered worlds of financed fantasy.

> **BUT IT'S JUST A MOVIE, RIGHT?**
> After seeing a decline in students embarking upon careers in science and engineering, the American Film Institute secured at least $25,000 in Pentagon research grants to train scientists on how to write movie screenplays. In the *New York Times* feature, "Pentagon's New Goal: Put Science Into Scripts," the article ponders: "And what better way to get a lot of young people interested in science than by producing movies and television shows that depict scientists in flattering ways?"[10c]

Five examples where Whites are presented as Affluent characters without much explanation as to how their material wealth was accrued include:

1) Wedding Crashers (2005)

» actor/character: Christopher Walken as United States Treasury Secretary William Cleary
» analysis: Cleary is clearly an excellent choice to keep watch of the nation's piggybank, considering that he himself is no financial slouch. For instance, after hosting a rather large and lavish wedding reception at Maryland's Eastern Shore, Cleary's family and his newfound guests, John Beckwith (Owen Wilson) and Jeremy Gray (Vince Vaughn), jettison off in Cleary's schooner yacht to his stately Annapolis mansion.

2) Billy Madison (1995)

» actor/character: Adam Sandler as Billy Madison
» analysis: Madison's family is more than well-off. In fact, the entire premise of the movie revolves around Madison having "done nothing" with his life in light of his – or rather, his father's – ample wealth. Madison attempts to meet his father's challenge by successfully completing his elementary and secondary education before becoming eligible for his inheritance.

3) Jurassic Park (1993)

- » **actor/character:** Richard Attenborough as John Hammond
- » **analysis:** The financial health of billionaire entrepreneur John Hammond is unquestioned since he is responsible for the creation and installation of the famously experimental theme park that goes awry.

4) Hitch (2005)

- » **actor/character:** Amber Valletta as Allegra Cole
- » **analysis:** Cole is the undisputed heiress of a large amount of money that Albert (Kevin James) is originally hired to help her manage. The movie's concluding wedding reception scenes at a stately mansion only reinforce the Assumed Affluent theme.

5) Casino Royale (2006)

- » **actor/character:** Daniel Craig as James Bond
- » **analysis:** James Bond is not just an international spy, but a *first-class* international spy. From the cars, to the suits, to the accessories (diamonds are forever, you know), to the first-class accommodations, Bond demonstrates that preserving peace in the world is not enough. Under the philosophy that "you only live twice," Bond's high-priced tastes and golden eye for exquisite living allow him to maximize the living daylights out of whatever situation he spies upon.

PROTOTYPE #2: THE FAMILY-TIED

White characters serve as the universal default for most mainstream roles, and the White family unit most often serves as the emotional anchor that grounds the movie. The *Family-Tied* prototype stresses the strength and value of relationships between White family members. This prototype maintains the eventual reunification or continued preservation of the core family unit as a consistent goal, despite the onset of various conflicts and tensions endured during the course of the movie.

It is striking to observe how many mainstream movies depict White characters as belonging to a larger familial group. Central White characters are rarely depicted without any familial, romantic or collegial interests. This

---

> **WHAT DO YOU THINK?** In ***The Hunger Games*** (2012), did you see evidence of the Affluent prototype?
>
> You might be thinking: "No! Katniss (Jennifer Lawrence) and her family start off the movie really poor and destitute, so no!"
>
> While this may be true, it is rare within a mainstream movie that movie producers keep our White protagonists below the poverty line. For the purposes of the movie, once she volunteers to be the tribute, she is whisked away on a luxury train, arrives in town where she is feted, dressed and "polished" while training for the games.
>
> Plus, after "winning" the games (uh, **spoiler alert** — we figured you knew they made two additional sequels), Katniss and her family were "getting by" quite nicely while living in the Victors' Village.
>
> Katniss did not start in poverty and remain there as a constant the way the Black female titular character Claireece Precious Jones (Gabourey Sidibe) in the 2009 Academy Award winning ***Precious*** did.
>
> **NOTE:** While the movies ***Precious*** and ***Hunger Games*** are from two different genres and appear vastly different on the surface, we nonetheless compare the two since they both were released within three years and both involve independent, central female protagonists who were sixteen-years old (in the movie) dealing with issues concerning coming-of-age and world view.

is a stark contrast to minority characters, who frequently appear in "isolation" in movies with predominately White casts.

The typical Family-Tied prototype is set up by a false conflict, meaning that there is tension present between prominent White characters that is not entirely "true" in its ultimate threat since it somehow becomes resolved by the movie's conclusion. A common scenario involves the self-absorbed White male professional who begins the movie on frosty terms with his estranged wife, but when faced with the challenge of persevering through some larger, overarching conflict, he realizes how much he truly loves her (e.g., **Die Hard, Shall We Dance?, True Lies**).

Another common scenario demonstrates the spiritual fortitude of White characters who band together and resist dissolution of their personal bonds when the children, avowed love interest, or entire family, are placed in some sort of peril (e.g., **Jurassic Park III, The Incredibles, Air Force One**). In all instances, the movie emphasizes resolution of individual character arcs that place White characters on stronger emotional footing by the movie's conclusion.

Case in point, let us revisit **Soul Plane** (profiled in *Chapter 6: Comic Relief*). Even though the movie was marketed widely as a "Black movie" and contains a predominately Black cast, a significant part of the story revolves around a White family (the only family unit in the movie) and the resolution of their character arcs. As a joke, the traveling White family members share a surname, the Hunkees, that is a double entendre reference to the racial slur. Although he is traveling with his girlfriend Barbara (Missi Pyle), Elvis Hunkee (Tom Arnold) and his two children, Heather and Billy (Arielle Kebbel and Ryan Pinkston), have character arcs that make the family members a more cohesive unit by the movie's end.

The presence of these White character arcs in a "Black movie" reinforce the notion that White characters and their interactions are always important. Further, in accordance with the **identification process**, developed White characters provide a hook for White audience members to stay engaged in the storyline. Lastly, although the Black lead protagonist, Nashawn Wade (Kevin Hart), has a romance storyline that develops, there ironically is no prominently visible *minority family unit* depicted utilizing the services of NWA Airlines – not even in the background.

Compare the involvement of the Hunkees in **Soul Plane** to movies like **Terminator 2: Judgment Day** and **Kill Bill: Vol. 1**, where minority (Black) characters have family ties in movies that are otherwise dominated

LIGHTS! CAMERA! INTERACTION! Watch *Lethal Weapon 4* to see whether you can spot the Family-Tied prototype at work. More specifically, look where two important characters, one White and one Black, are pregnant and deliver babies during the course of the movie.

The White women is Lorna Cole (Rene Russo), the longtime girlfriend of protagonist Marlon Riggs (Mel Gibson). The Black woman is Rianne Murtaugh Butters (Traci Wolfe), the daughter of protagonist Roger Murtaugh (Danny Glover). The Black baby's father is Detective Lee Butters (Chris Rock).

Compare and contrast the following: 1) the birthing processes, 2) the amount of screen time each baby receives and 3) the amount of attention movie characters give each baby.

What are the differences? What is the rationale for such decisions?

by White characters. Notice that their family bonds are not developed or actively maintained onscreen. In **Terminator 2**, Dr. Miles Bennett Dyson (Black actor Joe Morton), at a critical point in the movie, consciously eschews an opportunity for escape and sacrifices himself by self-inflicted detonation, without any familial resolution. Although Dr. Dyson's family is seen onscreen, Dr. Dyson's actions ironically help preserve the White family unit of Sarah and John Connor (Linda Hamilton and Edward Furlong). In **Kill Bill: Vol. 1**, Vernita Green is gruesomely killed at the very beginning of the movie as her daughter looks on, without any further resolution of the resulting effects.

Compare this dynamic to the number of superhero movies containing storylines that feature a White character seeking to balance the scales of justice in honor of a fallen family member (e.g., **Spider-Man, Batman Returns, The Punisher**, etc.). These White superheroes are able to internalize a painful familial experience and transform it into a motivational tool for bettering the lives of others. In the process, not only do they change their external selves through the donning of a costume, but they also transform their internal selves for the better.

Successful animated features such as **How to Train Your Dragon 2,** or **Finding Dory,** employ the White Family-Tied prototype freely where the whole movie revolves around a lone White-voiced protagonist who has everyone else concerned about the protagonist connecting with *their* family (*Note:* in the prequel **Finding Nemo**, even though they are represented as "neutral" fish or animals onscreen, the lead characters are all voiced by White actors). As with non-animated examples, the drive to maintain a White family core, despite the attendant odds, serves as a central, underlying theme that drives much of the movie's plot. In light of this fact, it is all the more salient to see when the traditional Family-Tied pattern is abandoned in mainstream animated movies featuring minority characters or minority-voiced characters.

Two notable examples of non-traditional family structures can be found in **Lilo & Stitch** and **Brother Bear**. In **Lilo & Stitch**, Lilo (voiced by Daveigh Chase) is a young, female Hawaiian protagonist, who is an orphan living with her older sister in a borderline-dysfunctional household. In **Brother Bear**, Koda (voiced by Black actor Jeremy Suarez) becomes an orphan by Kenai's (voiced by White actor Joaquin Phoenix) own doing – the movie begins with Kenai as a human hunter who kills the bear that is Koda's mother. These non-traditional minority families stand in stark contrast to the stable, middle-class, White family of four in the animated feature **The Incredibles**, and they stand out even further given the small number of minority or minority-voiced protagonists in mainstream animated features.

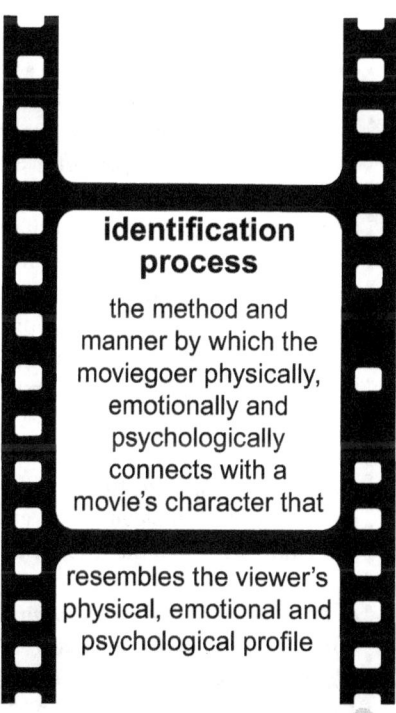

identification process

the method and manner by which the moviegoer physically, emotionally and psychologically connects with a movie's character that

resembles the viewer's physical, emotional and psychological profile

Five examples of mainstream movies that feature the White Family-Tied prototypes include:

1) Saving Private Ryan (1998)

» actor/character: Matt Damon as Private James Francis Ryan
» analysis: The title, **Saving Private Ryan**, encapsulates the overarching mission of Captain John H. Miller (Tom Hanks); namely to brave the dangers of foreign armed conflict, and risk his own life – and the lives of the men in his unit – so that he can successfully track down Private Ryan and safely return him to his expectant family back in the United States.

2) Bringing Down the House (2003)

» actor/character: Steve Martin as Peter Sanderson; Jean Smart as Kate Sanderson; Kimberly J. Brown as Sarah Sanderson; Angus T. Jones as Georgey Sanderson
» analysis: Despite initial indicators that Sanderson is separating from his wife, the proverbial White family of four is successfully reunited at the movie's conclusion.
» bonus: Notice how Queen Latifah as Charlene Morton fulfills the Angel Figure archetype by helping Sanderson maintain his family order. She defends his daughter's honor, agrees to don a pink "maid" outfit and serve the family to impress an elderly billionaire client, and exhorts Sanderson to "practice" aggressive sexual advances on her so that he can be a better lover to his estranged wife. In reference to this last point, one scene features Morton pointing at her breasts, commanding Sanderson to "Grab these!" to which he obliges. Later in the scene, after Morton instructs Sanderson that a woman wants a man "who knows how to ride her when she bucks," they

> **WHAT DO YOU THINK?**
> **Bringing Down the House** features a scene where in order to help lawyer Peter Sanderson (Steve Martin) land a billionaire client and make a good impression upon her, ex-convict Charlene Morton (Queen Latifah) agrees to serve Sanderson's family a dinner meal. Morton endures humiliation for Sanderson by preparing and serving the meal in a pink "maid" outfit (which includes cornbread with a full-toothed smile). Also, during dinner, Sanderson's guest, Mrs. Arness (Joan Plowright), begins singing an old "Negro spiritual" entitled "Mama, Is Massa Gonna Sell Us Tomorrow?"
>
> Did you know that the song by Mrs. Arness was a real slave song? The song was composed to describe the unfortunate uncertainty and familial insecurity that enslaved workers faced while living on plantations in the Old South, as documented by the book Unchained Memories.[10d]
>
> *In light of what the song communicates about the anxiety, apprehension and anguish over enslaved Black family separation, what did the filmmakers wish to communicate in using a real song for comedic value?*

both proceed to the couch where Sanderson straddles Morton and practices his "bucking." The scene concludes when Sanderson and Morton are interrupted by the entrance of his son and his shocked and appalled elderly neighbor, Mrs. Kline (Betty White), who covers Georgey's eyes and exclaims, "Mandingo!"

3) The Day After Tomorrow (2004)

» **actor/character**: Dennis Quaid as Jack Hall; Jake Gyllenhaal as Sam Hall; Sela Ward as Dr. Lucy Hall
» **analysis**: Natural disasters are not strong enough to rupture the bonds of family as Jack Hall battles against unusually severe weather in order to save his son.
» **bonus**: Notice how the White family also fulfills the Intellectual prototype (introduced on pg. 179) Jack Hall is a paleoclimatologist who is summoned to brief the President of the United States, Dr. Lucy Hall is a medical doctor, and Sam Hall is in New York to participate in an academic decathlon. To drive the point home about how "smart" Sam Hall is at the movie's beginning, Sam explains to his father that the reason why he received an "F" on his math final was because he computed all of the answers in his head. Jack Hall responds: "Well that's ridiculous! How can he fail you for being smarter than he is?"
» **note**: Since the movie is a disaster movie affecting the entire planet, several minority faces are *visible* in this movie, but nonetheless retain only peripheral influence. The most prominent minority characters are as follows: Brian Parks (Black actor Arjay Smith) as a "nerdy" teenage supporting character and Sam's academic decathlon teammate; "Statute of Liberty Guard" (Black actor Kwasi Songui), who leads everyone into the freezing cold despite Sam's admonition to heed his father's advice to stay inside of the library; Janet Tokada (Asian actress Tamlyn Tomita), who provides endearing assistance to Jack Hall (Dennis Quaid); Simon (Black actor Adrian Lester) as a fellow Background Figure scientist in the Scottish research facility where the massive storm is first discovered by the prominent (White) English scientist Terry Rapson (Ian Holm); and finally there is Luther (Black actor Glenn Plummer), a homeless man depicted with a yellow plastic shopping bag covering his hair. Luther contributes one-liners such as: "What about the garbage? Always something to eat in the garbage!"

4) War of the Worlds (2005)

» **actor/character:** Tom Cruise as Ray Ferrier; Miranda Otto as Mary Ann; Dakota Fanning as Rachel Ferrier; Justin Chatwin as Robbie Ferrier

» **analysis:** Supernatural disasters are not strong enough to rupture the bonds of family as Ray Ferrier battles against unusually ungracious extra-terrestial visitors to save his family members from harm.

» **key scene:** Aside from a few concluding thoughts from narrator Morgan Freeman, the movie's last scene culminates with the climactic reunion of Rachel and her mother. Although ex-wife Mary Ann and Ray are separated and Mary is pregnant with the child of her new love, the final scene centers on the "original" family unit and its survival through severe calamity. As Mary Ann embraces Rachel, she mouths the words "Thank you" to Ray who embraces his son Robbie in relief.

5) Flightplan (2005)

» **actor/character:** Jodie Foster as Kyle Pratt

» **analysis:** Pratt appears as an unflappable, determined and strong-minded woman who will not let anyone get in the way of her locating her "lost" child; not any flight attendants, not the Air Marshal nor the airline's captain will stand in the way of finding her child.

» **bonus:** Upon the movie's release, three labor unions representing 80,000 flight attendants urged a boycott of the movie since it portrays a flight attendant as a terrorist. The Association of Flight Attendants stated that the movie falsely portrays flight attendants as "rude, unhelpful and uncaring."[5] Should minorities have a similar reaction and urge boycotts whenever they are presented as "rude, unhelpful and uncaring?"

Conversely, while minority families do make appearances in mainstream movies (although less frequently in movies that contain a high ratio of White characters), minority family units are more prevalent in mainstream movies with strong comedic undercurrents. Not only is this comedic minority family strand evident in minority-themed comedies (e.g., *Nutty Professor II: The Klumps*, *Are We There Yet?*, *Johnson Family*

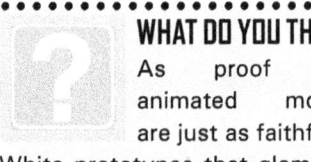

WHAT DO YOU THINK?
As proof that animated movies are just as faithful to White prototypes that glamorize White participation within the audience's central view, take a closer look at *Tangled* (2010).

The central protagonist is Rapunzel (Mandy Moore), a White, female princess with long, blond hair separated from her parents at birth unbeknownst to her. Her captor uses the magical powers in her hair to stay forever young.

Rapunzel's parents, who are King and Queen of Corona, release sky lanterns every year on Rapunzel's birthday along with the entire kingdom. This execution of this tradition accounted for likely one of the movie's most visually enthralling scenes, when Rapunzel saw the ritual for herself while singing the hit track "I See the Light" later in the movie.

After this point, the whole Kingdom of Corona and all of the movie audience becomes now focused upon and concerned about the (royal) White family becoming reunited again, of which they most certainly do (*spoiler alert!*).

Later in the movie, we see Rapunzel search, suffer and sacrifice, all for a "family" she never knew for eighteen years. Imagine if people would fight as hard for family members they do know, where society would be?!

Vacation, *Diary of a Mad Black Woman*) but also in mainstream comedies that contain White actors. In *Me, Myself & Irene*, Officer Charlie Baileygates' (Jim Carrey) three Black children represent a family construction involving minority characters used primarily for comedic purposes. Similarly, in *There's Something About Mary*, one of the movie's "surprise gags" involves the discovery that Mary Jensen's (Cameron Diaz) father Charlie Jensen (Keith David) is a Black male. In contrast, minority families are woefully represented in mainstream dramas or movies where the characters are supposed to be taken "seriously."

PROTOTYPE #3: THE HERO

The *Hero* is almost always personified by a White male and enjoys a status elevated far above that of your run-of-the-mill protagonist. The Hero is the destined one, the chosen one, the lucky one, or the smart one who, while maximizing his wits, is authorized to do whatever is necessary to complete his objective (which typically includes saving the world or making it better). Forceful, aggressive and decisive actions usually accompany this role. Virtually any action movie containing A-list White males like Arnold Schwarzenegger, Tom Cruise, Bruce Willis, Sylvester Stallone, etc. satisfies this prototype.

Frequently, the Hero shoulders the "White Man's Burden" to save the world or a large group of individuals to which the Hero often has no direct personal ties. Such a responsibility is commonly vested in White characters (even if it has yet to be discovered or acknowledged by the Hero early in the movie). This "responsibility" empowers the Hero to adopt a means-to-an-end philosophy, wherein all death, destruction and mayhem they leave in their wake is justified by the movie's cathartic end. The Hero, through keen wit or physical skill, not only helps others, but helps himself develop personally in the process of becoming a hero.

Armageddon, the meteoric disaster movie, is an excellent example, whereby every major White protagonist has a heroic story arc. Meanwhile, the "major" minority characters, Bear (Michael Clarke Duncan) and Lt. General Kimsey (Keith David), are ineffectual, inarticulate or in the way of the *heroism* of the White characters. A.J. Frost (Ben Affleck) assumes a take-charge leadership role when the drilling crew grows despondent about their mission's prospects in space, while Dan Truman (Billy Bob Thornton) is a NASA administrator who takes charge at Mission Control on the ground. Even Lev Andropov (Peter Stormare), the Russian Cosmonaut, lends his assistance to the American, er,

> **TOTAL ANECDOTAL**
>
> Indicative of the White character default norm that Hollywood studios operate by, for the movie *World Trade Center*, producers cast White actor William Mapother to play Marine Sergeant Thomas. Sergeant Thomas, both in the movie and in real life, gained notoriety for his role in helping rescue two police officers buried underneath twenty feet of rubble and debris during the aftermath of the World Trade Center attack on September 11, 2001. Although his name was known, not much was known about his identity as he selflessly vanished from the limelight after performing his deed.
>
> Shortly before the movie's release in August 2006, Sergeant Thomas learned about the upcoming movie and stepped forward to reveal himself as the selfless soldier. As it turns out, Sergeant Jason Thomas is Black.
>
> The movie's producer, Michael Shamberg, apologized to Sergeant Thomas, saying the mistake was realized only after production had begun.[10e]
>
> Given the fact that "Sergeant Thomas" could have been of any racial or ethnic background, the decision to cast a White male actor reflects the "knee-jerk" assumption that a White character could universally fulfill the heroic role that the movie's producers wished to portray.
>
> This "mistake" is all the more glaring in light of the painstaking efforts the filmmakers made to be sensitive to the families of the victims by "accurately" retelling such a horrific and painful story.

global mission to save planet Earth, using his adroit bomb-defusing skills. Lastly, there is Harry S. Stamper (Bruce Willis), who sacrifices himself for the good of all mankind and stays behind to detonate the meteor that would have hit planet Earth. In so doing, he sends A.J. Frost back off to Earth with his best wishes to care for his daughter, Grace Stamper (Liv Tyler).

Many blockbuster movies employ the "No-Name Hero" concept. Even though the Hero prototype suggests that these "larger-than-life" heroic roles would need to be portrayed by A-list actors, relatively unknown actors are intentionally selected for some of these heroic roles. Examples include Mark Ruffalo in **Hulk**, Christian Bale in **Batman Begins**, Brandon Routh in **Superman Returns**, and Daniel Craig in the latest installment of the James Bond series, **Casino Royale**. There is a paucity of comparable mainstream roles for minority characters.

Given movie studios' apprehensions over cultivating immediate mainstream appeal, minority actors must typically be "proven" entities (i.e., Black rappers and comedians) before this can happen. The second aspect of this "No-Name Hero" concept is the presence of the "ordinary" hero, wherein White male actors like Tobey Maguire, Harrison Ford and Tom Hanks often portray "everyman" characters that rise to the heights of heroism during the course of the movie. Although the two "No-Name" variations frequently overlap, they can exist mutually exclusive of one another. Such actors are often chosen because their name does not immediately "overshadow" the role itself, which highlights Hollywood's willingness to risk using lesser-known *White* protagonists in major mainstream movies.

Often, the Hero is self-sufficient, but occasionally yields to token help from minority archetypes. Compare this dynamic to the more isolated nature of minority heroes/protagonists in minority-driven movies (e.g., "Black movies"). Observe the following chart:

EXAMPLES OF HEROIC HELP BY MINORITY CHARACTERS			
MOVIE	**HERO**	**MINORITY**	**ARCHETYPE**
The Matrix	Neo (Keanu Reeves)	Morpheus (Laurence Fishburne)	Angel
Mission: Impossible	Ian McFarland (Tom Cruise)	Luther Stickell (Ving Rhames)	Angel, Background Figure
Lethal Weapon	Roger Murtaugh (Mel Gibson)	Martin Riggs (Danny Glover)	Comic Relief
Die Another Day	James Bond (Pierce Brosnan)	Jinx (Halle Berry)	Angel, Physical Wonder
The Sum of All Fears	Jack Ryan (Ben Affleck)	William Cabot (Morgan Freeman)	Utopic Reversal

Five additional mainstream movie examples showcasing the Hero prototype include:

1) Air Force One (1997)

» **actor/character:** Harrison Ford as President James Marshall
» **analysis:** Not only does President Marshall thwart the attempt to hijack his own plane by fighting the Kazakh terrorists onboard Air Force One, but his efforts are doubly heroic in that the President manages to *successfully pilot* the 747 jumbo jet and elude enemy fire during the movie's climax. Marshall then proceeds to stabilize and fly a severely damaged plane just long enough to safely evacuate his family, staff and self (in the nick o' time, naturally) before it crashes into the ocean.

2) Finding Nemo (2003)

» **actor/character:** Albert Brooks as the voice of Marlin; Ellen DeGeneres as the voice of Dory; Alexander Gould as the voice of Nemo
» **analysis:** In this animated feature, each of the main characters, who are all voiced by White actors, overcome personal impediments to achieve

heroism for themselves and for others. Marlin overcomes his own fears of the vast ocean and embarks upon an arduous journey far away from his familiar surroundings to track down his son, Nemo, who was captured and removed from the ocean by deep sea divers. Dory also overcomes her short-term memory to lend a helping hand (fin?) to Marlin. Not to be left out, Nemo himself overcomes an undersized fin through the coaching of Gill (William Dafoe) to help execute an escape plan for himself and his fellow comrades trapped in a dentist's aquarium. Additionally, moments after Nemo is rescued, young Nemo returns the favor by directing a school of fish trapped in a fishing net to use their collective strength to overcome the power of the fishing net's retractable motor and triumphantly escape.

3) Erin Brockovich (2000)

> **WHAT DO YOU THINK?**
> The makers of *Crimson Tide* were on their own in re-creating "authentic" military conditions since the Pentagon took issue with the movie's depiction of poor naval security measures for nuclear weapons. As a consequence, the Pentagon refused to offer their technical advice, which is customarily deemed valuable in providing viewing audiences a reasonably accurate naval fantasy.[10f]
>
> Do you think that the Pentagon's denial to assist with *Crimson Tide* represents an effort to prevent American servicemen from being portrayed as anything less than heroic?
>
> If so, what does this say about the power and influence of mainstream movies? *Or about the power of real societal institutions to influence what a fictional movie portrayal should look like?*

» **actor/character:** Julia Roberts as Erin Brockovich

» **analysis:** The title character finds justice in her own way, using her own way, which ultimately helps her get her own way (which, by the way, coincides with the desires of a larger group of citizens concerned about a California power company polluting the small town of Hinkley's water supply). As a divorced, single mother of three, the Family-Tied prototype also provides ample fodder for Brockovich's Manipulator prototype (introduced on pg. 184) since she *must* influence others in order to fulfill a heroic destiny. The overlapping of these various prototypes is summed up in her delivery of empowering lines like this (to her eventual employer): "I'm smart, I'm hardworking and I'll do anything, and I am not leaving without a job!"

» **bonus:** As recognition for her "strong" role and performance, Roberts won Best Actress in a Leading Role at the 2001 Academy Awards.

4) Batman Begins (2005)

» **actor/character:** Christian Bale as Bruce Wayne/Batman

» **analysis:** The movie's premise revolves around Bruce Wayne's personal dedication to justice for all of mankind (in general) and the citizens of Gotham City (in particular) after witnessing the murder of his parents as a child. Wayne is able to redirect his personal emotions of vengeance and anger and apply them in a constructive manner to the benefit of others.

» **bonus**: Notice the presence of the Affluent prototype with the stately opulence that surrounds Bruce Wayne, a billionaire industrialist and philanthropist.

5) The Lord of the Rings: The Fellowship of the Ring (2001)

» **actor/character**: Elijah Wood as Frodo Baggins
» **analysis**: The *Lord of the Rings* trilogy provides ample examples of White characters facing their fears and emerging triumphant after their bouts with evil forces. What is significant about *The Fellowship of the Ring* is that as the first installment of the trilogy, it introduces the "White man's burden" endured by Frodo Baggins. Frodo and *only Frodo alone* can successfully dispose of his "special" ring and defeat the pernicious evil that threatens to destroy all living creatures. Essentially, the balance of Middle Earth rests with Frodo. The entire trilogy, in addition to developing several smaller subplots and parallel stories, revolves around chronicling the courageous actions of the diminutive but determined Hobbit Frodo Baggins to carry out a responsibility that he cannot refuse.

PROTOTYPE #4: THE INTELLECTUAL

The *Intellectual* prototype encompasses the White character who is inherently knowledgeable about anything and everything. Omniscience is often displayed when this character takes on a leadership role, instructing and demonstrating others on better ways to do things: fight, build houses, catch a criminal or even fly planes at the last minute (even if seemingly outside the area of the character's expertise!). Movie audiences are trained and conditioned to look to White characters to provide vital and important information essential to the plot. Since most protagonists in mainstream movies are White characters, audiences by default rely on Whites to deduce and solve the movie's most pressing problems.

The Intellectual prototype may be presented as a successful cultural arbiter. This White character has the ability to "master" the "culture" of others, often benefitting both the character and the cultural "inhabitants." Movies along this thread include *The Last of the Mohicans*, *The Last Samurai*, *Malibu's Most Wanted*, *Bulworth*, *The Missing*, *Dances with*

WHAT DO YOU THINK?

If you like hero movies, then chances are high that you have likely seen *The Avengers* (2012) by now. To see how White prototypes glamorize White participation within the audience's central view, take a closer look at the most significant Black character: Samuel L. Jackson as Nick Fury.

Before analyzing Mr. Fury, let us list the other heroes in the movie:

- Robert Downey Jr. as **Iron Man**
- Chris Evans as **Captain America**
- Mark Ruffalo as **Hulk**
- Chris Hemsworth as **Thor**
- Scarlett Johansson as **Black Widow**
- Jeremy Renner as **Hawkeye**

All of the six aforementioned characters are played by White actors. The last two listed, Black Widow and Hawkeye, do not have superhero powers, but they do have definitive, specialized skills.

In contrast, what does the non-White character of Nick Fury bring to the table with respect to skills and powers? He only wields a gun and just happens if anything, to be physically impaired with his sporting of a black eye patch to match his two black leather jackets (one three-quarter length, one to waist, black pants and black boots.

If Fury (and *Hancock*?) qualifies as a "Black" hero literally in black, then does it hold on the other hand that all of our superheroes only come in the color "white?"

Wolves, and *The Air Up There*. A movie such as **Dangerous Minds** would also be included in this cultural arbiter subgrouping, since its "White person saves inner-city kids" storyline features Louanne Johnson (Michelle Pfeiffer) successfully navigating the "culture" of the inner-city. Johnson is able to successfully reach, organize and redirect minority youth that have previously been deemed unreachable.

Another example of this ability of White characters to understand cultures outside of their own can be found in *The Day After Tomorrow*, where Laura Chapman (Emily Rossum) is able to save trapped two individuals trapped in a taxi by providing commands in French where a police officer was previously unable to communicate.

Intellect is also expressed by the fact that virtually every time White characters appear in a social setting, their feelings, thoughts and personal liberties are deemed important enough to be respected, protected, articulated, and heard in full. For instance, White youth are frequently portrayed as intellectual "peers" with adults (e.g., **Home Alone, Sixth Sense, Star Wars Episode I: The Phantom Menace**). Consider the children characters in **Jurassic Park**, Tim and Lex Murphy (Joseph Mazzello and Ariana Richards), coherently bandying about Latin dinosaur names and saving the day with their knowledge of Linux-based software!

In contrast to the Intellectual prototype, minority characters (especially youth) are often depicted in isolation, have their intellect mocked and are portrayed as somewhat intellectually lacking. As referenced earlier with **Dangerous Minds** and the recurring theme of inner-city kids that need to be saved – these characters are prime examples of minorities lacking intellect that only White characters possess (also consider **Freedom Writers, Finding Forrester, One Eight Seven, Take the Lead**. To illustrate the point, here is a short list of minority youths and their compromised portrayals:

- *Cop Out* - Marcus I. Morton plays Tommy in this buddy cop comedy featuring Bruce Willis and Tracy Morgan. Tommy is a habitual criminal who at the tender age of eleven is "the biggest car thief in Brooklyn." Not only is Tommy's speech punctuated with harsh invective, but he proceeds to assault an officer by kicking him in the genital region and then sustains a punch to the groin himself by a grown adult male;
- *Meet the Fockers* Ray Santiago plays Jorge Villalobos, a Latino youth whose had no knowledge of his father and his "illegitimate bastard-child status" was the source of a running gag in the movie;

LIGHTS! CAMERA! INTERACTION!

Compare and contrast differing representations of intellect by both a White and minority actor for the same character in **Doctor Dolittle** (1967) and its remake (1998).

The premise for both the original movie and its remake is that Dr. John Dolittle has the uncanny ability to talk to animals and understand them in turn. In the 1967 original, Dr. Dolittle is played by White actor Rex Harrison, while in the 1998 remake, Black comedian Eddie Murphy fits the bill.

In particular, notice how each "discovers" his ability to talk to the animals. Harrison's White character proactively engages the intellectual challenge to learn as many languages as humanly possible (as exemplified by the Oscar-winning song "Talk to the Animals"). In contrast, Murphy's Black character has an unexplained, innate ability to understand animals and is forced to reconcile with his awkward talent after attempting to suppress it.

- ***Monster's Ball*** - Coronji Calhoun plays Tyrell Musgrove, an obese Black child with an uncontrollable sweet tooth and tempestuous relationship with his mother who is killed off in a car accident;
- ***Jerry Maguire*** - Jeremy Suarez plays a precocious but vulgar Black post-toddler youth in Tyson Tidwell who shouts, "That's my mo-fo," in reference to seeing his father Rod Tidwell, played by Cuba Gooding, Jr., make a great football play (*Note:* "mo-fo" is an abbreviation for the harsh invective of "mother f—er");
- ***Sky High*** - Dee Jay Daniels plays Ethan, a diminutive Black and nerdy youth;
- ***Role Models*** - Bobb'e J. Thompson plays Ronnie, an angry, petulant, foul-mouthed youth in need of a mentor since his father is absent;
- ***Doctor Dolittle*** - in this 1967 remake, Eddie Murphy as a young John Dolittle – complete with glasses – backs into an embarrassing situation when he smells his new principal's behind in efforts to "get to know" him upon the advice of his talking dog that only he can understand; and
- ***Spider-Man 2*** - after Tobey Maguire as Peter Parker performs a spectacular stunt using his "spider" reflexes to flip off his bike to avoid hitting a car, he tells Black actors Marc John Jefferies and Roshon Fegan – literally billed as "Amazed Kids" – that they can flip like him if they just eat and exercise right; although a very subtle intellectual slight, the innuendo is that they "wouldn't understand."

Antwone Fisher (based upon a true story) surfaces as an example of a mainstream movie where minority intellect is the movie's central focus. However, ***Antwone Fisher*** does not prominently feature White characters, somewhat suggesting that minority intellect "is free" to become the focus of a movie where more dominant White characters are not simultaneously competing for the viewing audience's attention. Additionally, perhaps as the victim of audiences unwilling to make a connective switch, ***Antwone Fisher*** did not perform well at the box office, despite the star presence and involvement of Oscar winner Denzel Washington (who produced, directed and starred in the movie).

Meanwhile, it is quite commonplace to see White characters coming together, pooling their intellectual resources to devise a solution to a problem, execute a scientific venture, navigate around an intellectual/legal/philosophical roadblock, or deduce a centuries-old unsolved mystery. ***The Mummy*** satisfies this prototype as lead characters Richard "Rick" O'Connell (Brendan Fraser) and Evelyn Carnahan (Rachel Wiesz) go "around the world" to solve an ancient archeological mystery. Contrast this storyline with that of *The Scorpion King*, a spinoff of *The Mummy* franchise starring former professional wrestler Dwayne "The Rock" Johnson, which is merely an action-driven, revenge-based plot that requires great physical exercise, but little to no intellectual exercise. The first two movies in the franchise (*The Mummy* and *The Mummy Returns*) featured archeological mysteries which provided the movie's participating White characters with more "intellectual weight." Meanwhile, the absence of a mystery plot-device in *The Scorpion King* only emphasizes the lack of an intellectual undertaking for the minority Physical Wonder archetype upheld by The Rock.

It cannot be overlooked that the Intellectual prototype is built upon the threshold assumption that the character is, in fact, correct. At some point in the movie, despite others initially rejecting the Intellectual's contribution, the Intellectual will be validated by truth or facts. The Intellectual validation is often the running theme in disaster movies, wherein a White character with know-how or clout (e.g., the scientists played by Jeff Goldblum in *Independence Day* and Dennis Quaid in *The Day After Tomorrow*, or the ex-Navy man played by Josh Lucas, the architect played by Richard Dreyfuss and the former firefighter *and* mayor of New York played by Kurt Russell in *Poseidon*) warns everyone around him about an impending crisis along with a (correct) responsive strategy.

Although the "I'm right, and everyone else is wrong" storyline presupposes that there are lots of other White characters who are indeed *wrong*, the fact that the White Intellectual victor's viewpoint is validated by movie's end virtually every time only reinforces an overall balance of positive racial capital. Hence, much of the movie's drama and suspense revolves around whether the White Intellectual is able to convince others to follow their logic. Ultimately, intellect transforms this character into an authority figure since there are often tangible consequences for those who fail to heed the Intellectual's "advice." As a result, other characters must obey the Intellectual in order to survive, and the audience must root for this character to "be correct" if they wish to see the Intellectual save the day.

Five examples of the Intellectual prototype include:

1) The Silence of the Lambs (1991)

» **actor/character**: Anthony Hopkins as Dr. Hannibal Lecter; Jodie Foster as Clarice Starling

» **analysis:** The chief source of the movie's suspense comes not from anticipated gore, but from the intellectual battle of wills waged between a "brilliant" lecherous murderer (Dr. Lecter) and a young but tenacious FBI agent focused on cracking a high-profile case (Clarice Starling).

» **bonus:** In 1992, Anthony Hopkins won a Best Actor in a Leading Role Oscar for his memorable performance as the sinister intellectual, despite a limited amount of screen time.

2) Twister (1996)

» **actor/character:** Helen Hunt as Dr. Jo Harding; Bill Paxton as Bill Harding

» **analysis:** Dr. Jo Harding and Bill Harding are researchers who chase tornadoes and try to warn locals about the intellectual knowledge that they possess — so much so that they are essentially able to outwit Mother Nature in implementing a new device they created to improve man's ability to predict future tornadoes.

» **bonus:** Notice the Family-Tied prototype present whereby Dr. Jo Harding is motivated to be an effective "storm chaser" since she lost her father to a tornado as a child and wants to save future lives from a similar fate. The movie begins with Bill Harding intending to deliver divorce papers to Dr. Jo Harding and ends with Bill's fiancée (Dr. Melissa Reeves played by Jami Gertz) leaving him because it is patently obvious that the Hardings still have strong feelings for one another.

3) Good Will Hunting (1997)

» **actor/character:** Matt Damon as Will Hunting

» **analysis:** This movie centers on Will Hunting's discovered genius and his difficulties interfacing with the world outside of his brilliant head.

» **bonus:** Not only did this movie win an Oscar for Best Screenplay, but Robin Williams also won an Oscar for Best Actor in a Supporting Role in 1998. Notice the twist on the Affluent prototype, wherein Hunting starts off the movie as a janitor working at the Massachusetts Institute of Technology (MIT). White protagonists in mainstream movies are rarely seen in janitorial positions (as compared to say, Morgan Freeman as "God" in *Bruce Almighty*), but his status as a janitor is transitive – not permanent – since he was an undiscovered genius in janitorial clothing the whole time! Nevertheless, he ultimately *turns*

>  **WHAT DO YOU THINK?**
> Another excellent example of Intellect on display comes in ***Sherlock Holmes*** (2009) starring Robert Downey, Jr. (Sherlock Holmes) and Jude Law (Dr. John Watson).
>
> Holmes' intellect not only on display in solving the crime, but in the way he solves the crime. He appears to be distracted, mildly interested and off-topic. Yet, he is a keen observer of human conduct and provides most of the information for the audience to follow, establishing the pace of the movie through his thoughts.
>
> Also, Holmes is portrayed as one who is always "thinking ahead," for more than one occasion, we see Holmes walk through his thoughts (in slow motion, of course) about how to break down his next physical attack upon some would-be henchman trying to thwart his investigation in painstaking detail.
>
> Then, the movie returns to real time and the audience sees Holmes walk through the steps that he accurately analyzed and predicted. Many of the rest of us might struggle to put together a "plan of attack" within a few nanoseconds so neatly and without panic.

down a lucrative employment opportunity in order to go "see about a girl."

4) National Treasure (2004)

» actor/character: Nicolas Cage as Ben Gates; Diane Kruger as Abigail Chase
» analysis: This movie features the quick-witted talents of Ben Gates and Abigail Chase who team up and put their heads together to progressively deduce clues to the location of a treasure left previously undiscovered for centuries.

5) Star Wars: Episode I - The Phantom Menace (1999)

» actor/character: Jake Lloyd as Anakin Skywalker
» analysis: Young Anakin is featured as an unusually prodigious and alert nine-year-old who not only wins his own freedom from slavery in a cut-throat pod race, but also receives a special invitation to leave home and embark upon Jedi training. Aspects of Young Anakin's brilliant personality include heady discussions with adults, his understanding of "alien" languages and his knowledge of pod racer parts and maintenance.
» key scene: Young Anakin Skywalker demonstrates his high aptitude for "the force" when he unwittingly places himself in harm's way by joining an intense battle with the Federation army while in the cockpit of a X-wing fighter jet. Nonplussed, he manages to fire proton torpedoes at the enemy ship's reactor, causing a chain-reaction explosion that destroys the ship. The torpedoes Anakin fires ultimately save his colleagues on the planet Naboo, who are fighting droids remotely controlled by the ship that Anakin destroys.
» bonus: Young Anakin also speaks the language of "native" space creatures, such as Watto on the desert planet of Tatooine, reinforcing the notion that Whites can fluidly fulfill the role of a cultural arbiter.

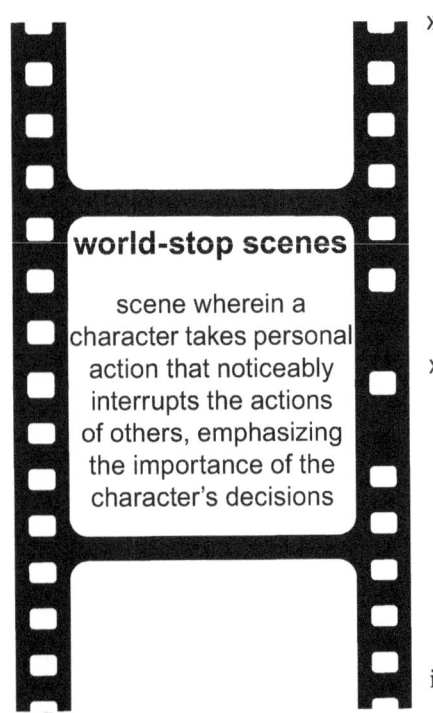

world-stop scenes

scene wherein a character takes personal action that noticeably interrupts the actions of others, emphasizing the importance of the character's decisions

PROTOTYPE #5: The Manipulator

When you see a White lead in a mainstream movie, that character is typically faced with some type of conflict that requires resolution. In our definition, the *Manipulator* prototype does not necessarily refer to a character exploiting another by means of unfairly gained leverage, but rather, refers to the ability of a White character to reject their circumstances at face value and manipulate or change them to fit their personal needs. As a result, White characters are frequently moving from a position where they lack control to the point where they become the primary person in control.

For this reason, the presence of the Manipulator is frequently marked by **world-stop scenes**, scenes in which the individual's goals are prioritized over the public's goals. To be clear, a world stop scene is not always marked by an occasion where the character is bent upon world domination. Rather, such a scene can appear quite innocuously as a destructive chase sequence that destroys a significant amount of public property, where the destruction is unpunished or justified by the character's personal goals (which may also match the interests of the larger public). World-stop scenes also manifest themselves when seemingly disinterested passerbys suddenly stop to applaud the consummation of a romance (e.g., the climactic kiss on the baseball field by Jimmy Fallon and Drew Barrymore's characters in **Fever Pitch**).

Ultimately, in world-stop scenes, the central character's actions affect a larger number of people on a personal level (e.g., "Johnny, if you do this one task, then you can save the entire world from destruction!"). Conversely, for many comedies featuring White actors, a prime source of material stems from a White protagonist's *inability* to control or master their environment, as in **Lost in Translation** and **Father of the Bride**. Nonetheless, in these "disoriented" comedies, the White protagonist ultimately achieves some level of "mastery" or somehow gains control of the situation by movie's end.

The Manipulator is perhaps exemplified by those characters that display a strong sense of entitlement. This character does not live by the rules, and often "must" break them in order to succeed. The movie revolves around this one person's axis of existence, since he is able to stop or alter society's normal functioning in order to advance his agenda, generally unburdened from consequence. A common vehicle for this prototype is a movie where the lone, morally-empowered citizen *must* "take the law into his own hands." This empowered character is generally free to perform whatever task he wants – including legally questionable acts – just to accomplish their goal of "justice." The audience is usually forgiving of such actions, especially when the righteous cause of our sympathetic vigilante is adequately explained.

The thoughts and feelings of the Manipulator are given significant value and attention over everyone else, demonstrating this person's importance

WHAT DO YOU THINK?

In contrast to the **Menace to Society** archetype, **Manipulator** prototypes often escape or thwart "normal" police and security procedures since the importance of their individual objective is justified.

During the climactic scene in *Fever Pitch*, Lindsey Meeks (Drew Barrymore) runs across the field during a Boston Red Sox game to stop Ben Wrightman (Jimmy Fallon) from selling his season tickets. After eluding security and police, Meeks finally greets Wrightman on the other side of the field. When the police finally catch up to Meeks and inform her that "You're outta here," Meeks absentmindedly shouts back, "Give me a second, okay? Just give me a second! Please! Please!" before continuing to profess her love to Wrightman.

After a spell, the police attempt again to arrest Meeks, informing Wrightman that he needs to "let her go." Wrightman defiantly states, "Never!" before drawing Meeks in for a kiss. Observant strangers then cheer and break out in applause, subsequently chanting "Let's go Red Sox!" The movie ends with Meeks and Wrightman kissing while exasperated police and security "helplessly" watch the protagonists soak in the full glory of their love.

The movie also ends here without any visual depiction of Meeks answering for her "illegal" behavior. *How many minority characters in mainstream movies do you recall successfully manipulating law enforcement in their favor?*

to society and affirming that what is good enough for this character is good enough for society. Moreover, Manipulators distort the amount of social power the "average" citizen has (or should responsibly use) in order to accomplish the most routine of tasks by minimizing (in exaggerated fashion) the true difficulty involved in marshaling personal power to accomplish such goals. As an example, consider the birth scene in *Lethal Weapon 4*, where Lorna Cole (Rene Russo) stops normal hospital protocol to have a wedding ceremony with Marlon Riggs (Mel Gibson) before the impending delivering of her forthcoming baby. Also note how she convinces a Rabbi to preside over the ceremony, even though neither Cole nor Riggs is Jewish.

> **WHAT DO YOU THINK?**
>
> In *The Island*, protagonists Lincoln Six Echo (Ewan McGregor) and Jordan Two Delta (Scarlett Johansson) enlist the aid of McCord (Steve Buscemi) to determine their true identity. McCord waffles on helping Lincoln and Jordan, since revealing their identity would expose a major scandal that might endanger his own life. Sensing his hesitation, Lincoln confidently and squarely addresses McCord with this scene-ending line: "We're not asking for your permission; we're asking for your help." McCord complies in the next scene.
>
> This self-directed, take-charge approach is typical of world-stop scenes, whereby the individual's desires take ultimate priority, regardless of the resulting effect for others. As it turns out in The Island, the individual quest of the protagonists ultimately benefits everyone.
>
> *Have you seen this character trait consistently displayed by minority characters in mainstream movies? Or is this domain exclusive to Whites?*
>
> As a contrast within the same movie, Starkweather (played by Black actor Michael Clarke Duncan) at one point attempts to escape "the bad guys" and prevent them from harvesting his organs. During his failed one-man coup, he also "asks" for help (in the presence of Lincoln), but no one comes to his aid, even though he is recognized as a celebrity figure in the movie (a professional football player). This scenario is akin to the No-Name Hero dynamic, wherein Lincoln, as an "average" White male, is able to enlist more help and sympathy than a minority celebrity! Notice how Starkweather's captors refer to him as "big fella" and "this guy," thereby shifting him from a celebrity to a nobody. Meanwhile, the White protagonists, over the course of the movie, shift from average "nobodies" to exceptional saviors/celebrities!

The Manipulator's actions are directed by a shared sense of moral authority with the viewing audience. In the process of developing White characters during a movie, motives for conduct are usually justified and explained, regardless of whether the character's motives are ultimately judged to be legal or illegal. In the movie *Fun with Dick and Jane*, Dick and Jane (Jim Carrey and Téa Leoni) embark on a life of crime to pay for the lifestyle that they lost when Dick "wrongfully" loses his job (right after obtaining a promotion and instructing Jane to quit her job).

Despite their patently illegal activities, Dick and Jane's criminal acts are not portrayed as morally offensive (as affirmed by the movie's title) and go unpunished. The movie culminates with a multi-million dollar bank heist that is presented as an act of justifiable revenge since Dick's former corrupt boss (Alec Baldwin as Jack McCallister) was the original morally corrupt transgressor who caused Dick to lose his job. Since the protagonists' actions are "justifiably" explained and placed in context relative to the greater misdeeds of another, the shared sense of moral authority with the viewing audience is not jeopardized, and the audience is free to "support" and root for the otherwise thieving protagonists.

Further evidence of the Manipulator prototype can be found in the following movies:

1) Anger Management (2003)

- » **actor/character**: Adam Sandler as Dave Buznik; Jack Nicholson as Dr. Buddy Rydell
- » **analysis**: During the movie's climax, notice the world-stop scene at the Yankees baseball game, where the entire crowd in attendance (along with Major League Baseball players Roger Clemens and Derek Jeter), stop to acknowledge and cheer the wedding proposal between the lead characters. The lead characters not only receive a supportive "You can do it!" from "Sir" Rudy Giuliani, but the ex-NYC mayor actually leads the crowd with the rallying cry "Kiss her Da-vid!" after Dave publicly proposes to Linda (Marisa Tomei).
- » **bonus**: Another world-stop scene takes place earlier in the movie when Dr. Rydell accompanies Dave to Dave's workplace. Dr. Rydell instructs Dave to stop his car during morning rush hour traffic in the middle of a New York City bridge and sing the ballad "I Feel Pretty" from the 1961 musical **West Side Story**. Further, the entire movie is a slight nod to the Intellectual prototypes fulfilled by Dr. Rydell and Linda. Even though Linda and Dr. Rydell did not to have a pre-existing relationship, the movie's conclusion reveals that the two thought out and collaborated on a plan to "help" Dave – a plan that was evidently executed without any significant mishaps.
- » **note**: As indicative of the largely contained and marginalized presence of minorities, even for a mainstream movie set in New York City, there are only a few minority characters that have speaking lines. Notice

> **WHAT DO YOU THINK?**
> If you were to start pre-production for a simple romantic-comedy that you planned to film, how hard or easy do you think it would be to have former Major League Baseball greats Derek Jeter and Roger Clemens appear *in the same movie* alongside the former New York City Mayor who oversaw the city's resilient stand against the 9/11 terrorist attacks?
>
> To secure the presence and participation of these three well-known and highly visible celebrities, *would it be a matter of Affluence? Influence? Or both?*

> **WHAT DO YOU THINK?**
> If you are unclear about what a **Manipulator** prototype looks like, then chances are high that you have not seen *How to Train Your Dragon* (2010).
>
> The word "manipulator" may conjure negative images of individuals influencing others' behavior patterns without their knowledge or for nefarious means.
>
> Not always.
>
> The teenage White male protagonist, Hiccup Horrendous Haddock III (Jay Baruchel) lives on an island within a small Viking village that is always at odds with the local dragons who constantly attack their village and raid its livestock.
>
> After another attack, Hiccup comes into contact with a rare "Night Fury" dragon which he names Toothless. While Toothless was injured, Hiccup figures out how to communicate with the dragon, devises a prosthetic fin that allows Hiccup to guide and fly the dragon while in flight. Hiccup, while shunned for not being a burly Viking who wants to "fight" all the time obtains validation and vindication through his inventions which now allow him to "train his own dragon" and fly to heights never dreamed of before. This training method allowed for Hiccup's village to successfully vanquish the evil Red Death dragon in the end.
>
> This exchange between Hiccup and Toothless (and others) is the very definition of manipulation, although it was for the "greater good."

how their roles fulfill minority archetypes and comport with the HARM theory (in order of appearance):

- *Air Marshal*: Black male Background Figure, Physical Wonder, Comic Relief.
- *Judge Brenda Daniels*: Black female Background Figure, Utopic Reversal.
- *Lou*: Latino male Background Figure, Physical Wonder, Comic Relief.
- *Angry Man #1*: Black male Background Figure. Not only is he not named and personalized, but he only flashes onscreen a few times during Dave's original anger management session and is conspicuously absent throughout the rest of the movie.
- *Angry Man #2*: Latino male Background Figure. Angry Man #2 suffers a similar fate to his similarly silent colleague, Angry Man #1. More revealing is the establishing scene for Dave's anger management group at roughly the 10:39 mark, where the overhead camera angle includes all of the speaking characters that will become Dave's friends to the exclusion of Angry Man #1 and Angry Man #2.
- *Unnamed Buddhist Monks*: Asian male Background Figures, Comic Relief.
- *Derek Jeter*: Black male Background Figure, Physical Wonder.

2) The Fugitive (1993)

» **actor/character:** Harrison Ford as Dr. Bruce Kimball
» **analysis:** Note the righteous indignation: the system is never wrong, except for when the system happens to the White protagonist.

3) Home Alone (1990)

» **actor/character:** Macaulay Culkin as Kevin McAllister
» **analysis:** In **Home Alone**, a young eight-year-old, Kevin, must cleverly manipulate his home environment to defend himself successfully against two burglars (Joe Pesci and Daniel Stern as Harry and Marv).

4) Legally Blonde (2001)

» **actor/character:** Reese Witherspoon as Elle Woods

» **analysis:** Elle Woods, a 4.0 major in Fashion Merchandising at California University Los Angeles (CULA), wills herself into law school just so she can exact revenge on the boyfriend who dumped her. In order to "make a point," Elle decides to alter her boyfriend's educational environment by personally injecting herself, despite her previous inclinations to avoid law school.

» **key scene:** At the movie's beginning, her application video in concert with her nearly perfect 179 Law School Admission Test (LSAT) score (out of a possible 180 points), demonstrates that Elle is willing to do whatever is necessary to satisfy existing standards, but on her own terms. Elle's determination and resolve to get her way is made manifest in this brief exchange:

> *CULA Counselor*: What are your back-ups?
> *Elle*: I don't need back-ups, I'm going to Harvard.
> *CULA Counselor*: Well then. You'll need excellent recommendations from your professors . . .
> *Elle*: . . . OK . . .
> *CULA Counselor*: . . . and a heck of an admissions essay, and at least a 175 on your LSATs.
> *Elle*: I once had to judge a tighty-whitey contest for Lambda Kappa Pi. Trust me, I can handle anything.

» **bonus:** If anything, notice how Elle's near perfect LSAT score reinforces the Intellectual prototype *and* serves to shatter conventional stereotypes regarding "blondes" as dull-witted and non-intellectual.

5) Minority Report (2002)

» **actor/character:** Tom Cruise as Chief John Anderton
» **analysis:** Note the righteous indignation: the futuristic and technologically advanced system of detecting crime before it happens is never wrong, except for when the system designates the White protagonist, Chief Anderton, guilty of murder.

PROTOTYPE #6: THE ROMANTIC

We frequently see mainstream movies showcasing love stories between two White protagonists, whether as a central story or a subplot. Romantic comedies, which serve as a large source of roles for White female protagonists, focus invariably on romantic overtures and sexual tensions between makeshift

---

LIGHTS! CAMERA! INTERACTION!
Watch *Die Another Day* (2002) to see whether you can spot the Romantic prototype at work. More specifically, look where two important characters, one White and one Black, share sex scenes with the central protagonist, James Bond (Pierce Brosnan).

The White woman is Miranda Frost (Rosamund Pike), a double-crossing M16 agent. The Black woman is Jinx (Halle Berry), who helps Bond as an NSA agent. Despite the fact that Frost proves to be a mole who dies in the movie, her love scene differs markedly from Bond's love scene with Jinx.

Compare and contrast 1) the type and amount of lighting involved, 2) the type of background music, 3) the amount and type of dialogue directly before, during and after sex, 4) the amount of nudity and 5) the amount of sensual "sound effects" emitted from each woman.

What are the differences? What is the rationale behind such decisions?

couples. However, even in action and adventure mainstream movies, which typically feature White male protagonists, the romantic connection involving at least one White character is a recurring theme; the protagonist often "gets the girl" at the movie's conclusion as a "trophy" for his accomplishments.

Further edifying this *Romantic* prototype are the frequent and fantastical match-ups that feature an "average" White male character paired with an attractive female character. Take the movie **Hitch** as a prime example, where the love interest for Albert (Kevin James) is Allegra Cole (Amber Valletta). Albert is a portly corporate employee who wears glasses. Meanwhile, Allegra is a rich heiress who fits the White Beauty Standard with respect to her appearance as a slender blonde White female (Valletta's White Beauty Standard is further confirmed by the fact that she got her start in "the business" as a fashion model). Over the course of the movie, as Albert's confidence in himself grows, so does Allegra's affinity for Albert. The eventual marriage of Albert and Allegra underscores how the White Romance prototype (as well as the Family-Tied prototype) serve as anchors for the White audiences, especially in movies like **Hitch** that has a minority protagonist (Will Smith).

Another variation on this average-male, above-average-female romance is when the White male protagonist falls for an otherwise unassuming girl who, after removing her glasses and letting her hair down, instantaneously transforms into a "hot" date. For example, consider Laura Chapman (Emmy Rossum) in *The Day After Tomorrow*. During her opening scenes of the movie, Chapman is plainly dressed with her hair in a pony tail, yet during a swanky reception later in the movie, she catches Sam Hall's (Jake Gyllenhaal) eye with her hair out and otherwise sexy appearance whilst clad in evening attire.

Judging by mainstream movie standards, it appears that love is not blind, or at least not colorblind. Interracial romances between White and minority characters almost always feature a *White male* and a *non-White female* (e.g., Matthew Perry and Salma Hayek in **Fools Rush In**, Clive Owen and Rosario Dawson in **Sin City**, Josh Hartnett and Lucy Liu in **Lucky Number Slevin**, Ralph Fiennes and Jennifer Lopez in **Maid in Manhattan**, Warren Beatty and Halle Berry in **Bulworth**, etc.). Conversely, romantic pairings in mainstream movies between A-list *non-White males* and *White females* rarely occur, especially between central characters (although Denzel Washington has been cast opposite White A-list stars like Julia Roberts in **The Pelican Brief** and Angelina Jolie in **The Bone Collector**, these onscreen pairings were devoid of any intimate passion).

LIGHTS! CAMERA! INTERACTION!

One pairing that possibly satisfies the White female-minority male romantic storyline featuring A-list actors is the 2004 movie **Shark Tale**. Will Smith and Renée Zellweger provide the voices for the romantic couple of Oscar and Angie. Incidentally, Shark Tale is an animated feature which does not depict or show a White female and minority male tangibly consummating a romance as human beings – we will allow for you to draw your own conclusions as to why.

How many "human" depictions of A-list White women and minority males can you think of in mainstream movies? How does the predominance of White males throughout the industry affect the imbalance of White male pairings in interracial romances?

In observance of Hollywood's aversion non-White male driven interracial romance, note the "ironic" gender change between *Guess Who's Coming to Dinner* and its remake *Guess Who*. The original version featured the mixed-race pairing of a Black male and a White female (Dr. John Wade Prentice and Joanna "Joey" Drayton played by Sidney Poitier and Katharine Houghton). The remake featured the mixed-race pairing of a White male and a Black female (Simon Green and Theresa Jones played by Ashton Kutcher and Zoe Saldaña). Compare the tepid romance from the original to the more "active" remake – which incidentally features a *White male* in the mixed-race relationship.

LIGHTS! CAMERA! INTERACTION!
Name a top minority actress that has not over the course of her career appeared in a mainstream movie involved in a romantic relationship with a White male.

Conversely, can a similar claim be made that the vast majority of top-flight White actresses have been paired romantically with minority lead male actors?

In *Guess Who's Coming to Dinner*, the physical "romance" is essentially limited to a peck kiss on the lips between Dr. Prentice and Joey as observed by audience through a taxi driver's rearview mirror. The pairing in *Guess Who* is much more sexually expressive (e.g., Theresa jumps on Simon and wraps her legs around him while smooching; Theresa describes Simon's penis size to her sister). Switching the gender of the races in *Guess Who* speaks to a larger dynamic of the general lack of romance for (and the isolation of) minority male protagonists. In nearly one hundred years of Hollywood filmmaking, the fact that the 1967 landmark movie, *Guess Who's Coming to Dinner*, is still a "landmark" movie about interracial romance (involving a Black male and a White female) demonstrates the inability of Hollywood's limitless imagination to cross imaginary boundaries.

WHAT DO YOU THINK?
As proof of the identification process at work, the Walt Disney Co. in teaming with designer Kirstie Kelly has launched a business whereby at "a cost of $1,100 to $3,000 for each gown, brides will be able to walk down the aisle in dresses inspired by Cinderella, Snow White, Belle, Sleeping Beauty, Jasmine or Ariel."

Those who identified with such Disney princesses as young girls are now able to fulfill their vision of beauty and splendor on their very own wedding day as adults. Not only does such a product speak to how some moviegoers relate to images put before them, but it also speaks to how a major movie studio —in creative fashion — seeks to establish long-term and lucrative consumer relationships with moviegoers. "In thinking of ways it could reach outside the core princess crowd of 3- to 6-year olds, Disney honed in on women who had grown up with the characters. Brides seemed an obvious target."

Consider how Kelly describes the different styles that match each princess. Of the six princesses listed, only Jasmine qualifies as an across-the-street minority.

Cinderella - "'classic glamour'" - her dresses come in high-shine satin with ball-gown skirts and make generous use of silver embroidery and crystals"
Snow White - "a slightly conservative more conservative look dubbed 'sweet elegance'"
Ariel - "who played the title role in 'Little Mermaid,'" has a 'sultry allure' and is 'comfortable showing her body'"
Jasmine - "from 'Aladdin,' is 'bohemian chic,' and her dresses are big on sheath and lace"[10g]

CHAPTER 10: WHITE BALANCING ACT

Five examples of Romantic prototypes include:

1) Bridget Jones's Diary (2001)

» **actor/character**: Renée Zellweger as Bridget Jones; Hugh Grant as Daniel Cleaver; Colin Firth as Mark Darcy

» **analysis**: The White protagonists seek, explore and eventually find out what true love truly means.

» **bonus**: Note the occurrence of a world-stop scene where a jumbotron scoreboard high above a public intersection (think of a mini-New York Times Square) reflects Bridget's diary thoughts at roughly the 26:34 mark. After Bridget first lands Daniel Cleaver, the scoreboard reads, "Weight: 131 lbs. Have replaced food with sex." A second message reads, "Cigarettes: 22 . . . . All post-coital." Although no other individuals "stopped" or interrupted their actions to defer to the protagonist, it nonetheless is a world-stop scene given that the audience witnesses the larger environment manipulated purely for Bridget's benefit, as if it were *her* environment exclusively.

2) Something's Gotta Give (2004)

» **actor/character**: Jack Nicholson as Harry Sanborn; Diane Keaton as Erica Jane Barry

» **analysis**: The White protagonists seek, explore and eventually find out what true love truly means.

» **bonus**: With this performance, Diane Keaton was nominated for a Best Actress in a Leading Role for the 2004 Academy Awards. Although she has a brief nude scene that was rather unremarkable, what is remarkable is the fact that this nude scene was Keaton's first in a movie career that began in 1970 (***Lovers and Other Strangers***). Compare Keaton's construction of a successful career spanning more than three decades to the high prevalence of nudity for minority female actresses starting their careers (see "What Do You Think?" pg. 126).

> **WHAT DO YOU THINK?**
> *Is there such a thing as "recycled romance"?* Look at the pairings below and determine whether they are merely random or formulaic?
>
> Tom Hanks and Meg Ryan
> *Sleepless in Seattle* (1993)
> *You've Got Mail* (1998)
>
> Richard Gere and Julia Roberts
> *Pretty Woman* (1990)
> *Runaway Bride* (1999)

3) How to Lose a Guy in 10 Days (2003)

» **actor/character**: Kate Hudson as Andie Anderson; Matthew McConaughey as Benjamin Berry

- » **analysis**: The White protagonists seek, explore and eventually find out what true love truly means.
- » **bonus**: Keep a sharp eye for Lori, played by Asian Canadian actress Samantha Quan. Her flitting appearances are made early in the movie, before the "serious" love story takes shape and before the emotional "heavy-lifting" takes place. Although Lori is a co-worker of Andie Anderson, observe how Lori's character, although seen floating *around* the protagonist, is nevertheless not seen *with* the protagonist. She remains socially isolated from the protagonist's inner circle unlike her two White colleagues and confidants (Kathryn Hahn as Michelle Rubin, and Annie Parisse as Jeannie Ashcroft).

4) Titanic (1997)

- » **actor/character**: Leonardo DiCaprio as Jack Dawson; Kate Winslet as Rose DeWitt Bukater
- » **analysis**: The White protagonists seek, explore and eventually find out what true love truly means.
- » **bonus**: Based upon box office sales, this movie is the second highest-grossing movie of *all-time*. Adding to its record-setting luster is the fact that *Titanic* netted eleven Oscars at the 1998 Academy Awards ceremony.

> **WHAT DO YOU THINK?**
> If you like romance movies, then chances are high that you have likely seen **La La Land** (2016) by now (starring Emma Stone and Ryan Gosling).
>
> What?! You actually want us to explain how this movie is "romantic?"
>
> While you must humor us here (because we are not going to explain how), we will tell you that this movie did win six Academy Awards out of fourteen nominations, which is a fair indication that this movie will be highly regarded for portraying how the White protagonists seek, explore and eventually find out what true love truly means...

5) What Women Want (2000)

- » **actor/character**: Mel Gibson as Nick Marshall; Helen Hunt as Darcy McGuire
- » **analysis**: The White protagonists seek, explore and eventually find out what true love truly means.
- » **key scene**: A particularly poignant (and lengthy) romantic scene comes at roughly the 1:25:45 mark when Marshall and McGuire share their first kiss and subsequently depart each other's company outside of The Back Door jazz club. Notice the dialogue, tight camera shots and accompanying background music that contribute to the scene's emotional appeal. Music also plays an important role in "setting the stage" for romantic at roughly the 1:38:05 mark when the two share a quiet, private, and innocently intimate dance.
- » **bonus**: Notice the Affluence prototype reinforced by the "modest" office spaces occupied by co-workers Marshall and McGuire, in addition

to that of their supervisor Dan Wanamaker (Alan Alda) at the Sloane Curtis ad agency.

» **double bonus:** At the beginning of the movie, keep a lookout for "Flo, the Doorwoman" (Loretta Devine). As a Black female character, notice how often Flo employs vulgarities within the short span of dialogue that she has in her limited time onscreen. Her servile function in the movie is made obvious with the numerous times that the phrase "Yes, sir" punctuates her speech. Finally, while many women in the movie are revealed to the audience as harboring secretly flattering thoughts about the protagonist Marshall, Flo is the only woman who proceeds to bellow out animalistic noises.

Just as the phases of the moon cannot be properly appreciated without an understanding of the moon's relationship to both the sun and Earth, race in mainstream movies cannot be analyzed purely in terms of minorities and their roles within Hollywood. Minority archetypes must be contextualized in terms of their relationship to White prototypes.

By analyzing how both minority and White characters are portrayed and utilized in mainstream movies, the true import of race in Hollywood becomes clearer. Minority archetypes are often more narrow in their import since minority characters are limited to a small, marginalized spectrum of behaviors. Despite the title or rank ascribed to a minority character, the archetypes demonstrate that overall screen time and substantive impact remain limited and contained in comparison to their White counterparts. White prototypes are broader in their application and scope, and serve to empower a wider range of characters audiences see in their mainstream movies.

In analyzing mainstream movies for general White patterns, bear in mind that, as with the minority archetypes, movies may employ multiple White prototypes (e.g., in ***Seabiscuit***, the Hero, Manipulator and Romantic prototypes all resonate strongly through the protagonist Red Pollard as played by Tobey Maguire). Discussing White balance is critical to any legitimate analysis of race in mainstream Hollywood. Many discussions about race and the movies focus only upon the impact (or lack thereof) of minority actors within Hollywood circles. What is required is a thorough examination of the other side of the coin, for, if minorities are not portrayed or depicted as powerful, intelligent and affluent members of society who can make the world a better place, then who is?

LIGHTS! CAMERA! INTERACTION!

Quick! Try to think of a mainstream movie starring at least one White character that does not contain a White character prototype. If you do find such a movie, walk through the six mainstream factors to ensure that it is a mainstream movie. Next, compare or relate what you find to the minority archetypes. What are the differences in how race is treated onscreen?

The Bottom Line #2: Color Me Bad

Hollywood mainstream movies routinely present a limited view of minorities, in stark contrast to the developed spectrum of White characters.

ACT 3: Resolution

CHAPTER 16:
AT A THEATER NEAR YOU

> *We have met repeatedly with industry executives to seek their attention to the problem of under-employment of women and minorities. Each time we received promises that they would do everything they could to provide more opportunities. The results prove that that is not enough..*

Jack Shea, Past President, Directors Guild of America[1]

CHAPTER 11:
AT A THEATER NEAR YOU

What do you suppose is happening right now in the lobbies of movie theaters nationwide? What about inside of coffeehouses, break rooms and homes across the nation? You guessed it — people are discussing mainstream movies. It seems that discussing movies is as much a pastime as watching the movies themselves.

But what exactly are people discussing? They are discussing the characters, events and implications of these movies, of course. What happened, to whom, and what did it mean. Whether a movie makes people happy, sad or confused, people undoubtedly discuss the images that they have just seen. It is only natural. After all, when was the last time you went to the movies accompanied by another and left the theater in pure silence (sour dates exempted) without discussing what had just transpired on the screen?

The full science and theory behind society's love for movies is probably the substance for a future doctoral thesis and is certainly beyond our scope here. Nonetheless, it is fairly evident that fans from all across the globe harbor a deep fascination with Hollywood mainstream movies. What else would explain the international fervor for the Academy Awards and the multitude of people who travel from around the globe to visit a funny-colored, star-laden sidewalk called Hollywood Boulevard? Movies possess a special quality – some might even say magic – that make their characters and their storylines resonate the world over. To this point, Jack Valenti, former long-time president of the MPAA, observed that, "[w]hat you offer consumers is an epic viewing experience and an alluring social adventure they cannot duplicate in their homes – stadium seating, huge screens with luminance, the sensuality of digital sound, unknown but enthusiastic companions of a single night – all responding to the skills of cinema artists who can make you laugh or cry or hold you in suspense."[2]

 **BUT IT'S JUST A MOVIE, RIGHT?**
Movies can also bring people together outside of the movie theater. Consider this statement by the Martha's Vineyard Chamber of Commerce in June 2005:

In 1974, a group of filmmakers arrived on Martha's Vineyard to make a movie, based on a popular best-selling novel. The movie — *Jaws*. The impact of that film on popular culture and the entertainment industry is legendary. Now, thirty years later in celebration of the 30th anniversary of the filming of *Jaws*, the Martha's Vineyard Chamber of Commerce will launch *Jaws Fest*, an annual three-day event for *Jaws* fans from around the globe.[11a]

Additionally, a movie convention held to celebrate the release of ***Star Wars: Episode III - Revenge of the Sith*** attracted no less than 30,000 fans.[11b] The high attendance rate serves as a reminder that movies can motivate, inspire and direct individual action long after the ending credits have left the screen.

199

> **BUT IT'S JUST A MOVIE, RIGHT?**
>
> Emblematic of the power of Hollywood imagery, in the wake of the deadly Columbine school shootings, President Bill Clinton directed Federal Trade Commission (FTC) Chairman Robert Pitofsky to study the entertainment industry's marketing of violent material with respect to young people. The FTC then issued a scathing report against Hollywood images.[11c]
>
> More interesting than the content of the report itself is the fact that it was ordered as a possible source of insight into a tragic real-life societal event.

PICTURE THIS

It is the endearing movie image which has the awesome power to communicate messages on a grand scale. Camera techniques, special lighting and slow-motion movement, combined with an inspiring classical music soundtrack, can make the most mundane of tasks appear majestic. Most moviegoers appreciate the emotion that develops when it takes a full three minutes for an explosion to occur, or when it takes a full five minutes for the game-winning home run to leave the ballpark, or when it takes a full fifteen minutes to complete a photo-finish horse race. The studios are well aware of the potential for movies to evoke strong emotional responses from its audience members.

If you have seen enough movies, then you are certainly familiar with the classic scenario where the protagonist hurriedly gets into a car and drives off. Given that time is money (especially in Hollywood), the director must make a decision about what is most important to communicate to the audience: is it more important to show a realistic portrayal of each logical step required for the protagonist to drive off in the first place, or is it more important to simply show that the protagonist drive off in a rush? Let us compare two possible versions of the same scene:

Scene 1 Take 1

After thwarting the surprise ambush in her apartment, Jane rushes out of the front door of her apartment and stops in front of her car. After fishing through her purse to locate her keys, Jane fumbles with the key ring to select the actual car key (as distinguished from her gym locker key).

Jane then inserts the key in the car door, unlocks the door, seats herself inside the car, closes the door, engages the seatbelt, adjusts the car seat forward, tilts the steering wheel downward, and adjusts the mirrors before putting the key in the ignition and starting the car. Jane first places the car in reverse (since she is parallel parked), and briefly checks her side mirrors for oncoming traffic before putting the car in drive and frantically speeding off.

BUT IT'S JUST A MOVIE, RIGHT?
On April 9, 2003, the Los Angeles City Council voted to use the name South Los Angeles (instead of South Central Los Angeles) in an effort to divorce it from its "international image of gang violence and poverty." Supporters specifically cited media and filmmakers as key players in utilizing the name change.[11d]

Scene 1 Take 2

After thwarting the surprise ambush in her apartment, Jane hurriedly gets into her car and drives off. Jane is next seen frantically adjusting her rear view mirror to see how close the bad guys are.

WHAT DO YOU THINK?

Do you think the power of movie images are inconsequential? Then consider these statements from Jack Valenti, former President of the MPAA, who viewed the primary task of the MPAA Ratings System (i.e., G, PG, PG-13, R, NC-17 and X) as providing "advance information about movies so that parents can decide what movies they want their children to see or not to see."[11e]

If parents know that movies are fictional, then why does the MPAA Ratings System exist to warn parents and protect children from certain images that they might see? Does the rationale supporting the ratings system implicitly acknowledge that movie images bear some actual impact on a child and their possible development and/or formation? If violent and/or sexual images may be deemed harmful and influential, then can the same not be said for disparaging images and stereotypes of minorities?

A study conducted by Children Now in 1998 entitled, "A Different World: Children's Perceptions of Race and Class in Media," supports that conclusion.[11f] Their research found that children associate White characters with various attributes: having lots of money, being well educated, being a leader, doing well in school, and being intelligent. Conversely, they associate minority characters with breaking the law, having a hard time financially, being lazy and acting foolish. Is the same type of influence possible for adults? What happens when the influenced children in this article grow up?

Consider these remarks from former President Bill Clinton: "We had a very good discussion, and I want to thank NATO President, Bill Kartozian, and his colleagues who are here with him, for the efforts they are making to make sure that we work together to prevent youth violence, and the ways the theater industry, in particular, can help in that cause."[11g] Do you believe that Hollywood impacts youth violence the way Clinton suggested?

Violence, sex and profanity in American movies increased significantly between 1992 and 2003, while ratings became more lenient, according to a Harvard University study. The research concluded that, "Parents must recognize their responsibility in choosing appropriate films with and for their children, and in discussing the messages in films with children to mediate any potential adverse effects and reinforce any potential beneficial effects."[11h]

Through the combination of editing and a variety of cinematic techniques, a three-minute scene can be communicated in less than thirty seconds. Chances are that your typical Hollywood director is going to choose *Scene 1, Take 2* over *Scene 1, Take 1* as the most efficient means of communicating the intended message. As realistic as the full sequence of events might be, when a director must communicate a long series of events within a short period of time, the edited version may be the most effective method of conveying the action. As simple as this sounds, many decisions are involved. The director must first decide which raw footage to shoot, which subjects to focus on, and from which angle. Then, the footage must be edited, a process that can involve everyone from the director and the editor to the producers and the studio executives, all in an effort to make the final cut.

The world of a mainstream movie is a **controlled universe**, and if the director loses control of the captured image, then the director loses control of the intended message. Suppose a director wishes to film two actors holding a conversation while walking down a busy New York street. What if someone were to obstruct the camera at precisely the moment when the director wanted a close-up? What if two passerbys randomly got into a fight during filming? Even worse, what if a crowd started to form behind the actors and stare at the production while they continued to act out their "natural" scene? Though the director could risk setting up a camera in the middle of an actual city street during a busy day, there is no guarantee that anyone besides the hired actors would behave exactly the way the director wished. Thus, what appears to the viewer to be a rather innocuous scene is actually the product of a lot of thought and planning by a lot of different people focused on achieving a certain "natural effect," even if such a scene lasts for only a few seconds.[3]

When the movie's creators successfully manipulate the controlled universe, they create a movie that appears to be as "natural" and believable as possible. Consider the grassroots buzz generated by ***The Blair Witch Project***, a wildly successful indie-crossover that had people canvas the state of Maryland town just to research this "real" witch that was completely fabricated.[4] Another example is the controversy over the website created in anticipation of the theater release of ***Godsend***, a movie about the controversial topic of human cloning.[5] Studios realize that the movie-watching experience is heightened when audiences are drawn into the believable storyline and characters, and do not spend time questioning the largely artificial and premeditated means utilized to facilitate the storyline.

---

controlled universe

a secured setting whereby the movie's creators are able to manipulate all objects and persons depicted on film to create a particular image captured onscreen

---

TOTAL ANECDOTAL

Many "spontaneous" actions in movies are actually quite controlled and premeditated. For instance, Sharon Stone refers to herself and Michael Douglas as the "horizontal Ginger Rogers and Fred Astaire." Stone is referring to the heavy amount of choreography involved in her well-known love scenes with Douglas in ***Basic Instinct***.[11i]

Some websites, such as *www.moviecliches.com*, point out the humor in common movie conventions that have become clichés as a result of their repeated use throughout mainstream movies over the years. By and large, these "clichés" are calculated "shortcuts" that allow filmmakers to convey a general point without having to interrupt the pacing of the storyline to do so. *In recognizing the strength of the visual image*, studios constantly make decisions about which images are most important to communicate. So what exactly does Hollywood choose to communicate about race?

I SEE WHITE PEOPLE

For those who openly question all the fuss about racial representation in mainstream movies, consider the interview with Hollywood producer Arnon Milchan (**Pretty Woman, Fight Club, Mr. & Mrs. Smith**) in Harvard history professor Henry Louis Gates' documentary series entitled *Beyond the Color Line*.[6] In the interview, Milchan candidly explained that a movie with two White stars gets greenlighted because it brings in double the box office take of a movie starring two Black stars. Milchan also suggested that the "girl next door" would likely opt to see two White stars in a movie before she wanted to see two Black stars.

Supposing that Milchan is correct, perhaps his comments are explained by the identification process. When the main stars more closely resemble the members of the majority audience – which is predominately

BUT IT'S JUST A MOVIE, RIGHT?
Movie studios often spare no expense in their efforts to make their fantasy tales appear as "real" as possible. For instance, Hollywood has always relied on the U.S. military for assistance (including access to tanks, aircraft carriers, helicopters and troops) that would be too expensive to recreate. In return for offering access and equipment, the Pentagon gets to approve the script to ensure the military is portrayed in a positive light.

Case in point, in the movie **Stealth**, the film crew was originally denied access to real aircraft carriers since the love story conflicted with the Navy's fraternization policy. Although this rift was eventually smoothed over, it is evidence of how seriously some institutions regard their portrayal in movies, even in a fictional story.

"These days, there is an unwillingness to criticize individual servicemen and women, which was quite common in the Vietnam era," says Phil Strub, who heads the Pentagon's film liaison office. "Americans are very disinclined to do that now, and we're very glad this attitude tends to pervade all entertainment."

This probably explains why the military actually has an "outreach" office in Hollywood. The FBI, CIA, Department of Defense, Office of Homeland Security and NASA all have their own liaison offices as well.

Additionally, since the premise of **Stealth** revolves around a plane that operates on artificial intelligence, producers arranged for an actual full-scale, remote controlled plane landing for the premiere![11j]

> **WHAT DO YOU THINK?**
> When Hollywood movie star Arnold Schwarzenegger ran for the office of California Governor in 2004, he toured the state with coach buses, two of which were called the *Running Man* and *Total Recall*, referencing movies he made bearing the same name.[11k]
>
> By interspersing aspects of his stardom and peppering his speeches with movie lines, how much did this contribute to Schwarzenegger's political advantage (and eventual victory)? How much did his movie career augment his visibility in terms of receiving votes? How much did voters identify with his Hollywood-crafted image? Did voters believe that his power, authority and heroism onscreen were characteristics that he also possessed offscreen?

White – then the movie becomes more appealing to that target market. As a result, White actors are deemed representative of the mainstream perspective. So using that very same logic, how are minority viewers supposed to connect and watch mainstream movies with stars that look nothing like them? Succinctly put, minorities have to adopt a "mainstream" perspective if they wish to enjoy these films.

In accordance with Arnon Milchan's logic, what would have happened if the roles of Tom Cruise and Cuba Gooding, Jr., were reversed in *Jerry Maguire*? Would the movie have been as commercially successful if Jerry Maguire (Tom Cruise) had played the football star, while Rod Tidwell (Cuba Gooding, Jr.), his smart, up-and-coming agent, found love, happiness and financial security? Why? Why not? Oh, and remember that the movie would instead be known as *Rod Tidwell*. Along this vein of role reversals, what if Tom Cruise taught Ken Wantanabe everything he knew in *The Last Green Beret* instead of the other way around in *The Last Samurai*? Or what if Michael Clarke Duncan "begrudgingly" executed Tom Hanks in *The Green Mile* after his gift restored Duncan's health and love life? Better yet, what about Renee Zellweger receiving an Oscar in part for an explicit love scene with Sean "Diddy" Combs in *Monster's Ball*? These role reversals likely feel "strange" to most moviegoers, even though most audience members do not even blink when they see and identify with the same scenarios in favor of White characters.

Most White moviegoers never have to "deal with" the concept of race in mainstream movies because most minorities have marginal roles and do not dominate the pace and action. If a movie *is* dominated by minority actors and themes, White audience members still have a wide variety of *other* movies to choose from. Since the inception of the mainstream movie business, there has not been a single day when a White moviegoer could not go to a mainstream theater and see a movie starring White characters. The opposite does not hold true for minority moviegoers.

Whites may tend not to think "in racial terms" because of a steady diet over time of **color-blind movies** containing White worlds and a miniscule or non-existent minority presence. Mainstream movies showcasing virtually all White actors have created a standard of Whiteness that moviegoers have come to expect. For example, who can argue that the second-highest grossing movie of all time, *Titanic*, is not a breathtaking romance story for all audiences? *Titanic* enjoys widespread appeal due to its general themes of youthful love and perseverance that resonate with so many movie patrons. Yet, *Titanic*

color-blind movie

a movie with an almost exclusively White cast and a miniscule or non-existent minority presence; although presented as "universal,"

"universal" or applicable to all races, the movie merely focuses on Whites and their experiences

YOU MEAN, THERE'S RACE IN MY MOVIE?

enjoys this broad appeal in spite of the fact that virtually every character in the movie is White.[7] Notwithstanding its "historically accurate" depiction of Atlantic passenger travel at the time, ironically the record-breaking success of **Titanic** is due in part to the financial patronage by plenty of non-White people around the world who saw the movie.

Hollywood, in search of maximum profits, caters to the large population of White moviegoers, further decreasing the need for Whites to "segment" their identity within minority-dominated movies. Are White audience members to blame if they identify more readily with movies that feature majority White casts? Are movie studios to blame if they tailor the majority of their movies to the majority White audience? If the answer to both questions is "No," then in the process of producing movies for predominately White mainstream audiences, is it necessary to marginalize minorities in the process?

If the answer to this last question is "No," then who shall be held accountable for the consistent pattern of minority marginalization that exists and how? This last question speaks to the **cycle of blamelessness** that has confounded minority groups for decades, for Hollywood, as a collective entity, provides very few overt clues to its racialized thinking. However, a lack of indisputably racist intentions does not necessarily mean there is no evidence of racial harm. Plainly put, *racist intent is not a necessary prerequisite for perpetuating the marginalizing minority archetypes.* Moreover, Whites' preference for Whites can still yield situations that do not allow for equal opportunity among all actors.

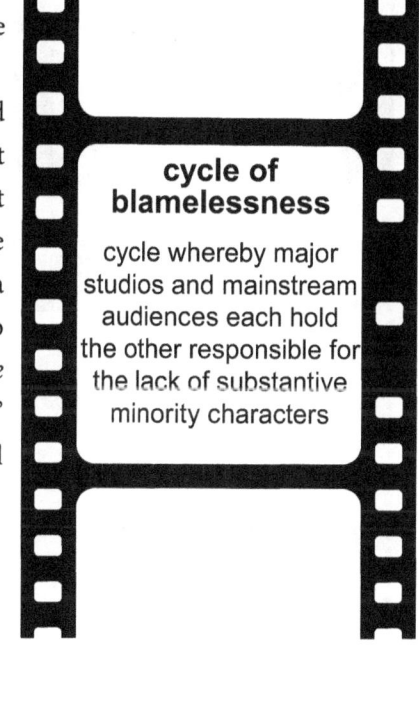

cycle of blamelessness

cycle whereby major studios and mainstream audiences each hold the other responsible for the lack of substantive minority characters

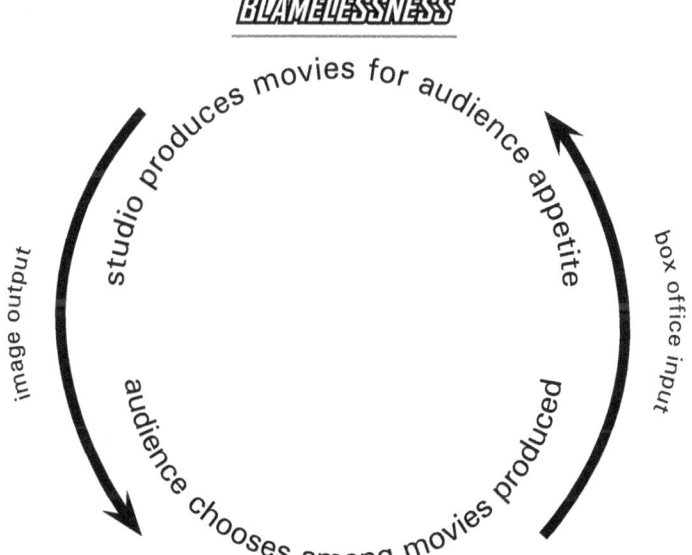

tipping point
the imprecise number where "too many" minorities involved in a movie brands it as a "minority movie," thereby curtailing its budget and "universal" appeal

Although there is no evidence of an organized effort to freeze out minorities from Hollywood, when "given the chance" to participate in mainstream movies, minorities are often restricted from the full participation experienced by their White counterparts. Statistical evidence points to the rise of *physical* participation by minority actors, meaning, the ability to count bodies on a movie set. However, closer analysis reveals that the typical minority character is largely a non-factor. The reflexive, if not unconscious, manner in which minorities are marginalized and limited onscreen (and perhaps offscreen as well) serves as the true source of concern, for their collective status amounts to that of second-class citizenry that is accepted without much fanfare or critical scrutiny. Since the entire environment is permissive of such minority depictions, it is plausible that individual screenwriters, directors, actors and studio executives are not intentionally carrying out racist agendas. They are simply going along with the systematic "formula" that Hollywood follows in order to successfully create mainstream movies, a formula that places Whites at the center and excludes minorities to the margins.

NO WHITE CRIME

In real estate, the **tipping point** refers to the imprecise percentage of minorities who can move into a predominately White neighborhood before Whites start to move out. This phenomenon parallels the attitudes of movie studios and audiences alike that begin to view a movies as less desirable in proportion to the number of minorities it has in key, leading roles. It is important to note that this negative branding not only occurs by audience members that fail to patronize such movies in the theater, but also by movie studios who trim production and marketing budgets due to "internal" valuations long before these movies are ever presented to the audience.

If a studio produces a movie and stacks it with "too many" minority actors, the risk is that audience members will see and brand the movie as a "minority-movie" aimed as *primarily*

WHAT DO YOU THINK?

Paramount Pictures produced and released *World Trade Center*, a movie directed by Oliver Stone directed movie about the September 11 terrorist attacks. The movie is about two policemen who survive the collapse of the World Trade Center buildings, with Nicolas Cage starring as one of the policemen.

To show sensitivity to the families of the victims from the actual event, an Associated Press story entitled "Stone Begins Shooting 9/11 Movie in N.Y." details how Paramount studios hired Jennifer Brown, a "former vice president for community development at the Lower Manhattan Development Corp.," to act as a liaison with the victim community. In fact, Brown set up and facilitated more than a dozen meetings "with business, community, family and survivor groups, along with police and fire officials." Brown also said that people grew very supportive once they understood that the story Paramount was telling was specifically about the officers and not about the entire story of September 11. "What we've heard mostly, is just to be real," she said.[11]

Why would survivor groups be concerned about "unrealistic" portrayals in the movie? Does the movie studio have a responsibility to be sensitive and responsive to how onscreen imagery might affect its potential audience? If so, how would this "responsibility" change the way studios portray minorities?

YOU MEAN, THERE'S RACE IN MY MOVIE?

for minorities. As a consequence, the studios calculate that they will not stand to make as much money off of these movies as opposed to those movies that rely on more "traditional" mainstream formulas. When A-list minority stars like Denzel Washington and Will Smith are cast in protagonist roles, they are usually surrounded by key White characters to allay the effects of the tipping point (e.g., *The Bone Collector, Hitch, I, Robot, Independence Day, Inside Man, Legend of Bagger Vance, Man on Fire, Manchurian Candidate, Shark Tale, Training Day, Wild Wild West*, etc.). Otherwise, studio executives run the risk of investing hundreds of millions of dollars into a movie that White moviegoers of the "general" audience may not pay to see, since they may think that the movie will not apply to them. Since most minority characters and minority movie stars fit consistently within the archetypes, they are generally not regarded as "universal" as it pertains to Hollywood movies. As such, the rationale behind the tipping point becomes a self-fulfilling prophecy in the minds of many Whites (and others). Yet, given the cycle of blamelessness, there is no convenient target to blame.

>
> **LIGHTS! CAMERA! INTERACTION!**
> Perhaps as evidence of movie studios not wanting to transgress the tipping point, high-profile mainstream movies such as **Inside Man** (Denzel Washington), **I, Robot** (Will Smith), **Around the World in 80 Days** (Jackie Chan), **X-Men** (Halle Berry), and **Wild Hogs** (Martin Lawrence) all feature an A-list minority character that is racially isolated amongst all White co-stars. None of these movies contain any other A-list minority leads and the minority star has virtually no familial or romantic ties to other characters of the same race.
>
> Can you think of a movie where a White A-list actor was racially isolated with A-list minority characters (e.g., Ben Stiller stars alongside Will Smith, Denzel Washington and Don Cheadle)?
>
> If you can think of such a movie, is the White character devoid of romantic and/or familial relationships with other Whites?

A movie can contain universal themes and still contain a majority of minority actors. However, the tipping point discourages Whites from watching the movie due to the effort required to make the connective switch. This reasoning begs the question, what specifically makes color-blind movies so "universal"? How can movies containing little to no minorities apply "to all audiences"? How come movies containing elevated levels of minority actors suffer from more limited production budgets and marketing efforts despite the presence of universal themes? It appears as if studios make a conscious decisions regarding racial matters, which is contrary to the notion that the studios "unwittingly" carry out racialized strategies. Studios deliberately devise marketing plans that take into consideration how to market a movie like *Brown Sugar* as a "Black movie" while marketing a movie with White leads like *You, Me and Dupree* as enjoyable comedy for *all* audiences.

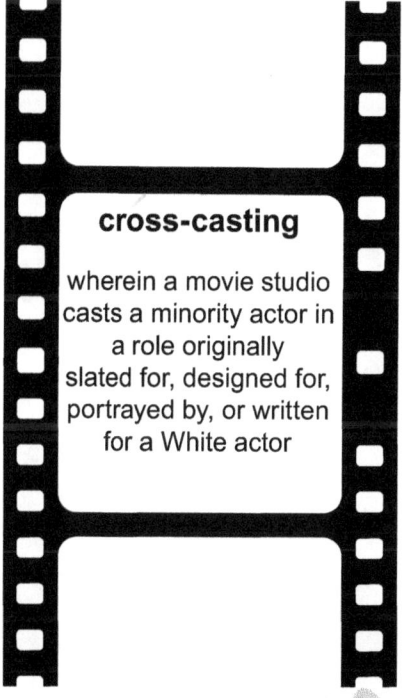

cross-casting

wherein a movie studio casts a minority actor in a role originally slated for, designed for, portrayed by, or written for a White actor

Some studios, as a means of breaking these casting boundaries, have engaged in **cross-casting.** Cross-casting is where a studio casts a minority in a movie role originally designed for or occupied by a White actor. Often seen as markers of progress, remakes like *The Nutty Professor, Guess Who, Doctor Dolittle* and *The Honeymooners* feature minority characters in leading roles once occupied and made popular by White characters. In deciding to create a remake, the studios first minimized their risk by choosing projects that were previously proven to be both popular and profitable. Secondly, the aforementioned examples all shared in common the genre classification of *comedy*, further minimizing the studios' risk by not presenting a product that would not demand a large connective switch by its mainstream audience.

Critics point out that it is no coincidence that the majority of this cross-casting comes from remakes and sequels, "which are less risky and typically less imaginative" for studios to produce.[8] For instance, *The Hollywood Reporter* opined that in **King's Ransom**, Anthony Anderson plays "the sort of arrogant businessman who, in a demonstration of how far racial equality has come, has in the past generally been played by elderly Caucasians."[9]

Hollywood is a movie *business* and not a movie *service*. Movie studios, seeking to minimize risk and maximize profits, cater to majority White audiences. In spite of the industry's apparent racial progress, your run-of-the-mill Hollywood mainstream movie will still more than likely be written by Whites, directed by Whites, produced by Whites and feature mostly White characters. Consequently, heavy minority involvement and participation does not comport with the familiar business models studios employ when looking for the next blockbuster hit. However, the reality is that not all movies featuring Whites are guaranteed to be financially successful. In fact, a significant percentage of movies starring Whites fail every year. This means that implicitly there is even greater pressure on the "minority-themed" movie to succeed, even though normal business procedure at most studios allows for an expected amount of failed movie projects!

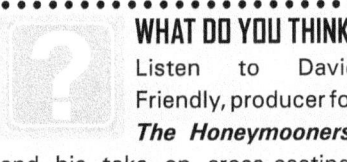

WHAT DO YOU THINK?
Listen to David Friendly, producer for *The Honeymooners*, and his take on cross-casting: "It wasn't calculated enough to say, 'Let's do *The Honeymooners* black and let's write it for African Americans.' If that had been the case, the dialogue would have been blacker."[11m]

What do you think Friendly meant by the word "blacker"?

TESTING, TESTING, 1,2,3

When studios create and distribute a movie, they are often acutely aware of how their intended audience will perceive the movie and accordingly seek to manipulate this perspective to their advantage. Studios often have privately held test screenings for select audiences before a movie's official release to determine whether to modify the product or the movie's marketing strategy.[10] These screenings are not just intended to find out if people like or dislike the movie, but also to find out audience attitudes towards particular characters, plot devices and scenes. These screenings also help studios determine potential audience demographics. Ideally, a movie is able to maximize its profitability when it is able to have its target audience identify fully with the characters and the overall storyline.

In today's age, Hollywood's mainstream movies are more about entertainment than art. Studios make practical business decisions are made about the quality and type of entertainment produced for public consumption. While mainstream entertainment may have some artistic value that challenges the status quo, for the most part, formulaic conventions will always prevail. By the movie's end, moviegoers exit the theater relieved that the status quo has been honored, that the world has been saved, that justice has prevailed and that our Hero "got the girl" at the end.

As we have already discussed, the mainstream movie business is a significant business indeed. Movies accounted for $9.5 billion in worldwide box office sales in 2004.[11] The lucrative nature of the movie business is even more staggering when factoring in additional revenue streams such DVD/VHS sales and rentals, soundtracks, licensed merchandise, endorsement deals, and video game spinoffs, just to name a few. Since movies produced in Hollywood are shown in more than 150 countries worldwide, suffice to say the United States film industry provides the majority of movies seen in millions of homes throughout the world.[12] American mainstream movies enjoy unparalleled exposure throughout the nation and the world over.

BUT IT'S JUST A MOVIE, RIGHT?

Consider the following decisions made by movie studios before the release of a movie.[11n]

Collateral Damage, a movie about a firefighter (Arnold Schwarzenegger) who searches out those responsible for a terrorist bombing that killed his family, was originally set to be released in October 2001. Instead, the release was pushed back four months to February 2002. Warner Bros. Pictures delayed the release out of sensitivity for the horrific terrorist attacks that decimated the World Trade Center in New York and damaged the Pentagon in Washington, D.C., on September 11, 2001. Columbia Pictures also pulled certain ***Spider-Man*** marketing materials, including movie trailers and posters, featuring the World Trade Center's Twin Towers.

Swordfish was withdrawn from cinemas shortly after the terrorist attacks on New York City and Washington, D.C., on September 11, 2001, due to a scene involving an exploding building. Blockbuster, the nation's largest video rental chain, affixed stickers to ***Swordfish*** boxes stating, "In light of the acts of terrorism on September 11, 2001, please be advised that this product contains scenes that may be considered disturbing to some viewers."

In 1992, riots broke out in the wake of the acquittal of four Los Angeles Police officers accused of using excessive force against Black motorist Rodney King. Universal Pictures not only changed the title of the movie ***Looters*** to ***Trespass***, but they also used a different marketing strategy. In order to distance the movie from negative associations linked to the riots, the release date was pushed back from the summer of 1992 to later in the year.

These decisions communicate Hollywood studios' belief that audience sentiment will adversely impact the movie's performance at the box office. *What else do these decisions communicate about studio perceptions of disparaging minority images? Do studios continue to adhere to the HARM theory only because paying audiences have not voiced any displeasure? Do studios even expressly contemplate any negative repercussions upon minority audiences when making movies that appeal to the greatest possible audience?*

With this unparalleled exposure comes unparalleled influence for mainstream movies. Given the high-risk investment opportunity that mainstream movies present, there is a great deal of care and planning invested into each and every one of them, even for those that are "bad" or commercially unsuccessful. A lot of time, energy and thought goes into how a movie's images are portrayed and what feelings they will evoke if properly depicted. Taking into consideration the practical financial influences and pressures involved with producing and distributing a mainstream movie, hundreds of employees often dedicate thousands of hours towards creating the exact and precise movie images most likely to contribute to the movie's commercial success.

Mainstream movies are seen by millions of people with the potential of making hundreds of millions of dollars. With this in mind, how much can actually be left to chance and happenstance? Nothing. It is not enough for the moviegoer to dismiss the fleeting presence of a minority as insignificant simply because the character's *performance* was insignificant. In the larger context, the attentive moviegoer must understand that the movie's director is attempting to communicate a message, and that every scene as arranged contributes to that message. Given the numerous amount of individuals who participate in the process of making a mainstream movie, everything must be meticulously thought out: scenes and camera angles are discussed before they are shot; dialogue is revised; the positioning of the actors is contemplated; and makeup and wardrobe must be planned well in advance. Essentially, nothing that comes out in the final print is an accident when hundreds of millions of dollars are at stake. Since each scene is carefully mapped out, planned and choreographed, any marginalized representation of minorities cannot be dismissed or regarded as mere coincidence.

TOTAL ANECDOTAL

Movie studios pay close attention to the feedback from their potential audiences, oftentimes even before the movie is officially released! In an effort to better protect their overall investment, studios will preview some movies to select audiences to solicit feedback prior to the official release. Based upon the feedback, studios may decide to re-edit or in some cases reshoot scenes completely. For example, according to *www.imdb.com*, the final postscript scene in **The Bourne Supremacy** was shot just weeks before its release in response to preview crowds who thought the original ending was too bleak.

When Paramount made the decision to reshoot certain scenes for **The Stepford Wives**, they regarded the costs as "necessary expenses to protect their investment." Another well-known example involves **Fatal Attraction**, where the original ending had Glenn Close's character commit suicide, but was changed to its present form since many pre-screening audience members wanted to see some form of revenge.[11o]

THE SACRIFICIAL SOFA

Many minority actors, without access to large reserves of racial capital, must individually accumulate personal power in order to choose their roles and shape their Hollywood persona over time. Some actors willingly accept roles under the belief that they are on par with their White counterparts, although such roles often perpetuate the larger pattern of marginalization. Other minority actors – especially those who have yet to establish themselves – often spend time on the **sacrificial sofa**, feeling the pressure to accept a marginal or racially disparaging role, all in hope of getting the opportunity for more roles in the future. This "sacrificing" of the racial image is analogous to the "casting couch" phenomenon in Hollywood, where typically a female actor performed sexual favors in exchange for an "in" to the business.[13] Due to an overall dearth of racial capital in Hollywood, many minority actors find themselves limited to a narrow range of roles that require them to negatively "sacrifice" their minority image.

sacrificial sofa

where an actor feels the need to accept a marginal or racially disparaging role for the opportunity for more lucrative and satisfying roles in the future

Generally speaking, minority actors who *do* recognize that their role is compromised rationalize their acceptance using two primary justifications: the *short-term benefit* and the *long-term benefit*. The short-term benefit recognizes the social cost of playing a role potentially harmful to the individual's image, but proceeds on the basis that the role will at least be financially beneficial to the individual. Market forces dictate that the number of actors is greater than the number of available roles, and the number of roles available to minority actors is even smaller. Some actor will eventually benefit financially from the compromised role, so it might as well be them. After all, actors must *act* in order to pay their bills.

The long-term benefit rationale also recognizes the social cost of a compromised role, but justifies the role as part of a long-term plan. In order to gain experience, exposure, contacts, etc., the actor accepts the role so as to position themselves better for a more improved image in the future. One could make the argument that Jamie Foxx' career is an example of one who, over time, improved his image with each new project. He went from cross-dressing as an ignorant woman named Wanda on the television variety show *In Living Color*, to having his own sitcom, *The Jamie Foxx Show*. He then started netting significant roles in mainstream movies, such as **Any Given Sunday** and **Ali**. In 2004, Jamie Foxx played Ray Charles in the biographical epic **Ray**, a role for which Foxx claimed the Academy Award for Best Actor. This award is widely regarded as the highest honor an actor can receive in the profession.

Due to the overall lack of control and investment that minorities claim within Hollywood, the pervading fear is that by refusing a role – no matter how unflattering – another opportunity may not come again. One could easily argue that many White actors must endure similar decision-making processes. However, with the larger amount of racial capital at their disposal, White actors have a much greater chance for upside gain given the wide range and volume of roles available to them. For those minority actors who take the larger political import of their role into consideration, sometimes the reality of the situation dictates that principles are nice, but profits are nicer.

While minority actors are now more prevalent in a wide range of mainstream movies, the HARM theory still limits how favorably they are portrayed. For example, compare how Black and White women were portrayed in the top movies of 1996 according to research by Robert M. Entman and Andrew Rojecki in their book, *The Black Image in the White Mind*.[14] The authors charted behavior of Black and White female behavior patterns with respect to using profanity, being physically violent and being restrained. Granted, there is nothing inherently discriminatory or racist about a minority character using profanity. However, given the sparse number of roles for Black women within mainstream movies, the fact that nearly nine out of every ten Black female characters (in contrast to only 17% of all White female characters) used some type of vulgar language in expressing themselves magnifies the overall disparaging effect according to the premium of proportion theory. The juxtaposition between minority archetypes and White prototypes remains stark indeed:

BLACK AND WHITE FEMALE PORTRAYALS IN THE TOP GROSSING MOVIES OF 1996		
DESCRIPTION OF BEHAVIOR	WHITE FEMALES (% of racial group)	BLACK FEMALES (% of racial group)
shown using vulgar profanity	17%	89%
shown being physically violent	11%	56%
shown being restrained	6%	55%

Source: *The Black Image in the White Mind*

It is conceivable that none of the individual directors who made a movie in 1996 featuring a Black woman were being intentionally racist by having her use a profane word or two. The character may have called for it. The scenario may have required it. The script may have been modified by unnamed studio executives. Whatever the case, although you may find an alarming disparity in the use of profane language, it is unlikely that you will find an inflammatory memorandum circulating in Hollywood outlining a larger plan to make Black women look "less refined" than White women through more frequent displays of physical violence and restraint holds.

Consider the role of Vernita Green played by Vivica A. Fox in ***Kill Bill: Vol. 1***. Although her character appears onscreen for a total of less than eight minutes in the entire movie, Green utters at least fifteen profanities within that time (with such dialogue interrupted by a lengthy and *violent* fight scene with Uma Thurman's character). Taken individually, this "vulgar" role from ***Kill Bill: Vol. 1*** might not be particularly noteworthy. Nevertheless, when viewed in the aggregate with other similarly profane roles fulfilled by Black actresses, we begin to recognize a subtle yet consistent representation of Black women as a group (note that ***Kill Bill: Vol. 1*** was released not in 1996, but in 2003).

The aforementioned statistical numbers strongly suggest that Black female characters are depicted less favorably than their White counterparts. Here, the premium of proportion dynamic is relevant, for the Black characters most likely have significantly less screen time than their White counterparts (a la Vivica Fox as compared to Uma Thurman), presenting viewers with a more compressed window with which to see an "alternate" view of these characters. Also note that the "Black and White Female Portrayals in the Top Grossing Movies of 1996" chart does not take into account other "undesirable" qualities, such as being unattractive, overweight, or holding an "undesirable" profession such as a stripper or a prostitute. Since most moviegoers do not compile statistical data of this nature, such a pattern is likely to go unnoticed and remain "invisible" to the eye on an

WHAT DO YOU THINK?

What does the data in the *Black and White Female Portrayals in the Top Grossing Movies of 1996* chart (pg. 212) suggest about the quality and type of roles available for Black women? Is there any obligation on behalf of the movie studios to even out these percentages? If not, what will be the residual effect upon audience members if these ratios continue unabated? Does this vulgarity inform current aesthetic portrayals of Black women?

Take the scenario of a Black woman who has packed up all of her possessions and moved out to Hollywood in hopes of fulfilling her dream of becoming an actress. She becomes the proverbial "starving actress" who waits tables at night while searching for her big break during the day. After months of unsuccessful auditions, her phone finally rings.

If she is offered a role, does she reject a supporting role that requires her to use a high rate of vulgarity and act physically violent just because it goes against her principles? What are her practical financial pressures in accepting a role that she does not like? If she wishes to turn down the role, what about the fact that word may get around that "she is difficult to work with," thereby jeopardizing the possibility of her receiving future callbacks? Further, how does she discern the difference between a racially marginalizing role and a role that simply requires her to play a character that the audience is "not supposed to like." After all, she is an actress, so the expectation is that she should be able to play a range of roles, some of which may be positive and some of which may be negative.

Have roles for Black women in mainstream movies changed significantly since 1996?

CHAPTER 11: AT A THEATER NEAR YOU

isolated level without taking on a larger, institutional dimension. Thus, in merely accepting a movie role, many a Black female may have spent time on the sacrificial sofa without even realizing it.

JUST PLAYING MY PART

Granted, not every minority actor must seek out and accept roles that "glorify" their race. Take **Soul Plane** for instance. Not every minority in the country supported the movie, nor did the movie perform terribly well at the box office. Still, the modest public display of support for **Soul Plane** is somewhat surprising since the movie contained many references and gags that played upon age-old stereotypes, many of which have been notoriously contentious and sensitive topics in American race relations. For example, when serving the in-flight meal, a flight attendant hands out individual pieces of fried chicken to customers in their seats directly out of a *Popeyes Chicken & Biscuits* box, while in another scene, a White woman becomes sexually aroused when she sees a Black male on a magazine cover whose penis is seen bulging underneath his shorts at the mid-point of his thigh.

Perhaps some of the actors were not *directly* endorsing the stereotyping, but were merely endorsing a "take-what-you-can-get-and-be-thankful" philosophy (note D.L. Hughley's quote on pg. 104). Yet, with so little existing work for minority actors in Hollywood, those actively looking for an opportunity to work are likely to take full advantage of any available acting gig that presents itself to gain exposure and "further" their career. This thinking *seems* quite rational and logical, yet it is inherently flawed.

An overall paucity of minority-populated mainstream movies skews the audience's attitude towards these films. When a mainstream movie featuring minorities is released, many minorities feel obligated to support the movie – regardless of content or quality – in recognition of the fact that such movies are released infrequently. The resulting hunger for alternate images produces a "chilling effect," whereby minorities – both inside *and* outside of the industry – may be slower to critically analyze the substance

CUT!

OK! So why would a minority actor willingly accept a role that makes him look "bad," especially when no one is forcing him to take the role? Theoretically, the premium of proportion theory should encourage more conservatism in role selection from groups with small amounts of racial capital in Hollywood. A minority whose racial group has infrequent participation within mainstream movies should be more selective about accepting a marginalized role. However, the overall limited availability of roles for minorities tends to increase the pressure for minority actors during the process of deciding whether to accept or reject a role.

Once an actor has a role and is on the movie's payroll, if approached to deliver a line or told to act out a scene he deems racially insensitive or personally objectionable, the actor has limited options. If the actor protests, the producers can just as easily find someone else who is willing to play the part (see *But, It's Just a Movie, Right?* on pg. 159).

More significant is that fewer of the "problematic" roles in contemporary movies are inherently "demeaning" in the way that most people look for overtly racist imagery. This is what makes continued analysis of minority archetypes so compelling and so pervasive: larger patterns of marginalization are often difficult for the individual actor to recognize. Such patterns usually cannot be appreciated until seemingly racially innocuous roles are viewed collectively for their overall impact and significance within mainstream cinema and society.

of such images and may actually defend the movie's ability to denigrate minority images without advocating for the creation and production of more redeeming ones.

It is safe to say that the average minority actor does not pursue a lifelong passion for acting in hopes of playing a drug addict, criminal, maid or passerby when finally afforded that ever-elusive chance. To avoid this negative typecasting, many minorities readily accept archetypal roles that do not individually qualify as stereotypes, but nonetheless preserve a larger pattern of marginalization.

With the corresponding reality of *offscreen* disfranchisement for many minorities,[15] perhaps it is not surprising to see so many minority actors lining up to portray roles that are unflattering. Due to the decision-making inequities that persist, many minorities are reluctant to speak out about these roles out of fear of the consequences of not receiving any additional acting opportunities *at all*, let alone unflattering ones.

TO CATCH AN AUDIENCE

Marketing a movie is just as important as making a movie, so a studio must pay detailed attention to a movie's **umbrella image**, the defining visual rendering indelibly associated with the movie's central theme. When wrapping up any major movie production, specific **key art**, ranging from standard movie posters to online ads, is commissioned in order to encapsulate the entire feeling of a movie in only a few seconds worth of viewing. Not only must the umbrella image communicate the feeling associated with the storyline, but it must also stimulate the viewer to be intrigued, reminded or inspired to see the movie. Key art is instrumental in communicating this message of the movie in succinct fashion, frequently relying on the movie's most provocative images and showcasing recognizable A-list stars where possible. The careful selection of the proper umbrella image may prove critical in the overall success of the movie.

Given our discussion about the power of image, such analysis is relevant. Walk through the following scenario to see if you have had a similar experience. You enter the video rental store with several movies in mind that you would like to see. Unable to find anything, you start randomly browsing the aisles, looking for box covers that catch your eye. You end up choosing a movie that you have never even heard of before, based at least in part upon the movie cover that superficially appeared most interesting or attractive to you. If anything like this has happened to you, then you understand *first-*

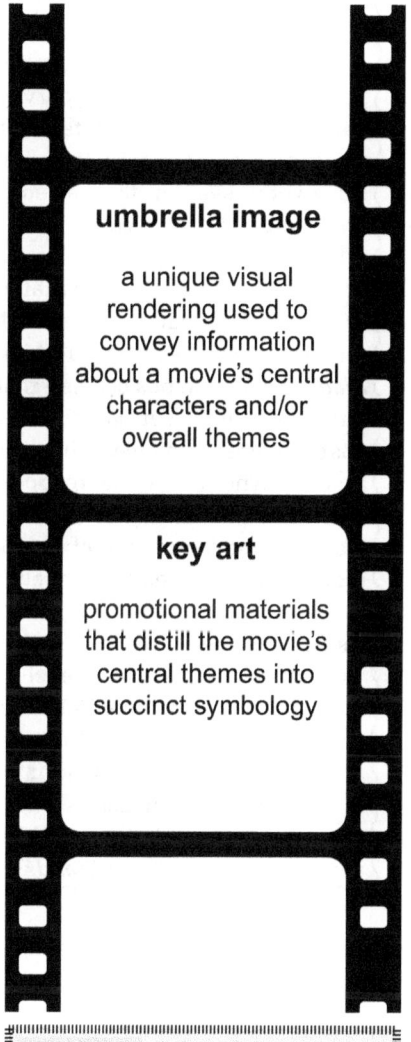

umbrella image

a unique visual rendering used to convey information about a movie's central characters and/or overall themes

key art

promotional materials that distill the movie's central themes into succinct symbology

TOTAL ANECDOTAL
The Hollywood Reporter Key Art Awards have been taking place since 1972.[11p] Awards are given out to the professional community responsible for the best movie advertising campaigns and advertising art.

CUT!

But c'mon! You can't possibly be talking about a mass conspiracy here. Hollywood studios make movies independent from one another. Their decisions are influenced primarily by the market, not by social movements. So what is your hang up? We agree that there is probably no official conspiracy in place. Ironically, chasing conspiracy theories only further clouds the issue, since that misleads people to believe that the pervading problems are perpetuated by a select few. There is a pattern of minority marginalization entrenched in the Hollywood system that affects minorities both onscreen and offscreen.

This feeling is probably what prompted Wesley Snipes to file a lawsuit against New Line Cinema for reportedly failing to pay him his full salary in *Blade: Trinity*. Snipes claimed that the studio's true intention was to set up spinoffs for other (White) cast members, movies that would not include Snipes, who is largely responsible for creating the Blade franchise. Snipes felt that this "covert" plan resulted in, among other creative restrictions, reduced screen time for himself in his own movie.

Oscar winner Halle Berry also had a "misunderstanding" about receiving less screen time than she expected in the *X-Men* series, even though she shared the screen with "less bankable" White actors. Berry created a minor storm by threatening to leave the project unless she was assured of a more prominent role in the third installment of the series, *X-Men: The Last Stand*.[11q]

hand how important movie art is in encapsulating and communicating the image of the movie.

Not only does the movie's key art reinforce an important theme or symbol, but it can also serve as the selling point for a movie previously unknown to potential viewers. Key art is far more than the mere musings of a few graphic artists. Key art is an involved thought process that involves marketing executives, movie producers, entertainment lawyers and a litany of other specialists. As key art signals potential consumers about the leading characters and the possible avenues of heroism that they might pursue, it may also signal exactly who *will not* be prominently featured and who will play a less significant role in the movie.

Are movie posters really that important? Maybe you and I take them for granted, but perhaps that is because you and I are not entertainment lawyers. Movie stars frequently negotiate set ratios by which their image will appear in key art via "equal size and likeness" clauses. For instance, Tom Cruise's contracts often call for him to be the lone actor in key art for any movie in which he has a starring role (check out the key art for movies like **Mission: Impossible**, **The Last Samurai**, **The Minority Report**, etc.). Yet Cruise allowed DreamWorks SKG to drop his face from **Collateral** posters in some urban areas to better focus on co-star Jamie Foxx during its promotional run in the summer of 2004. DreamWorks deliberately split the marketing campaign despite plans to show the same movie to both "urban" and mainstream audiences alike.[16]

If race influenced the marketing campaign of **Collateral**, then what other marketing campaigns might be influenced by race and how? If the plan for **Collateral** suggested that Foxx was more marketable to "urban audiences," then can we also infer that the studio viewed him as *less* marketable in "mainstream," predominately White markets? Recall that **Collateral** preceded his Academy Award winning performance in **Ray**, which elevated his star status.

Key art is instrumental in both creating and confirming consumer expectations. Case in point, original key art for **Get Rich or Die Tryin'** depicted rap artist 50 Cent with his thoroughly tattooed back to the viewer, seen holding an infant child while simultaneously brandishing a firearm. *Get Rich or Die Tryin'* was a "Black movie" in an urban setting, telling the redemptive tale of "survival on the streets" based upon the true story of former-drug-dealer-and-gunshot-victim-turned-multi-platinum-selling-rap-artist, 50 Cent. The original key art was designed to create expectations of violence associated with the treacherous world of urban living. The studio modified its key art promoting the movie after protests from civil rights and watchdog organizations both domestically and abroad.[17]

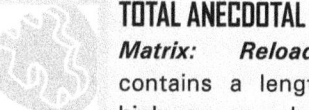

TOTAL ANECDOTAL
Matrix: Reloaded contains a lengthy highway chase scene that took three months to shoot. Instead of backing up real traffic for filming, a 1.4 mile highway model was constructed on the Alameda Point Naval Base. This highway illustrates the expense and the length that studios will go to in order to achieve a certain visual effect, if only for a few moments of usable footage.[11r]

FINANCING FANTASY

Well, if minorities fight an uphill battle against marginalization within traditional mainstream circles, the question remains, how come more minorities do not write "better" screenplays and make more movies if they are genuinely dissatisfied with the current crop of movies that Hollywood produces? The short answer is that in addition to significant racial capital, many Whites enjoy unparalleled access and opportunity to economic and social capital when making movies in their image. Conversely, many minority filmmakers remain burdened by more limited resources, which in turn tangibly affects the bounds of imagination that they can test during the course of making a movie. This is the principle of **finite fantasy**. The finite fantasy concept makes the process of simply making "better movies" more of a challenge than people may think.

This finite fantasy phenomenon can most likely be explained as a convergence of several factors: 1) due to the lack of images and alternatives, many minority filmmakers start with "what they know," which may consist of very practical and cathartic expressions of "reality" to fill existing voids of the minority experience within the public media sphere; 2) studios are not willing to invest the additional cost for a project normally considered harder to sell domestically and internationally; and 3) movie producers and audiences alike may reject such movies ideas for their lack of "realism."

finite fantasy

many mainstream movies spearheaded by minorities are limited in the spectrum of social experiences that they portray due to a limitation of resources

As an illustration of this point, compare the quality and frequency of special effects in mainstream movies with that of independent films or – more to the point – to mainstream movies that do not feature White leads. Most minority-themed mainstream movies deal with more "realistic" human-interest themes that do not test the bounds of natural laws. Such limitations of minority-themed movies may reflect uninspired screenplay writing or may also reflect a lack of the necessary economic muscle by minorities to produce such movies. The resulting effect is that minority characters do not appear to

> **WHAT DO YOU THINK?**
> To successfully create the engaging emotion and feeling that moviegoers experience, movie studios often perform research to base their fictional stories on factual occurrences, if only to improve the believability of their fictional stories.
>
> As part of the pre-production process, the studios often gain access to the objects, people, phenomena and institutions that they wish to emulate in their movies.
>
> Consider Will Ferrell's comments about the filming of the race car comedy *Talladega Nights: The Ballad of Ricky Bobby*: "Once we got NASCAR involved, they provided us with a lot of access." Also see what John Lasseter, director of the animated feature, Cars, had to say about "getting up to speed" on the NASCAR experience: "I got access from the garages and the pits to the owners' boxes and the infield with the campers in Redneck Hill (in the middle of the track between turns one and two)."[11s]
>
> Or consider how about Oscar-winning director Sofia Coppola obtained unprecedented access to areas within the Palace of Versailles that are normally off-limits in filming *Marie Antoinette*![11t]
>
> What do the three above examples say about the *Minority Cycle of Movie-Making* and the ease or difficulty in obtaining access to existing institutions and resources? How does unfettered access improve the quality and marketability of a movie intended for mainstream audiences?
>
> *Can you think of an example where a minority-driven movie was shot and filmed at a historic landmark, or where such a movie was permitted to use an otherwise "off-limits" location or equipment?*

have as many opportunities to explore the bounds of imagination and fantasy, unlike their White counterparts.

The practical nature of the movie-making business is that the studios are willing to spend hundreds of millions dollars for the production of a single movie (e.g., **Waterworld, Titanic, Terminator 3: Rise of the Machines, Troy, Kong, Chronicles of Narnia: The Lion, the Witch and the Wardrobe**, etc.). The Minority Cycle of Movie-Making is such that movies starring minority leads (and supporting casts) are generally regarded as less financially lucrative as movies starring White leads, which in turn justifies less financial support from the movie studios, which ultimately inhibits the movie's potential to become financially lucrative, and thus the cycle continues.

Movie studios, in their attempts to limit their exposure on "riskier" minority projects, often allocate less funding for the production budget, salaries, marketing campaign, special effects and the like, which all ultimately affect the quality of the project's final appearance. The limitation of resources allocated to "riskier" minority-involved projects thereby limits the range of minority images that can be produced. Due to a smaller budget, fantastic elements that are taken for granted in movies featuring mostly Whites may be logistically out of reach for movies produced by minorities featuring primarily minority characters.

Practically speaking, movie studios must literally "buy in" to the principle that empowering minority images are also profitable. It is entirely too easy to place the onus on minorities to just "make their own movies." Such rationale also undermines the point that Hollywood (theoretically) is for all moviegoers to share, regardless of race. Hollywood produces movies that they hope are patronized by the greatest possible audience, which undoubtedly includes minorities. Nevertheless, Hollywood demonstrates a consistent reluctance to employ meaningful, substantive and "universal" minority characters.

Despite a corresponding increase in independent minority productions, the high cost of producing mainstream movies proves a formidable barrier. It is difficult for these newer production companies to compete with established major studios and their $100 million dollar budgets. Such difficulty becomes evident with the type and quality of movie images created during production. Quite simply, less money means less special effects, less scenes shot on location, less highly-

BUT IT'S JUST A MOVIE, RIGHT?

With respect to the ability of Hollywood studios to influence consumer choices, check out the following excerpt from the *Business Week* article entitled "Selling high: Red Stripe beer, The Firm":

Placement can enhance brand value at strategic times. When Tom Cruise visits Gene Hackman in the Cayman Islands [in the movie **The Firm**], Hackman suggests that he "grab a Red Stripe," so Cruise opens the fridge for a bottle of the Jamaican-brewed beer. Within a month of the film's release, Red Stripe sales in the U.S. had increased by more than 50%, and just a few weeks later, company owners sold a majority stake in their brewery for $62 million to Guinness Brewing Worldwide.[11u]

Take a look at some other notable product placements in mainstream movies:

- **E.T.** - Reese's Pieces
- **Jurassic Park** - Ford Explorer
- **Analyze This** - Merrill Lynch
- **Austin Powers** - Heineken Beer
- **Men in Black** - Ray Ban shades
- **The Da Vinci Code** - Volvo
- **Transformers** - General Motors
- **The Sixth Sense** - Zoloft
- **Sahara** - Jeep
- **Back to the Future** - Pizza Hut
- **Home Alone** - Budget Rentals
- **Sideways** - Pinot Noir wines
- **I, Robot** - Converse sneakers
- **Minority Report** - Lexus

Also note that after **Night at the Museum** debuted in theaters, the American Museum of Natural History in New York (the museum which served as the movie's setting) sustained a 20% boost in attendance.[11v]

If major corporations invest significant sums into product placement believing that such visual association will influence consumers to act in their favor, then what about the influential quality of the placement of minority archetypes? Does it not follow that the archetypal behavior of minority characters onscreen also affects attitudes towards minorities offscreen?

---

priced and recognizable actors, less elaborate costumes, less custom-built sets and less money to market the final product. Also note, despite the existence of several minority-owned production companies, a "movie production company" is not synonymous with a "movie studio." Production companies *create* movies, but it takes a movie studio to *market* and *distribute* these movies. This means that minorities are behind both in terms of *production* and *distribution* based on a studio system.

It is uncommon to see minority-owned production companies finance high-priced features germane to mainstream movies. Many minority filmmakers simply lack the social capital enjoyed by major movie studios – social capital amassed over the years that contributes to long-standing and enduring relationships with financiers, distributors, movie theaters and the press alike. Yet, Hollywood is not for Whites only. As the country's population continues to grow more diverse, Hollywood will need to make movies more inclusive of minority imagery if it continues to rely on minority dollars to remain profitable.

BUT IT'S JUST A MOVIE, RIGHT?

Three years before production began for the sci-fi thriller **The Minority Report**, Steven Spielberg assembled a team of sixteen future experts in Santa Monica to brainstorm out the year 2054 for him. This team included Neil Gershenfeld of the Media Lab at MIT; Shaun Jones, director of biomedical research at DARPA (Defense Advanced Research Projects Agency); William Mitchell, dean of the school of architecture at MIT; Peter Calthorpe, the New Urbanism evangelist; and Jaron Lanier, one of the inventors of virtual reality technology.[11w]

IMAGE IS EVERYTHING

Hollywood's ability to touch people's imagination is so strong that even the Central Intelligence Agency (CIA) called Hollywood for a few pointers. Addressing what the September 11 Commission said was one of the main failures of government — imagination — a senior CIA official said that the spy agency was willing to "push beyond the traditional boundaries of intelligence.... We had our terrorism and counternarcotics analysts meet with Hollywood directors, screenwriters and producers. People who are known for developing the summer blockbusters or the hit TV show that often have a terrorism theme."[18]

Why else would politicians on Capitol Hill argue about the influence of movies on American youth and families? The fact that mainstream movies can serve as cultural trendsetters has not been lost on corporate advertisers, who often pay hefty premiums for product placement in mainstream movies. Quite simply, what else can explain the production of cable television specials such as *Party, Politics & Movies* (where U.S. Senators such as Orin Hatch talk about movies influential to them), *What Hollywood Taught Us About Sex*, *Movies That Shook the World*, or *The Science of Superman*.[19] Is it possible that movies can affect our bodies in addition to our minds? Well, a research team from the University of Michigan might have us believe just that, suggesting that hormone levels in both men and women can increase, disposing them to feel more romantic just by watching a movie. Says Oliver Schultheiss, the psychology professor who led the study, "When you're watching movies, your hormones are responding, not just your mind."[20]

Well, what about movies affecting the *body politic* as well? With the release of the unprecedented documentary blockbuster **Fahrenheit 9/11**, it achieved unique status by successfully crossing over into the mainstream spotlight. Once the documentary was injected into the mainstream, questions began to mount around how much influence it would have on mainstream culture and politics. Debates raged among political analysts whether **Fahrenheit 9/11** would actually make a discernible impact at the polls during the November 2004 elections, but the fact that the movie was even included in such *national* conversations hints at the power of widely distributed and disseminated

BUT IT'S JUST A MOVIE, RIGHT?
For another example of how the mainstream press has written about the unwitting effect that movies have had on real-life political matters, see "Politics Creates a Disturbance in the Force."[11x]

In the article, George Lucas defends **Star Wars Episode III: Revenge of the Sith** as an apolitical work, stating that the movie was not an attack on President George W. Bush's administration and foreign policy in Iraq, although some conservatives saw the movie differently.

The point of the matter is not whether the article cited is "factually" correct, but the fact that this article was even composed at all! The production of the article by mainstream media attests to Hollywood's presence and power to influence minds outside of Hollywood.

movies throughout mainstream outlets. In fact, the popularity garnered by director Michael Moore earned him a seat in the Presidential box with former President Jimmy Carter at the Democratic National Convention in July 2004![21]

As further indication of the national prominence of Hollywood movies, consider that the Library of Congress has a national film registry to help preserve movies significant to American culture.[22] Movies matter in the political sphere and Hollywood has maintained relationships with government agencies, such as the military and Congress, to ensure that American principles are not violated or broken in the making of these movies.

The influential nature of movies is often taken for granted, if not underestimated entirely. Movies are clearly influential enough to be monitored by an independent body, the MPAA, and to be directly recruited by the nation's President for assistance to "work together to prevent youth violence" during periods of national crisis.[23] For this reason, Hollywood's **moral compass** is deeply encoded in its mainstream movies. Very rarely does one see a mainstream movie where evil prevails and justice fails. Bad guys are punished and perpetrators receive their comeuppance somehow, almost without exception.

For better or for worse, movies are considered a "social event," even though they largely require almost no physical movement and verbal interaction by the viewer. In the midst of our drudgery, movies can provide an escape. There, in the comfort of your movie theater seat, you can travel to Camelot, or see what battle would be like in space. Movies are also evocative, for what else can explain people crying in theaters, unintended moaning and groaning, laughing out loud, regurgitating, or even jolting in their seats? Studios understand full well that movies are a "low-risk" way for moviegoers to experience fantasy. Mainstream movies can even function as a pseudo-educational mixture of fantasy and truth. **Pararealistic movie** like these are highly influential in that they are commonly used as powerful analogies and teaching tools. These movies combine historical knowledge with the imagination so that the director can "take us there," often serving as a "tangible" representation of historical events, even in spite of historic

---

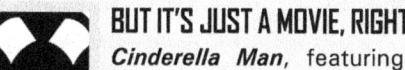

BUT IT'S JUST A MOVIE, RIGHT?

Cinderella Man, featuring Russell Crowe, is about a boxer living through the Depression Era in America. Russell believes the movie serves an instructional purpose: "A really important part of making this film is to remind America that the current abundance they are experiencing is not an absolute right."[11v] But movies are strictly just to entertain, right?

What does Crowe's opinion say about actors viewing their roles as vehicles for political statements? If Crowe's approach is the rule and not the exception, then how should minority actors view and approach their roles?

If Crowe's A-list status and accompanying leading role provide him with a political/social platform, then what effect do marginalizing archetypes have on minority actors?

---

moral compass

the unwritten rule guiding major studios so that they consistently produce mainstream movies communicating the ultimate victory of "good over bad"

pararealistic movie

a mainstream movie crafted or based upon a historical event containing a mixture of hyperbolized or fictional accounts, usually out of necessity to maintain the movie's entertainment value and mainstream appeal

inaccuracies and artistic liberties. This is why many teachers throughout the country show the movie **Pearl Harbor** in class when discussing World War II in history class, **Amistad** while discussing slavery, or **Schindler's List** when discussing the Holocaust.[24]

Moreover, movie-watching is a highly social interaction, especially when experienced with another person. Think about the scores of movie dates that take place in our nation's theaters (despite the ironic notion that one can "get to know" someone on a date by sitting next to them in relative silence in a darkened theater). How many times have you gone to the movies with other people and then chatted about the movie afterwards, or struck up a conversation with a complete stranger over a favorite movie? Movies draw their connective power from the fact that you and everyone else who has seen them now have the exact same set of images to draw upon for future conversations and cultural references.

We all may have different schools and teachers, but we all share the same **Harry Potter** experience at Hogswarth Hill. As proof of the "shared" Hollywood experience, take an informal poll to see how many of your friends and family members are familiar with the phrase "Show me the money!" or "I'll be back . . . ." The images contained in mainstream movies have an impact because they are seen, processed and discussed by millions of people the world over.

Now if these movies have demonstrated the ability to affect people, then how does consistently marginalizing racial imagery contained within mainstream movies affect audiences? After all, **Jaws** made some people afraid to go into the ocean. The death of **Bambi**'s mother made some grown men remorseful about hunting. The opening debut of **Star Wars I: The Phantom Menace** prompted otherwise responsible adults to "play hooky" and miss work just to see the movie on opening day (at the estimated tune of a $239 million "loss" in productivity for the nation's economy).[25] Given the expansive reach and influence of Hollywood, the potential (and real) harm caused by marginalized images of minorities cannot be ignored.

WHAT DO YOU THINK?

If you want to read about the state of the diamond industry and its continued aversion to "conflict diamonds," gems sold for the primary purpose of financing armed conflicts in Africa, go to *www.diamondfacts.org*.

The website is sponsored by the World Diamond Council (WDC) trade organization and was created in anticipation of the release of **The Blood Diamond**, starring Leonardo DiCaprio and Djimon Hounsou (for which he received a Best Supporting Actor Oscar nomination). In fact, the WDC president, Eli Izhakoff remarked: "We've intensified our efforts because of this upcoming movie."[11z]

Why is it that the WDC would launch a proactive public relations campaign more than three months before the movie's scheduled mid-December 2006 release? How much of an impact do you think the WDC estimated such a movie would have? Was the WDC wise to "preempt" such a movie with potentially negative imagery about its industry? What precipitated the WDC's actions? Actual harm or perceived harm?

Movie studios use mainstream movies to illustrate in incomparable fashion the greatest aspects of human nature. Would heroic movies such as **Batman Begins, Lord of the Rings, Harry Potter** or **Pirates of the Caribbean** have been as successful if the protagonists failed in saving the world from evil, and the audience knew *beforehand* that failure was the imminent outcome? Probably not. We watch movies like **Hunger Games** and **Hacksaw Ridge** not just for their entertainment value, but also for the inspiration supplied from the protagonists' triumphs in the face of the seemingly insurmountable obstacles that they had to overcome.

Studios knowingly exploit the identification process for millions of Americans who otherwise do not know each other, but who otherwise share and identify with a common medium. Membership to the *Hollywood Audience* has paid dividends with respect to providing a common context and source of communication. Unfortunately, within the shared memory of the *Hollywood Audience*, studios have yet to consistently invest in the creation of minority characters or actors that convincingly depart from minority archetype character patterns. Meanwhile, the shared memory of mainstream Hollywood productions worldwide contain positive associations for White protagonists, at the virtual exclusion of minority characters, who remain marginalized in their status and importance. The archetypes affect *everyone's* perceptions of minorities, including minorities themselves! Studio-generated imagery helps form and reinforce a presumption of minority irrelevance that is not limited to the boundaries of the walls inside the movie theater.

CHAPTER 12:
AUDIENCE PARTICIPATION

Sometimes people don't realize how degrading it is to see some of these things. Like when people clap their hand over their mouth and make that sound: 'woo woo.' I don't think that even comes from Indian people. I believe it comes from the movies.

Joseph Bohanon, Professor, University of Southern Mississippi[1]

CHAPTER 12:
AUDIENCE PARTICIPATION

Have you ever, at any point in your life, seen a movie inside of a movie theater? If so, then consider yourself part of one of the largest informal clubs in the world: the *Hollywood Audience*. Try this at home: locate someone you know personally (including yourself) who has not seen a Hollywood-produced mainstream movie – *ever* – in their entire lifetime. If this task poses you some difficulty, then it speaks to the degree that Hollywood has been able to penetrate your social circle. Not only are you familiar with Hollywood, but you unwittingly have familiarized yourself with characters that inspired you with awe or commanded your respect. It is the widespread popularity and unparalleled distribution of Hollywood movies that contributes to their unique power. While many individuals casually switch between radio stations, read different newspapers and watch a wide range of television shows, there is only one Hollywood that we all share. Nearly everyone knows about the latest mainstream movies, even if they have not seen any of them personally.

But what makes the *Hollywood Audience* experience unique? What makes the bonds of this shared community so strong, yet so loose? Allow us to explore several factors that will bring us closer to the answer.

EYES WIDE SHUT

The identification process describes the reflexively personal decision-making process that most moviegoers use when deciding on which movie they will patronize. A moviegoer's first factor for consideration often revolves around whether the movie contains characters with whom the moviegoer personally identifies. The moviegoer may admire the projected traits of a particular character or simply be a fan of the actor portraying that character. Usually, the most obvious target for such identification is the movie's protagonist(s). For example, moviegoers watching **Batman Begins** would most

---

TOTAL ANECDOTAL
Did you know that *Gone with the Wind*, regarded as a classic and one of the mainstays of American cinema, gets its title from the foreword shown during the movie's introduction?

"There was a land of Cavaliers and Cotton Fields called the Old South. Here in this pretty world, Gallantry took its last bow. Here was the last ever to be seen of Knights and their Ladies Fair, of Master and of Slave. Look for it only in books, for it is no more than a dream remembered, a Civilization gone with the wind."

Big deal, right? But what if you had relatives that were adversely affected by this "Civilization" and were on the darker side of this "pretty world"? Are the fetters of slavery part of a "dream remembered"? How does your perspective about race affect how you regard the images in this "classic" movie? *Does your personal perspective influence how you identify with Scarlet O'Hara? Rhett Butler? Or Mammy?*

likely identify with Bruce Wayne/Batman (Christian Bale) first and foremost, and the movie's experience is organized around this character accordingly.

Not surprisingly, the majority of movies produced by the major Hollywood studios prominently feature storylines that revolve around White characters and actors. This is due in large part to the majority-White population in the country, but also because Whites – like any other race of people – can more readily identify with people of their own racial background. This is not to say that Whites cannot identify with characters and actors of other races. The identification process is more about a positive attitude *in favor of* something rather than a dislike for an alternative, much in the same way that being right-handed does not inherently suggest a disdain for one's left hand (despite an acknowledged preference to use the right hand for "important" tasks and functions given the higher comfort level associated therewith).

Most Whites never have to consciously confront this issue since there is always a wide variety of movies to choose from that prominently feature White characters and actors. Minority viewers, on the other hand, must undergo a different identification process given the dearth of minority protagonists with which to identify. Thus, a dual-consciousness develops in minority moviegoers whereby, in order to make the connective switch and fully partake in the viewing experience,[2] they must make adjustments to view the movie from a "White" point of view, which is otherwise labeled as the "mainstream" point of view. Many minority moviegoers make this identification process without even thinking about it, having been conditioned by the overwhelming number of movies starring Whites. For most White moviegoers, the identification process is "natural" since, based upon the abundant presence of White images and perspectives, they are not placed in a position where they are asked or forced to "switch."

It makes simple business sense to target mainstream movies to garner the greatest possible audience. That way, the movie improves

---

LIGHTS! CAMERA! INTERACTION!

The first "talking picture" (the first movie with sound) was **The Jazz Singer** (1927), featuring Al Jolson's immortal words: "Wait a minute . . . wait a minute. You ain't heard nothin' yet!" Due to its historical significance, many people still continue to review and circulate this movie, notwithstanding the fact that Jolson performs in the movie in blackface.

Similarly, since **The Birth of a Nation** (1915) was a groundbreaking movie in terms of its various cinematic elements and its wide distribution, it continues to be viewed and discussed in hundreds of film theory books and film classes across the nation, despite a storyline that prominently glorifies members of the Ku Klux Klan as heroic figures.

For those who object to the continued use of the above movies, are their objections still valid or are they unfounded? Is it possible to objectively parse content from quality? What about the fact that the DGA had its prestigious lifetime award for "distinguished achievement in motion picture direction" named in honor of D.W. Griffith, the director of **The Birth of a Nation**?

Starting in 2000, the DGA renamed the award to the DGA Lifetime Achievement Award. Go to *www.dga.org* and look up honoree Steven Spielberg's comments on the name change when he received the award in 2000.

its chances of generating the greatest possible profit. Theoretically, in light of the common color-blind adage of "I see no color," any American should be able to enjoy any movie featuring any other American, despite their race or ethnicity. After all, millions of minorities knowingly patronize and enjoy movies that do not prominently feature minority characters every weekend at the box office.

White moviegoers, however, have a different choice to make. Given the vast majority of White-dominated movies, Whites always have the luxury of deciding whether to patronize movies prominently featuring White characters. In actuality, it is the *minority viewers* who need to be color-blind when *they* go to the movies. A sporadic minority presence in Hollywood means that when minorities watch a movie, they cannot afford to "discriminate" and choose a movie featuring only members from their race. In contrast, since Whites constitute the numerical majority, they have the luxury to be color conscious and can simply decide not to see a movie that does not reflect their own perspective.

Movie studios are well aware of the large number of choices confronting moviegoers on a Friday night. This desire to have the greatest possible audience identify with a movie influences greatly which projects they will greenlight for production. Given that the majority of moviegoers are White, movie studios are concerned that a movie that does not prominently feature Whites as the central characters will truncate the potential size of the audience and, consequently, the resulting profits. The studios, being well aware of this identification process, often include "prominent" minority characters in ancillary roles to help draw a larger portion of the minority audience. Thus, if and when minorities are featured in mainstream movies, their presence is usually ancillary to a central White protagonist that drives the story, while complex minority protagonists in mainstream movies remain uncommon.

IT'S JUST A MOVIE, RIGHT?
Moviegoers are not the only ones that undergo the identification process. Check out what ***Spider-Man*** director Sam Raimi said about his connection to the web-crawling superhero:

"As a child, I dreamed of being Spider-Man, and I always wanted to be a motion-picture director," said Raimi. "So in writing, I get to be both. I really relate to Peter Parker. I really worry about him."[12a]

WHAT DO YOU THINK?
Check out the following excerpts from movie reviews published in *The Hollywood Reporter*. The reviews are for movies featuring predominately minority casts: ***ATL***, starring rapper Tip Harris (also known as T.I.), ***Phat Girlz***, starring comedienne Mo'Nique, and ***The Last King of Scotland***, starring Forest Whitaker (bold italics added):

➤ ***ATL*** (2006):
'ATL' is set for a quick payoff with urban youth audiences. The film has little crossover potential.[12b]

➤ ***Phat Girlz*** (2006):
After a short run in urban areas, this Fox Searchlight release could perform better on home video.[12c]

➤ ***The Last King of Scotland*** (2006):
Much of 'Scotland' is an extraordinary piece about naivete caught up short in terrible events. Box office looks substantial in sophisticated urban venues in North America.[12d]

The last movie netted Whitaker a Best Actor Oscar for his role as Ugandan dictator Idi Amin. Yet, does the term "sophisticated urban venues" imply that the "urban" audience is normally unsophisticated?

What do these reviews say about the universal appeal of these movies? What is it about these movies that limits them to "urban only" appeal?

THE YOUNG AND THE RACELESS

Although complicity – let alone "fault" – is difficult to assess in the cycle of blamelessness, the identification process nonetheless provides clues to audience agency. The identification process often comes into full view when a mainstream movie is released that features an all-minority leading cast. Such a movie is likely to be branded as "only" being a "Black movie" or said to appeal to "urban audiences" (e.g., a "Black movie"), even though it may contain general themes that are common to many mainstream movies. The same cannot be said for a movie featuring White worlds, even though it may be as racially exclusive – if not more so – than the "Black movie." For example, the **Lord of the Rings: The Fellowship of the Ring** does not receive a corresponding label of being a "White movie," and the series is broadly marketed as having universal appeal, despite featuring a virtually all-White cast. The industry uses terms like "the urban audience" to serve as a "raceless" marker for the identification process. Such a label functions more so as a "warning" to White moviegoers rather than an invitation to minorities (or "urbanites").

Smaller production and marketing budgets, smaller distribution deals, fewer showings on opening weekend, as well as limited marketing campaigns, all communicate the studio's belief that the movie has limited capacity to connect successfully with mainstream audiences. When a movie is branded as a "Black movie" within mainstream media and is specifically marketed as a "Black movie" by the studio, the presumption is that White movie patrons will have to make a connective switch just to partake in the viewing experience. The movie studios and the media may suggest that they are enhancing such a movie's appeal by specifically describing the target audience, but branding a movie as a "Black movie" limits its applicability to a wider audience, notwithstanding its potentially universal themes that could apply to any moviegoer.

One cannot make the blanket statement that Hollywood studios are "racist." That would be irresponsible. However, one *can* say that the movie studios function as for-profit businesses whose goal is to maximize profits. In order to attract the greatest possible audience, movie studios

BUT IT'S JUST A MOVIE, RIGHT?
Here is what nationally syndicated columnist Arianna Huffington (i.e., *The Huffington Post*) had to say about the hit movie **Legally Blonde 2**:

> Sitting between my teenage daughters while watching Elle (Reese Witherspoon) take on the U.S. Congress, I was struck by the palpable effect it had on them: They left the theater inspired, empowered, and talking about the things they wanted to change and the ways they might be able to change them. None of which would have happened as a result of a lecture from mom.[12e]

Do you think the fact that Huffington and daughters are all White made it easier for them to connect with Reese Witherspoon's character? Do you think that her observation would have been the same had the movie starred a young Asian actress instead? Would they still have gone to see the movie had this been the case? **Would the same movie starring a non-white actress even have been greenlit in the first place?**

must create stories and characters that their audiences can identify with; otherwise, the audience will not connect with and patronize their movies. Consequently, studio executives feel compelled to make movies that the "girl next door," or any "average American" citizen, will find enjoyable. By virtue of demographic statistics, this "average American" citizen is White. After all, the movie studios are not charged with the mission of expanding racial equality. The studios have an obligation to their shareholders to place the most economically sound products out on the market. In a sense, they are obligated to give the girl next door what they believe she wants.

The girl next door unwittingly becomes a catalyst in the minority marginalization process. When the girl next door goes out to the movies with the boy down the street, she makes decisions that influence the studios when they are making their decisions regarding which movies to produce.[3] Is it her fault if there are no dramas, legal thrillers, or fantasy quest movies featuring primarily minority characters? And if there is one available, does she have to feel compelled to watch it? What if she did not like the title, the lead character, or the description of the plot? Is it her fault that of the fourteen movie selections at her suburban multiplex, that she may not feel like choosing the one movie featuring minority characters? The girl next door may just be making a simple decision based on her preference and may not be making a conscious decision based on race. Nevertheless, the girl next door and her seemingly innocuous decisions are influential, and affect the types of movies the studios make . . . and the ones they do not make.

I, RACE NOT

Given the crossover appeal of certain minority A-list actors like Eddie Murphy, Denzel Washington and Will Smith, it is clear that White audiences, both domestically and internationally, are willing to accept certain minority characters in leading roles. However, upon closer inspection, it is apparent that high-profile minority actors must often be buttressed with a high number of supporting White characters to help "broaden" the movie's general appeal. Otherwise, studios run the risk of breaching the tipping point and having their movie branded as a "minority-oriented" movie, which may adversely impact the movie's earning potential.

Thus, even when making the financial commitment to produce a mainstream movie starring a minority actor, studios still observe the identification process by blunting as much as possible the potentially large connective switch required by majority-White audiences. For instance, it is

WHAT DO YOU THINK?

The steady access that White Hollywood celebrities have had with major movie studios has resulted not only in access for the individual celebrities, but in many cases for their progeny as well. Several examples of "second generation" Hollywood stars include:

- Oscar-winning actress *Angelina Jolie* (daughter of Oscar-winning actor Jon Voight)
- Oscar-winning actress *Jane Fonda* (daughter of Oscar-winning actor Henry Fonda)
- actress *Kate Hudson* (daughter of Oscar-winning actress Goldie Hawn)
- actress *Jamie Lee Curtis* (daughter of actors Janet Leigh and Tony Curtis)
- *Nicolas Cage* (nephew of Oscar-wining director Francis Ford Coppola and Talia Shire)
- Oscar winner *Sofia Coppola* (daughter of Oscar-winner Francis Ford Coppola, granddaughter of Oscar-winner Carmine Coppola)
- actress *Drew Barrymore* (daughter of actor John Barrymore, niece of actress Diana Barrymore, goddaughter of Oscar-winning director Steven Spielberg)

Do you see this similar trend reflected for minority actors? If not, does this "natural selection" process amount to a form of nepotism for Whites? **Does the identification process *suggest* that White directors and producers feel "more comfortable" in drawing upon a talent pool that reflects their personal tastes?**

not uncommon to see a leading minority character co-star with a White lead (e.g., *Men in Black* series) or become motivated by a tragic incident involving Whites (e.g., *Man on Fire*). An excellent example of this White-oriented identification process comes from *I, Robot,* starring Will Smith as Detective Del Spooner. *I, Robot* is a particularly unique example since it was a widely marketed summer blockbuster featuring a Black male protagonist *in a non-comedic role*. Observe the following relationship chart:

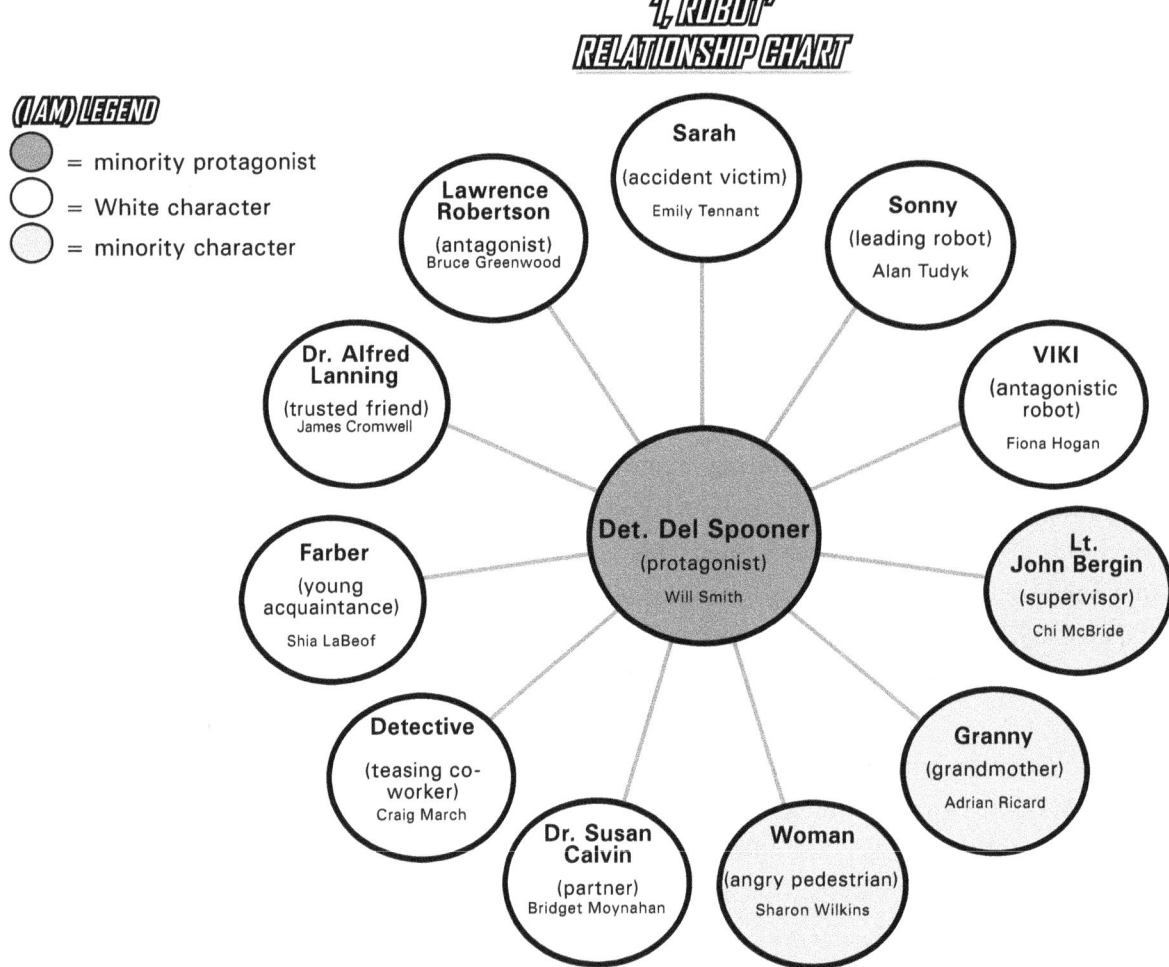

Yet, Det. Spooner remains essentially isolated from other *prominently featured* minorities. Det. Spooner's "circle of influence" during the heart of the movie's climactic action and drama sequences involve White characters only, while most of Detective Spooner's interactions throughout the movie are with White characters. The three minorities Detective Spooner interacts with are all Black: Lt. John Bergin (Chi McBride), Spooner's supervisor; Granny, Spooner's grandmother; and "Woman" (which is the name listed in the credits), an overweight Black woman who curses Spooner for accosting her robot. Will Smith's status as an "independent" minority lead actor is countered by his character's predominately White circle of relationships. To illustrate this point, consider the "'I, Robot' Relationship Chart" on the opposing page that outlines the various characters that Det. Spooner interacts with during the movie.[4]

In contrast to White Hero prototypes profiled in *Chapter 10: White Balancing Act*, note the lack of complex and emotionally redeeming relationships for Det. Spooner, including immediate family or romantic leads. Of the three minority characters in Det. Spooner's relationship circle, none of them are central to the storyline. Of the White characters in his relationship circle, five of them are absolutely vital to the plot's development:

- *Dr. Alfred Lanning* – Dr. Lanning invented the robot, Sonny, that stars throughout the movie. Lanning's death also sets the entire movie in motion; through prior planning, Lanning orchestrates a strategic plan to provide Det. Spooner "clues" to solving his premeditated suicide, which eventually leads Spooner to solving a larger problem of robot corruption that Lanning could not solve personally. Lanning's plan purposely manipulated Spooner's overzealous "prejudice" of robots in order to overthrow the centralized robotic brain, VIKI, that controlled all the robots. Dr. Lanning is also responsible for supplying Det. Spooner with his surgically repaired robotic arm.
- *Dr. Susan Calvin* – Dr. Calvin is a robopsychologist who helps Det. Spooner "solve" the crime behind Dr. Lanning's murder. In spite of the "natural" romantic possibilities (at least based on standard White Hero movie conventions), there is no intimacy between Det. Spooner and Dr. Calvin.
- *Sarah* – An accident victim that Det. Spooner could not save in his past, Sarah is a young White girl that serves as Spooner's "mortality" tale and humanizes him for the (White) audience. The loss of Sarah fuels Spooner's prejudice against robots.
- *Lawrence Robertson* – dubbed the "richest man in the world" by Det. Spooner, Robertson is the owner of U.S. Robotics, the company that manufactures robots like Sonny. Robertson serves as the movie's principal antagonist and the main conspirator that Det. Spooner must thwart.

- ***Sonny, the robot*** – Sonny's status as a central figure is undeniable. Although an "animated character" in the movie, for all intents and purposes Sonny is a "White character" since not only does the robot have "blue eyes," but it is also voiced by a White actor (Alan Tudyk).

If the movie's producers had cast minorities (e.g., Black actors) in Dr. Lanning, Dr. Calvin's, Sarah's, Robertson's and Sonny's roles, the movie may have required a greater connective switch for White viewers, which may have undermined its broad appeal.

Ironically, the most influential character in Detective Spooner's relationship circle is the character with the least amount of screen time: Sarah. Sarah is the young twelve-year-old girl who Detective Spooner sees quite frequently in his nightmares. Spooner is tortured by the memory that he was unable to save her life. Although Spooner had no previous ties to Sarah, they were both trapped underwater as a result of a car accident. A rescuing robot calculated that it had a greater logistical chance to save Spooner's life, conflicting with his belief that the robot should have saved Sarah so that she could have lived beyond her youth. The robot's "coldhearted" decision to save Det. Spooner – not Sarah – fuels his hatred for robots, which ultimately serves as an integral part of the plot development.

Spooner, as a protagonist motivated by the loss of a child, is not novel unto itself. For example, Chief John Anderton (Tom Cruise) in ***The Minority Report*** had lost his son as a result of a kidnapping, and that incident had (evidently) chewed at him emotionally, to the point where he took drugs to cope while rehashing the memory of his son. This "humanizing" reminder of mortality invites the audience to make a personal and emotional connection with the heroic protagonist, both in the case of Anderton *and* Det. Spooner. However, while Anderton's grief is motivated by a deeply personal loss of family, Det. Spooner's emotional wrenching results from the death of a "complete stranger," through no fault of his own, no less. While Anderton's familial loss is consistent with the Family-Tied prototype, Det. Spooner's anguish only reinforces his racial "isolation," devoid of any deeply personal relationships with other Black characters in need of rescue or romance.

It cannot be overlooked that Sarah was White, for since Detective Spooner is a Black male protagonist, the insertion of Sarah provides an emotional foothold for which many White viewers can grab onto, much in the same way the White audience relates to the "Angelic" relationship between

Creasy and Pita (Denzel Washington and Dakota Fanning) in **Man on Fire**. Had Sarah been cast as a Black girl, the studio might have been nervous about the movie transforming into a "Black movie," which might have adversely affected box office receipts.

LIGHTS! CAMERA! INTERACTION!

To see how race itself plays a subtle context in the storyline development of movies take note of these two particular themes in *I, Robot*.

- **Poverty**. Compare Det. Del Spooner's residence to that of Dr. Susan Calvin's for subtle distinctions of class status. Notice how Spooner's residence resonates with proverbial themes of impoverished Blacks as water pipes are externally visible in his bathroom and he has a functioning aerial fan (presumably in lieu of air conditioning) – in the year 2035! In fact, at roughly the 1:02:13 mark, a joke is made over Spooner's "antiquated" stereo system that Dr. Calvin cannot operate purely by verbal commands (as she is clearly accustomed). Spooner's impoverished status (relative to the other prominent White characters) is subtly affirmed by his frequent references to money (e.g., asking whether coffee offered to him was "free" at the 12:29 mark).

- **Prejudice**. Det. Del Spooner was openly "prejudiced" towards robots "and their kind." Although the audience learns that a prior negative experience colors his perception of robots, his prejudice was nonetheless regarded as irrational by others in light of the fact that no robot ever committed a crime (prompting his boss to request that he turn in his police badge). Further underscoring the theme of prejudice is the subtext of "free will," analogous to arguments proffered during the civil rights era for minorities. For instance, at roughly the 1:09:11 mark, Sonny, in illustrating the vision of robots assembled en masse in his dreams, explains, "Look, you can see them here as slaves – to logic. And this man on the hill comes to free them." By movie's end, Spooner learns the error of his logic, and learns to accept the robots as his friends. Spooner's epiphany comes after realizing that Dr. Lanning used Spooner's overzealous disdain for robots to set in motion a plan to save humans from the corrupted robot, VIKI, and her plans for a robotic revolution. At roughly the 1:42:45 mark, Det. Spooner confesses to Sonny: "Lanning was counting on my prejudice to lead me right to you."

Given the racial overtones of the two themes described above, would there have been "any difference" had an A-list White actor been cast in Det. Spooner's role instead of Will Smith? To what degree did Will Smith's race make the contrast of "reverse discrimination" of a Black character (Spooner) against a White character (Sonny) more poignant or ironic to moviegoers?

Although White mainstream audience members may not fully identify and connect with Will Smith as a Black male lead, they are still provided with the acknowledgment and affirmation of their significant onscreen presence vis-à-vis other characters and themes depicted throughout the movie. White characters – that coincidentally fulfill prototype patterns of glamorization – seen supporting a minority lead help minimize the studio's risk by providing White audience members with a concrete, visual means of drawing them into the movie. Additionally, the heavy use of White supporting characters helps the movie avoid the negative stigma of being branded as a "minority-themed" intended for minority audiences only. The insertion of the White prototypical characters helps narrow the connective switch gap and expands the identification process to ensure the movie retain its broad-based, "universal" appeal.

CATEGORICAL DENIAL

In Hollywood's earlier days, it was a more clear-cut case to assert that minorities were restricted from performing in certain high-profile roles. Today, the general perception is that these restrictions have relaxed. However, upon closer scrutiny and analysis, it appears that such restrictions have relaxed only under certain conditions.

There are only so many original storylines in the world with which you are well familiar: boy meets girl, boy loses girl, boy wins girl back, etc. The creative beauty is to see these familiar themes of love, persistence, trust and courage manifested in slightly different ways each time. Movies are separated into different genres based upon the different themes and styles of storytelling that they contain. For the purposes of our text, the main genres that we focus upon are: *1) comedy, 2) action & adventure* and *3) drama*.

Our genre scope is purposefully broad as our intention is not to list every possible classification possible inasmuch as we wish to illustrate how moviegoers generally identify with the characters therein, based upon thematic elements alone. Our goal is not to parse out the finer points between science-fiction and thrillers, but rather to illustrate a broader thematic continuum by which many audience identification patterns are gauged.

The genre of a movie affects the underlying identification process, whereby the primary function of the protagonist in a movie is to serve as the conduit for the movie's emotional experiences. Generally speaking, the audience is expected to identify with the main character. Otherwise, *the moviegoer may not fully feel or appreciate the viewing experience as intended by the director and the producers of the movie*. Part of the challenge is creating "believable" protagonists who have characteristics with which any audience member can identify. A movie's genre dictates the connective switch threshold, or rather, the emotional and mental "distance" that one has to travel to identify with the characters.

For this reason, different levels of audience identification are required based upon the movie's genre. If we were to create a spectrum, then comedies require less concentration and identification with primary characters than serious romances would. As it stands, most comedies, especially those with slapstick elements, contain symbology that general audiences can share and understand. After all, who can resist laughing at the sight of someone tripping and falling in an exaggerated manner? At the other end of the genre spectrum, dramas are more nuanced since the "drama" requires that the audience emotionally identify with the specific struggles and cathartic experiences of the protagonist. Our genre spectrum is as follows:

1. Comedy

Since comedy is considered "lighter fare," the content and material tends not to be too serious and the need for a connective switch is lower. Accordingly, many minorities have been prominently featured in comedies, often taking first billing or enjoying significant screen time. Based upon the identification process and the need for a connective switch, it is not surprising to see minorities featured in movies where a lesser emotional commitment is required from the audience to "laugh at" the protagonist and other minority characters therein (e.g., see "Lights! Camera! Interaction!" on pg. 153).

It is within the refuge of humor that many writers and directors feel safe to be more politically incorrect in their expression of common thoughts and ideas. Although it is not politically correct to express deep-seated feelings of racial superiority by Whites, it is nonetheless acceptable to make comedic movies poking fun at minorities. Further, it is less offensive if the minority protagonists are the ones carrying out the racially-charged humor. Minorities are by no means exempt from self-deprecating humor. The central problem is that, unlike White characters who appear in comedic situations, the "culture" of minority characters is often used as the basis for most of the jokes and humor. Minorities do not enjoy nearly as many roles where humor is developed from aspects of their personalities or derived from complex social situations.

For example, take **Head of State,** starring comedian Chris Rock as the President of the United States of America, with fellow comedian Bernie Mac serving as the Vice President. The running joke is that the President is Black, and the humor ensues by looking at the resulting differences in style and

> **WHAT DO YOU THINK?**
> *Harold & Kumar Go to White Castle*, is a "landmark" movie in many ways in that it gained mainstream acceptance starring two minority males from racial groups infrequently seen in leading roles; Korean-American John Cho and Indian-American Kal Penn.
>
> This comedic indie-crossover is largely considered to be a "breakout" film for both actors, although they both had taken bit roles in several movies prior.
>
> In view of how studios observe the identification process in selecting new projects to greenlight, do you think Cho and Penn would have had the same chance to achieve breakout status while co-starring in a drama? Or a moderately priced action/adventure movie? *Was having Cho and Penn co-star in a comedy a "safer bet" for the studio? Why or why not?*

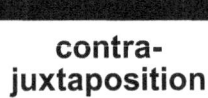

contra-juxtaposition

an exaggeration of an existing minority stereotype contrasted against "typical" White middle-class norms

substance as contrasted – both explicitly and implicitly – against a prototypical White President. This comedy plays upon the political reality that there has never been a Black President of the United States in our nation's history (up until that time). The same comedic premise would not have worked if the protagonist was White, given the fact that the President has always been White.

Contrast the comedic premise of **Head of State** to other presidential comedies like **Dave** and **The American President**, where situational factors – not race – serve as the comedic fodder. In **Dave**, the President, played by Kevin Kline, falls ill and must temporarily replaced by his identical twin, also played by Kevin Kline; the comedy ensues thereafter. In **The American President**, Michael Douglas plays an eligible bachelor who must balance the trials and tribulations of dating with the responsibilities of running the nation. Like **Head of State**, this movie plays upon a political reality – the President is *always* supposed to be married – but once again the crux of the humor is largely independent of race and based primarily on the situations therein. Conversely, the explicit dependence upon the Comic Relief archetypes and other race-based humor in **Head of State** was evident in the movie's marketing campaign, with the tagline stating, "The only thing white is the house."

Comedies like these decrease the need for a strong connective switch for White moviegoers, serving as a "safe" space for Whites to enjoy otherwise politically incorrect racial humor. A common comedic technique is **contra-juxtaposition,** which showcases a racial group's "worst" contrasted against another racial group's "best." Examples include **How High** (rappers Method Man and Redman star as two guys from the ghetto who get into Harvard University by smoking magic marijuana), **Friday After Next** (showcasing Ice Cube as an urbanite who moves out to the suburbs), **B.A.P.S.** (featuring Halle Berry and Natalie Desselle as two ghetto fabulous "homegirls" who care for the rich old man played by Martin Landau) and **Bringing Down the House** (Queen Latifah as an ex-convict who seeks the help of a rich lawyer, Steve Martin, to exonerate her). The above list is just a sampling of movies where upper-class, privileged Whites are juxtaposed against minorities of inferior socioeconomic status, whose social behavior is inherently deemed socially "inappropriate."

Within the comedy genre, Comic Relief archetypes are commonly exposed by Whites who identify the inappropriate behavior, while their accompanying reaction to that behavior is what provides fodder for most of the jokes. One clichéd variation on this theme is to have an old, conservative rich White person join in "hip hop dance moves" with their diametrically opposed, young, jive-talking, baggy-pants wearing, inner-city Black "homie." The dancing itself is not so much the target of parody as much as it is emblematic of the idea that these are two members of socially stratified groups who are so unlikely to ever cross paths, let alone on such unlikely terms. Further, when the "worst" of minorities are juxtaposed against the "best" of another racial group, the "best" is usually (always?!) White. Can you think of an "opposite" example?

Moreover, we must compare these characterizations of minorities in the comedy genre with that of Whites. When Whites are involved with comedy, the recent trend is to invest hundreds of millions of dollars into these movie projects. Movies like *Talladega Nights: The Ballad of Ricky Bobby*, *Evan Almighty* and *Night at the Museum* have been budgeted at figures that were once reserved for blockbuster action movies.

White comedic actors may very well engage in cartoonish humor whereby they are the "victim" of slapstick jokes, make "bug eyes" and the like. White "culture" (or usually a "subset": thereof) can even occasionally be used as fodder for humor (*Note:* Indicative of how some White humor is "cultural" and is not necessarily patently universal is the fact that *Talladega Nights*, showcasing the distinctly "American" sport of NASCAR, grossed more than $148 million domestically, but only grossed less than $15 million abroad).

However, unlike the frequent "culture as fodder" dynamic that surrounds the minority Comic Relief archetype, the humor dynamic changes when studios decide to invest millions of dollars into movies featuring White characters as the principal driving force, often employing high-priced, A-list

> **LIGHTS! CAMERA! INTERACTION!**
>
> Think about how many minority leads are known for comedic roles or roles with comedic elements. What follows are but a few examples to get you started:
>
> - Eddie Murphy (*Norbit, The Nutty Professor* series)
> - Kal Penn (*Harold & Kumar Go to White Castle*)
> - Queen Latifah (*Bringing Down the House*)
> - Jackie Chan (*Shanghai Noon*)
> - Chris Rock (*Head of State*)
> - Chris Tucker (*Rush Hour* series)
> - Will Smith (*Bad Boys* series)
> - Martin Lawrence (*Big Momma's House* series)
> - Ice Cube (*Are We There Yet?, Friday* series)
> - Samuel L. Jackson (*Snakes on a Plane, The Man*)
> - Shawn and Marlon Wayans (*White Chicks, Scary Movie*)
> - Cedric the Entertainer (*Johnson Family Vacation*)
> - Bernie Mac (*Guess Who, Mr. 3000*)
> - Danny Glover (*Lethal Weapon* series)
>
> Contrast this listing with the number of minority leads that you can think of that you would "automatically" associate with dramas (besides Denzel Washington).
>
> If you are having difficulty with the second listing, perhaps it demonstrates to what extent you personally associate top minority actors with comedy, as opposed to how few you readily associate with serious drama – based upon the images that Hollywood has provided you, of course.
>
> As a final contrast, how many White actors can you list that you immediately associate with serious and/or emotionally-involving movies?

actors in the process (e.g., Jim Carrey, Will Ferrell, Adam Sandler, Ben Stiller, etc.). With "so much" on the line – including a multi-million dollar payday for the A-list actor – the studios construct moralistic storylines that involve broad character arcs that merely *include* comedic effects (e.g., **Click**, **40 Year Old Virgin**, **Dodgeball**, **Wedding Crashers**, **Bruce Almighty**, etc.). Thus, "White comedies" are more than just a collection of *comedic events*; they are comedic *stories*. By design, the principal White characters cannot be rendered insignificant by jokes made at their "cultural" expense without explanation or meaning. Comparatively, minority characters often make fleeting appearances in color-blind movies, often at their own cultural expense – 1) *literally*, since they are not nearly as substantially compensated as the top White comedic actors, and 2) *figuratively* since the joke is on them and they remain powerless to do anything about it.

The key point of distinction here is the *type* of comedy for which White actors and minority receive compensation. In pointing out the fact that leading A-list actors score more financially rewarding deals for comedic stories, we do not suggest that the personal "cost" of self-deprecating humor is necessarily mitigated just because they are handsomely compensated for such "disparaging" work. At face value, this logic seems to support the short-term benefit rationale minority actors use when contemplating whether or not to spend time on the sacrificial sofa (see pg. 211 in *Chapter 11: At a Theater Near You*). Prominent minority comedic figures such as Martin Lawrence, Chris Tucker and Tyler Perry have all have been paid quite well for their work. Yet, when factoring into the equation the low racial capital and high premium of proportion for minority actors, the *individual* "gain" of a few minority comedic figures does not outweigh the *collective* cost for other minority actors following in their wake. In evaluating the negative "cost" of such humor, is there an acceptable "price point" for such "disparaging" and marginalizing work?

Given that it is somewhat acceptable to see minority leads in mainstream comedies, how come we do not see more mainstream romantic comedies featuring minority-led casts?

> **WHAT DO YOU THINK?**
> What is the color of love? In a MSNBC Online article entitled "Was Race An Issue in 'Hitch' Casting?", Will Smith, who starred opposite Latina actress Eva Mendes in **Hitch**, speaks to Hollywood's rationalization of minority marginalization:
>
> > There's sort of an accepted myth that if you have two Black actors, a male and a female, in the lead of a romantic comedy, that people around the world don't want to see it.[12f]
>
> **How does the connective switch theory factor into Will Smith's assessment?** This interview echoes how White audiences are resistant or perceived to be resistant by movie studios to minority images that serve to displace favorable White ones. Many studio executives use the connective switch rationale to defer culpability for marginalized minority roles to a faceless "American society" that knows intuitively what imagery it will pay to see. **What do Smith's comments say about his lack of power and control within the Hollywood machine, in spite of being one of the most – if not the most – powerful minority actors of his time?**

Romantic comedies, which often have more "dramatic" elements that "standard" comedies, require a connective switch, which is why we see so few mainstream romantic comedies featuring minority leads, and virtually none featuring a minority male paired with an A-list White female. This pattern of racial separation along gender lines speaks to the stark contrast between White prototypes and minority archetypes, and the thwarted sexuality of the minority male. On a basic level, the audience must have some attraction to the characters; otherwise they will not identify with many of the feelings portrayed by the characters. The fact that many movie studios cater to White audiences is evident in the volume of all-White romantic comedies that contain minimal minority presence. A countless number of mainstream movies reflect similar decision-making, allowing primarily for wide-ranging displays of intimacy by Whites, while comparable opportunities for minorities are more limited in frequency and scope.

It is the *romance* – one of the *White* prototype themes – that precludes us from seeing more mainstream minority-led romantic comedies. Despite the comedic elements in these movies, the audience must identify with the intimacy between the two protagonists, as well as identify with the emotions and desires of each particular character. This is why so many of the romantic comedies featuring White characters are heavy with dialogue that prioritizes their thoughts, ideas and feelings as central to the moviegoer's experience. Furthermore, romantic comedies are often led by protagonists that fit or approach the White Beauty Standard, typically as it relates to the female protagonist, but occasionally as it pertains to the (White) male lead as well (e.g., Richard Gere, Hugh Grant, etc.). This effectively truncates many of the opportunities minorities might have to star in such movies. For example, consider the virtual absence of romantic comedies starring Denzel Washington and Halle Berry, both of whom have long been considered two of the most attractive (minority) actors in Hollywood. While romantic comedies like **Hitch** have performed extremely well at the box office, it still remains a rare case – and even **Hitch** contained a White romance (that culminated in marriage!) as a developing subplot.

2. ACTION & ADVENTURE

Action and adventure movies are the proverbial fare of blockbuster movies that Hollywood releases every summer. Such movies are designed to appeal to a broad audience, and are built to inspire viewing members with larger-than-life images of heroism and triumph over the evil villain against all odds. The Hero prototype dominates this genre as the lead character.

LIGHTS! CAMERA! INTERACTION!
Take a look at some classic movies featuring everyday White American families (e.g., **E.T., Home Alone, Honey, I Shrunk the Kids, Back to the Future**). Do you think that any of these movies would have been as financially successful had they featured a minority family to serve as the "prototypical" American family? Would the same identification process have occurred? Do you think that any of these movies would have been socially as popular had there been a need for a large connective switch for White audiences?

This Hero usually has extraordinary qualities that moviegoers either wish to emulate (e.g., Spider-Man) or has exceedingly ordinary qualities that most can sincerely appreciate (e.g., Harry Potter). The purpose of this section is not to re-hash the Hero prototype profiled in *Chapter 10: White Balancing Act*, but rather is to illustrate that the identification process for viewing members is stronger than comedic movies, yet less so than dramas. While the actions of the protagonist may contain occasional humoristic elements, the majority of the protagonists actions are not designed to induce laughter. Quite the contrary, the protagonist is often working to solve (or resolve) an important problem, one that usually affects a large number of people.

WHAT DO YOU THINK?
What do you think about this quote from *The Washington Post*?

The role of John McClane (from the *Die Hard* series) set the template for Willis in big-screen hero mode — the wise-cracking Everyman, wincing between white-hot rounds of semi-automatic gunfire. Superpowers wouldn't befit this guy. He's supposed to struggle like any of us in a jam, only with sharper aim and better quips.[12g]

When author David Segal references Willis as an "Everyman," can this term refer to anybody regardless of race, or ***does it expressly convey this White author's ability to specifically identify with this White character?***

If minority characters take the lead in an action and adventure movie – especially if it is a big-budget, blockbuster movie – then they are typically surrounded by other important White characters in order to soften the larger connective switch that majority White audiences must make. Minority characters are "acceptable" in action movies as protagonists, but the "penalty" of such roles is that they are often socially and racially isolated (e.g., as noted in the "'I, Robot' Relationship Chart" on pg. 230), and display many characteristics of the Comic Relief archetype (see the "Lights! Camera! Interaction!" popout on pg. 153), or are dehumanized in some way (e.g., the animalistic nature of Jet Li in *Unleashed*, the otherworldly nature of Wesley Snipes in *Blade* and the underworldly nature of Michael Jai White in *Spawn*).

To see how race informs action and adventure movies, consider the ***Lethal Weapon*** series featuring Mel Gibson and Danny Glover. Mel Gibson's character (Martin Riggs) is single, while Danny Glover's character (Roger Murtaugh) is married. The sexual tension and romantic possibilities therefore revolve around Riggs. Murtaugh, as the more stable and conservative of the two, does have a family. However, his family, and more importantly Murtaugh himself, are all fodder for humor. In ***Lethal Weapon 2***, his daughter appears in a condom commercial; in ***Lethal Weapon 4***, the humor is centered on his daughter's pregnancy, with comedian Chris Rock playing the expectant father (Detective Lee Butters). In observance of the identification process, the producers decided that they would yield more from their audience if they channeled any "serious" romance angles through Mel Gibson's character.

Although Riggs and Murtaugh are "equal" partners, notice how throughout the entire ***Lethal Weapon*** series that Riggs performs most of the "heavy-lifting" for the pair's detective work. More often than not, it is Riggs who takes charge, provides directives, initiates confrontations, brainstorms ideas and discovers clues. Murtaugh has the appearance of being Riggs' equal partner, but in reality serves a glorified Angel role since he is merely present to serve Riggs, along with serving as a foil for Comic Relief. This construction for the two characters is based upon the studio's desire to minimize discomfort associated with a large connective switch, and to merely exploit the "more natural" emotional connection that majority White audience members make with Riggs' more powerful White character.

The connective switch required for majority White audiences grows stronger in accordance to the more "serious" nature of heroism required of a protagonist in action and adventure movies. Thus, it is not without coincidence that minority characters – let alone minority *protagonists* – appear less frequently in action and adventure movies. If and when minority characters appear, studios typically shunt minority roles into familiar and formulaic archetypes (e.g., the Background Figure, Menace to Society villains, or "the Black guy that dies first," as emblematic of an expendable character with whom the audience identifies with the least) out of "concern" that a minority lead may not have the same box office draw as a White one.

While themes of power and romance are typically burlesqued in comedies, they retain more importance in action and adventure movies as they provide insight to the protagonist's development and state of mind. Frequently, romance or a sexual reward is part of the White Hero's story arc; such prolonged sexual tension (intertwined with the tension prompted by the plot itself) between minority characters would once again tax the connective switch needs for Whites. Case in point, although several action/adventure movies exist with Asian male leads, rarely are they depicted as developing any ongoing sexual tension, nor is there any climactic consummation of their romance with another female character – let alone a White female character.

3. DRAMA

Dramas, as a general rule, are harder to market since they often lack the allure of the big-budget special effects of action movies, which are viewed as more marketable to wider audiences. Dramas require that the viewer identify with the personal issues experienced by the central characters. Whereas comedies *allow* for disassociation from movie characters, and action and adventure movies allow for association with heroic characters, dramas *require* association with leading characters. As previously mentioned, dramas typically lack major special effects, which are often used to hide poorly written

BUT IT'S JUST A MOVIE, RIGHT? Speaking of audience members identifying with onscreen imagery, some mediators use mainstream movie characters as interpretive and metaphorical tools (e.g., ***Kramer v. Kramer, War of the Roses, Braveheart***).[12h]

Even the Director General of the Canadian Conflict Management Program cites ***Changing Lanes***, starring Ben Affleck and Samuel L. Jackson, as a prime example of how a conflict between two people can escalate![12i]

storylines (or conversely, because of the high entertainment value of high-cost special effects, an involved storyline becomes less necessary). Without these effects, the viewer's attention in a drama is focused upon the lead character(s) dialogue, thoughts and emotions. In contrast to an action and adventure movie, most viewers will state their preference to start watching a drama from the very beginning so that they can "get into" the movie, as opposed to an action movie that requires less context for viewer participation.

Effective dramas freely employ themes that revolve around intimacy, either through familial love or romantic relationships. To this end, there are very few mainstream movies that depict minorities in serious, emotionally charged and intimate settings. Although the observant movie watcher may quickly offer up movies such as **The Preacher's Wife** or **The Joy Luck Club**, movies like these are rare and often fail to qualify as *mainstream* movies. Moreover, minorities depicted as intimate with Whites — particularly minority men with White women — is still a rarity.[5] For example, in **Pulp Fiction,** Ving Rhames, a Black male, plays Marsellus Wallace. His wife, Mia, is played by Uma Thurman, a White actress. Despite being "married," there is no physical contact between the two of them, and they only briefly appear together in the same scene once. Instead, one of the movie's most famous scenes features Vincent Vega (John Travolta) dancing and doing the twist with Mia.

Due to the high emotional context required for audience participation, studios primarily create dramas that revolve around White protagonists. The elevated emotional investment required of viewers translates into the most difficult connective switch that White audiences would have to make if the movie starred minority protagonists. Think of movies like **Good Will Hunting** or **Erin Brockovich**, when the stories depend upon the audience's "intimate" understanding of the White protagonist's dreams, motivations and inspirations. Since the identification process is at its strongest with dramas, studios operate from the premise that White moviegoers will become *more selective* and *more particular* about the race of the protagonists in these movies, more so than they would be in action and adventure movies and comedies.

THE GREATEST OF SMALL-TIME

Studios and audience members alike would have us to believe that there is supposedly no one to blame for this curiously consistent pattern of minority marginalization. Yet, there is one place where we can look for help: the box office. After all the workshops, seminars, initiatives and training sessions on diversity have concluded, people are left free to do what they want.

This means that on Friday night, when it is time to enjoy a movie, whether it be with the family, a spouse, a date, a friend or your own shadow, invariably the unstated goal is to watch a good movie and avoid wasting time and money. When people are standing in line with their eyes glazing over umpteen movie titles in red digital lettering, they reflexively pick a movie that they have an interest in or that they believe that they will enjoy. In selecting a movie that features mostly White characters, it is unlikely that anyone is taking the time to be "racist" at that moment. People are simply trying to make the best individual consumer decision that they can based upon the limited choices available.

WHAT DO YOU THINK? Given that *The Lion King* is set somewhere in Africa, is it "inconsistent" that the protagonist, Simba, is voiced by White actors (Jonathan Taylor Thomas as young Simba and Matthew Broderick as adult Simba) while Simba's parents are voiced by Black actors (James Earl Jones as Mufasa; Madge Sinclair as Sarabi)?[12] Would the movie have been as universally marketable had Simba been voiced by Black actors? *If race was not a factor, then what was the rationale behind this casting decision?*

If a moviegoer is more apt to become "invested" and emotionally involved in the protagonist's life, it is easier to do so when there is a shorter distance to cross in terms of personal identification. Due to the large amount of racial capital that Whites enjoy week in and week out at movie theaters across the country, White moviegoers rarely need to take time to parse out their connective switch needs. Meanwhile, since minorities have considerably less amounts of racial capital in Hollywood than Whites, the unspoken message is that minorities will, as a matter of course, have to make a connective switch. In order to identify with the White protagonists in mainstream movies, minorities must accept or adopt the protagonist's perspective if they wish to see and fully "participate" in the mainstream movie viewing experience.

Movie studios accommodate the largest segment of their audience with a full spate of mainstream movies prominently featuring White protagonists. On occasion, a movie studio will break from the conventional formula and will feature a minority lead in a movie. This is where the seemingly innocuous choices made by the girl next door resonate deeply with the movie studios that look to benefit financially from satisfactorily satisfying her tastes. The studios rely on the formulaic casting patterns – the White prototypes and the minority archetypes – in order to minimize the connective switch required of White moviegoers, which in turn reduces their financial risk by "broadening" the movie's appeal. As a direct result, the genre affects the type and caliber of minority characters and themes that appear in mainstream movies. Fewer minority leads appear in the more serious and emotionally involved genres, where the need for a connective switch is greater. Conversely, there is a heavier presence of minorities in comedies, where a connective switch is not a prerequisite to *laugh at* the characters and partake in the humor.

Certainly minority actors do more than just comedy, yet the plethora of comedic leads for minority actors contrasts sharply with the lack of more serious leading roles. There is often a comedic element involved when minorities are top-billed and directly involved with driving the story development. This comedic element "lessens the blow" of the minority's autonomy and the resulting connective switch elements needed for the White audience.

As with the "Lights! Camera! Action!" popout on pg. 153, take note of how many minority *leads* are known for comedic roles or roles with comedic elements. Of those non-comedic movies that do feature minority leads, the storylines rarely call for the audience to be deeply involved in the minority character's personal family life or romantic affairs since the protagonist is often isolated socially – especially from other minorities.

There is a general lack of opportunities for minority actors – both aspiring and established – to secure roles in Hollywood *that are normally only available to White actors*. This dearth of opportunities is underscored by the virtual absence of *serious* mainstream movies featuring two (or more) top-billed minority protagonists. Look up some of the top minority actors that you know and see how few of them have ever been top-billed with another minority actor, even in movies that *were not* mainstream!

Of the few existing examples where two or more minorities appeared together, the overwhelming number of these movies are comedies. Even in those comedies, it is *still* rare to see two *big* minority stars paired together. Of those that are dramas, many of them are biopics based upon stories of extraordinary minorities that triumphed in real life (e.g., **Cesar Chavez, Frida, Malcolm X, Ray, Hotel Rwanda, Ali**). There is nothing inherently wrong about redeeming stories about minority icons. Yet, the "real-life" aspect of these movies minimizes the "fantasy" involved (since the events therein occurred in reality), subsequently reducing the connective switch required by White moviegoers. Even the mainstream success **Dreamgirls** – while not a biopic – was a musical *based* upon real events. These movies – like so many other mainstream movies featuring minority leads – do not explore fantasy scenarios common to many mainstream movies that feature White leads. Over time, the message is therefore communicated that minorities are constrained to "reality-based" movies and are not entrusted with leading viewers into fantasy worlds (e.g., see the list of minority-led biopics on pg. 142). Meanwhile, White protagonists are suitable for leading *universal* adventures, crusades, missions and quests that any viewer can identify with and support.

On the audience side of the equation, mainstream movie audiences traditionally have not patronized (en masse) movies that feature mostly minority characters. Movie audiences have a valid defense: the studios have not provided many opportunities for patrons to see such movies. However, the box office does provide some insight into the "culpability" of the audience. To underscore how both the identification process and the connective switch reverberate with viewing audiences, take a look at the top grossing movies of all-time.[6]

We look at the top ten grossing movies because the box office is an indicator of "popularity" and patronage. Financially successful movies generate large box office sales because of their ability to appeal to a large number of viewers who *successfully* identify with the protagonist and their personal situation. Movies that require a large connective switch presumably will not generate substantial blockbuster sales due to the difficulty involved in selling a product that does not appeal to the largest section of the paying public (i.e., White moviegoers).

Consider the following chart:

TOP TEN ALL-TIME WORLDWIDE GROSSING MOVIES
[AS OF 2/17]

	BOX OFFICE GROSS ($)	TITLE
1.	2,788,000,000	**Avatar** (2009)
2.	2,186,000,000	**Titanic** (1997)
3.	2,068,000,000	**Star Wars: The Force Awakens** (2015)
4.	1,670,000,000	**Jurassic World** (2015)
5.	1,518,000,000	**Marvel's The Avengers** (2012)
6.	1,516,000,000	**Furious 7** (2015)
7.	1,405,000,000	**Avengers: Age of Ultron** (2015)
8.	1,341,000,000	**Harry Potter and the Deathly Hallows Part 2** (2011)
9.	1,276,000,000	**Frozen** (2013)
10.	1,214,000,000	**Iron Man 3** (2013)

Source: Box Office Mojo

Of the ten top-grossing movies of all time, some minority actors with notable screen presence are:

- **Iron Man 3** – Chinese actor Xueqi Wang as the villainous Doctor Wu, Don Cheadle as Colonel James Rhodes/Iron Patriot, Rebecca Hall as Maya Hansen (father is English, mother is American and of Dutch, Scottish, Sioux and African American origin). Hansen is killed before the movie's end for having a change of heart and tries to thwart the Mandarin villain while fulfilling the Angel Figure. Col. Rhodes also fulfills the Angel Figure archetype by helping his buddy, Tony Stark (Robert Downey, Jr.) in the climactic scene.

- **Star Wars: Episode VII - The Force Awakens** – John Boyega as Finn, Lupita Nyong'o as the voice of animated character Maz Kanata, Emun Elliott (father of Persian descent, mother is Scottish, changed name from Emun Mohammedi) as Brance, Yayan Ruhian as Tasu Leech, Ken Leung as Admiral Statura, Crystal Clarke as Ensign Goode, Jeffery Kissoon as Rear Admiral Guich and Philicia Saunders as Tabala Zo. All characters listed above with the exception of Finn and Maz Kanata can easily be classified as Background Figures. Lupita, while making the front cover of the 2017 *Vanity Fair* Hollywood issue, lent her voice to a quite old, orange, bespectacled CGI alien who nonetheless fulfilled the Angel Figure role to Rey (Daisy Ridley). And then there is Finn. Betrothed his name by fighter pilot extraordinaire Poe Dameron (Oscar Isaac), this former Death Star sanitation worker (see *Key Scene* commentary about Morgan Freeman's "God" character on p. 147) serves up Comic Relief moments as he is unable to negotiate the terms of his own Empire defection and is incompetent to handle flying military weaponry. Unable to wield the force (Utopic Reversal), he is knocked unconscious during the movie's most crucial moments, never to be heard from the remainder of the movie.

- **Jurassic World** – Irrfan Khan as Masrani, BD Wong as Dr. Henry Wu, Omar Sy as Barry, Brian Tee as Hamada. Hamada (Utopic Reversal) as head of island security ends up getting stepped upon and crushed by the Indominus Rex dinosaur. Dr. Wu (Menace to Society) secretly made hybrid dinosaurs to function as weapons. Masrani was the failed successor and CEO of Jurassic World who crashed and burned in a helicopter he claimed he knew how to fly. Barry was an Angel Figure and "buddy" of White male protagonist Owen Grady (Chris Pratt).

- **Avatar** – see pp. 82 - 83.

- **Frozen** – As the palace prepares to open its doors for Elsa's coronation early in movie, sharp eyes have detected Black princess Tiana (*The Princess and the Frog*) as one of the guests in the background — no speaking part though.

The only movie located in the top ten that features a top-billed minority actor (i.e., ABC Movie "starring" XYZ actor) is possibly *Star Wars Episode VII: The Force Awakens*, with Nigerian-British actor John Boyega (born as John Adedayo Adegboyega) portraying the role of Finn, as humanized from his First Order stormtrooper designation of FN-2187. Yet, this formulation of Finn "starring" in this movie quite frankly may be stretching it. Perhaps starring credits may be awarded to Dwayne "The Rock" Johnson (father is black, mother of Samoan background) in *Furious 7*, although he is preceded in the credits by Vin Diesel (who refuses to acknowledge or discuss publicly his multicultural background although typically is cast as White characters a la Jennifer Lopez), Paul Walker (who died during filming), English actor Jason Statham, Latina actress Michelle Rodriguez (of Dominican and Puerto Rican descent), Brazilian-American Jordana Brewster, and Black crossover musicians Tyrese Gibson and Ludacris.

In contrast to the Comic Relief moments that pepper the non-white male performances listed in the preceding paragraph, the other top-grossing movies feature "more serious" White protagonists, wherein the identification process is stronger for viewing audiences than it is for comedic roles. One of the most financially successful movie that Hollywood has ever produced – *Titanic* – is a drama with strong themes of romance ("the greatest love story ever told"), but also contains many elements typically reserved for action & adventure movies (i.e., big-budget special effects). The movie is also color-blind since it contains a virtually all-White cast, and as such is filled with White prototypes. All of these elements combine to make a movie that is broadly appealing due to its mainstream elements, but one that also resonates strongly with the White audience since there is little need for a connective switch. The success of *Titanic* helps illustrate how the more *mainstream* a movie is, the more likely it is to rely on the formulaic nature of the prototypes and archetypes. The miniscule presence of minorities within the top ten grossing movies of all time – most of which were released in the last ten years – is a reminder of how "little" progress Hollywood has made, even in our post-racial age of imputed racial inclusivity.

The perceived ability of the *Hollywood Audience* to identify with racial imagery within mainstream movies directly influences the creation of mainstream images. Movie studios make decisions about which movies to greenlight, which movies to market heavily, and whom to cast based upon their projections and beliefs about what the audience will want. Conversely, potential audience members make consumer choices

> **WHAT DO YOU THINK?**
> Given the international proliferation and accessibility of Hollywood movies, to what extent do you think that American mainstream movies influence or assist members of the international audience in learning English?
>
> If movies can help people learn the language, then what else might the foreign viewer learn through mainstream imagery about race in America?

about whether they identify with a movie's theme and its characters – often with limited information – before they decide to sit down and watch it. Thus, the "Top Ten All-Time Worldwide Grossing Movies" chart reflects the global distribution of widely popular movies that are not only virtually devoid of minority characters, but also consistent in their use of minority archetypes and White prototypes.

ACT LOCALLY, APPEAL GLOBALLY

For the many international audience members who have never set foot on American soil, our inquiry begs the question: how influential are mainstream minority archetype (and White prototype) patterns in shaping their perceptions of American people and American culture?

American movies represent the country's "second-largest export after aircraft,"[7] so it is important to take notice of what racial images are internationally distributed for paid consumption. There is no doubt that Hollywood is the international trendsetter with respect to feature films. The U.S. dominates world trade in movies, television programs, and sound recordings, as evidenced by the fact that as recent as ten years ago, U.S. movies made up 71.4% of Europe's movie market.[8] As another example of Hollywood's influence, according to the British Film Institute, the most watched movie of all time in England is *Gone with the Wind*. Some 35 million people have seen *Gone with the Wind* since its release in Britain in 1940, according to estimated attendance records.[9]

Before we dismiss the "entertainment-only" quality of mainstream movies as non-influential, let us take note of where Hollywood's influence is tangibly felt. It is common for A-list celebrities to serve as high-profile ambassadors, product endorsers, and special guests of presidents and royalty alike. One such example of the power of celebrities comes by way of Angelina Jolie and her high-profile appointment as goodwill ambassador to the Office of the United Nations High Commissioner for Refugees (UNHCR). The implicit power of high-profile mainstream movie stars is evident in news headlines such as, "Angelina Jolie, [Condoleeza] Rice Spotlight World's Refugees," that give the actress "top billing" over the nation's Secretary of State![10]

Another example of Hollywood's global influence occurred when the United Nations (UN) not only agreed to on-location filming of *The Interpreter*, starring Nicole Kidman and Sean Penn, but publicly expressed that such an experience was an effective public relations move (see the popout entitled "It's Just a Movie, Right?" on this page). After all, what better way to de-mystify a verifiable global organization than with a fictional movie?

BUT IT'S JUST A MOVIE, RIGHT?

The 2005 release of the action-thriller *The Interpreter*, featuring Nicole Kidman and Sean Penn, translated into a somewhat historic public relations success. The United Nations (UN) granted the movie's producers permission to film at their facility after years of spurning other Hollywood requests. This was the rationale, as articulated by Shashi Tharoor, the UN undersecretary-general for public affairs: "It could be, in effect, a free commercial for the U.N. – a thriller made by a top-notch filmmaker with a stellar cast."

Tharoor, who was instrumental in getting approval for the film, also noted that the movie "will reach far more millions of people than any public relations initiative that I could have come up with. And we are satisfied that the values in the story reflect our principles."[12k]

The UN can raise its profile through a mainstream movie since Hollywood's movies are distributed in just about every country in the world. Today, Hollywood movies, whether through DVDs and videocassettes, purchase and/or rental, satellite and cable delivery, parcel post mail or online delivery, are all widely available in the international market. The widespread distribution of these movies does not automatically mean that they are widely

> ### BUT IT'S JUST A MOVIE, RIGHT?
> As evidence of the power of mainstream movie images, it is striking to see how many examples abound of people engaging in copycat behavior and imitating conduct displayed on the big screen — even to the point of risking serious injury. When the Disney football movie **The Program** was released in 1993, articles soon surfaced about kids lying in the street while cars would run past them, imitating a particular scene in the movie. The disputed scene was cut after a number of similar incidents occurred across the U.S., many resulting in tragic injuries.[12l]
>
> Copycat behavior can also endanger the health of animals, as illustrated by some of the fans of **Finding Nemo**. The movie contributed to an increase in the ownership of clown fish, the type of brightly colored orange fish featured in the animated movie. "Everyone who comes in says they want Nemo," declared Michael Diaz, manager of a West Palm Beach pet store. Additionally, in imitation of the climactic scene in the movie where Nemo is successfully flushed down the toilet to escape captivity, several children (unsuccessfully) did the same for their fish. The Roto-Rooter plumbing dispatch center in Valencia, California, said it received approximately 70 calls about kids flushing their fish down toilets after the movie's release. "I hear kids crying in the background," says Margie Valadez, a dispatcher for Roto-Rooter. "But there's nothing we can do. They're gone."[12m]

accepted. Overseas censorship and movies that have been banned abroad further underscore the point that the images in mainstream movies *do* matter.

Dan Glickman, the head of the MPAA, is no stranger to the wide-ranging reach and impact of Hollywood movies. A former Congressman from Kansas who served as the Secretary of Agriculture under President Bill Clinton, Glickman stated the following when he took the lead role over the MPAA from *president emeritus*, Jack Valenti: "What enthuses me is the work of sustaining and enlarging MPAA's role in international cinema. As America's most wanted export, the American movie is also a great source of economic growth. I am eager to begin working closely with my new colleagues at MPAA, here and abroad, with the Congress, the federal government, state legislatures, *with officials of nations on all the continents, as well as the global creative community.*"[11]

But it's just a movie, right?

Not according to President George W. Bush, who created an Office of Global Communications to work with Hollywood to shape America's image abroad.[12] The President recognized that movies have the power to influence perceptions of American people and the American way of life. America's

copycat behavior

when individuals imitate behavior displayed in a mainstream movie

movie industry remains virtually unchallenged with respect to its worldwide distribution, penetration and influence.

This "imbalance of trade" was the impetus behind the international Convention on the Protection and Promotion of the Diversity of Cultural Expressions passed by the United Nations Educational, Scientific and Cultural Organization (UNESCO) in October of 2005. The convention was described as an effort to "combat the homogenizing effect of cultural globalization" of which American movies are considered a key component. Theoretically designed as a measure to allow countries to limit the influx of Hollywood movies in their domestic markets, the convention passed with 148 votes in its favor and only two against it.[13] Although this vote was treated as a minor detail within the American press, it was actually a significant issue of international proportions. The result of the vote suggests that many foreign countries recognize the cultural and financial impact of the worldwide proliferation of Hollywood movies.

TOTAL RECALL

The movie-viewing experience and the identification process is so strong that many moviegoers openly admit to having their imagination excited and inspired by fantasy characters like Spider-Man and Indiana Jones. A sliding scale typically ensues whereby the more one likes a movie, the more influential the movie's imagery will become. For instance, after watching ***Star Wars***, some moviegoers express their support and belief in the franchise in various ways: one might purchase a humorous coffee mug in the shape of Darth Vader's head; another might display a "cool" movie poster in their home; another might make an even larger commitment, spending thousands of dollars on "movie-quality" costumes for public appearances;[14] countless others may simply cup their mouths and breathe heavily while delivering their best impression of James Earl Jones' Darth Vader voice. In every case, the identification process plays a vital part in communicating universal themes embodied in the movie which speak to different moviegoers in different ways. If moviegoers can become fanatically inspired by "real" movie characters that they strongly identify with, then moviegoers can also be negatively impacted by the exclusion and marginalization of minority characters.

Do you recall ***Total Recall***? The premise of this action/adventure thriller was that Douglas Quaid (Arnold Schwarzenegger) was the victim of a "virtual vacation memory" that went wrong — or did it? At any rate, the audience learns that in the future, the memory of a desired vacation could be

---

TOTAL ANECDOTAL

Speaking of "total" anecdotal, as further proof of the "same, but different" philosophy that guides many major studios' decision-making process, the mainstream hit movie, ***Total Recall*** was remade in 2012 with Colin Farrell.

Perhaps some tasks are better left undone. The 1990 original starring Arnold Schwarzenegger grossed $119M at the box office with a budget of $65M while the budget for the remake was $125M with a final gross of $58M. The $119M gross in 1990 is worth $227M in 2017 dollars.

implanted in the brain without having to physically endure the tribulations of travel. The brain would then be unable to distinguish the "real" memories from the implanted ones, thereby allowing the imported experience to seamlessly enter into the realm of complete consciousness. The virtual vacation memory would render the same effect as the memory of a real vacation, thereby "saving time" for those who did not have time to take a vacation in the first place.

The metaphor described in this mainstream movie may be similar to how many of us interact with mainstream movies. Perhaps after a considerable amount of time importing "memories" in the form of two-hour mainstream movies, it becomes difficult for the brain to distinguish which memories are "real" or implanted. With the more subtle, unspoken, details of life as reflected in our mainstream movies, such imagery – viewed over time – may be more influential than it initially appears. Hypothetically speaking, consider the girl next door who has frequently watched mainstream movies for the last three consecutive decades. Also consider that the overwhelming majority of mainstream movies she has watched consistently excluded or belittled minority presence through the use of the archetypes. Further consider that within these same movies over the past three decades, the girl next door was simultaneously bombarded with positive impressions of White characters via her exposure to the prototypes. *If this is the case*, it would not be too far fetched to conclude that ideas reflecting minority marginalization and White glamorization will either take hold in some part of her consciousness or be reinforced by repeated exposure.

MPAA president Dan Glickman encapsulated this "sentiment" when he stated, "I think I am one of the luckiest guys in the world and I intend to dedicate myself fully to this industry that has given me so many wonderful memories."[15] The statement echoes the notion that mainstream movie images are an important and integral part of our social fabric. Mainstream movies have an exceedingly high social value and function. Although they are not

> **BUT IT'S JUST A MOVIE, RIGHT?**
> Can movies impact moviegoers in a way to promote racial intolerance, including anti-Semitism? See what the National Director of the Anti-Defamation League (ADL) had to say about **The Passion of the Christ**, directed by Mel Gibson.
>
> "The film unambiguously portrays Jewish authorities and the Jewish mob as the ones responsible for the decision to crucify Jesus," said Abraham H. Foxman, ADL National Director, who actually met with Vatican leaders. "We are deeply concerned that the film, if released in its present form, could fuel the hatred, bigotry and anti-Semitism that many responsible churches have worked hard to repudiate."[12n]
>
> What does Foxman's statement imply about the power of mainstream movie images? Are such "made-up" images completely benign or can they contribute to actual hatred? Are we to believe that a movie could stand to be so influential? Should we seriously consider the implication that the movie may contain negative images that are destructive to the global image of Jews?
>
> While one may add the caveat that this movie was merely an "interpretation" of real events, note how influential and "factual" many people regarded this "fictional" account of what transpired. Also, note the amount of concern over "one" potentially anti-Semitic movie. **What then are the implications over the repeated use and consumption of marginalizing minority archetypes?**

vital for daily subsistence to the human body, it is difficult to imagine a world without the movies we share. It is undeniable that these high-revenue generating mainstream movies have a measure of influence on American culture identity formation. Given the country's relatively "young" history in comparison to other nations, movies help to concretize in "tangible" form American culture and make it "accessible" through its commercial exportation. Although not nearly as old, the blockbuster **Forrest Gump** is as American as the Hunchback of Notre Dame is French. In many ways, Rocky Balboa is as "real" and tangible an icon as any other famous patriot who still lives on within mainstream memories as a "Treasure of American History."[16]

Mainstream movies reflect as well as reveal mainstream culture's identity. Although some casual movie patrons may dismiss a two-hour movie as temporal and *non-influential*, for many, movies take on a much bigger role. Movies in many cases do not just communicate messages and imagery about life, but movies *are life itself.* The *Los Angeles Times* encapsulated the "larger-than-life" quality that movies retain when it remarked upon the death of screen legend Katharine Hepburn that she "transcended her screen roles by showing several generations how to be a woman in a way that combined sublime beauty and sexuality with fiery intelligence."[17] Audience members cannot completely discount the ability of mainstream movie images to transcend the silver screen into something larger, especially when mainstream media asserts and affirms that movie roles and actors take on a socially instructive function.

The common tendency of mainstream moviegoers to identify with central White characters, whether through deliberate choice or out of "necessity," undergirds the slow, steady and subtle construction of a racial hierarchy in the minds of millions. When moviegoers consistently identify with White protagonists over time, the cumulative effect is that viewers automatically distinguish White characters as "important" and worthy of attention. Meanwhile, minority characters become further entrenched and confined to the limited world of the formulaic archetype patterns.

Based upon principles surrounding the identification process and the connective switch, it is not without coincidence that the top-grossing movies of all time contain a limited minority presence and are primarily driven by White characters with whom majority White audiences can identify.

The Bottom Line #3: *Emotion Pictures*

Given Hollywood's extensive reach and economic impact, mainstream movies, through the use of consistently marginalized minority images, reflect and reinforce messages of racial imbalance worldwide.

CHAPTER 13:
THE BOTTOM DIME

*It's the movies that have really
been running things in America
ever since they were invented.
They show you
what to do,
how to do it,
when to do it,
how to feel about it,
and how to look
how you feel about it.*

Andy Warhol, artist and social commentator[1]

CHAPTER 13:
THE BOTTOM DIME

The *theory* behind Hollywood's approach to diversity is much different than the actual *practice*. Despite the numerous diversity initiatives over the years, a pattern of minority exclusion and marginalization persists in mainstream Hollywood nonetheless. Virtually all minority imagery in mainstream movies is constrained by Hollywood's Acting Rule for Minorities – the HARM theory – which states that if and when a minority character appears in a mainstream movie, their image will be compromised in some way, shape or form. The HARM theory, in concert with the consistent use of minority archetypes over time, combine to create a pecking order that separates racial groups in hierarchical fashion. The recurring emphasis on White character development and omnipresence of the White prototypes, coupled with the absence of minorities in comparable roles, communicates the message that minorities are simply unfit to portray characters outside of their "traditional" roles as background and support figures whose actions revolve around White characters. For those minority characters that *do* obtain starring roles, not only are they often isolated, but they often are made "palatable" to the White audience by evincing a comedic quality. Ultimately, this imbalanced image cycle helps to reinforce a racially segregated space in the minds of moviegoers, even within the boundless world of fantasy and make-believe.

Although Hollywood is a White-dominated industry, it formulaically produces lucrative mainstream movies designed to appeal universally to large, broad audiences of all races. Despite this universal appeal, Hollywood mainstream movies routinely present a limited view of minorities, in stark contrast to the developed spectrum of White characters. Given Hollywood's extensive reach and economic impact, mainstream movies – through the consistent use of marginalized minority images – reflect and reinforce messages of racial imbalance worldwide. So, how exactly did we get here?

READING THE WRITING ON THE SCREEN

For starters, we outlined the six mainstream movie factors to establish the parameters for movies that fit within our analysis:

> **MAINSTREAM MOVIE FACTORS**
>
> 1. FULL-LENGTH RELEASE
> 2. WIDESPREAD DISTRIBUTION
> 3. PRODUCTION/MARKETING COSTS
> 4. LARGE BOX OFFICE SALES
> 5. A-LIST TALENT
> 6. MAINSTREAM MEDIA EXPOSURE

Additionally, we provided several bonus considerations that further indicate a movie's mainstream status:

> **MAINSTREAM MOVIE BONUS FACTORS**
>
> 1. SPINOFF
> 2. SPUNOFF
> 3. PROMOTIONAL TIE-INS
> 4. PARAPHERNALIA
> 5. THEME PARK RIDES
> 6. LONG LEAD TIME
> 7. ACADEMY AWARD NOMINATION/WIN

We then introduced and analyzed in detail the six common minority character patterns, known as the archetypes, that are utilized in mainstream movies:

> **MINORITY ARCHETYPES**
>
> 1. THE ANGEL
> 2. THE BACKGROUND FIGURE
> 3. THE COMIC RELIEF
> 4. THE MENACE TO SOCIETY
> 5. THE PHYSICAL WONDER
> 6. THE UTOPIC REVERSAL

From there we proceeded to outline and discuss the six prototypes for White characters in mainstream movies:

> **WHITE PROTOTYPES**
>
> 1. THE AFFLUENT
> 2. THE FAMILY-TIED
> 3. THE HERO
> 4. THE INTELLECTUAL
> 5. THE MANIPULATOR
> 6. THE ROMANTIC

Let us now revisit the *Bottom Line* posted at the end of *Act 1: Introduction*, *Act 2: Conflict & Climax* and *Act 3: Resolution*. These three summations provide transparent insight into how moviegoers interpret racial imagery in mainstream movies:

ADDING UP THE BOTTOM LINE

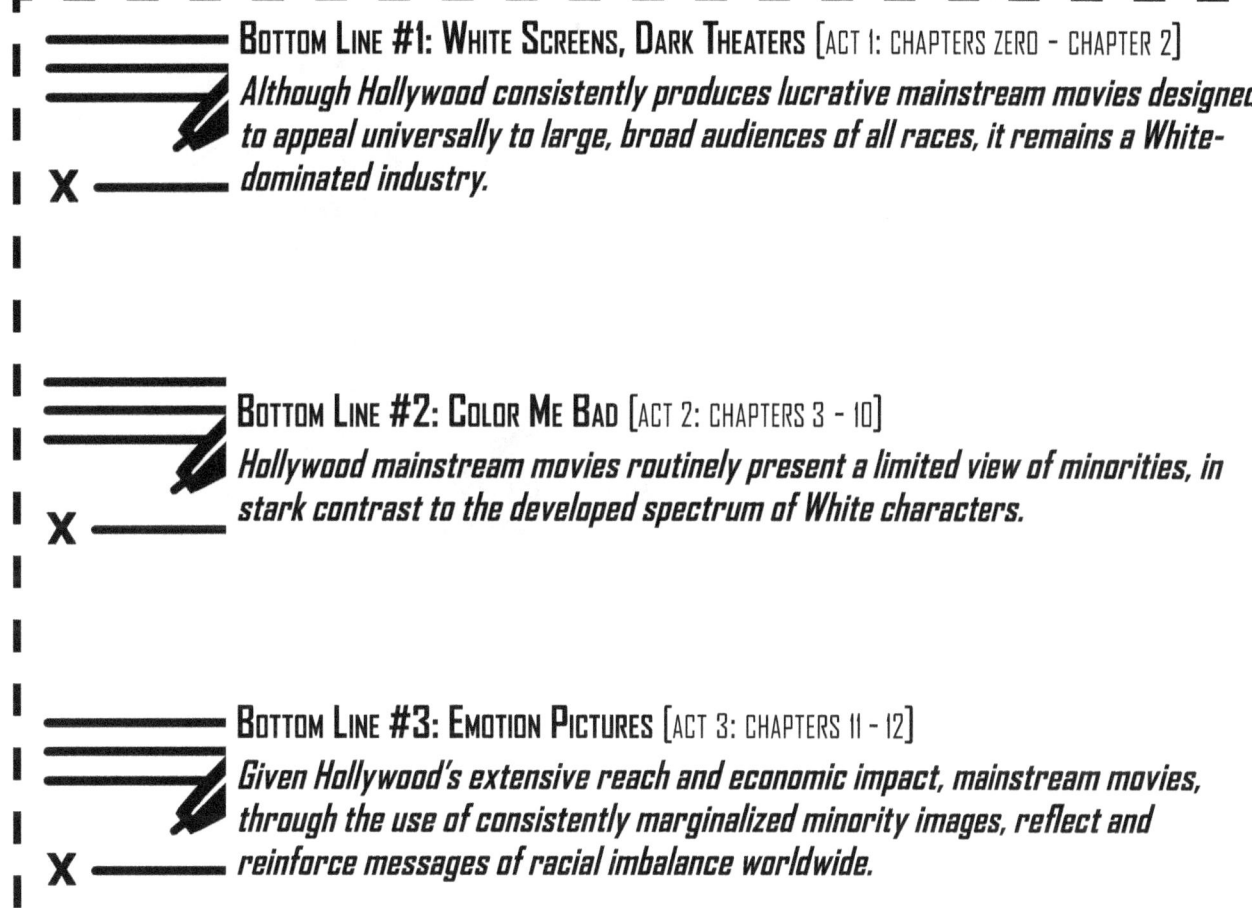

BOTTOM LINE #1: WHITE SCREENS, DARK THEATERS [ACT 1: CHAPTERS ZERO - CHAPTER 2]
Although Hollywood consistently produces lucrative mainstream movies designed to appeal universally to large, broad audiences of all races, it remains a White-dominated industry.

BOTTOM LINE #2: COLOR ME BAD [ACT 2: CHAPTERS 3 - 10]
Hollywood mainstream movies routinely present a limited view of minorities, in stark contrast to the developed spectrum of White characters.

BOTTOM LINE #3: EMOTION PICTURES [ACT 3: CHAPTERS 11 - 12]
Given Hollywood's extensive reach and economic impact, mainstream movies, through the use of consistently marginalized minority images, reflect and reinforce messages of racial imbalance worldwide.

THE SMOKELESS GUN

The available statistics merely bear out what you already know to be true: Hollywood is a White-dominated industry.[2] To this end, Hollywood has gone to great lengths to ensure that White imagery is accepted universally. Whites have fashioned themselves to be "culture-masters" and remain "culture-less" at the same time. Not surprisingly, high participation and high racial capital levels translate into the universality of the White image in the vast majority of mainstream movies, not just domestically, but around the globe.

If we are to issue an indictment for the consistent marginalization of minority images in mainstream movies, the larger question is who (or what) do we indict? If we agree that there is a pattern of marginalization that requires remedying, who or what is ultimately responsible for such change? This is the billion dollar question! Look at the following diagram and see what you find when you stare at the spaces located between the black squares:

The key to this optical illusion is that if you stare at the blank spaces in between the black squares, faint gray spots will appear, even though none are drawn on the page. This gray "square-dance" exercise serves as an appropriate metaphor for the relationship between the movie studios and audience members. If the movie studios represent the black boxes and the audience represents the white spaces running throughout the boxes, then determining who exactly is most responsible for the gray boxes that keep stubbornly appearing will not be easy. Studios produce the movies, while audience demand and box office results dictate what types of movies will be made in the future, and which movies will not be made at all.

The answer, of course, is that the gray boxes are produced by virtue of both the white spaces and the black boxes co-existing in one space. The visual illusion is analogous to the continued perpetuation of minority marginalization in mainstream movies. No movie studio will stand up and say that it is purposely trying to compromise minority images in its movies. Instead, the studio will emphasize its obligation to supplying general audience demand. Conversely, in today's purported "color-blind" age, rare is the moviegoer who will publicly approve – let alone seek out – material that overtly disparages another racial group. Each side can legitimately argue against its culpability, yet the reality is that the gray spots persist nonetheless.

PRESUMED INNOCENT

Neither movie studios nor audience members will claim responsibility for continued minority marginalization in mainstream movies, even though both parties acknowledge that it occurs. In *Chapter 11: At a Theater Near You*, we analyzed the studio's role in consciously creating marginalizing and disparaging minority images, while in *Chapter 12: Audience Participation*, we looked at how moviegoers contribute to the cycle of minority marginalization.

Movie studios must accept a large portion of the "shared blame," since they ultimately control the images released to the mainstream public. Moreover, the unwavering consistency of minority archetypes, despite being produced by separate and independent studios, shows that there is little variation in the behavior of the producers and distributors of these images. There is less evidence (even if true) to suggest that White audience members "consistently" avoid movies (of comparable production value) featuring minority characters. Movies that were well produced (budget-wise) and marketed (e.g., **Hitch**, **Bad Boys II**, **Rush Hour II**) performed quite well at the box office. These movies, while not immune from the HARM theory, affirm that there are still millions of people worldwide willing to see minority characters as protagonists.

Despite the overwhelming number of examples of studios producing movies containing the minority archetypes, there are still very few examples of big-budget movies (i.e., movies exceeding $100 million in production costs alone) starring minority characters in leading roles akin to the White prototypes. Consider the last time that you saw a movie featuring primarily minority characters with a production budget upwards of a hundred million dollars. Chances are that you can likely recall only a handful of such movies that you have seen over the course of your entire lifetime! Contrast this with the volume of big-budget movies offered by the studios containing virtually all-White casts – and zero to minimal minority presence – that are released every year (e.g., **Interstellar, Troy, Titanic, Braveheart, Lord of the Rings**, etc.). Given the dearth of similarly budgeted movies starring minorities in leading roles, one could hardly claim to have enough evidence of "failure" to preclude others from making such movies in the future. Hence, is it fair to give the audience equal blame when it has not had an *opportunity* to "reject" (or accept) minority characters in leading roles?

If no one is willing to acknowledge responsibility for the persistent pattern of minority marginalization in mainstream movies, then where do we go from here? Perhaps it would make our job easier if there was a "smoking gun" or a scathing memo that we could locate, isolate and study for clarity. Unfortunately, the issues surrounding race in mainstream movies are not as black and white as that. As illustrated in the previous chapters, race in the movies can be quite a layered, complex and gray conversation. However, the apparent difficulty involved in parsing out such issues should not act as a barrier to doing so altogether, in spite of the lack of transparent racial data (as referenced in the "Minority Reports" section of *Chapter 2: The Cast of Caricatures*). It is most likely the case that the majority of moviegoers do not intentionally wish for the image of racial minorities to be compromised on the big screen. The studios, in turn, can legitimately argue that minorities are no longer limited to "stereotypical" roles of the past and that, more importantly, they are merely producing movies that meet the demands of their audience. We must understand this relationship between the movie studios and the audience to see how those pesky gray boxes make their appearance and help perpetuate a pattern of marginalization.

By maintaining a cloak of "invisibility," subtle patterns such as the minority archetypes simply become part and parcel of the standard operating business practices in Hollywood. Once it becomes standard practice to cast minority actors in certain types of roles, it becomes "normal." Once a practice is considered normal, it is part of the mainstream. Once a practice is part of the mainstream, it simply becomes part of the "American way." Thus Hollywood argues that "fun and harmless" racial jokes communicated through mainstream movies should not be taken personally against any one individual minority or any particular racial group — it is simply a matter of maintaining American habit and custom. Darn. The gray boxes strike again.

THE PRICE OF PARITY

The continued marginalization of minorities, although explained and analyzed in detail within the preceding pages, is nonetheless inexcusable given the socially acceptable push for "inclusion" and the high valuation of diversity. Hollywood employs vast amounts of intellectual and financial capital to create a few seconds of cinematic magic for patrons throughout the world to enjoy. Yet, Hollywood still finds it difficult to make more meaningful minority characters appear onscreen. Many Hollywood studios and audience members advance justifications of spotty minority participation in mainstream movies based upon explanations of "market forces" – explanations which support the cycle of blamelessness – but which nonetheless do not provide concrete insight into the steady and perpetual presence of the HARM Theory and minority archetypes. Although mainstream movies are designed to appeal to audience emotions, the negative repercussions of minority marginalization in mainstream movies can be distilled into two distinct costs:

1) Financial Cost

Patterns of minority marginalization and White glamorization have appeared in so many movies over the years that their image patterns are now commonplace. Movie audiences have been conditioned to understand that to repeat these patterns is not to be racist *per se*, but rather to employ prudent business sense as dictated by available statistical data, market pressures and market research. Thus, it is important to stress that much of the "natural" tendency of mainstream audiences to identify with White characters is the result of conditioning over time, a by-product of millions of marketing dollars that have consciously fueled this "unconscious" behavior. With respect to minorities, these formulaic patterns are particularly problematic considering that minority images are often sparse, unflattering and sometimes outright disparaging. Nevertheless, the minority archetypes continue to be regarded as part of the general formula for successfully making and marketing a mainstream movie.

As a result, minorities continue to pay a large financial price by having their images consistently compromised and packaged for global consumption. The limited array of minority roles *directly translates into limited opportunities for financial success for minority actors*. The prevalence of minorities fulfilling roles with limited speaking parts and limited screen time means limited opportunities for financial gain for an aspiring minority actor with dreams of establishing a fruitful and successful career as a mainstream Hollywood actor. Hollywood stars are not born, *they are created*. Without repeated exposure in prominent roles in a variety of mainstream movies, being a minority – or rather, *not being White* – significantly impacts an actor's opportunities for financial success. Since Whites constitute the overwhelming majority of screenwriters, producers and directors, minorities are seldom on the forefront of studio executives' minds as they plot the creation of their next major blockbuster movie project.

To date there has been no true financial incentive for Hollywood to change. Movie studios profit handsomely from movies that marginalize minority images, and there appears to be no shortage of minority actors willing to sit for a spell on the sacrificial sofa, all in the name of economic survival. So long as Hollywood studios continue to see tangible profits, there will be no abstract reason to change the current business practice.

Hollywood has invested very little in multi-dimensional minority roles, displaying at times a most *disingenuous* approach to diversity. What else could explain Hollywood's willingness to disparage and mock minorities (e.g., casting Asian females in **Austin Powers: Goldmember** as Fook Yu and Fook Mi) and their *reluctance* to showcase minorities as leading characters and central protagonists? Nevertheless, Hollywood continues unapologetically to reach out to minority-paying moviegoers for continued patronage of its mainstream movies. As long as Hollywood is able to sell "skin-deep" diversity as a substitute for penetrating parity, then Hollywood will not have any motivation to change or modify its offerings. As it stands, the increased use of superficial diversity has helped to placate many critics, thereby muting many of the ongoing conversations about race in Hollywood. For those who have long rallied against negative stereotypes and can no longer find them as frequently in contemporary movies, their critical eyes are not losing sight – they are merely looking for the wrong things. Minority archetype patterns represent the newer and often more subtle strain of discrimination with which informed moviegoers must contend.

Minorities, if and when they do appear in a mainstream movie, must be able to quickly and correctly recognize if their images are marginalized in relation to the dominant White images. Hollywood is under no obligation to include minorities in mainstream movies, *inasmuch as they have a financial incentive to do so*. Likewise, minority groups are under no obligation to patronize movies that make them look unfavorable in the eyes of both domestic and international audiences. There is a choice for both groups: minority audiences can vote more forcefully with their purses and wallets, thereby empowering minority actors to become more selective about the roles they accept; Hollywood, with knowledge that certain minority character patterns are limiting, insulting and disparaging, can choose not to employ these formulas, while seeking simultaneously to expand its market base.

The studios must stop hiding behind industry statistics and desist blaming the international audience for continued disparities in racial representation onscreen. Until we have a representative sampling of "equally-budgeted" movies (i.e., movies prominently featuring minorities that have budgets similar to those starring Whites) to show the success (or failure) of racial parity in Hollywood, then their "data" is merely another excuse to continue the unabated history of minority marginalization. *The bottom line is the bottom dime.*

2) Social Cost

Given the broad and penetrating scope of the minority archetypes, it is of little consequence whether the major Hollywood studios are producing marginalized minority images intentionally or unwittingly. The search for that one tell-all memo where a studio executive admits that he wanted to humiliate minority characters all along will prove fruitless. Hollywood has dramatically improved its track record for diversity in recent years, but occasional visual evidence of "progress" does not necessarily mean that Hollywood is *progressive*.

In the final analysis, the minority archetype patterns are too rampant to be random or the result of mere coincidence, as illustrated by the extensive examples cited in this text. Even though we illustrated the archetypes and prototypes with a wide variety of examples, we only presented a mere sampling out of the multitude of mainstream movies, which ultimately means that our examples merely scratch the surface of these deep-seated Hollywood patterns. Mainstream movie images are premeditated by definition since they take months – if not years – to make. Given the size, scale and cost of a mainstream movie, scenes are painstakingly planned out in vigorous detail before they are captured on camera. It is ironic that an industry so governed by high-pressure deadlines and budgets on one hand can be so lax with decades-old timelines for improving diversity on the other.

The statistical improvement of diversity is only part of the solution, especially since numbers only tell part of the story. Movies like **The Last Samurai** are statistical boons for diversity since they contain lots of minority actors. Yet, when all is said and done, a White actor is still the central protagonist (Tom Cruise) who saves the day. Although Hollywood has slowly gravitated away from traditional stereotypes, it nonetheless pulls audiences toward minority archetypes that individually may appear flattering or benign, but collectively support an overarching pattern of marginalization.

Although the archetypes have emerged to replace antiquated stereotypes, their discriminatory substance and function remain largely the same. It is just as amazing as it is alarming that the *Angel, Background Figure, Comic Relief, Menace to Society, Physical Wonder* and *Utopic Reversal* archetypes still apply to the vast majority of minority characters in the vast majority of mainstream movies, despite documented statistics reflecting "progress" in minority participation. The statistics only speak to *numeric* improvement, but the brutal reality is that the White prototypes of the *Affluent, Family-Tied, Hero, Intellectual, Manipulator* and *Romantic* have rarely been applicable to minority characters in mainstream movies.

What is clear and unambiguous is that Hollywood studios – and audiences alike – have invested in the strength and conviction of White characters. Whites have been favorably depicted as being able to confront their problems, outthink the killer, restore/maintain/enforce/uphold justice, experience intimacy and romance, achieve stability and security, manipulate their fate, realize their destiny, explore their fantasy, lose their temper, take charge of the situation, enjoy extravagant material possessions, obsess about insignificant details, take personal liberties where appropriate, break laws and violate rules where necessary, make their voice heard, and, of course, save the world.

Minority characters have yet to "breakthrough" and attain the broad character range that audiences have universally taken for granted with White characters. When a mainstream movie "just happens" to feature a lone minority character, and that lone minority character is only onscreen for a limited period of time in a disparaging role, it only heightens the minority's juxtaposition against sustained themes of White glamorization.

FRONT ROW AND CENTER

Understandably, Hollywood's charge is not to serve as an agent for social activism; Hollywood's charge is to provide entertainment for a fee, and to make money for all the vested interests involved. However, upon close scrutiny of the minority character patterns, which have persisted unabated throughout the years, it is disingenuous for Hollywood to continuously pat itself on the back upon the latest report of a statistical increase in "diversity." Not only is it disingenuous, but it is troubling that Hollywood claims to be "unaware" of a conscious manipulation of race. The strength, depth, scope and consistency of the pattern reveal quite the opposite and suggest that those in Hollywood are astutely aware of how they deal with race.

Hollywood studios rely on clever marketing techniques as a means of attracting more minority consumers to pay for their products – even when the movies they are marketing do not feature minority characters that impact the overall storyline or plot development. By doing this, Hollywood studios communicate the underlying and disturbing message that they expect minority moviegoers to pay the full cost of *admission* while simultaneously enduring the price of *omission* from the mainstream movie experience.

In the simplest sense, Hollywood is no longer racist; just *racialized*. Although minority inclusion is at an all-time high, true substantive infusion has yet to take place on a consistent basis. Many of Hollywood's historically racist intentions to purposely exclude minorities have morphed over the years into "unintentional omissions," both of which ultimately produce a similar marginalizing effect. Further, although some in Hollywood make concerted attempts to include diversity in their movies, an increase in the *quantity* of minority characters without an increase in the *quality* of these roles render these results shallow and disingenuous. Hollywood's push for diversity is not complete just because **Crash**, a low-budget, independent-crossover about racial tensions in Los Angeles, won an Academy Award for Best Picture in 2006. If anything, the fervent interest in **Crash** suggests that the subject of race is very much on the mind of many moviegoers.

By continuing to merely modify the archetypal patterns over the years, Hollywood has communicated a more disturbing message that minorities lack the emotional and intellectual capacity to live life like their White counterparts — *even in the realm of fiction*. Mainstream movie audiences and movie studios alike, both of which are dominated by Whites, engage in a cyclical conversation devoid of blame, whereby no stock is invested in the concept that minorities are anything other than role players within a larger, more important White hierarchy.

Minority character archetypes have been employed so long that they are accepted as a conventional part of mainstream movies. Minority archetypes are incorporated as a "normal" part of the average moviegoing experience. The commonplace nature of minority archetypes results in the casual acceptance of minority marginalization, with only the most egregious and stereotypical examples attracting national attention and criticism. Although racial imagery has certainly come a long way, long-term change will only manifest itself through continued mainstream audience exposure to more complex minority characters and minority-driven scenarios. In effect, mainstream audiences must be willing to accept average minorities as "stars," much in the same way the principles of White glamorization work to elevate the primacy and importance of "average (White) Americans" onscreen.

Hollywood cannot be taken seriously any longer if the studios continue to spend hundreds of millions of dollars and years of pre-production just to tweak the right dialogue, the right lighting and the right shot, only to profess ignorance about the inability to find time to include more minorities. Granted, Hollywood is under no obligation to include minorities in its movies.

Yet, in the infamous words of Hannibal Lecter (*The Silence of the Lambs*), *quid pro quo* is most appropriate. Hollywood counts on minority financial participation and patronage at the box office but simultaneously plans for minority marginalization onscreen. Time has certainly shown that Hollywood has the creative ability to do "what it wants." Innovative minds have figured out ways to build replicas of the Titanic, have mapped out intricate storylines, and created new camera and editing techniques that we all enjoy, but for some reason Hollywood has failed to figure out how to "find" and market more minority actors and minority-based storylines.

Discussions about diversity and equity within Hollywood rarely focus on the systematic ordering of the White hierarchy and patronage that facilitates the universal distribution and acceptance of White imagery. While both minorities and Whites contribute to Hollywood's current racial climate, a common refrain is that minorities, if uncomfortable or dissatisfied with Hollywood's current formulaic arrangement, should just "make their own movies." However, the mainstream movie business is well established, and those who wish to make such movies must deal with unions (and other labor groups and outlets), which means that more than likely Whites will be involved along the way, despite concerted attempts to involve as many minorities as possible. Also, even if minorities were to take the lead in making "different" movies, this still does not address the fact that *Hollywood* continues to marginalize minorities. Minorities should not bear the *entire* responsibility for changing their own image, nor should they completely absolved of contributing to the current climate. The same can be said of the White people working in Hollywood. Who is more "responsible" for producing the marginalizing images in a movie like **Little Man**: the Wayans brothers or the White producers from Sony Pictures Entertainment, Revolution Studios and/or Revolution Royal Productions?

Ultimately, everyone mistakenly presumes their own innocence simply because they believe that they are not *completely* guilty of causing the problem. Everyone can justify their decisions in financial terms, which makes the individual actors who use this rationale almost as "guilty" as the studio executives that do the exact same thing, albeit at a larger scale with much greater implications. We must continue to take a hard-hitting look at how *all* parties involved guiltily maintain their innocence.

LIGHTS! CAMERA! INTERACTION!

Now that you have familiarized yourself with the minority archetypes and White prototypes, we present you with an invitation to continue the conversation any and every time you would like. Visit *The Pupil's Army Pages* at **www.theracedoc.com** where you can do any of the following:

1) join the *Pupil's Army*, where you can share what you see at the movies regarding race
2) explore our *Popout Pantry* to catch anecdotes and updates about race at the movies
3) use the *Watchdog Guide* document to quickly analyze the quantity and quality of race at your movies

Ultimately, we wish to observe: **How hard or easy is it to find minority and White characters that without question, depart from archetype and prototype patterns and the overarching HARM Theory?**

Stay tuned to see whether the historical, social and financial issues surrounding race at the movies will continue to generate sequels. In the meantime, we shall see you at the movies . . .

As avid movie lovers, we appreciate Hollywood movies and their social function – in spite of their racial imperfections – because they are an important part of American culture. Join **The Race Doctor** as we continue to identify and examine minority marginalization and White glamorization in mainstream movies. The ability to detect patterns and make relational associations on a large scale is vital since mainstream Hollywood must be judged by its total body of work, and not by singular cases or exceptions. Although you, *the Protagonist*, will now walk away with a heightened sensitivity about mainstream movie images, you will nonetheless be able to enjoy movies while simultaneously recognizing the subtle patterns and imagery that shape the racial landscape of mainstream movies. Now that you know that the answer is, "Yes, perhaps there is indeed race in your movie," from here on out, we promise that *you will NEVER see movies the same way again* . . .

BONUS FEATURES

BONUS FEATURES

GLOSSARY OF TERMS

GLOSSARY OF TERMS

In parentheses is the page number upon which each vocabulary word first appears (as defined) within the text.

A

A-list actor – (pg. 12) an actor deemed über-important within mainstream society and worthy of constant attention due to their ability to consistently draw a large following; as a result this actor is able to command and receive significant financial compensation for their work.

across-the-street minority – (pg. 63) a character whereby little ambiguity exists as to their racial identity or minority status based upon their physical appearance.

Affluent – (pg. 164) a White prototype pattern where the plot or a character arc is facilitated by affluence or access to significant capital. Most representations of prototypical Affluence are depicted through two nuanced means: *Assumed Affluent* and *Financing Fantasy*.

anchor – (pg. 158) the moral, political and social orientation of a character around which events in the movie revolve.

Angel – (pg. 56) a minority archetype character usually found in a servile position or functioning as a sidekick, serving as a source of spiritual strength, guidance and support to the central character(s). Frequently, this character occupies a "teacher" type role, imparting insightful perspectives or life lessons, despite the smaller amount of privilege and screen time that they may command relative to the protagonist.

archetype – (pg. 12) benign, but reoccurring character patterns that while not explicitly or overtly racist on the surface, nonetheless within the aggregate contribute towards larger patterns of marginalization.

asymptote – (pg. 62) a non-White actor whose physical attributes approach the White Beauty Standard or allow the actor to portray White characters. As with the mathematical concept that shares the same name, although this actor closely resembles or can be made to resemble the mainstream paradigm for beauty (e.g., for women: long, flowing hair, waif shape), she cannot reproduce the paradigm completely since she is not White. No matter how much she does externally to try and approach the paradigm, her culture or race still serves as a mark of social distinction.

B

Background Figure – (pg. 56) a minority archetype character that is rather inconsequential to the overall storyline and does not perform actions or recite dialogue that advances the plot in any meaningful way; serves as mere "window dressing" onscreen.

bankability – (pg. 20) the degree to which an actor or director's name alone can raise 100% financing up-front for a movie.

blockbuster – (pg. 17) a movie which proves to be an overwhelming financial success at the box office. In common usage a "blockbuster" is a movie that has a box office of typically more than $100 million upon its release in North America.

C

catharsis – (pg. 72) an emotional or psychological release of tension, resulting in revelation or personal growth for a character.

character arc – (pg. 41) the charting of the emotional or psychological change that occurs within a character as they progresses through a story.

color-blind movie – (pg. 204) a movie with an almost exclusively White cast and a miniscule or non-existent minority presence; although presented as "universal," or applicable to all races, the movie merely focuses on Whites and their experiences.

Comic Relief – (pg. 56) a minority archetype character where culture serves as fodder for most the jokes that they are involved in. Typical conduct includes loud, improper grammar, intense emotion, exaggerated motions and expressions.

common denominator – (pg. 28) a broad theme that most people can recognize or relate to based upon their general human experience.

connective switch – (pg. 66) the ability of a viewer to adopt the perspective of a character in order to form an emotional connection with that character.

contra-juxtaposition – (pg. 98) an exaggeration of an existing minority stereotype contrasted against "typical" White middle-class norms.

controlled universe – (pg. 202) a secured setting whereby the movie's creators are able to manipulate all objects and persons depicted on film to create a particular image captured onscreen.

copycat behavior – (pg. 249) when individuals imitate behavior displayed in a mainstream movie. Acts can range from physical demonstrations to mere recitation of dialogue (e.g., "Show me the money!" from *Jerry Maguire*).

cross-casting – (pg. 207) wherein a movie studio casts a minority actor in a role originally slated for, designed for, portrayed by, or written for a White actor.

cycle of blamelessness – (pg. 205) cycle whereby movie studios and mainstream audiences each hold the other responsible for the lack of substantive minority characters.

E

emasculation – (pg. 91) the process whereby the male identity of a minority character is overtly compromised or challenged in the face of conventional gender roles.

ethnicity – (pg. 33) specific group affiliation based upon particular cultural ties, often related to a shared country of origin.

F

Family-Tied – (pg. 169) a White prototype pattern that stresses the strength and value of relationships between White family members. This prototype maintains the eventual reunification or continued preservation of the core family unit as a consistent goal, despite the onset of various conflicts and tensions endured during the course of the movie.

faux presence – (pg. 30) whereby the marketing campaign misleadingly suggests that a minority character has a more prominent role (or more screen time) than actually depicted in the movie. Within a color-blind movie, the promised but perfunctory minority presence that initially attracted minority moviegoers to the movie essentially amounts to a "bait and switch."

finite fantasy – (pg. 217) due to the socioeconomic effects of living a "racialized life," many mainstream movies spearheaded by minorities are limited in the spectrum of social experiences that they portray due to a limitation of resources.

first-run movie – (pg. 16) a feature typically ninety minutes to three hours in length that is first exhibited to the public in national and regional movie theater chains.

G

greatest possible audience – (pg. 14) the ideal number of available consumers willing to purchase or view a particular mainstream movie.

greenlight – (pg. 30) process whereby an idea for a movie project receives authorization for filming by a major movie studio, matched with financial backing.

H

Hero – (pg. 175) during the course of the movie, this White prototype pattern is an otherwise "normal" character who after some trial or initiation, is annointed to become something larger than their previous self, thereby enjoying an elevated status above that of an average individual. Most usually personified by a White male, this character is frequently authorized or justified in using forceful, aggressive and decisive actions to complete his objective(s).

Hollywood's Acting Rule for Minorities (HARM theory) – (pg. 56) holds that if and when a minority character appears in a mainstream movie, their character will be compromised in some way, shape or form.

Hollywood's Racial Makeup – (pg. 33) refers to the five racial categories consistently acknowledged by Hollywood onscreen in mainstream movies: Asian, Black, Latino, Other and White. These categorizations are based upon the most frequent and prominent races that mainstream Hollywood overtly depicts consistently on the silver screen, and are not to be taken as an exhaustive detailing of all possible racial images that may appear onscreen.

I

identification process – (pg. 170) the method and manner by which the moviegoer physically, emotionally and psychologically connects with a character that resembles the viewer's physical, emotional and psychological profile.

Intellectual – (pg. 179) a White prototype character that appears to be inherently knowledgeable about anything and everything; this protoype is deceptively important to movie audiences since this character often provides vital and important information essential to the plot.

K

key art – (pg. 215) promotional materials that distill the movie's central themes into succinct symbology. It also represents the official art produced and distributed by the movie studio that signifies the movie's principal themes and promotes the movie. A movie poster is a common example of key art.

M

mainstream culture – (pg. 22) the prevailing, yet intangible current of contemporary thought within society.

mainstream injection – (pg. 28) the attempt to distribute a mainstream movie within the mainstream pipeline, thereby improving its chances of becoming embedded or infused within mainstream culture.

mainstream movie – (pg. 11) a movie designed, produced and marketed with the purpose of reaching the greatest possible audience.

mainstream pipeline – (pg. 21) the assortment of major media outlets that reach the greatest possible audience due to nationwide marketing and distribution networks. This network consists of radio programs, newspapers, magazines, television shows and movies that are seen by vast numbers of people throughout the country at or around the same time, thereby serving as an informal means of sharing information, centralizing thought and organizing loose societal networks.

major movie studios – (pg. 11) the corporate conglomerates responsible for the majority of mainstream distribution. The six major distributors and producers of movies are: 1) Buena Vista Pictures Distribution (The Walt Disney Company), 2) Paramount Pictures Corporation, 3) Sony Pictures

Entertainment Inc., 4) Twentieth Century Fox Film Corporation, 5) Universal City Studios LLP, and 6) Warner Bros. Entertainment Inc. The Chairmen and Presidents of these companies all serve on the board of directors for the MPAA. See *Motion Picture Association of America,* "Members Page," n.d., <http://www.mpaa.org/AboutUsMembers.asp> (15 July 2007).

Manipulator – (pg. 184) a White prototype character who rejects their circumstances at face value and changes them to fit their personal needs. This prototype frequently moves from a position where they lack control to the point where they become the primary person in control.

masking – (pg. 67) whereby an actor is able to hide his racial identity on or offscreen and blend in with the White majority through a superficial change (e.g., bleaching of hair, change of surname)

Menace to Society – (pg. 57) this minority archetype character is portrayed as possessing a value system that poses a threat to civil "normalcy," either through violence (or potential violence) and/or moral corruption.

Minority Cycle of Movie-Making – (pg. 166) few opportunities exist for minorities to make movies due to risk-averse studios, which accounts for fewer opportunities to overcome the risk.

minstrelsy – (pg. 97) a wildly popular form of entertainment that denigrated Blacks and lampooned their status as victims of systemic racism. Minstrel shows frequently featured both Whites and Blacks who donned "blackface" make-up.

moral compass – (pg. 221) the unwritten rule guiding major studios so that they consistently produce mainstream movies communicating the ultimate victory of "good over bad." Many movie studios, perhaps under an informal moral obligation to provide audiences with redeeming messages, freely use the protagonist onscreen as the ultimate visual metaphor of triumph over tribulation. After all, most movies would strike audiences as rather uninteresting if there was not some sort of tension or conflict that required resolution. Nonetheless, the overwhelming majority of mainstream movies ensure that bad acts are punished and that good acts obtain recognition before the credits roll. So, in its most simplistic terms, movies feature "problems" that audience members pay for the privilege of vicariously experiencing and solving through the protagonist.

O

one-way culture sharing – (pg. 74) where one racial group's cultural "resources" are exploited chiefly to benefit a White character without a reciprocal exchange.

P

pararealistic movie – (pg. 221) a mainstream movie crafted or based upon a historical event containing a mixture of hyperbolized or fictional accounts, usually out of necessity to maintain the movie's entertainment value and mainstream appeal.

Physical Wonder – (pg. 57) this minority archetype character is regarded for their physical or sexual prowess, typically at the sacrifice of intellectual or emotional capacities.

premium of proportion – (pg. 54) the amount of impact a character image possesses relative to their entire racial group. Isolated and unfavorably depicted minority roles disproportionately disparage the overall group image to which the representative character belongs, primarily due to a lack of other available images with which to provide balance.

protective stereotype – (pg. 111) exaggerated images of bigotry or hatred that allow common White audience members to distance themselves from such abnormal and obvious displays of anti-social behavior. Such a character is "protective" in that it masks more subtle and common representations of discrimination more likely to be prevalent within contemporary society.

prototype – (pg. 163) general patterns of common traits shared or exhibited by White characters in mainstream movies. These overarching character patterns reflect the most consistent methods in which White characters assert an exclusive and domineering presence onscreen. These prototypes prioritize Whites as central characters whose the thoughts, feelings, sentiments and actions become a primary concern for the viewing audience. Moreover, these characters typically serve as emotional anchors for the movies in which they appear, often harnessing and marshaling their stated attributes in order to achieve some measure of cathartic growth or achieve resolution for their individual character arc.

R

race – (pg. 33) general group affiliation based upon physically observable characteristics or physical constructs, such as skin color or hair type.

racial capital – (pg. 41) the amount of power (economic, political or social) ascribed collectively to a particular racial group.

racial requirement – (pg. 34) where a minority actor fulfills a specific role, often stereotypical in nature, that is not deemed to be a universal character playable by a person of any other race, let alone a White actor.

Romantic – (pg. 189) a White prototype character that seeks, explores and eventually finds out what true love truly means.

S

sacrificial sofa – (pg. 211) where an actor feels the need to accept a marginal or racially disparaging role for the opportunity for more lucrative and satisfying roles in the future.

stereotype – (pg. 34) a negative classification based upon specific conduct or characteristics ascribed to a particular racial group.

T

tipping point – (pg. 206) the imprecise number where "too many" minorities involved in a movie brands it as a "minority movie," thereby curtailing its budget and "universal" appeal.

U

ugly American – (pg. 86) minorities that display "undesirable" behaviors or characteristics to serve as a contrast with the "normal" American protagonist.

umbrella image – (pg. 215) a unique visual rendering used to convey information about a movie's central characters and/or overall themes. Movie studios often rely on the umbrella image also to stimulate, remind or inspire the viewer to see the movie.

unclean hero – (pg. 144) whereby a minority protagonist represents the driving force of a movie, yet does not experience the pure moral, financial and/or sexual victories typically associated with White mainstream heroic characters.

Utopic Reversal – (pg. 57) found occupying a high social position (e.g., police chief, judge, etc.), they in actuality are a pseudo-authority figure since their level of power and authority is undercut (either explicitly or implicitly) in relation to other characters onscreen, thereby rendering their authority or position as mostly symbolic in nature.

V

visible continuum – (pg. 116) the observable part of a movie's timeline as portrayed and shown to the movie audience between the beginning and ending credits. *Note:* In theory, there is no beginning or end to a movie since a sequence of events led up until the time when the visible continuum began, and additionally, there will be a future chain of events after the movie's viewing window closes. Oftentimes, this timeline is manipulated and the audience is allowed to see in the past via flashbacks or glimpse into the future via time travel. The movie's creators must therefore select finite points within a larger story to form the boundaries of the visible continuum, or those segments of time that the audience is allowed to see.

W

White balance – (pg. 158) due to high levels of positive racial capital, negative roles for White characters do not disproportionately represent the full range of White characters.

White Beauty Standard – (pg. 61) actresses who approach (or are made to approach) the White aesthetic (e.g., small hips and slender build; long or lightened, flowing hair).

world-stop scene – (pg. 184) scene wherein a character takes personal action that noticeably interrupts the actions of others, emphasizing the importance of the character's decisions. This scene is common to White Manipulator prototypes.

NOTES

CHAPTER ZERO

1. *City News Service*, "SAG Minorities," 20 December 2000, available from Lexis-Nexis [database online]. *Note:* Dr. Metoyer occupied this position of affirmative action director at the time in which she made these comments. Subsequently, Dr. Metoyer was involved in litigation with SAG, which she accused of firing her on bogus grounds after she accused SAG superiors of discrimination and misrepresenting the true number of minorities on staff at the guild. It is one of several such lawsuits filed against SAG in recent years. See *Daily Variety*, "SAG Faces 7th Lawsuit for Racial Discrimination," 9 December 2002, pg. 82; *Daily Variety*, "SAG Sees 8th Suit over Firing," 14 April 2003, pg. 10.

2. See the section entitled "Minority Reports" in *Chapter 2: The Cast of Caricatures*. It simply is not possible to replace the word "White" with another racial category in order to obtain a truer statement (e.g., "mainstream movies have been an almost exclusively *Native American* domain") as the available statistics would demonstrate otherwise.

3. Hattie McDaniel's legacy as the first minority Oscar winner was crystallized when she was honored by the United States Postal Service in its Black Heritage commemorative stamp series. See *United States Postal Service*, "Hattie McDaniel, First African American To Win An Academy Award, Featured On New 39-Cent Postage Stamp," 25 January 2006 <http://www.usps.com/communications/news/stamps/2006/sr06_005.htm> (28 February 2006).

4. In 2007, eight of the twenty Best and Best Supporting Actor nominees were minority actors. Adriana Barraza and Rinko Kikuchi were nominated for their supporting roles in **Babel**; Jennifer Hudson claimed Best Performance by an Actress in a Supporting Role for **Dreamgirls**; Djimon Hounsou was nominated for Best Supporting Actor in **Blood Diamond**; Penélope Cruz received a Best Actress nomination for **Volver**; Will Smith received his second Best Actor in a Leading Role nomination for **The Pursuit of Happyness**; and Forest Whitaker claimed the Best Actor in a Leading Role Oscar for **The Last King of Scotland**.

5. Stephen Rea, "Oscar Hugs and Shrugs; The Academy Award Nominations Show Unusual Diversity this Year and, in the Case of 'Dreamgirls,' an Oddity," *The Philadelphia Inquirer*, 24 January 2007, pg. F1.

6. "Contemporary movies" are movies released within the fifteen to twenty years.

7. Words initially appearing in bold throughout the text are "framed for analysis" or profiled inside of movie reels dispersed throughout the text for increased emphasis and understanding. In order to ensure

coordination between the editors and the reader, please note that many vocabulary words contain definitions that differ from their assumed conventional meaning.

8   For example, see generally: Stephen Schaefer, "Under 'Siege' - Filmmakers Fend Off Criticisms from Arab-American Groups," *Boston Herald*, 4 November, 1998, available from Lexis-Nexis [database online]; *The Record*, "Black Artists Shunned?; Racial Bias Seen in Oscar Nominations," 22 March, 1996, available from Lexis-Nexis [database online]; Susan Dominus, "Why Isn't Maggie Cheung a Hollywood Star?" *The New York Times*, 14 November 2004, available from Lexis-Nexis [database online]; Lewis Beale, "H'wood Has a Bad Accent Book, Stars Say Hispanics Still Mostly Villains," *Daily News*, 24 January 2001, available from Lexis-Nexis [database online]; Steve Chagollan, "The Myth of the Native Babe: Hollywood's Pocahontas," *The New York Times*, 27 November 2005, available from Lexis-Nexis [database online].

9   For instance, eminent African American film scholar Donald Bogle has penned the seminal work *Toms, Coons, Mulattoes, Mammies & Bucks: An Interpretive History of Blacks in American Films,* (New York: Continuum International Publishing Group, 2001), which analyzes negative stereotypes for Black characters in early American film. Bogle's work, first published in 1973, essentially builds upon scholar Sterling Brown's mapping of common negative character patterns for Black fictional characters some four decades prior. See Sterling A. Brown, "Negro Character as Seen by White Authors," *The Journal of Negro Education*, Vol. 2, No. 2 (Apr., 1933), pp. 179-203. **The Race Doctor** aims to build upon existing scholarship by critically analyzing to what extent negative racial imagery for minorities persists in contemporary mainstream movies. Although stereotypical terms such as "coon" and "buck" are widely considered politically incorrect and are not verbalized openly, they nonetheless exist in substance, but merely in a different format, and known by a different name (i.e., archetypes).

CHAPTER 1

1   Joshua Rich, "Piracy King: The MPAA Crowns A New Movie Boss," *Entertainment Weekly*, 16 July 2004, pg. 18.

2   "Industry experts say the rising cost of films, the pressure on studios to make a bundle at the box office in the opening weekend and an aversion to risk are all behind the remake madness." Susan Wloszczyna, "A Remake by Any Other Name; Hollywood Is Big about Borrowing from the Past," *USA Today*, 14 April 2004, pg. 1D.

3   This book will follow standard literary conventions that recognize "actor" as a gender-neutral term.

4   *Note:* the term "A-list actor" is not necessarily synonymous with "top-flight actor," meaning, the most popular actors are not necessarily the most talented or skilled.

5   Sean Connery (1962-1967, 1971), George Lazenby (1969), Roger Moore (1973-1985), Timothy Dalton (1987-1989), Pierce Brosnan (1995-2002) and Daniel Craig (2006 to the present). See Casey Seiler, "Shaken, not Stirred, by a Bond with Bond," *The Times Union*, 20 November 2005, pg. G1.

6   For instance, the U.S. government states that, "U.S. films dominate the foreign feature films in Hong Kong. They satisfy about 90 percent of the total foreign feature film demand." United States Commercial Service "Doing Business in Hong Kong & Macau: Country Commercial Guide for U.S. Companies," 4 February 2005, <http://www.buyusainfo.net/docs/x_7423798.pdf> (15 July 2007).

7. For example, a well-known Academy Award winning movie like **Ray** made as much in one week of DVD sales ($75 million) as it did during an entire five months at the box office. See Gary Thompson, "Hollywood DVD Sales Prop Up Weak Box Office," *The San Diego Union-Tribune*, 31 July 2005 <http://www.signonsandiego.com/uniontrib/20050731/news_1a31slump.html> (15 July 2007).

8. Albert C. Outler, "Confessions, Book 11, Chapter 14," *Institute of Practical Bible Education, The Electronic Public Library*, 2005 <http://www.iclnet.org/pub/resources/text/ipb-e/epl-01/agcon-18.txt> (15 July 2007).

9. See Scott Bowles, "Hollywood Frets Over Fickle Fans," *USA Today*, 29 August 2005, <http://www.usatoday.com/life/movies/news/2005-08-28-fickle-fans_x.htm> (15 July 2007).

10. Worldwide gross as of February 2017 was $2.78 billion. See *Box Office Mojo*, "'All Time Box Office: Worldwide Grosses," n.d., <http://www.boxofficemojo.com/alltime/world> (14 February 2017). This number does not include an estimated 7.09 million units sold of Blu-ray Discs.

11. See *Motion Picture Association of America*, "2015 Theatrical Statistics Summary," n.d., <http://www.mpaa.org/wp-content/uploads/2016/04/MPAA-Theatrical-Market-Statistics-2015_Final.pdf> (14 February 2017). Please note that 2015's domestic box office ticket sales are down from 2005's total of 1.4B. Still, the attendance totals are significant given the increase in quality of home theaters, the decrease in turn-around time for DVD releases, and the increase in cost of ticket prices.

12. See Pamela McClintock, "$200 Million and Rising: Hollywood Struggles with Soaring Marketing Costs," *The Hollywood Reporter*, 31 July 2014, <http://www.hollywoodreporter.com/news/200-million-rising-hollywood-struggles-721818.html> (14 February 2017). This number can increase for major productions.

13. Notably, **The Simpsons Movie** began its marketing campaign by showing movie trailers announcing its arrival more than a year before its theatrical release. See Scott Bowles, "Mmmm, Popcorn: A 'Simpsons' Film in '07," *USA Today*, 3 April 2006, pg. 1D.

14. See Ronald Blum, "Baseball Picks 'Spider-Man' Off Base," *The Associated Press State & Local Wire*, 7 May 2004, available from Lexis-Nexis [database online].

15. See Gail Schiller, "Brand Warfare," *The Hollywood Reporter*, 10-16 May 2005, pg. S-4.

16. See David Koenig, "7-Elevens become Simpsons 'Kwik-E-Marts,'" *The Associated Press State & Local Wire*, 1 July 2007, available from Lexis-Nexis [database online]. In addition to the twelve stores that underwent facelifts (complete with industrial foam and new signage), most stores throughout the entire *7-Eleven* chain sold products featured in the movie (and television show). Underscoring how some major corporations wish to exploit the power of mainstream movies, the article states, "7-Eleven executives loved the idea. They had surveys showing a strong overlap between their customers and fans of the show – both tend to be young and male. It sounded like cash registers ringing."

17. See Michael McCarthy, "'Star Wars' Goes Utterly Commercial: Get Ready to Be Bombarded with Toys, Games, Lots of Ads," *USA Today*, 25 April 2005, pg. 2B.

18. See Kathy M. Kristof, "'Covenant' Leads a Lackluster Box Office; Weekend Totals Are the Worst of the Year. Still, 'Pirates' Hits $1 Billion in Cumulative Sales," *Los Angeles Times*, 11 September 2006, pg. C1; Pat O'Brien, "Yo Ho Ho and a Revamped Ride; Jack Sparrow and other Characters from Disney's Films Join the Crew on Pirates of the Caribbean Attraction," *The Press Enterprise*, 7 July 2006, pg. AA18.

[19] See note 13, *supra*.

[20] See Kit Bowen, "Miramax Looking for the Oscar Bounce," *Hollywood.com*, 13 February 2003, <http://www.hollywood.com/news/Miramax_Starts_Its_Oscar_Campaigns/1707579> (15 July 2007).

[21] See Orlando Ramirez, "Drawn to Controversy: Many Race-based Cartoon Stereotypes Aren't Acceptable Now but Still Remain Accessible," *The Press-Enterprise*, 28 May 1995, pg. E1.

[22] In fact, in the Winter Holiday season of 2004, it was commonplace to find "Wise-crackin' Donkey" for sale, who would regale consumers with several "gut-busting" phrases such as "Are we there yet?" and "Do you smell something?" or "Do I have something on my teeth?" See *Hasbro*, "Instructions: 'Shrek 2' Wise Crackin' Donkey," n.d., <http://www.hasbro.com/common/instruct/Shrek_2_Wise-Crackin'_Donkey.pdf> (15 July 2007). Hasbro also sells a Wise-Crackin' Shrek, but the Donkey was a "hotter sell" according to Jim Silver, co-publisher of *Toy Wishes* magazine. See Teri Goldberg, "Blockbuster Toys: This Summer's Movies Have Inspired Some Must-have Toys," *MSNBC Online*, 2 August 2004, <http://www.msnbc.msn.com/id/5263229/> (15 July 2007).

[23] The quote was attributed to Congressman Henry Hyde (R-Ill.). Lisa Friedman, "Valenti Building Has Its Preview," *The Daily News of Los Angeles*, 23 June 2005, pg. B1.

[24] "The worldwide hunger for U.S.-made entertainment helps steer our own culture, by encouraging projects that will sell overseas and discouraging those that foreign audiences are thought to spurn." Sharon Waxman, "Hollywood Attuned to World Markets," *Washington Post*, 26 October 1990, pg. A1.

[25] Take *Troy* for example, starring Brad Pitt. The movie "only" made $133.3 million domestically, a number that was practically tripled with its $364 million overseas take. See *Box Office Mojo*, "'Troy' Box Office Data," n.d., <http://www.boxofficemojo.com/movies/?id=troy.htm> (15 July 2007).

[26] "Cuba Gooding Jr. blurs by as Texas-born Doris Miller, a black mess cook on the USS West Virginia who becomes a self-made hero by blasting a Japanese plane out of the sky. The film's trailer promises a substantial part for Gooding, but he gets about five minutes out of the film's 183." Chris Garcia, "'Pearl Harbor' Bombs Out," *Cox News Service*, 24 May 2001, available from Lexis-Nexis [database online]; "Movie trailers today have nothing to do with what the movie is actually about. You'd think from 'Pearl Harbor's' trailer that the surprise attack and Cuba Gooding Jr. are major components of the film. In fact, the battle lasts barely a fifth of the film and Gooding Jr. is onscreen about 10 minutes." Steve Lowery, "A Naked Chick, Please!," *OC Weekly*, 1 June 2001, pg. 22.

[1a] See Kelly Carter, "Studios' Views of Black Films May Undercut Their Success," *USA Today*, 11 April 2001, pg. 4D.

[1b] See Bruce Orwall, "Glut of Big-Budget Movies Raises Risks for Them All," *Wall Street Journal*, 2 July 2003, pg. B1.

[1c] See *Internet Movie Database*, "Trivia for 'Ice Age,'" n.d., <http://www.imdb.com/title/tt0268380/trivia> (15 July 2007).

[1d] See Walt Williams, "Report: Paleontologist 'Fudged' Discovery to Promote Movie," *Bozeman Daily Chronicle*, 12 May 2005, <http://www.bozemandailychronicle.com/articles/2005/05/12/news/01horner.txt> (15 July 2007).

¹ᵉ See *Internet Movie Database*, "Trivia for Pearl Harbor," n.d., <http://www.imdb.com/title/tt0213149/trivia> (15 July 2007).

¹ᶠ See John Burman, "Setting the Pace: Cruise, Hanks and Roberts in Photo Finish As the Most Bankable Players in 'The Hollywood Reporter's' 2002 Star Power Survey," *The Hollywood Reporter*, 1 August 2004 <http://thehollywoodreporter.com/thr/starpower/article_display.jsp?vnu_content_id=1294804> (15 July 2007).

¹ᵍ See Alex Veiga, "Sony to Pay $1.5M Over Fake Movie Critic," *The Associated Press State & Local Wire*, 3 August 2005, available from Lexis-Nexis [database online].

¹ʰ *Indiana State Museum*, "Lord of the Rings, Motion Picture Trilogy Exhibition," n.d., <http://www.in.gov/ism/MuseumExhibits/lotr.asp> (15 July 2006).

¹ⁱ See Jason Szep, "'Star Wars' Becomes Tool to Teach Modern Technology," *Red Orbit*, 24 October 2005, <http://www.redorbit.com/news/entertainment/282724/star_wars_becomes_tool_to_teach_modern_technology/> (15 July 2007).

¹ʲ See Holli Chmela, "Did You Know Androids Could Eat Mail?," *The New York Times*, 22 March 2007, pg. A19; *United States Postal Service*, "Citizens' Stamp Advisory Council," <http://www.usps.com/communications/organization/csac.htm> (15 July 2007).

¹ᵏ See SI Wire, "Super Bowl Commercials: How Much Does a Spot Cost in 2017?," *Sports Illustrated*, 16 January 2017, <http://www.si.com/nfl/2017/01/26/super-bowl-commercial-cost-2017.html> (14 February 2017).

¹ˡ *The Associated Press State & Local Wire*, "Mandela Praises Oscar Winner Theron," 11 March 2004, available from Lexis-Nexis [database online].

¹ᵐ See Andy Seiler, "Something to Offend Everyone: Minority Groups Say Hit Films Fill Screens with Stereotypes," *USA Today*, 28 June 1999, pg. 1D.

¹ⁿ See *Internet Movie Database*, "Trivia for 'Wallace & Gromit in the Curse of the Were-Rabbit.'" n.d., <http://www.imdb.com/title/tt0312004/trivia> (15 July 2007).

¹ᵒ Suzanne Fields, "Bridging the Hollywood-D.C. Gap," *The Times Union*, 4 April 2005, pg. A9.

¹ᵖ See Hy Hollinger and Cynthia Littleton, "International Markets Have Long Been Crucial to Film Biz," *The Hollywood Reporter*, 28 July 2005, pg. S-1.

¹ᑫ See Dustin Rowles, "A Bunch of American Box-Office Disappointments Were Global Hits in 2016," *Uproxx*, 1 January 2017, <http://www.uproxx.com/movies/american-box-office-bombs-internationally> (14 February 2017).

¹ʳ See T.L. Stanley, "The Color of Money: Hollywood Diversifies," *Advertising Age*, 30 August 2004, pg. 3.

CHAPTER 2

1. Anthony Breznican, "Jet Li Punches Back Against Formulaic Action Movies," *The Associated Press State & Local Wire*, 24 August 2004, available from Lexis-Nexis [database online].

2. **Hollywood's Racial Makeup** refers to those racial groups most consistently featured by characters in Hollywood movies: Asian, Black, Latino, Other and White. These categorizations are based upon the *most prominently* featured races that mainstream Hollywood overtly depicts in its movies, and is not necessarily an exhaustive list that details all racial imagery set to appear in a mainstream movie. See *Chapter 3: The Cast of Caricatures* or the vocabulary entry in the glossary for additional information. **NOTE FOR THIS TEXT:** We acknowledge that

there are some practical limitations in grouping vast groups of people within "catchall categories." However, we find it most effective to analyze race through the paradigm that Hollywood provides us. Although the "Asian" category includes Pacific Islanders, "Asian" in this instance is synonymous with East Asian culture (e.g., Chinese, Japanese or Korean) and does not necessarily signify someone that hails from India, even though "East Indians" are "Asian" as well. The "Black" category includes Africans and descendants from the African Diaspora. The "Latino" category includes those persons of Hispanic descent and includes references to both Latino and Hispanic. The "Other" category includes smaller, yet recognizable racial groups that appear too infrequently to warrant separate categories, although Native Americans and Middle Easterners comprise the largest groups within this "Other" category. The "Other" category will also include characters that appear racially ambiguous onscreen that do not otherwise satisfy the other four categories. The "White" category includes all ethnic classifications and differentiations that all share White skin, and are not of Hispanic descent. Even though they are only colors, "Black" and "White" will be capitalized in the text when used to describe broad racial groupings.

3   In this text, the "Asian" definition does not include "East Indians" or persons from the country of India.

4   Played by Tadao Tomomatsu. As an anecdotal glimpse into the limited world of Asian mainstream character roles, look at the history of Tomomatsu's other roles to see what patterns emerge. See *Internet Movie Database*, "Full Cast and Crew for 'Inspector Gadget,'" n.d., <http://www.imdb.com/title/tt0141369/fullcredits> (15 July 2007). Racial requirements are employed for White characters as well, whereby only a White actor is "best suited" to play a particular role due to historical context or credibility. For example, would the premise of two divorce lawyers crashing weddings to "score babes" in **Wedding Crashers** still receive a greenlight from a major Hollywood studio if the two leads were anything other than White males? As a clue to the racial transparency required by the characters, the movie's website contains a "Crasher Kit," which contains helpful accessories and tactics on how to successfully crash weddings. Among them is a *Name Tag Marker*, where to "really blend in you need a culturally appropriate name tag." Upon clicking on the name tag inside of the open briefcase on the website, the user receives these instructions:

> Choosing an appropriate fake name for the wedding you're attending is vital. Enter your details and print off your own culturally sensitive name tag.
> **Step 1.** Enter your name;
> **Step 2.** Choose a culture to make the name conversion:
> ☐American ☐Irish ☐Chinese ☐Jewish ☐Indian;
> **Step 3.** Print out your name tag and blend in!"

See *WeddingCrashersMovie.com*, "Crasher Kit," n.d., <http://www.weddingcrashersmovie.com> (15 July 2007).

5   See Martha M. Lauzen, "The Celluloid Ceiling: Behind-the-Scenes and On-Screen Employment of Women in the Top 250 Films of 2002," *Movies Directed By Women*, 7 July 2003, <http://www.moviesbywomen.com/marthalauzenphd/stats2003.html> (15 July 2007).

6   See Michael Speier, "The Bronze Screen: 100 Years of the Latino Image in Hollywood Cinema," *Variety*, 8 October 2002, <http://www.variety.com/review/VE1117919004?categoryid=32&cs=1&query=the+and+bronze+and+screen&display=the+bronze+screen> (15 July 2007).

7   Tatiana Siegel, "Latinos in Entertainment: With a Number of High-profile Projects on the Horizon, Hollywood Appears Ripe for a Hispanic Revolution," *The Hollywood Reporter*, 14 June 2005, <http://www.

hollywoodreporter.com/thr/film/feature_display.jsp?vnu_content_id=1000957036> (15 July 2007).

8 In *Pocahontas* at roughly the 1:06:24 mark, the scene containing the song "Savages" begins. While both the settlers and the Native Americans have song verses "disparaging" the other, note the stereotypical rants from the English Settlers, as opposed to the more defensive critiques from the Native Americans:

English Settlers	Native Americans
Governor Ratcliffe	*Chief Powhatan*
What can you expect	This is what we feared
From filthy little heathens?	The paleface is a demon
Here's what you get when the races are diverse	The only thing they feel at all is greed
Their skin's a hellish red	*Kekata*
They're only good when dead	Beneath that milky hide
They're vermin, as I said	There's emptiness inside
And worse	*Native Americans*
English Settlers	I wonder if they even bleed
They're savages! Savages!	They're savages! Savages!
Governor Ratcliffe	Barely even human
Barely even human	Savages! Savages!
English Settlers	*Chief Powhatan*
Savages! Savages!	Killers at the core
Governor Ratcliffe	*Kekata*
Drive them from our shore!	They're different from us
They're not like you and me	Which means they can't be trusted
Which means they must be evil	*Powhatan*
We must sound the drums of war!	We must sound the drums of war
English Settlers	*Native Americans*
They're savages! Savages!	They're savages! Savages!
Dirty shrieking devils!	First we deal with this one
Now we sound the drums of war!	Then we sound the drums of war

The lyrics reflected in this note were transcribed by **The Race Doctor** during viewings of the movie. This song was performed by David Ogden Stiers, Jim Cummings and Chorus for *Pocahontas: Original Motion Picture Soundtrack,* (Burbank: Walt Disney Records, 1995).

9 See Jim Beckerman, "Entertainers Face Risks if Politics Get into the Act," *The Record*, 25 July 2004, pg. E1.

10 Bruce Adler, "Arabian Nights," *Aladdin: Original Motion Picture Soundtrack*, (Burbank: Walt Disney Records, 1992).

11 *United States Census Bureau,* "2014 National Population Projections: Publications," n.d., <http://www.census.gov/population/projections/data/national/2014/publications.html> (14 February 2017).

12 *Motion Picture Association of America,* "Valenti Reports Record-Breaking Box Office Results, Continued Decrease in Production Costs and Praises Movie Industry War Efforts in ShoWest Address," 5 March 2002, <http://www.mpaa.org/jack/content.htm> (15 December 2005). According to a survey conducted by the MPAA, 42% of Blacks and 45% of Latinos, as compared to 33% of Whites, were frequent moviegoers (i.e., seeing more than one movie a month), indicating that minorities do participate in the Hollywood Experience at a high rate, just not onscreen. See Erin Texeira, "More Hollywood Remakes Cast Minorities in Roles Once Filled by Whites," *The Associated Press State & Local Wire*, 8 June 2005, available from Lexis-Nexis [database online].

13   *Ibid.*

14   *Screen Actors Guild-American Federation of Television and Radio Artists*, "About Us," n.d., <http://www.sagaftra.org/content/about-us> (14 February 2017). NOTE: SAG merged with AFTRA in 2013.

15   *Screen Actors Guild-American Federation of Television and Radio Artists*, "2007 & 2008 Casting Data Reports," 2008, <http://www.sagaftra.org/files/sag/documents/2007-2008_CastingDataReports.pdf> (14 February 2017), p.13. For comparative data going back to 1998, see *Screen Actors Guild*, "Ethnicity Share of All 2003 SAG TV/Theatrical Roles (Excluding Animation)," n.d., <http://www.sag.org/Content/Public/03castingdatarpt-eth1.pdf> (15 July 2007). To access the latest casting data report, go to the SAG home page at <http://www.sag.org>, click on the "Diversity" option in the "Resources" box on the right side of the page, and then select "Reports." Underscoring the dearth of widely-available racial data in Hollywood, observe how the most recent report available was published on October 6, 2004, containing data from the 2003 year.

16   The SAG spokesperson at the time acknowledged this fact. See Anthony Breznican, "More Minority Actors in Hollywood," *The Associated Press State & Local Wire*, 13 August 2001, available from Lexis-Nexis [database online]. Hence, statistical improvements in diversity may not accurately reflect the sentiments of viewers who still see minorities limited to roles of inferior quality onscreen, despite an increase in the overall number of roles.

17   *Directors Guild of America*, "About the DGA," n.d., <http://www.dga.org/The-Guild/History.aspx> (14 February 2017).

18   *Directors Guild of America*, "DGA Annual Report on Women and Minority Hiring Reveals Bleak Industry Record for 1999," January 2001, <http://www.dga.org/news/v25_5/news_minorityhire.php3> (15 July 2007). The data in this report is particularly useful in that it parses out the "total days worked" by race as opposed to more general membership composition statistics. See also *Directors Guild of America*, "Feature Film Director Report," 2014, <http://www.dga.org/The-Guild/Diversity/Industry-Reports.aspx> (14 February 2017).

19   Interestingly enough, information on total membership is not readily conspicuous on the WGA website. For a recent estimate of membership as of 2012, see *Directors Guild of America*, "Writers Guild of America, West, The 2014 Hollywood Writers Report, Turning Missed Opportunities into Realized Ones," July 2014, <http://www.wga.org/uploadedFiles/who_we_are/HWR14.pdf> (14 February 2017), p.32.

20   *Writers Guild of America*, "1998 Hollywood Writers Report" 1998, <http://www.wga.org/manual/Report/minority.html> (30 June 2005). Indicative of the difficulty in obtaining consistently reliable data about race in Hollywood directly from the service unions themselves, it appears that only five reports were commissioned over a period spanning nearly two decades (1987, 1998, 1998, 2005 & 2007). According to the WGA website, 1987 marked the first year that the Guild started tracking employment statistics.

21   Within the 2005 Hollywood Writers Report, see Section V entitled "Minority Writers" on pg. 25. *Writers Guild of America*, "2005 Hollywood Writers Report," 2005, <http://www.wga.org/subpage_whoweare.aspx?id=922> (15 July 2006). This study, released seven years after its predecessor, represents one of the most comprehensive, publicly available report about minority writers in the entertainment industry.

22   Seven minority stagehands filed a lawsuit against the International Alliance of Theatrical and Stage Employees (IATSE) which at the time, boasted more than 1,500 members. The lawsuit claims that only 150

members are minorities, providing a rough calculation of nearly 90% White membership if the number of minority stagehands is close to the 150 cited. See *City News Service,* "Stagehands Claim Insider Hiring Results in Discrimination," 24 July 2002, available from Lexis-Nexis [database online].

23 For an example of past diversity initiatives and efforts, see Christina Hoag, "Diversity in Hollywood: Are Women and Minorities Treated Fairly?" 5 August, 2016, *CQ Researcher,* <http://www.library.cqpress.com/cqresearcher/document.php?id=cqresrre2016080500>, (14 February 2017). The statement "Roles for African Americans changed after 1942, when the NAACP, a civil rights organization, won pledges from studios to end stereotyped casting and hire more blacks for production jobs" indicates that Hollywood studios were well aware of the diversity issues that marred its magical work and have been "making efforts" to correct such issues ever since.

2a See *Pittsburgh Tribune Review,* "Marshall Defends Controversial 'Geisha' Casting Decision," 7 March 2005, available from Lexis-Nexis [database online].

2b Public Enemy, "Burn Hollywood Burn," *Fear of a Black Planet,* (New York: Def Jam Records, 1994).

2c Jadakiss, "Why?" *Kiss of Death,* (New York: Ruff Ryders Records, 2004).

2d Scott Bowles, "Black Actors' Breakthrough Year, Influence 'Turns Corner,'" *USA Today,* 7 February 2005, pg. 1D.

2e Stanley, "The Color of Money: Hollywood Diversifies."

2f *Internet Movie Database,* "Biography for Salma Hayek," n.d., <http://www.imdb.com/name/nm0000161/bio> (15 July 2007).

2g *Internet Movie Database,* "Biography for Patrick Gallagher," n.d., <http://www.imdb.com/name/nm0302466/bio> (15 July 2007).

2h See Dale Gavlak, "Ricky Martin Seeks End to Arab Stereotypes," *The Associated Press State & Local Wire,* 25 July 2005, available from Lexis-Nexis [database online].

2i See Soraya Sarhaddi Nelson, "Protesters Say Hollywood Favors White Stunt Workers; Bias: Group Says Caucasians Are Made Up to Look Like the Minority Actors They Double for in Film and TV, Costing People of Color Jobs," *Los Angeles Times,* 28 September 1999, pg. B1.

2j *United States Census Bureau,* "U.S. Summary: 2015;" *Motion Picture Association of America,* "2015 Theatrical Statistics Summary."

2k See notes 11, 15, 18 & 21, *supra.*

2l The Academy noted in a press release that should "'Adaptation' win for Adapted Screenplay, the two credited writers will share a single Academy Award." Pat Nason, "Hollywood Digest," *United Press International,* 11 February 2003, available from Lexis-Nexis [database online].

2m See Richard Benke, "Apaches Praise 'The Missing' for Accuracy, Send Students to Learn About Language," 16 December 2003, *The Associated Press State & Local Wire,* available from Lexis-Nexis [database online].

2n See "Blacks, Latinos Make Movie Gains," published August 8, 2003 by *United Press International,* available from Lexis-Nexis [database online]. Overseas, the same information was touted under the headline "Acting Roles for Minorities Increase." See *BBC News* "Acting Roles for Minorities Increase," 8 August 2003, <http://news.bbc.co.uk/2/hi/entertainment/3135147.stm> (15 July 2007).

CHAPTER 3

1. In 1939, Hattie McDaniel was the first minority actor, male or female, to ever win an Academy Award for Best Supporting Actress for her rendition of Mammy in **Gone with the Wind**. Lisa Bornstein, "More Than 'The Maid;' A Play Welcomes Hattie McDaniel Back to Denver More than 50 Years after Oscar Winner's Death," *Rocky Mountain News*, 23 February 2004, available from Lexis-Nexis [database online].

2. Nancy McCarthy, "ABA Study Finds Minority Lawyers Have 'Miles to Go' in the Profession," California Bar Journal, March 2005, <http://www.calbar.ca.gov/state/calbar/calbar_cbj.jsp?sCategoryPath=/Home/Attorney%20Resources/California%20Bar%20Journal/March2005&sCatHtmlPath=cbj/2005-03_TH_03_ABA-minorities.html&sCatHtmlTitle=Top%20Headlines> (15 July 2007).

3. See generally, Timothy McNulty, "How Un-PC Can You Be?" *Pittsburgh Post-Gazette*, 16 April 2006, pg. E1. See also, note 5 for *Chapter 8: Physical Wonder*.

4. Cameron Diaz' father is Cuban-American, while her mother is of Italian, Native American and German descent. Diaz' career has certainly not been staked on her "Latina" status, but rather upon her acting talent as a "tall, strikingly attractive, blue-eyed natural blonde." To look up her biography, see *Internet Movie Database*, "Biography for Cameron Diaz," n.d., <http://www.imdb.com/name/nm0000139/bio> (15 July 2007). To further illustrate her onscreen malleability, in **Any Given Sunday**, she played an Italian woman named Christina Pagniacci, and in **Being John Malkovich** and **In Her Shoes**, she fulfilled Jewish roles as Lotte Schwartz and Maggie Feller respectively.

5. **Spy Kids** is undoubtedly unique in that it stars a "mostly Latino cast" in a blockbuster action-adventure family movie centering around a Latino family of four (the Cortez family). Yet, closer inspection of the principal lead actors reveals an interesting subplot. The father, Gregorio Cortez, is played by European Antonio Banderas (he hails from Spain). The mother, Ingrid Cortez, is played by Italian-American actress Carla Gugino. The older daughter, Carmen Cortez, is played by Alexa Vega, who is half-Colombian and half-(White) American. The younger brother, Juni Cortez, is played by Daryl Sabara, who is of Jewish heritage. Thus, even in presenting to the audience a Latino family, the studio, perhaps wary of the possibility that the audience might not identify with the characters (i.e., successfully make a connective switch), made the decision to cast actors who collectively did not share much of a formal association with Latino heritage. Certainly, Latino actors and actresses exist in Hollywood. Yet, the ultimate question for studios is whether any Latino actors exist that mainstream audiences will pay to see. Until Latino actors are cast in such "Latino roles," this question will remain unanswered.

3a. See *WENN Entertainment News Wire Service*, "Foxx Furious over 'Miami Vice' Race 'Joke,'" 9 September 2005, available from Lexis-Nexis [database online].

3b. See "The 2017 Hollywood Issue" cover of *Vanity Fair* released January 2017.

3c. *Internet Movie Database*, "Berry Returns to 'X-Men' for Bigger Role," 12 May 2004 <http://www.imdb.com/news/wenn/2004-05-12> (15 July 2007).

3d Henry Meller, "Halle: There are No Great Roles for Black Women," *Daily Mail*, 25 January 2005, <http://www.mailonsunday.co.uk/pages/text/print.html?in_article_id=335302&in_page_id=1773> (15 July 2007).

3e See Bruce Westbrook, "Actor Says Big Break Won't Go Up in Smoke," *The Houston Chronicle*, 4 August 2004, pg. 1.

3f Reinforcing the idea that some Jews purposely concealed their identity, according to <www.jewhoo.com>, within some Jewish circles, people play a game called "Locate the Landsman," where they attempt to identify famous or noteworthy fellow Jews. Landsman is a Yiddish word for "countryman," however within the United States, it is often used to refer to another Jew. See "Notes on Playing Locate the Landsman (LTL)" at <http://www.jewhoo.com/editor/landsman.html> for more information (15 July 2007).

3g See Patricia Erens, *The Jew in American Cinema*, (Bloomington: Indiana University Press, 1984), pg. 114.

CHAPTER 4

1   Joe Morgenstern, "Holy Melancholy, 'Batman'! Tale of Superhero's Origins Is Vivid, Stylish — and Dour," *Wall Street Journal*, 17 June 2005, pg. W1.

2   Educators using this text are free to use the provided examples or are otherwise encouraged to substitute more recent works of their own choosing to serve as illustrative examples.

CHAPTER 5

1   Joanne Weintraub, "Strong, Loving Black Families Don't Exist in Most of TV's World," *The San Diego Union-Tribune*, 27 June 2000, pg. E10.

5a *The New York Post*, "Studio Too Far Out on a Limb," 23 October 2006, pg. 12.

5b *Box Office Mojo*, "'Harry Potter and the Sorcerer's Stone' Box Office Data," n.d., <http://www.boxofficemojo.com/movies/?id=harrypotter.htm> (15 July 2007).

CHAPTER 6

1   Seiler, "Something to Offend Everyone."

2   For a more general overview about the history of minstrelsy in America, reference William J. Mahar's *Behind the Burnt Cork Mask: Early Blackface Minstrelsy and Antebellum American Popular Culture*, (Urbana: University of Illinois Press, 1999).

3   See generally Kiku Day, "Totally Lost in Translation: The Anti-Japanese Racism in Sofia Coppola's New Film Just Isn't Funny," *Guardian*, 24 January 2004, <http://www.guardian.co.uk/comment/story/0,,1130137,00.html> (15 July 2007).

4   See note 4, *Chapter 2: The Cast of Caricatures, supra*.

6a See *Box Office Mojo*, "'Zoolander' Box Office Data," n.d., <http://www.boxofficemojo.com/movies/?id=zoolander.htm> (15 July 2006); *Box Office Mojo*, "Dukes of Hazzard," n.d., <http://www.boxofficemojo.com/movies/?id=dukesofhazzard.htm> (15 July 2007).

6b See Mark Sommer, "Tribute to Jolson Brings Back an Anguished Debate over Blackface," *Buffalo News*, 10 July 2002, pg. D1.

6c Go to the **Soul Plane** movie website at <http://www.soulplane.com> and click on "Technical Notes (Production Information)" followed by "Synopsis." In creating and illustrating the "fantasy" of a Black-owned airline, the writers burlesque the "power" of Black capital in "the real world." The airline was only created after the founder, Nashawn Wade (Kevin Hart) received a dubious $100 millon settlement after a humiliating experience suffered on a commercial flight. This plot device suggests that Nashawn Wade would probably have been unable to ever afford or facilitate the purchase of an airline without the "good fortune" of the $100 million settlement.

6d Mark de la Viña, "Nothing but the Truth, Topical Humor Puts the Shocking but Unapologetic D.L. Hughley at the Top of His Field," *Mercury News*, 9 June 2005, pg. E1.

CHAPTER 7

1 Bowles, "Black Actors' Breakthrough Year Influence 'Turns Corner.'"

2 Just out of curiosity, does anyone know why we do not have a "genderblind" age? What if people ran around all day saying "I don't see gender, there is narry a chauvinist bone in my body!" This rationale, while bordering absurdity when applied to gender or age (i.e., an "ageblind" society), nonetheless retains appeal for many Whites when applied to matters of race in an ideal "colorblind" society" (e.g., "I see no color; just people").

3 Sam Slovick, "Thugs on Film," *LA Weekly*, 14 March 2003, pg. 32.

7a See Susan King, "History Fires the Imagination; The Past Guided 'Apocalypto's' Makers but Still Left Them Room to Create Their Tale of a Maya World," *Los Angeles Times*, 7 December, 2006 pg. E6.

7b Lawrence Van Gelder, "Movies, Performing Arts/Weekend Desk; Arts, Briefly," *The New York Times*, 8 December, 2006, pg. E4. Additionally, "Ignacio Ochoa, director of the Nahual Foundation, which promotes Maya culture, said, 'Gibson replays, in glorious big-budget Technicolor, an offensive and racist notion that Maya people were brutal to one another long before the arrival of Europeans and thus they deserved, in fact needed, rescue.'"

CHAPTER 8

1. Allison Samuels, "Angela's Fire." *Newsweek,* 1 July 2002, pg. 54.
2. The Black Buck stereotype is that of a Black male character featured primarily for the physical prowess that he brings to the screen. A Jezebel stereotype is that of a Black female character that is sexually salacious and of questionable morality, representing the opposite of White middle-class respectability. See generally Donald Bogle, *Toms, Coons, Mulattoes, Mammies & Bucks: An Interpretive History of Blacks in American Films* (first referenced in note #8 from *Chapter Zero: Behind the Scenes*).
3. See Bob Strauss, "Latino Stars Share in Celebrity Spotlight," *The Times Union,* 9 March 1995, available from Lexis-Nexis [database online].
4. See *IAI Presentations, Inc.,* "The Peking Acrobats®," n.d., <http://www.chineseacrobats/com/pa.html>.
5. Nancy Tartaglione-Vialatte, "Cannes Film Festival; 'Ocean's' Crew Cavorts, but Seriously . . .; The Jokes Fly at a News Conference. Then a Journalist Raises an Issue about Shaobo Qin's Role," *Los Angeles Times,* 26 May 2007, pg. E7. In this article, compare Soderbergh's "defense" of racially-themed humor in **Ocean's Thirteen** ("I think we're an equal opportunity offender") with that of *7-Eleven* marketing executive Rita Bargerhuff's comments about a national promotional tie-in with **The Simpsons Movie** (see note 15, *Chapter 1: What is a Mainstream Movie?*). 7-Eleven agreed to convert a dozen stores into *Kwik-E-Marts*, the fictional chain that generally lampoons convenience stores in both the movie and television show. *Kwik-E-Mart* is owned and operated by Apu, an (East) Indian male who speaks with a thick and heavy foreign accent. In referencing the reaction of Indian *7-Eleven* franchisees to the promotional campaign, Bargerhuff acknowledged that "there was definitely a concern of offending people." However, Bargerhuff further explained that, "they seemed to understand that 'The Simpsons' makes fun of everybody. The vast majority saw this as a great opportunity."

8a. Carla Meyer and Ruthe Stein, "Oscars' Split Decision, Best Picture 'Chicago,' 'Pianist' Divide Top Awards," *The San Francisco Chronicle,* 24 March 2003 <http://sfgate.com/cgi-bin/article.cgi?f=/c/a/2003/03/24/MN269661.DTL> (15 July 2007).

CHAPTER 9

1. Cheri Matthews, "The Late Inmage [sic] Hollywood Expanding Its View," *Modesto Bee,* 13 October 1991, pg. D1.

CHAPTER 10

1. See **Spider-Man** director Sam Raimi's take in the interview, "Sam Raimi and his 'Spider-Man' Actors Show Great Power and Responsibility," *Science Fiction Weekly,* 6 May 2002, <http://www.scifi.com/sfw/issue263/interview.html> (15 July 2007).

2   For an example of each reference, see generally Gregg Kilday, "Film Reporter; Ganis Looking to Spell Success with 'Akeelah,'" *VNU Entertainment News Wire*, 17 March 2006, available from Lexis-Nexis [database online]; Neal Travis, "Hayek Reaching for New High," *The New York Post*, 26 November 2000, pg. 13.

3   *Propertyinsight*, "517 Third Street," n.d., <http://www.propertyinsight/ca/517-third-street-new-westminster-bc-grznlpu2drlt> (14 February 2017).

4   Bythewood shared his thoughts with Harvard African American Studies professor Henry Louis Gates in "the Hollywood episode" of a four-part documentary series entitled *America Beyond the Color Line with Henry Louis Gates, Jr.* The series first aired on PBS on February 4, 2004. See *America Beyond the Color Line*, directed by Dan Percival and Mary Crisp, 220 minutes, PBS Home Video, 2003, DVD.

5   Micheline Maynard, "'Flightplan' Irks Flight Attendants," *The New York Times*, 28 September 2005, pg. E2.

10a See Degen Pener and Cindy Pearlman, "Dealing with the Devil, Two Exacting Stars and a Runaway Budget Made Filming the 'Devil's Own' a Hellacious Headache," *Entertainment Weekly*, 11 April 1997, <http://www.ew.com/ew/report/0,6115,287407_1_0_,00.html> (15 July 2007).

10b *The Associated Press State & Local Wire*, "Purple Hearts Pulled from 'Crashers' Site," *MSNBC Online*, 26 July, 2005, <http://www.msnbc.msn.com/id/8701080> (15 July 2007).

10c See David M. Halbfinger, "Pentagon's New Goal: Put Science Into Scripts," *The New York Times*, 8 August 2005, pg. E1.

10d Home Box Office, *Unchained Memories: Readings From the Slave Narratives*, (Boston: Bulfinch Press, 2002), pg. 22. The book was released as a companion guide to the HBO documentary special entitled *Unchained Memories* released in 2003. The foreword was composed by Harvard African American Studies professor Henry Louis Gates referenced in note 3, *supra*.

10e See David Caruso, "Mystery 9/11 Rescuer Reveals Himself," *CBS News*, 14 August, 2006, <http://www.cbsnews.com/stories/2006/08/14/ap/national/mainD8JGFMKO0.shtml> (15 July 2007).

10f See Christopher Hanson, "Hollywood, Pentagon Uneasy Allies," *The Times Union*, 30 April 1997, pg. D1.

10g Merissa Marr, "Fairy-Tale Wedding? Disney Can Supply the Gown; Princess-Inspired Designs Aim to Attract Older Crowd; Subtle Mermaid Styling," *The Wall Street Journal*, 22 February 2007, pg. B1.

CHAPTER 11

1   Jack Shea, "January 2001, President's Report," *Director's Guild of America*, January 2001, <http://www.dga.org/news/v25_5/dept_presreport.php3> (15 July 2007). Michael Apted was elected President of the DGA in June, 2003 after Jack Shea retired.

2   See Gregg Kilday, "Valenti Makes Final Appearance, Touts Biz's Strengths," *The Hollywood Reporter*, 24 March 2004, <http://www.hollywoodreporter.com/hr/search/article_display.jsp?vnu_content_id=1000469708> (15 July 2007).

3   Although movies in their final form appear to be "seamless," they are actually intricate projects involving hundreds of employees and hundreds of millions of dollars that require considerable pre-planning and strategizing. Ken Kamins,

manager of director Peter Jackson, compared filming *The Lord of the Rings* trilogy "to playing three-dimensional chess for every minute of every day for 15 straight hours." Merissa Marr, "Pirates' Treasure? Storms, Delays Drive Up Cost of Sequels Shot Back to Back, but Disney Hopes for Two Hits," *The Wall Street Journal*, 30 June 2006, pg. B1.

4   Luke Y. Thompson, "Witch Is Which?; 'Blair Witch 2' Blurs Fact and Fiction, but the Truth Is, It Ain't Scary," *Dallas Observer,* 26 October 2000. Database online; available from Lexis-Nexis.

5   William Booth, "A Ruse Awakening on the Web, Realistic Sites Are Being Created as Marketing Ploys," *Washington Post,* 24 April 2004, pg. C1.

6   The documentary, the brainchild of the Harvard African American Studies professor Henry Louis Gates, first aired on PBS, February 4, 2004. See *America Beyond the Color Line,* directed by Dan Percival and Mary Crisp, 220 minutes, PBS Home Video, 2003, DVD. In "Part IV: Black Hollywood," the following dialogue between Arnon Milchan and Gates ensues at roughly the 1:17:11 mark:

> **Gates:** Of course. I mean, you have to make money.
> **Milchan:** Yes.
> **Gates:** So, you're only going to put these people in roles if they draw in the crowds.
> **Milchan:** The easiest thing to do is with the guy or the girl next door. The guy or the girl next door, in context of the pie of the moviegoers, are blond with blue eyes, or they're definitely not Mexicans, they're definitely not African American, uh, they don't have accents, they're kinda . . . they're cheerleaders, they're . . .
> **Gates:** All-American.
> **Milchan:** . . . they're, all-American. So, **Panic Room** - you put **Panic Room** - you'll put a black girl in **Panic Room** or a Mexican - and I'm saying . . .
> **Gates:** Yes . . .
> **Milchan:** . . . it will be a smaller movie.
> **Gates:** A smaller movie. How much smaller? How much smaller? How much was **Panic Room** ?
> **Milchan:** **Panic Room** did . . . let's say a $100 million dollars?
> **Gates:** OK . . .
> **Milchan:** If it was with um, let's say Halle Berry?
> **Gates:** OK, with Halle Berry, how much?
> **Milchan:** Half.
> **Gates:** With Halle Berry, half?
> **Milchan:** Yeah.
> **Gates:** So that's the economics, that's the bottom line.
> **Milchan:** Of that, of that configuration of that movie - not of every movie.
> **Gates:** All right, let me ask you this. Love story - with Halle Berry and Denzel Washington as the leads, how much would you make? Great script - everything's perfect.
> **Milchan:** Beautiful question actually - you're right. I will make 'X' and then I will make twice as much with the white couple.
> **Gates:** No kidding. Fifty to a hundred again.
> **Milchan:** Yeah, yeah. I think so, I think so because there would be this white righteous whatever, bill billies - God knows whatever you call them - people don't like to see, um a black woman and a black man - even going to bed!
> **Gates:** But Russell Crowe and Halle Berry, $100 million.
> **Milchan:** Ah, $200 million. $200 million. You know? No different than Whitney Houston and Kevin Costner.
> **Gates:** Right.
> **Milchan:** That's kinda . . .
> **Gates:** Yeah, because it's got that edge. Friction (?) . . .
> **Milchan:** The problem is educating the consumer. So, they wanna buy black and black and red and yellow, sure we have it!

7   At roughly the 2:10:28 mark, there appears to be a "minority" family having difficulty reading the signs in the hallway while the ship is sinking. The father figure is standing in front of a sign that reads, "E Deck, Berthing, Cabin N°s 140-159," as he flips through what may very well be a dictionary of some kind. He has a pained expression on his face as he attempts to literally interpret what everyone else instinctively knows: the *Titanic* is sinking and escaping out of the hold is the only viable chance for survival. Note that the family does not speak English during their limited time onscreen (± four seconds) and their "foreignness" is further reinforced by their dress, where the women's heads are covered and the father figure is wearing a distinctive hat.

8   Texeira, "More Hollywood Remakes Cast Minorities in Roles Once Filled by Whites."

9   Frank Scheck, "'King's Ransom,'" *The Hollywood Reporter*, 25 April 2005, <http://www.hollywoodreporter.com/thr/reviews/review_display.jsp?vnu_content_id=1000894467> (15 July 2007).

10 A good example of how test screenings make a difference is illustrated in ***My Best Friend's Wedding*** starring Julia Roberts and Hugh Grant. Many of the test screeners did not like the original ending of ***My Best Friend's Wedding*** since they felt that the Julia Roberts' character did not adequately repent for her selfishness. "'They didn't think Julia had gotten her comeuppance,' says [producer Jerry] Zucker, who produced the film. 'So we changed it. It made a huge difference.' Roberts' teary-eyed redemption scene translated into U.S. $126 million." See Nancy Griffin, "Secrets and Wives." *Sydney Morning Herald*, 12 June 2004, <http://www.smh.com.au/articles/2004/06/11/1086749889818.html?from=storyrhs> (15 July 2007).

11 *Motion Picture Association of America*, "MPAA President Dan Glickman Addresses ShoWest."

12 "Today, U.S. films are shown in more than 150 countries worldwide and American television programs are broadcast in over 125 international markets. The U.S. film industry provides the majority of home entertainment products seen in millions of homes throughout the world." *Motion Picture Association of America*, "About Us," n.d., <http://www.mpaa.org/AboutUs.asp> (15 July 2007).

13 As indicative of the serious nature of this casting couch phenomenon, the SAG website contains a message from the City Attorney of Los Angeles about how to protect oneself from sexual battery crimes. See Rocky Delgadillo, "Trust Your Instinct - Your Life May Depend on It," *Screen Actors Guild*, n.d., <http://www.sag.org/sagWebApp/Content/Public/rockydelgadillo.htm> (15 July 2007). To access the open letter, go online to the <http://www.sag.org> home page, click on the "Tips and Tools" option in the "Resources" box on the right side of the page, and then select "LA City Attorney Rocky Delgadillo: Trust Your Instinct."

14 Robert M. Entman and Andrew Rojecki, *The Black Image in the White Mind*, (Chicago: The University of Chicago Press, 2000), pg. 198. The authors selected the twenty-five top-grossing movies of 1996-97. First they coded named characters according to race. Then they coded the characters based upon researched behaviors.

15 For instance, the Pew Hispanic Center reported that both Latinos and Blacks on average "have less than ten cents for every dollar in wealth owned by White households." See Rakesh Kochhar, "The Wealth of Hispanic Households: 1996-2002," *Pew Hispanic Center*, October 2004, <http://pewhispanic.org/files/reports/34.pdf> (15 July 2007). Additionally, a report issued by the National Urban League (NUL) in 2005 asserted that a Blacks on average experience only three-quarters the prosperity that Whites experience. See John Moreno Gonzales, "Worry Over Racial Economic Gap; Urban League Study Finds Indicators for Blacks Are

Stagnant or in Decline When Compared with Whites'," *Newsday*, 7 April 2005, pg. A26. Contact the NUL directly for a copy of *The State of Black America 2004* report at <http://www.nul.org>.

16 See T.L. Stanley, "The Color of Money: Hollywood Diversifies."

17 Larry Fine, "Flap over Billboards Paying Dividends for Rapper 50 Cent; Some Say Ads Are Too Graphic - but Film Star Thinks It Will Help Sell Tickets," *The Seattle Times*, 1 November 2005, pg. E4. Take note of 50 Cent's response to criticism from British moviegoers who protested his firearm imagery; he observes that "mum's the word" for British fans of James Bond, whose '007' logo contains an image of a gun; *WENN Entertainment News Wire Service*, "50 Cent: 'I'm No Worse Than James Bond,' 18 January 2006, available from Lexis-Nexis [database online].

18 Tabassum Zakaria, "CIA Checking if Life Imitates Art," *Reuters*, 5 August 2004, <http://www.reuters.com/newsArticle.jhtml?type=reutersEdge&storyID=5876235> (30 June 2005).

19 *Party, Politics & Movies* first debuted on Turner Classic Movies (TCM) in August, 2004; *What Hollywood Taught Us About Sex* first debuted on the E! Channel in June, 2005; *Movies That Shook the World* first debuted on the American Movie Channel (AMC) in September, 2005; and *The Science of Superman* first debuted on the National Geographic Channel (NGC) in June, 2006.

20 Reuters, "Movies Can Put You in the Mood: Study Says Certain Films Can Boost Hormone Levels," *MSNBC Online*, 22 July 2004, <http://msnbc.msn.com/id/5490731/> (15 July 2006).

21 Mike Glover, "Fahrenheit 9/11 Making GOP Nervous," *The Associated Press State & Local Wire*, 22 July 2004, available from Lexis-Nexis [database online].

22 Conduct this simple exercise for the movies selected to the National Film Registry in 2004 and see: 1) if any minority characters are prominently featured in any of the top twenty-five films and 2) if so, how such characters fulfill or depart from the HARM theory and minority archetypes. *National Film Registry 2004*, "Films Selected to the National Film Registry, Library of Congress - 2004," 28 December 2004, <http://www.loc.gov/film/nfr2004.html> (15 July 2007).

23 See Bill Clinton, "Speech by President to Theater Owners Association," *Clinton Foundation*, 8 June 1999, <http://www.clintonfoundation.org/legacy/060899-speech-by-president-to-theater-owners-association.htm> (15 July 2007). Clinton made this speech less than two months after the "Columbine" shooting took place, where two students unleashed one of the nation's most tragic shooting rampages at Columbine High School in Colorado. The shooting took place on April 20, 1999.

24 See Dina Gerdeman, "Class Movies; Films Brought in to Teach, Not to Entertain," *The Patriot Ledger* 19 January 2000, pg. 1.

25 Mark Skertic and Jennifer Cassell, "'Star Wars' Fans Play Hooky," *Chicago Sun-Times*, 20 May 1999, Jedi Journal, pg. 4.

11a *Martha's Vineyard Chamber of Commerce*, "JawsFest," n.d., <http://www.mvy.com/jaws/> (15 July 2006).

11b César G. Soriano, "Lucas Rules Fans' Empire: Creator of 'Star Wars' Helps Convention Celebrate Final Film," *USA Today*, 25 April 2005, pg. 1D.

11c See *Boston Herald*, "FTC Tells Hollywood: Clean Up Your Act," 12 September 2000, available from Lexis-Nexis [database online].

11d See Peter Bowes, "LA Trouble Spot 'Wiped' From Map," *BBC News*, 23 April 2003, <http://news.bbc.co.uk/2/hi/americas/2969645.stm> (15 July 2007).

11e *Motion Picture Association of America*, "How Movies are Rated," n.d., <http://www.mpaa.org/Ratings_HowRated.asp> (15 July 2007).

11f *Children Now*, "A Different World: Children's Perceptions of Race and Class in Media," May 1998, <http://publications.childrennow.org/publications/media/differentworld_1999.cfm> (15 July 2007). As of July 15, 2007, a free copy can be downloaded from the non-profit organization Media Awareness Network at <http://www.media-awareness.ca/english/index.cfm> and by typing in "a different world" in the search box.

11g See note fifteen for this chapter, *supra*; Bill Clinton, "Speech by President to Theater Owners Association."

11h *CBS News*, "Movies Change, Ratings Don't," 14 July 2004, <http://www.cbsnews.com/stories/2004/07/14/entertainment/main629582.shtml> (15 July 2007). The research was conducted by the Kids Risk Project at the Harvard School of Public Health. See also *MSNBC Online*, "Movies Heavily Shape Teen Smoking, Study: 40 Percent of Youths Try Smoking Because They Saw It in Films," 7 November 2005 <http://msnbc.msn.com/id/9949432/> (15 July 2006).

11i See Cassie Carpenter, "Fakin' It, Actors Discuss the Ins and Outs of Making a Successful Sex Scene," *MSN Movies*, n.d., <http://movies.msn.com/movies/article.aspx?news=193121&GT1=6657> (15 July 2007).

11j See César G. Soriano and Ann Oldenburg, "With America at War, Hollywood Follows," 8 February 2005, *USA Today*, pg. 1A. The unmanned plane landing was reported in the July 19-25, 2005 issue of *The Hollywood Reporter* on pg. 16 under the caption "Flying High." See also Mimi Hall, "Hollywood, Pentagon Share Rich Past," *USA Today*, 7 March 2005, <http://www.usatoday.com/life/2005-03-07-hollywood-pentagon_x.htm> (15 July 2007); Scott Bowles, "These Big-Studio Films Won't Fake You Out," *USA Today*, 13 April 2005, pg. 5D.

11k Thoralf Schwanitz, "Press Access Limited on Bus with Arnold," *The Oakland Tribune*, 5 October 2003, available from Lexis-Nexis [database online].

11l See Amy Westfeldt, "Stone Begins Shooting 9/11 Movie in N.Y.," *The Associated Press State & Local Wire*, 2 November, 2005, available from Lexis-Nexis [database online].

11m Texeira, "More Hollywood Remakes Cast Minorities in Roles Once Filled by Whites."

11n See Carolyn Feibel, "Activists Say 'Collateral Damage' Insults Colombians and Firefighters, Exploits Sept. 11," *The Associated Press State & Local Wire*, 3 February 2002, available from Lexis-Nexis [database online]; *The New York Post*, "H'wood Pulls 2 Terror Flicks," 13 September 2001, pg. 66; Peter M. Nichols, "Home Video; A Terror Alert On New Stickers," *The New York Times*, 5 October 2001, pg. E26; Caryn James, "Filmview; What's Under the Tree? Stiffs and Hoods," *The New York Times*, 13 December 1992, Sec 2, pg. 20.

11o See *Internet Movie Database*, "Trivia for 'The Bourne Supremacy,'" n.d., <http://www.imdb.com/title/tt0372183/trivia> (15 July 2007). See also Griffin, "Secrets and Wives."

11p See generally Minju Pak, "Creative Spark, The Key Art Awards Give Movie Marketers an Annual Moment in the Sun," *The Hollywood Reporter*, 28 April 2005, pg. S-4; Cythnia Littleton, "34th Annual Key Art Awards," *The Hollywood Reporter*, 9 May 2005, pg. 6.

11q See Jesse Hiestand, "Snipes Suing NL over 3rd 'Blade,'" *The Hollywood Reporter*, 21 April 2005, pg. 4. See also *Internet Movie Database*, "Berry Returns to X-Men for Bigger Role."

11r See *Internet Movie Database*, "Trivia for 'The Matrix Reloaded,'" n.d., <http://www.imdb.com/title/tt0242653/trivia> (15 July 2007).

11s See Mike Snider, "NASCAR, Hollywood Share the Fast Lane," *USA Today*, 8 June 2006, pg. 1A.

11t See Todd Hill, "Getting Inside the Life of Marie Antoinette," *The Seattle Times*, 18 October 2006, pg. F4.

11u *Business Week* "A Product-Placement Hall of Fame," 11 June 1998, <http://www.businessweek.com/1998/25/b3583062.htm> (15 July 2007). See also, Schiller, "Brand Warfare."

11v See Colleen Long, "Thousands Visit Natural History Museum after Ben Stiller Movie," *The Associated Press State & Local Wire*, 9 January 2007, available from Lexis-Nexis [database online].

11w Jonathan Karp, "'Minority Report' Inspires Technology Aimed at Military," *Wall Street Journal*, 12 April 2005, pg. B1. See also *Internet Movie Database*, "Trivia for 'Minority Report,'" n.d., <http://www.imdb.com/title/tt0181689/trivia> (15 July 2007).

11x See César G. Soriano, "Politics Creates a Disturbance in the Force," *USA Today*, 18 May 2005, pg. 1D.

11y See *BBC News*, "Actor Crowe's Message for America, Russel Crowe Has Launched His Depression-era Film 'Cinderella Man' at the Venice Film Festival Saying the US Cannot Take Its Wealth for Granted," 5 September 2005 <http://news.bbc.co.uk/1/hi/entertainment/film/4215040.stm> (15 July 2007).

11z Maria Aspan, "The Good Side of Diamonds, Before a Movie Shows the Bad," *The New York Times*, 4 September 2006, pg. C4. "U.S. officials, worried that a new Leonardo DiCaprio film about the trade of 'conflict diamonds' to finance African warfare might misinform the public, say international efforts to combat the illicit commerce have been successful." The United States State Department also held briefings in advance of the movie's release. See also Desmond Butler, "U.S. Officials, Alarmed by New Film, Call Efforts to Eliminate Conflict Diamonds Successful," *The Associated Press State & Local Wire*, 6 December 2006, available from Lexis-Nexis [database online].

CHAPTER 12

1 Gary Pettus, "American-Indian Traditions, Stereotypes Survive," *The Associated Press State & Local Wire*, 28 November 2005, available from Lexis-Nexis [database online].

2 To explore the theory of double-consciousness or twoness even further, see generally W.E.B. DuBois, *The Souls of Black Folk*, (Oxford: Oxford University Press, 2007). Please note that this manuscript was originally published in 1903.

3 For more on this thought, consider Hollywood producer Arnon Milchan's conversation with Harvard African American History professor Henry Louis Gates at note 6, *Chapter 11: At a Theater Near You, supra*.

4 Although Det. Del Spooner shares words with a "Woman" (credited character name as rendered by Sharon Wilkins) who is in fact Black, this is their only encounter and Woman is not seen onscreen again. Spooner accosts the Woman's personal robot under the belief that the robot stole her purse.

The exchange between Det. Del Spooner and "Woman" is as follows:

> **Detective Del Spooner:** I said STOP! [commotion after tackling robot] Relax, relax. I'm a police officer.
> **Woman:** You [referencing Spooner] . . . are an *asshole*.
> **Detective Del Spooner:** Ma'am, is that your purse?
> **Woman:** Of course it's my purse! I left my inhaler at home. He [the robot] was running it out to me.
> **Detective Del Spooner:** I saw a robot running with a purse and naturally, I. . . I assumed . . .
> **Woman:** What? Are you crazy?
> **Robot:** I'm sorry for this misunderstanding, officer.
> **Woman:** [to robot] Don't apologize – you're doing what you're supposed to be doing. [to Spooner] But what are you doing?
> **Detective Del Spooner:** Have a lovely day ma'am.
> **Woman:** You lucky I can't breathe – or I'd walk all up and down your ass.

The "Woman" character not only fulfills the Background archetype, but is also consistent with the higher rates of Black female vulgarity as cited on pg. 66. She also fulfills the *stereotypical* image of the brusque, heavy-set Black woman with an ornery attitude, which is typically ascribed to minority inhabitants of the inner city (the movie is set in a futuristic Chicago). Further, the "Woman" character's presence perhaps serves as an indirect message that as technology improves and integrates innovative robotic technology within daily societal life in the year 2035, that stereotypical disparaging images of minorities will remain largely unchanged! The scene described above begins at roughly the 7:17 mark. Be sure to check out other roles played by Sharon Wilkins, namely her role in **Bad Boys II** as "Heavy Black Woman."

5   For those of you who are thinking about Halle Berry and Billy Bob Thornton's sex scene in **Monster's Ball**, the scene would hardly be characterized as "intimate."

6   For the top-grossing movies for all time, see *Internet Movie Database*, "All-Time Worldwide Boxoffice," n.d., <http://www.imdb.com/boxoffice/alltimegross?region=world-wide> (1 April 2007).

7   See Hollinger, "International Markets Have Long Been Crucial to Film Biz."

8   Susan Newman-Baudais, "Partnering Europe: Access to the European Market for Non-European Films - A Statistical Analysis," *European Audiovisual Observatory*, n.d., <http://www.obs.coe.int/online_publication/expert/filmdistribution_mif2005.pdf.en> (15 July 2007).

9   As judged by the British Film Institute. See *British Film Institute*, "The Ultimate Film Chart," n.d., <http://www.bfi.org.uk/features/ultimatefilm/chart/details.php?ranking=1> (15 July 2007).

10 Emma Burgin, "Angelina Jolie, Rice Spotlight World's Refugees," *Knight Ridder/Tribune News Service*, 15 June 2005, available from Lexis-Nexis [database online].

11 Emphasis added. *PR Newswire*, "Dan Glickman to Succeed Jack Valenti as Head of MPAA; Valenti Resigns After 38-Year Tenure," 1 July 2004, available from Lexis-Nexis [database online].

12 Elizabeth Becker and James Dao, "A Nation Challenged: Hearts and Minds; Bush Will Keep the Wartime Operation Promoting America," *The New York Times*, 20 February 2002, pg. A11.

13 Alan Riding, "UNESCO Adopts New Plan Against Cultural Invasion," *The New York Times*, 21 October 2005, pg. E3. Israel and the United States represent the two votes against passage. Australia, Honduras, Liberia and Nicaragua abstained from voting.

14. See *The Associated Press State & Local Wire*, "Movie Buffs to Represent the State in Rose Parade," 30 December 2006. The article profiles Joe Kerley IV, who has spent at least $3,000 on his detailed Clone Trooper costume – in fact, a "microphone and amplifier setup adds static to his speech, just like in the movie."

15. *Motion Picture Association of America*, "The Movie Industry Is a Vital Part of the American Economy." See also *Hollywood Fictions: The Dream Factory In American Popular Culture*, which quotes David Fine as stating that "this collapse of the boundary between reality and illusion, fact and fantasy, has been the central theme of novels about Los Angeles and Hollywood from the 1930s to the present." John Parris Springer, *Hollywood Fictions: The Dream Factory In American Popular Culture,* (Norman: University of Oklahoma Press 2000), pg. 63.

16. See Ann Sanner, "'Rocky' Goes to the Smithsonian Boxer's Gloves, Robe, Shorts," *The Associated Press State & Local Wire*, 6 December 2006, available from Lexis-Nexis [database online]. The memorabilia will be placed in a "Treasures of American History" exhibit.

17. See Geraldine Baum, "Classy Film Feminist Had Brains, Beauty, That Voice," *Los Angeles Times,* 30 June 2003, <http://www.calendarlive.com/movies/la-me-hepburn30jun30,0,6382172.story?coll=cl-movies-features> (30 June 2005).

12a. See Sean Smith, "Along Came Spidey," *Newsweek*, 28 June 2004, <http://www.msnbc.msn.com/id/5251416/site/newsweek/> (15 July 2007).

12b. Kirk Honeycutt, "Reviews: 'ATL,'" *The Hollywood Reporter*, 31 March - 2 April, 2006, pg. 8.

12c. Honeycutt, "Reviews: 'Phat Girlz,'" *The Hollywood Reporter*, 10 April 2006, pg. 10.

12d. Howie Movshovitz, "Reviews: 'The Last King of Scotland,'" *The Hollywood Reporter*, 7 September 2006, pg. 11. For further indication of how movies featuring minority leads are not regarded as universal movies, consider the following line from the review for **Little Man**, "[i]t might never make an AFI list, but the picture generates sufficient blasts of laughter to ensure brisk crossover business for Sony." Michael Rechtshaffen, "Reviews: 'Little Man,'" *The Hollywood Reporter*, 14-16 July 2006, pg. 14.

12e. See Arianna Huffington, "'Legally Blonde 2': People Power Hits the Big Screen," *Nashville City Paper*, 1 July 2003, <http://www.nashvillecitypaper.com/index.cfm?section=40&screen=news&news_id=24265> (15 July 2006).

12f. See Jeanette Walls, "Was Race an Issue in 'Hitch' Casting?" *MSNBC Online*, 24 February 2005 <http://www.msnbc.msn.com/id/7019342/> (15 July 2007).

12g. See David Segal, "Bruce Willis' Tragic Mask," *Washington Post*, 10 March 2005, pg. C1.

12h. See Robert D. Benjamin, "The Movies - Constructions of Reality and Sources of Metaphors," *Mediate.com*, April 2001, <http://www.mediate.com/articles/benjamin2.cfm> (15 July 2007).

12i. See Assistant Deputy Minister of Canada, "Conflict Management Program," *CF Personnel, Canadian Forces Personnel Newsletter*, 19 November 2003 <www.forces.gc.ca/hr/cfpn/pdf/cfpn11_03_e.pdf> (15 July 2006).

12j *Internet Movie Database*, "Full Cast and Crew for 'The Lion King,'" n.d., <http://www.imdb.com/title/tt0110357> (15 July 2007).

12k See *The Times Union*, "Now at the U.N., Lights, Camera, Action," 30 January 2004, pg. A2.

12l See David Van Biema, "Lie Down in Darkness, Does a Death On the Highway Implicate the Entertainment Industry?" *Time Magazine*, 1 November 1993, pg. 49.

12m See Kathleen Flynn and Allison T. Hoffman, "Fish Flushers Learn Life Does Not Imitate 'Nemo,'" *Los Angeles Times*, 26 June 2003, pg. B1.

12n See *Anti-Defamation League*, "ADL Concerned Mel Gibson's 'Passion' Could Fuel Anti-Semitism If Released in Present Form," 11 August 2003, <http://www.adl.org/NR/exeres/B383494F-8B0F-45B0-8F03-EBAC865C9098,0B1623CA-D5A4-465D-A369-DF6E8679CD9E,frameless.htm> (15 July 2007).

CHAPTER 13

1 See Fred Shuster and Jennifer Errico, "Warhol's World; His Touch Transcends the Art World and Is Reflected in Everyday Life," *The Daily News of Los Angeles*, 23 May 2002, pg. U11.

2 See "Minority Reports," *Chapter 2: The Cast of Caricatures*.

REFERENCES

ARTICLES

Aspan, Maria. "The Good Side of Diamonds, Before a Movie Shows the Bad." *The New York Times*, 4 September 2006, pg. C4.

The Associated Press State & Local Wire. "Hollywood Writers Vote for New President Under Federal Monitoring." 21 September 2004, available from Lexis-Nexis [database online].

___. "Mandela Praises Oscar Winner Theron." 11 March 2004, available from Lexis-Nexis [database online].

___. "Movie Buffs to Represent the State in Rose Parade," 30 December 2006, available from Lexis-Nexis [database online].

___. "Purple Hearts Pulled from 'Crashers' Site." *MSNBC Online,* 26 July, 2005, <http://www.msnbc.msn.com/id/8701080> (15 July 2007).

BBC News. "Acting Roles for Minorities Increase." 8 August 2003, <http://news.bbc.co.uk/2/hi/entertainment/3135147.stm> (15 July 2007).

___. "Actor Crowe's Message for America, Russel Crowe Has Launched His Depression-era Film 'Cinderella Man' at the Venice Film Festival Saying the US Cannot Take Its Wealth for Granted." 5 September 2005 <http://news.bbc.co.uk/1/hi/entertainment/film/4215040.stm> (15 July 2007).

Baum, Geraldine. "Classy Film Feminist Had Brains, Beauty, That Voice." *Los Angeles Times*, 30 June 2003, <http://www.calendarlive.com/movies/la-me-hepburn30jun30,0,6382172.story?coll=cl-movies-features> (30 June 2005).

Beale, Lewis. "H'Wood Has a Bad Accent Book, Stars Say Hispanics Still Mostly Villains." *Daily News,* 24 January 2001, available from Lexis-Nexis [database online].

Becker, Elizabeth and James Dao. "A Nation Challenged: Hearts and Minds; Bush Will Keep the Wartime Operation Promoting America." *The New York Times*, 20 February 2002, pg. A11.

Beckerman, Jim. "Entertainers Face Risks if Politics Get into the Act." *The Record*, 25 July 2004, pg. E1.

Benjamin, Robert D. "The Movies - Constructions of Reality and Sources of Metaphors." April 2001, <http://www.mediate.com/articles/benjamin2.cfm> (15 July 2007).

Benke, Richard. "Apaches Praise 'The Missing' for Accuracy, Send Students to Learn About Language." 16 December 2003, *The Associated Press State & Local Wire*, available from Lexis-Nexis [database online].

Blum, Ronald. "Baseball Picks 'Spider-Man' Off Base." *The Associated Press State & Local Wire*, 7 May 2004, available from Lexis-Nexis [database online].

Booth, William. "A Ruse Awakening on the Web, Realistic Sites Are Being Created as Marketing Ploys." *Washington Post,* 24 April 2004, pg. C1.

Bornstein, Lisa. "More Than 'The Maid;' A Play Welcomes Hattie McDaniel Back to Denver More than 50 Years after Oscar Winner's Death." *Rocky Mountain News*, 23 February 2004, available from Lexis-Nexis [database online].

Boston Herald. "FTC Tells Hollywood: Clean Up Your Act." 12 September 2000, available from Lexis-Nexis [database online].

Bowen, Kit. "Miramax Looking for the Oscar Bounce." *Hollywood.com*, 13 February 2003, <http://www.hollywood.com/news/Miramax_Starts_Its_Oscar_Campaigns/1707579> (15 July 2007).

Bowes, Peter. "LA Trouble Spot 'Wiped' From Map." *BBC News*, 23 April 2003, <http://news.bbc.co.uk/2/hi/americas/2969645.stm> (15 July 2007).

Bowles, Scott. "Black Actors' Breakthrough Year, Influence 'Turns Corner.'" *USA Today*, 7 February 2005, pg. 1D.

___. "Hollywood Frets Over Fickle Fans." *USA Today*, 29 August 2005, <http://www.usatoday.com/life/movies/news/2005-08-28-fickle-fans_x.htm> (15 July 2007).

___. "Mmmm, Popcorn: A 'Simpsons' Film in '07." *USA Today*, 3 April 2006, pg. 1D.

___. "These Big-Studio Films Won't Fake You Out." *USA Today*, 13 April 2005, pg. 5D.

Breznican, Anthony. "Jet Li Punches Back Against Formulaic Action Movies." *The Associated Press State & Local Wire*, 24 August 2004, available from Lexis-Nexis [database online].

___. "More Minority Actors in Hollywood." *The Associated Press State & Local Wire,* 13 August 2001, available from Lexis-Nexis [database online].

Brown, Sterling A. "Negro Character as Seen by White Authors." *The Journal of Negro Education*, Vol. 2, No. 2 (Apr., 1933), pp. 179-203.

Burgin, Emma. "Angelina Jolie, Rice Spotlight World's Refugees." *Knight Ridder/Tribune News Service,* 15 June 2005, available from Lexis-Nexis [database online].

Burman, John. "Setting the Pace: Cruise, Hanks and Roberts in Photo Finish As the Most Bankable Players in 'The Hollywood Reporter's' 2002 Star Power Survey." *The Hollywood Reporter*, 1 August 2004 <http://thehollywoodreporter.com/thr/starpower/article_display.jsp?vnu_content_id=1294804> (15 July 2007).

Business Week. "A Product-Placement Hall of Fame." 11 June 1998, <http://www.businessweek.com/1998/25/b3583062.htm> (15 July 2007).

Butler, Desmond. "U.S. Officials, Alarmed by New Film, Call Efforts to Eliminate Conflict Diamonds Successful." *The Associated Press State & Local Wire*, 6 December 2006, available from Lexis-Nexis [database online].

CBS News. "Movies Change, Ratings Don't." 14 July 2004, <http://www.cbsnews.com/stories/2004/07/14/entertainment/main629582.shtml> (15 July 2007).

Carpenter, Cassie. "Fakin' It, Actors Discuss the Ins and Outs of Making a Successful Sex Scene." *MSN Movies*, n.d., <http://movies.msn.com/movies/article.aspx?news=193121&GT1=6657> (15 July 2007).

Carter, Kelly. "Studios' Views of Black Films May Undercut Their Success." *USA Today*, 11 April 2001, pg. 4D.

Caruso, David. "Mystery 9/11 Rescuer Reveals Himself." *CBS News*, 14 August, 2006, <http://www.cbsnews.com/stories/2006/08/14/ap/national/mainD8JGFMKO0.shtml> (15 July 2007).

Chagollan, Steve. "The Myth of the Native Babe: Hollywood's Pocahontas." *The New York Times*, 27 November 2005, available from Lexis-Nexis [database online].

Chmela, Holli. "Did You Know Androids Could Eat Mail?" *The New York Times*, 22 March 2007, pg. A19.

City News Service. "SAG Minorities." 20 December 2000, available from Lexis-Nexis [database online].

___. "Stagehands Claim Insider Hiring Results in Discrimination." 24 July 2002, available from Lexis-Nexis [database online].

Daily Variety. "SAG Faces 7th Lawsuit for Racial Discrimination." 9 December 2002, pg. 82.

___. "SAG Sees 8th Suit over Firing." 14 April 2003, pg. 10.

Day, Kiku. "Totally Lost in Translation: The Anti-Japanese Racism in Sofia Coppola's New Film Just Isn't Funny." *Guardian*, 24 January 2004, <http://www.guardian.co.uk/comment/story/0,,1130137,00.html> (15 July 2007).

de la Viña, Mark. "Nothing but the Truth, Topical Humor Puts the Shocking but Unapologetic D.L. Hughley at the Top of His Field." *Mercury News*, 9 June 2005, pg. E1.

Dominus, Susan. "Why Isn't Maggie Cheung a Hollywood Star?" *The New York Times*, 14 November 2004, available from Lexis-Nexis [database online].

Feibel, Carolyn. "Activists Say 'Collateral Damage' Insults Colombians and Firefighters, Exploits Sept. 11." *The Associated Press State & Local Wire*, 3 February 2002, available from Lexis-Nexis [database online].

Fields, Suzanne. "Bridging the Hollywood-D.C. Gap." *The Times Union*, 4 April 2005, pg. A9.

Fine, Larry. "Flap over Billboards Paying Dividends for Rapper 50 Cent; Some Say Ads Are Too Graphic - but Film Star Thinks It Will Help Sell Tickets." *The Seattle Times*, 1 November 2005, pg. E4.

Flynn, Kathleen and Allison T. Hoffman, "Fish Flushers Learn Life Does Not Imitate 'Nemo.'" *Los Angeles Times*, 26 June 2003, pg. B1.

Friedman, Lisa. "Valenti Building Has Its Preview." *The Daily News of Los Angeles*, 23 June 2005, pg. B1.

Garcia, Chris. "'Pearl Harbor' Bombs Out." *Cox News Service*, 24 May 2001, available from Lexis-Nexis [database online].

Gavlak, Dale. "Ricky Martin Seeks End to Arab Stereotypes." *The Associated Press State & Local Wire*, 25 July 2005, available from Lexis-Nexis [database online].

Gerdeman, Dina. "Class Movies; Films Brought in to Teach, Not to Entertain." *The Patriot Ledger* 19 January 2000, pg. 1.

Germain, David. "Strong Finish Too Late to Dig Hollywood out of Box-office Dumps." *The Associated Press State & Local Wire*, 13 December 2005, available from Lexis-Nexis [database online].

Glover, Mike. "Fahrenheit 9/11 Making GOP Nervous." *The Associated Press State & Local Wire*, 22 July 2004, available from Lexis-Nexis [database online].

Goldberg, Teri. "Blockbuster Toys: This Summer's Movies Have Inspired Some Must-have Toys." *MSNBC Online*, 2 August 2004, <<http://www.msnbc.msn.com/id/5263229/> (15 July 2007).

Gonzales, John Moreno. "Worry Over Racial Economic Gap; Urban League Study Finds Indicators for Blacks Are Stagnant or in Decline When Compared with Whites'." *Newsday*, 7 April 2005, pg. A26.

Griffin, Nancy. "Secrets and Wives." *Sydney Morning Herald*, 12 June 2004, <http://www.smh.com.au/articles/2004/06/11/1086749889818.html?from=storyrhs> (15 July 2007).

Halbfinger, David M. "Pentagon's New Goal: Put Science Into Scripts." *The New York Times*, 8 August 2005, pg. E1.

Hall, Mimi. "Hollywood, Pentagon Share Rich Past." *USA Today*, 7 March 2005, <http://www.usatoday.com/life/2005-03-07-hollywood-pentagon_x.htm> (15 July 2007).

Hanson, Christopher. "Hollywood, Pentagon Uneasy Allies." *The Times Union*, 30 April 1997, pg. D1.

Hiestand, Jesse. "Snipes Suing NL over 3rd 'Blade." *The Hollywood Reporter*, 21 April 2005, pg. 4.

Hill, Todd. "Getting Inside the Life of Marie Antoinette." *The Seattle Times*, 18 October 2006, pg. F4.

Hollinger, Hy and Cynthia Littleton. "International Markets Have Long Been Crucial to Film Biz." *The Hollywood Reporter*, 28 July 2005, pg. S-1.

The Hollywood Reporter. "Flying High." 19-25 July 2005, pg. 16.

Honeycutt, Kirk. "Reviews: 'ATL.'" *The Hollywood Reporter*, 31 March - 2 April, 2006, pg. 8.

___. "Reviews: 'Phat Girlz.'" *The Hollywood Reporter*, 10 April 2006, pg. 10.

Huffington, Arianna. "'Legally Blonde 2': People Power Hits the Big Screen." *Nashville City Paper*, 1 July 2003, <http://www.nashvillecitypaper.com/index.cfm?section=40&screen=news&news_id=24265> (15 July 2006).

James, Caryn. "Filmview; What's Under the Tree? Stiffs and Hoods." *The New York Times*, 13 December 1992, Sec 2, pg. 20.

Karp, Jonathan. "'Minority Report' Inspires Technology Aimed at Military." *Wall Street Journal*, 12 April 2005, pg. B1.

Kilday, Gregg. "Film Reporter; Ganis Looking to Spell Success with 'Akeelah.'" *VNU Entertainment News Wire*, 17 March 2006, available from Lexis-Nexis [database online].

___. "Valenti Makes Final Appearance, Touts Biz's Strengths." *The Hollywood Reporter*, 24 March 2004, <http://www.hollywoodreporter.com/hr/search/article_display.jsp?vnu_content_id=1000469708> (15 July 2007).

King, Dennis. "Review: 'Memoirs of a Geisha.'" *Tulsa World,* 23 December 2005, pg. S4.

King, Susan. "History Fires the Imagination; The Past Guided 'Apocalypto's' Makers but Still Left Them Room to Create Their Tale of a Maya World." *Los Angeles Times*, 7 December, 2006 pg. E6.

Koenig, David. "7-Elevens become Simpsons 'Kwik-E-Marts.'" *The Associated Press State & Local Wire*, 1 July 2007, available from Lexis-Nexis [database online].

Kristof, Kathy M. "'Covenant' Leads a Lackluster Box Office; Weekend Totals Are the Worst of the Year. Still, 'Pirates' Hits $1 Billion in Cumulative Sales." *Los Angeles Times*, 11 September 2006, pg. C1.

Littleton, Cythnia. "34th Annual Key Art Awards." *The Hollywood Reporter,* 9 May 2005, pg. 6.

Long, Colleen. "Thousands Visit Natural History Museum after Ben Stiller Movie." *The Associated Press State & Local Wire*, 9 January 2007, available from Lexis-Nexis [database online].

Lowery, Steve. "A Naked Chick, Please!" *OC Weekly*, 1 June 2001, pg. 22.

MSNBC Online. "Movies Heavily Shape Teen Smoking, Study: 40 Percent of Youths Try Smoking Because They Saw It in Films." 7 November 2005 <http://msnbc.msn.com/id/9949432/> (15 July 2006).

McCarthy, Michael. "L'Oreal to 'Celebrate Beautiful Women' with Oscar Ads." *USA Today*, 25 February 2005, pg. 1B.

___. "'Star Wars' Goes Utterly Commercial: Get Ready to Be Bombarded with Toys, Games, Lots of Ads." *USA Today*, 25 April 2005, pg. 2B.

McNulty, Timothy. "How Un-PC Can You Be?" *Pittsburgh Post-Gazette*, 16 April 2006, pg. E1.

Marr, Merissa. "Fairy-Tale Wedding? Disney Can Supply the Gown; Princess-Inspired Designs Aim to Attract Older Crowd; Subtle Mermaid Styling." *The Wall Street Journal*, 22 February 2007, pg. B1.

___. "Pirates' Treasure? Storms, Delays Drive Up Cost of Sequels Shot Back to Back, but Disney Hopes for Two Hits." *The Wall Street Journal*, 30 June 2006, pg. B1.

Matthews, Cheri. "The Late Inmage [sic] Hollywood Expanding Its View." *Modesto Bee*, 13 October 1991, pg. D1.

Maynard, Micheline. "'Flightplan' Irks Flight Attendants." *The New York Times*, 28 September 2005, pg. E2.

Meller, Henry. "Halle: There are No Great Roles for Black Women." *Daily Mail*, 25 January 2005, <http://www.mailonsunday.co.uk/pages/text/print.html?in_article_id=335302&in_page_id=1773> (15 July 2007).

Meyer, Carla and Ruthe Stein. "Oscars's Split Decision, Best Picture 'Chicago,' 'Pianist' Divide Top Awards." *The San Francisco Chronicle*, 24 March 2003 <http://sfgate.com/cgi-bin/article.cgi?f=/c/a/2003/03/24/MN269661.DTL> (15 July 2007).

Morgenstern, Joe. "Holy Melancholy, 'Batman'! Tale of Superhero's Origins Is Vivid, Stylish — and Dour." *Wall Street Journal*, 17 June 2005, pg. W1.

Movshovitz, Howie. "Reviews: 'The Last King of Scotland.'" *The Hollywood Reporter*, 7 September 2006, pg. 11.

Nason. "News from Hollywood." *United Press International*, 11 February 2003, available from Lexis-Nexis [database online].

Nelson, Soraya Sarhaddi. "Protesters Say Hollywood Favors White Stunt Workers; Bias: Group Says Caucasians Are Made Up to Look Like the Minority Actors They Double For in Film and TV, Costing People of Color Jobs." *Los Angeles Times*, 28 September 1999, pg. B1.

The New York Post. "H'wood Pulls 2 Terror Flicks." 13 September 2001, pg. 66.

___. "Studio Too Far Out on a Limb." 23 October 2006, pg. 12.

Nichols, Peter M. "Home Video; A Terror Alert On New Stickers." *The New York Times*, 5 October 2001, pg. E26.

O'Brien, Pat. "Yo Ho Ho and a Revamped Ride; Jack Sparrow and Other Characters from Disney's Films Join the Crew on Pirates of the Caribbean Attraction." *The Press Enterprise*, 7 July 2006, pg. AA18.

Orwall, Bruce. "Glut of Big-Budget Movies Raises Risks for Them All." *Wall Street Journal*, 2 July 2003, pg. B1.

Pak, Minju. "Creative Spark, The Key Art Awards Give Movie Marketers an Annual Moment in the Sun." *The Hollywood Reporter*, 28 April 2005, pg. S-4.

Pener, Degen and Cindy Pearlman. "Dealing with the Devil, Two Exacting Stars and a Runaway Budget Made Filming the 'Devil's Own' a Hellacious Headache." *Entertainment Weekly*, 11 April 1997, <http://www.ew.com/ew/report/0,6115,287407_1_0_,00.html> (15 July 2007).

Pettus, Gary. "American-Indian Traditions, Stereotypes Survive; kh/jac/int/je." *The Associated Press State & Local Wire*, 28 November 2005, available from Lexis-Nexis [database online].

Pittsburgh Tribune Review. "Marshall Defends Controversial 'Geisha' Casting Decision." 7 March 2005, available from Lexis-Nexis [database online].

PR Newswire. "Dan Glickman to Succeed Jack Valenti as Head of MPAA; Valenti Resigns After 38-Year Tenure." 1 July 2004, available from Lexis-Nexis [database online].

Ramirez, Orlando. "Drawn to Controversy: Many Race-based Cartoon Stereotypes Aren't Acceptable Now but Still Remain Accessible." *The Press-Enterprise*, 28 May 1995, pg. E1.

Rea, Stephen. "Oscar Hugs and Shrugs; The Academy Award Nominations Show Unusual Diversity this Year and, in the Case of 'Dreamgirls,' an Oddity." *The Philadelphia Inquirer*, 24 January 2007, pg. F1.

Rechtshaffen, Michael. "Reviews: 'Little Man.'" *The Hollywood Reporter*, 14-16 July 2006, pg. 14.

Record, The. "Black Artists Shunned?; Racial Bias Seen in Oscar Nominations," 22 March, 1996, available from Lexis-Nexis [database online].

Reuters. "Movies Can Put You in the Mood: Study Says Certain Films Can Boost Hormone Levels." *MSNBC Online*, 22 July 2004, <http://msnbc.msn.com/id/5490731/> (15 July 2006).

Rich, Joshua. "Piracy King: The MPAA Crowns A New Movie Boss." *Entertainment Weekly*, 16 July 2004, pg. 18.

Riding, Alan. "UNESCO Adopts New Plan Against Cultural Invasion." *The New York Times*, 21 October 2005, pg. E3.

Samuels, Allison. "Angela's Fire." *Newsweek*, 1 July 2002, pg. 54.

Sanner, Ann. "'Rocky' Goes to the Smithsonian Boxer's Gloves, Robe, Shorts." *The Associated Press State & Local Wire*, 6 December 2006, available from Lexis-Nexis [database online].

Schaefer, Stephen. "Under 'Siege' - Filmmakers Fend Off Criticisms from Arab-American Groups." *The Boston Herald*, 4 November, 1998, available from Lexis-Nexis [database online].

Scheck, Frank. "'King's Ransom.'" *The Hollywood Reporter*, 25 April 2005, <http://www.hollywoodreporter.com/thr/reviews/review_display.jsp?vnu_content_id=1000894467> (15 July 2007).

Schiller, Gail. "Brand Warfare," *The Hollywood Reporter*, 10-16 May 2005, pg. S-4.

Schwanitz, Thoralf. "Press Access Limited on Bus with Arnold." *The Oakland Tribune*, 5 October 2003, available from Lexis-Nexis [database online].

Science Fiction Weekly. "Sam Raimi and his 'Spider-Man' Actors Show Great Power and Responsibility." 6 May 2002, <http://www.scifi.com/sfw/issue263/interview.html> (15 July 2007).

Segal, David. "Bruce Willis's Tragic Mask." *Washington Post*, 10 March 2005, pg. C1.

Seiler, Casey. "Shaken, not Stirred, by a Bond with Bond." *The Times Union*, 20 November 2005, pg. G1.

Seiler, Andy. "Something to Offend Everyone: Minority Groups Say Hit Films Fill Screens with Stereotypes." *USA Today*, 28 June 1999, pg. 1D.

Shuster, Fred and Jennifer Errico. "Warhol's World; His Touch Transcends the Art World and Is Reflected in Everyday Life." *The Daily News of Los Angeles*, 23 May 2002, pg. U11.

Siegel, Tatiana. "Latinos in Entertainment: With a Number of High-profile Projects on the Horizon from Latino Directors, Hollywood Appears Ripe for a Hispanic Revolution." *The Hollywood Reporter*, 14-20 June 2005, <http://www.hollywoodreporter.com/thr/film/feature_display.jsp?vnu_content_id=1000957036> (15 July 2007).

Skertic, Mark and Jennifer Cassell. "'Star Wars' Fans Play Hooky." *Chicago Sun-Times*, 20 May 1999, Jedi Journal, pg. 4.

Slovick, Sam. "Thugs on Film." *LA Weekly*, 14 March 2003, pg. 32.

Smith, Sean. "Along Came Spidey." *Newsweek*, 28 June 2004, <http://www.msnbc.msn.com/id/5251416/site/newsweek/> (15 July 2007).

Snider, Mike. "NASCAR, Hollywood Share the Fast Lane." *USA Today*, 8 June 2006, pg. 1A.

Sommer, Mark. "Tribute to Jolson Brings Back an Anguished Debate over Blackface." *Buffalo News*, 10 July 2002, pg. D1.

Soriano, César G. "Lucas Rules Fans' Empire: Creator of 'Star Wars' Helps Convention Celebrate Final Film." *USA Today*, 25 April 2005, pg. 1D.

___. "Politics Creates a Disturbance in the Force." *USA Today,* 18 May 2005, pg. 1D.

___ and Ann Oldenburg, "With America at War, Hollywood Follows." 8 February 2005, *USA Today*, pg. 1A.

Speier, Michael. "The Bronze Screen: 100 Years of the Latino Image in Hollywood Cinema." *Variety*, 8 October 2002, <http://www.variety.com/review/VE1117919004?categoryid=32&cs=1&query=the+and+bronze+and+screen&display=the+bronze+screen> (15 July 2007).

Stanley, T.L. "The Color of Money: Hollywood Diversifies." *Advertising Age*, 30 August 2004, pg. 3.

Strauss, Bob. "Latino Stars Share in Celebrity Spotlight." *The Times Union*, 9 March 1995, available from Lexis-Nexis [database online].

Szep, Jason. "'Star Wars' Becomes Tool to Teach Modern Technology," *Red Orbit*, 24 October 2005, <http://www.redorbit.com/news/entertainment/282724/star_wars_becomes_tool_to_teach_modern_technology/> (15 July 2007).

Tartaglione-Vialatte, Nancy. "Cannes Film Festival; 'Ocean's' Crew Cavorts, but Seriously . . .; The Jokes Fly at a News Conference. Then a Journalist Raises an Issue about Shaobo Qin's Role." *Los Angeles Times*, 26 May 2007, pg. E7.

Texeira, Erin. "More Hollywood Remakes Cast Minorities in Roles Once Filled by Whites." *The Associated Press State & Local Wire*, 8 June 2005, available from Lexis-Nexis [database online].

Thompson, Gary. "Hollywood DVD Sales Prop Up Weak Box Office." *The San Diego Union-Tribune*, 31 July 2005 <http://www.signonsandiego.com/uniontrib/20050731/news_1a31slump.html> (15 July 2007).

Thompson, Luke Y. "Witch Is Which?; 'Blair Witch 2' Blurs Fact and Fiction, but the Truth Is, It Ain't Scary." *Dallas Observer,* 26 October 2000. Database online; available from Lexis-Nexis.

The Times Union. "Now at the U.N., Lights, Camera, Action." 30 January 2004, pg. A2.

Travis, Neal. "Hayek Reaching for New High." *The New York Post*, 26 November 2000, pg. 13.

United Press International. "Blacks, Latinos Make Movie Gains." August 8, 2003, available from Lexis-Nexis [database online].

Van Biema, David. "Lie Down in Darkness, Does a Death On the Highway Implicate the Entertainment Industry?" *Time Magazine*, 1 November 1993.

Van Gelder, Lawrence. "Movies, Performing Arts/Weekend Desk; Arts, Briefly." *The New York Times*, 8 December, 2006, pg. E4.

Veiga, Alex. "Sony to Pay $1.5M Over Fake Movie Critic." *The Associated Press State & Local Wire*, 3 August 2005, available from Lexis-Nexis [database online].

Walls, Jeanette. "Was Race an Issue in 'Hitch' Casting?" *MSNBC Online*, 24 February 2005 <http://www.msnbc.msn.com/id/7019342/> (15 July 2007).

Waxman, Sharon. "Hollywood Attuned to World Markets." *Washington Post*, 26 October 1990, pg. A1.

Weintraub, Joanne. "Strong, Loving Black Families Don't Exist in Most of TV's World." *The San Diego Union-Tribune*, 27 June 2000, pg. E10.

WENN Entertainment News Wire Service. "50 Cent: 'I'm No Worse Than James Bond.' 18 January 2006, available from Lexis-Nexis [database online].

___. "Foxx Furious over 'Miami Vice' Race 'Joke." 9 September 2005, available from Lexis-Nexis [database online].

Westbrook, Bruce. "Actor Says Big Break Won't Go Up in Smoke." *The Houston Chronicle*, 4 August 2004, pg. 1.

Westfeldt, Amy. "Stone Begins Shooting 9/11 Movie in N.Y." *The Associated Press State & Local Wire*, 2 November, 2005, available from Lexis-Nexis [database online].

Williams, Walt. "Report: Paleontologist 'Fudged' Discovery to Promote Movie." *Bozeman Daily Chronicle*, 12 May 2005, <http://www.bozemandailychronicle.com/articles/2005/05/12/news/01horner.txt> (15 July 2007).

Wloszczyna, Susan. "A Remake by Any Other Name; Hollywood Is Big about Borrowing from the Past." *USA Today*, 14 April 2004, pg. 1D.

Zakaria, Tabassum. "CIA Checking if Life Imitates Art." *Reuters*, 5 August 2004, <http://www.reuters.com/newsArticle.jhtml?type=reutersEdge&storyID=5876235> (30 June 2005).

BOOKS

Bogle, Donald. *Toms, Coons, Mulattoes, Mammies & Bucks: An Interpretive History of Blacks in American Films*. New York: Continuum International Publishing Group, 2001.

DuBois, W.E.B. *The Souls of Black Folk*. Oxford: Oxford University Press, 2007.

Entman, Robert M. and Andrew Rojecki. *The Black Image in the White Mind*. Chicago: The University of Chicago Press, 2000.

Erens, Patricia. *The Jew in American Cinema*. Bloomington: Indiana University Press, 1984.

Home Box Office. *Unchained Memories: Readings From the Slave Narratives*. Boston: Bulfinch Press, 2002.

Mahar, William J. *Behind the Burnt Cork Mask: Early Blackface Minstrelsy and Antebellum American Popular Culture*. Urbana: University of Illinois Press, 1999.

Springer, John Parris. *Hollywood Fictions: The Dream Factory In American Popular Culture*. Norman: University of Oklahoma Press 2000.

OTHER

Adler, Bruce. "Arabian Nights." *Aladdin: Original Motion Picture Soundtrack*, Burbank: Walt Disney Records, 1992.

America Beyond the Color Line. Directed by Dan Percival and Mary Crisp. 220 minutes. PBS Home Video, 2003. DVD.

Ass't Deputy Minister of Canada. "Conflict Management Program." *CF Personnel, Canadian Forces Personnel Newsletter*, 19 November 2003 <www.forces.gc.ca/hr/cfpn/pdf/cfpn11_03_e.pdf> (15 July 2006).

Children Now. "A Different World: Children's Perceptions of Race and Class in Media." May 1998, <http://publications.childrennow.org/publications/media/differentworld_1999.cfm> (15 July 2007).

Clinton, Bill. "Speech by President to Theater Owners Association." *Clinton Foundation*, 8 June 1999, <http://www.clintonfoundation.org/legacy/060899-speech-by-president-to-theater-owners-association.htm> (15 July 2007).

Delgadillo, Rocky. "Trust Your Instinct - Your Life May Depend on It." *Screen Actors Guild*, n.d., <http://www.sag.org/sagWebApp/Content/Public/rockydelgadillo.htm> (15 July 2007).

Jadakiss. "Why?" *Kiss of Death*, New York: Ruff Ryders Records, 2004.

Kochhar, Rakesh. "The Wealth of Hispanic Households: 1996-2002." *Pew Hispanic Center*, October 2004, <http://pewhispanic.org/files/reports/34.pdf> (15 July 2007).

Lauzen, Martha M. "The Celluloid Ceiling: Behind-the-Scenes and On-Screen Employment of Women in the Top 250 Films of 2002." *Movies Directed By Women*, 7 July 2003, <http://www.moviesbywomen.com/marthalauzenphd/stats2003.html> (15 July 2007).

McCarthy, Nancy. "ABA Study Finds Minority Lawyers Have 'Miles to Go' in the Profession." *California Bar Journal*, March 2005, <http://www.calbar.ca.gov/state/calbar/calbar_cbj.jsp?sCategoryPath=/Home/Attorney%20Resources/California%20Bar%20Journal/March2005&sCatHtmlPath=cbj/2005-03_TH_03_ABA-minorities.html&sCatHtmlTitle=Top%20Headlines> (15 July 2007).

Newman-Baudais, Susan. "Partnering Europe: Access to the European Market for Non-European Films – A Statistical Analysis." *European Audiovisual Observatory*, n.d., <http://www.obs.coe.int/online_publication/expert/filmdistribution_mif2005.pdf.en> (15 July 2007).

Outler, Albert C. "Confessions, Book 11, Chapter 14." *Institute of Practical Bible Education, The Electronic Public Library*, 2005 <http://www.iclnet.org/pub/resources/text/ipb-e/epl-01/agcon-18.txt> (15 July 2007).

Public Enemy. "Burn Hollywood Burn." *Fear of a Black Planet*, New York: Def Jam Records, 1994.

Shea, Jack. "January 2001, President's Report." *Director's Guild of America*, January 2001, <http://www.dga.org/news/v25_5/dept_presreport.php3> (15 July 2007).

Stiers, David Ogden, Jim Cummings and Chorus. "Savages (Part 1)." *Pocohantas: Original Motion Picture Soundtrack*, Burbank: Walt Disney Records, 1995.

Vanity Fair. "The 2004 Hollywood Issue." March 2004, cover.

WEBSITES

Anti-Defamation League. "ADL Concerned Mel Gibson's 'Passion' Could Fuel Anti-Semitism If Released in Present Form." 11 August 2003, <http://www.adl.org/NR/exeres/B383494F-8B0F-45B0-8F03-EBAC865C9098,0B1623CA-D5A4-465D-A369-DF6E8679CD9E,frameless.htm> (15 July 2007).

Box Office Mojo. Box Office Mojo, "'Dukes of Hazzard' Box Office Data." N.d., <http://www.boxofficemojo.com/movies/?id=dukesofhazzard.htm> (15 July 2006).

___. "'Harry Potter and the Sorcerer's Stone' Box Office Data." N.d., <http://www.boxofficemojo.com/movies/?id=harrypotter.htm> (15 July 2007).

___. "'Titanic' Box Office Data." N.d., <http://www.boxofficemojo.com/movies/?id=titanic.htm> (15 July 2007).

___. "'*Troy*' Box Office Data." N.d., <http://www.boxofficemojo.com/movies/?id=troy.htm> (15 July 2007).

___. "'Zoolander' Box Office Data." N.d., <http://www.boxofficemojo.com/movies/?id=zoolander.htm> (15 July 2007).

British Film Institute. "The Ultimate Film Chart." N.d., <http://www.bfi.org.uk/features/ultimatefilm/chart/details.php?ranking=1> (15 July 2007).

Directors Guild of America. "The DGA; Basics; Welcome." N.d., <http://www.dga.org/index2.php3?chg=> (15 July 2007).

___. "DGA Annual Report on Women and Minority Hiring Reveals Bleak Industry Record for 1999." January 2001, <http://www.dga.org/news/v25_5/news_minorityhire.php3> (15 July 2007).

Hasbro, "Instructions: 'Shrek 2' Wise Crackin' Donkey." N.d., <http://www.hasbro.com/common/instruct/Shrek_2_Wise-Crackin'_Donkey.pdf> (15 July 2007).

IAI Presentations, Inc., "The Peking Acrobats®." N.d., <http://www.chineseacrobats/com/pa.html>.

Indiana State Museum. "Lord of the Rings, Motion Picture Trilogy Exhibition." N.d., <http://www.in.gov/ism/MuseumExhibits/lotr.asp> (15 July 2006).

Internet Movie Database. "All-Time Worldwide Boxoffice." N.d., <http://www.imdb.com/boxoffice/alltimegross?region=world-wide> (1 April 2007).

___. "Berry Returns to 'X-Men' for Bigger Role." 12 May 2004 <http://www.imdb.com/news/wenn/2004-05-12> (15 July 2007).

___. "Biography for Cameron Diaz." N.d., <http://www.imdb.com/name/nm0000139/bio> (15 July 2007).

___. "Biography for Patrick Gallagher." N.d., <http://www.imdb.com/name/nm0302466/bio> (15 July 2007).

___. "Biography for Salma Hayek." N.d., <http://www.imdb.com/name/nm0000161/bio> (15 July 2007).

___. "Full Cast and Crew for 'Inspector Gadget.'" N.d., <http://www.imdb.com/title/tt0141369> (15 July 2007).

___. "Full Cast and Crew for 'The Lion King.'" N.d., <http://www.imdb.com/title/tt0110357> (15 July 2007).

___. "Trivia for 'The Bourne Supremacy.'" N.d., <http://www.imdb.com/title/tt0372183/trivia> (15 July 2007).

___. "Trivia for 'Ice Age.'" N.d., <http://www.imdb.com/title/tt0268380/trivia> (15 July 2007).

___. "Trivia for 'The Matrix Reloaded.'" N.d., <http://www.imdb.com/title/tt0242653/trivia> (15 July 2007).

___. "Trivia for 'Minority Report.'" N.d., <http://www.imdb.com/title/tt0181689/trivia> (15 July 2007).

___. "Trivia for 'Pearl Harbor.'" N.d., <http://www.imdb.com/title/tt0213149/trivia> (15 July 2007).

___. "Trivia for 'Wallace & Gromit in the Curse of the Were-Rabbit.'" N.d., <http://www.imdb.com/title/tt0312004/trivia> (15 July 2007).

Jewhoo. "Notes on Playing Locate the Landsman (LTL)." N.d., <http://www.jewhoo.com/editor/landsman.html> (15 July 2007).

Martha's Vineyard Chamber of Commerce. "JawsFest." N.d., <http://www.mvy.com/jaws/> (15 July 2006).

Motion Picture Association of America. "About Us." N.d., <http://www.mpaa.org/AboutUs.asp> (15 July 2007).

___. "How Movies are Rated." N.d., <http://www.mpaa.org/Ratings_HowRated.asp> (15 July 2007).

___. "MPAA President Dan Glickman Addresses ShoWest 'The Movie Industry Is a Vital Part of the American Economy.'" 15 March 2005, <http://www.mpaa.org/press_releases/2005_03_15b.pdf> (15 July 2007).

___. "Members Page." N.d. <http://www.mpaa.org/AboutUsMembers.asp> (15 July 2007).

___. "Valenti Reports Record-Breaking Box Office Results, Continued Decrease in Production Costs and Praises Movie Industry War Efforts in ShoWest Address." 5 March 2002, <http://www.mpaa.org/jack/content.htm> (15 December 2005).

National Film Registry 2004. "Films Selected to the National Film Registry, Library of Congress - 2004." 28 December 2004, <http://www.loc.gov/film/nfr2004.html> (15 July 2007).

Screen Actors Guild. "About SAG." N.d., <http://www.sag.org/sagWebApp/application;JSESSIONID_sagWebApp=D1O1kvwpXFVY6eL2mj9dZcpkJ0VlJXlggrTkYHlYFevQPb0hkDIk!-409041021!NONE?origin=hnav_bar.jsp&event=bea.portal.framework.internal.refresh&pageid=Inside+SAG> (15 July 2005).

___. "Ethnicity Share of All 2003 SAG TV/Theatrical Roles (Excluding Animation)." N.d., <http://www.sag.org/Content/Public/03castingdatarpt-eth1.pdf> (15 July 2007).

Soulplane.com. "Technical Notes." N.d. <http://www.soulplane.com> (15 July 2007).

United States Census Bureau. "U.S. Summary: 2000." July 2002, <http://www.census.gov/prod/2002pubs/c2kprof00-us.pdf> (15 July 2007).

United States Commercial Service. "Doing Business In Hong Kong & Macau: Country Commercial Guide for U.S. Companies." 4 February 2005, <http://www.buyusainfo.net/docs/x_7423798.pdf> (15 July 2007).

United States Postal Service. "Hattie McDaniel, First African American To Win An Academy Award®, Featured On New 39-Cent Postage Stamp." 25 January 2006. <http://www.usps.com/communications/news/stamps/2006/sr06_005.htm> (28 February 2006).

___. "Citizens' Stamp Advisory Council." <http://www.usps.com/communications/organization/csac.htm> (15 July 2007).

WeddingCrashersMovie.com. "Crasher Kit." N.d. <http://www.weddingcrashersmovie.com> (15 July 2007).

Writers Guild of America. "1998 Hollywood Writers Report." 1998, <http://www.wga.org/manual/Report/minority.html> (30 June 2005).

___. "2005 Hollywood Writers Report." 2005, <http://www.wga.org/subpage_whoweare.aspx?id=922> (15 July 2006).

INDEX

The following listings do not cite entries made in the Glossary, Notes or Reference sections.

16 Blocks, 37
40 Year Old Virgin, The, 101, 238
50 Cent, 37, 216, 217

A

A Few Good Men, 54, 55
A Time to Kill, 53, 113, 166
Academy Award, 4, 22, 23, 25, 39, 44, 53, 54, 111, 132, 146, 178, 192, 193, 199, 211, 216, 256, 265
across-the-street minority, 63, 65, 106, 191
Adaptation, 44
Affleck, Ben, 116, 175, 177, 241
Affluent prototype, 163-66, 168, 169, 183, 256, 264
After the Sunset, 129, 147
Agent Cody Banks, 153
Air Force One, 166, 170, 177
Air Up There, The, 180
Akeelah and the Bee, 35
Aladdin, 40, 191
Alba, Jessica, 61, 65, 126, 135
Alexander, 120, 126
Ali, 142, 211, 244
A-list actor, 12
American Pie, 126
American President, The, 236
Amistad, 113, 222
Analyze This, 154, 219
anchor, 158, 163, 169, 190
Anderson, Anthony, 102, 153, 208
André Benjamin, 37
Angel archetype, 56
    Asian, 75
    Black, 76
    Latino, 77
    Other, 80

Anger Management, 128, 187
Aniston, Jennifer, 61, 147
Anthony, Marc, 78, 120, 149, 165, 166
Antwone Fisher, 35, 181
Antz, 27
Any Given Sunday, 211
Aoki, Devon, 65, 126
Apocalypse Now, 67
archetype
    general definition, 12
    categorical definitions
        Angel, 56
        Background Figure, 56
        Comic Relief, 56
        Menace to Society, 57
        Physical Wonder, 57
        Utopic Reversal, 57
Are We There Yet?, 35, 37, 174, 237
Armageddon, 13, 37, 129, 153, 175
Around the World in 80 Days, 207
Asian archetypes
    Angel, 75
    Background Figure, 87
    Comic Relief, 100
    Menace to Society, 114
    Physical Wonder, 130
    Utopic Reversal, 143
Asuka, Nao, 101
asymptote, 62-66, 92, 119, 126, 135, 246
ATL, 227
Austin Powers: Goldmember, 37, 65, 100, 117, 129, 262

B

Bacalso, Joanna, 94
Back to the Future, 24, 219, 239

Background Figure archetype, 56
    Asian, 87
    Black, 88
    Latino, 90
    Other, 93
Bad Boys II, 34, 37, 40, 44, 65, 128, 150, 151, 166, 237, 259
Bad Company, 37, 98, 153
Bai, Ling, 143
Bale, Christian, 176, 178, 226
Bambi, 222
Banderas, Antonio, 73, 93, 129, 246
bankability, 20, 21, 38
B.A.P.S., 236
Barbershop, 23, 37, 158
Barry, Raymond, 116
Basic Instinct, 202
Bassett, Angela, 63, 124, 159
Batman Begins, 13, 22, 44, 111, 153, 176, 178, 223, 225
Be Cool, 37, 128
Beach, Adam, 80
Beauty and the Beast, 27
Beauty Shop, 35
Bedard, Irene, 136
Bedazzled, 117
Bend It Like Beckham, 28, 40
Benet, Eric, 132
Berenger, Tom, 116
Berry, Halle, 4, 12, 61, 65, 120, 126, 132, 146, 159, 177, 189, 190, 192 207, 216, 236, 239
Best Man, The, 36, 167
Beverly Hills Cop, 98, 153
Bewitched, 13, 22
Big Daddy Kane, 36
Big Momma's House series, 37, 153, 237
    Big Momma's House, 128
    Big Momma's House 2, 77, 128, 159
Biker Boyz, 167
Billy Madison, 168
Birth of a Nation, The, 4, 226
Black archetypes
    Angel, 76
    Background Figure, 88
    Comic Relief, 101
    Menace to Society, 115
    Physical Wonder, 132
    Utopic Reversal, 146
Black Buck, 27, 129
Blade series, 240
    Blade, 35
    Blade: Trinity, 216

Blair Witch Project, The, 28, 202
Blanchett, Cate, 118, 120
blockbuster, 17, 23, 24, 27, 37, 154, 166, 176, 208, 209, 220, 230, 237, 239, 240, 245, 252, 261
Blood Diamond, 88, 222
Blow, 40
Bogle, Donald, 27
Bohanon, Joseph, 224
Bone Collector, The, 145. 190, 207
Bourne Supremacy, The, 210
Boyd, Jenna, 118
Boyz n the Hood, 167
Brando, Marlon, 39
Braugher, Andre, 92
Braveheart, 241, 259
Breakfast Club, The, 67
Bridget Jones's Diary, 192,
Bringing Down the House, 37, 53, 72, 80, 164, 172, 236, 237
Broderick, Matthew, 243
Brody, Adrien, 132
Brokeback Mountain, 4
Brooks, Albert, 177
Brosnan, Pierce, 147, 177, 189
Brother Bear, 26, 27, 171
Brothers, The, 36, 167
Brown, Dan, 22
Brown, Kimberly J., 172
Brown Sugar, 36, 167, 207
Brownlee, Mongo, 102, 117
Bruce Almighty, 147, 148, 183, 238
Bulletproof, 153
Bulletproof Monk, 74, 75
Bulworth, 179, 190
Buscemi, Steve, 186
Bush, George W., 220, 249
Butterfly Effect, The, 117, 119
Bythewood, Reggie Rock, 167

C

Cage, Nicolas, 80, 184, 206, 229
Calhoun, Coronji, 180
Cansino, Margarita. *See* Hayworth, Rita
Carell, Steve, 101
Carrere, Tia, 123
Carrey, Jim, 102, 175, 186, 238
Cars, 27, 218
Casino Royale, 44, 120, 153, 169, 176
Casseus, Gabriel, 117

casting couch, 211
catharsis, 72, 74, 75, 79, 81, 102, 117, 160
Cat in the Hat, The, 21
Cedric the Entertainer, 37, 237
Chan, Charlie, 34
Chan, Jackie, 99, 127, 153, 207, 237
Changing Lanes, 115, 241
Chappelle, Dave, 117, 135
character arc, 41, 72, 73, 99, 102, 161-64
Charles, Ray, 211
Charlie and the Chocolate Factory, 44
Charlie's Angels: Full Throttle, 18, 61
Chase, Daveigh, 171
Chatwin, Justin, 174
Cheadle, Don, 66, 108, 147, 207
Cheaper by the Dozen, 13
Chiba, Sonny, 76
Chicago, 37, 88
Cho, John, 236
Christensen, Erika, 115
Chronicles of Narnia: The Lion, the Witch, and the Wardrobe, 218
Church, Thomas Haden, 131
Cider House Rules, 37
Cinderella Man, 221
Cleese, John, 61
Click, 100, 238
Clinton, Bill, 200, 201, 249
Clinton, William J. *See* Bill Clinton
Clooney, George, 40, 90
Clueless, 23
Coach Carter, 142
Coburn, James, 94
Collateral, 31, 148, 153, 216
Collateral Damage, 209
Collette, Toni, 152
color-blind movie, 204, 207, 238, 247
Combs, Sean "Diddy," 115, 117, 204
Comic Relief archetype, 56
    Asian, 100
    Black, 101
    Latino, 105
    Other, 106
common denominator, 28
Con Air, 117, 129, 135
connective switch, 66, 67, 89, 181, 207, 208, 226, 228, 229, 232, 234-36, 238-47, 252
Connelly, Jennifer, 61, 88
Connery, Sean, 41, 144
contra-juxtaposition, 98, 99
controlled universe, 202

Coppola, Carmine, 229
Coppola, Ford, 229
Coppola, Sofia, 101, 218, 229
copycat behavior, 249
Cradle 2 the Grave, 37
Crash, 37, 40, 53, 62, 120, 153, 265
Crichton, Michael, 22
Crimson Tide, 35, 145, 178
cross-casting, 207, 208
Crowe, Russell, 221
Cruise, Tom, 31, 38, 82, 92, 144, 148, 174, 175, 177, 189, 204, 216, 219, 232, 263
Culkin, Macaulay, 188
Curious George, 23, 24
Curtis, Cliff, 40, 119
Curtis, Jamie Lee, 229
Curtis, Tony, 229
cycle of blamelessness, 205, 207, 228, 261

D

Da Vinci Code, The, 22, 219
Dafoe, William, 178
Damon, Matt, 77, 90, 172, 183
Daniels, Dee Jay, 181
David, Keith, 153, 175
Dawson, Rosario, 65, 120, 126, 190
Day After Tomorrow, The, 35, 153, 173, 180-82, 190
De Niro, Robert, 105, 117, 154
Deep Impact, 13
DeGeneres, Ellen, 177
Deja Vu, 94
Del Rio, Dolores, 129
Del Toro, Benicio, 4, 120, 135, 148, 153
Demsky, Issur Danielovich. *See* Kirk Douglas
Desselle, Natalie, 236
Deuce Bigalow, Male Gigolo, 37
Devil's Advocate, The, 55
Devil's Own, The, 159
DeVito, Danny, 90
Diary of a Mad Black Woman, 35, 128, 165, 175
Diaz, Cameron, 63-65, 126, 175, 246, 247, 249
DiCaprio, Leonardo, 88, 193, 222
Die Another Day, 114. 177, 189
Die Hard series, 240
    Die Hard, 170
    Die Hard: With a Vengeance, 86, 166
Directors Guild of America (DGA), 42, 45, 47, 226
Dirty Pretty Things, 126
DMX, 37

Doctor Dolittle, 105, 106, 180, 181, 206
Dodgeball: A True Underdog Story, 134, 160, 161, 165, 238
Dogma, 126, 136
Doom, 22
Douglas, Kirk, 67
Douglas, Michael, 132, 202, 236
Downey, Jr., Morton, 146
Dreamgirls, 4, 244
Dreyfuss, Richard, 92, 182
Drumline, 30
Duff, Jamal, 134, 161
Dukes of Hazzard, The, 13, 22, 97
Dumbo, 26
Duncan, Michael Clarke, 26, 76, 77, 107, 117, 120, 128, 129, 134, 175, 186, 204
Dunst, Kirsten, 61
Durand, Kevin, 117, 119, 121,
Dutton, Charles S., 120, 146

E

Ebert, Roger, 11
emasculation, 91, 128, 129, 134, 144-46, 161
Entman, Robert M., 212
Erens, Patricia, 68
Erin Brockovich, 178, 242
Estevez, Emilio, 67
Estevez, Ramon. *See* Martin Sheen
E.T., 24, 219, 239
ethnicity, 33, 99, 227

F

Fahrenheit 9/11, 220
Family-Tied prototype, 163, 169-72, 178, 183, 190, 232, 256, 264
Fanning, Dakota, 73, 78, 91, 120, 149, 174, 233
Fast and Furious, The, 68
Fatal Attraction, 210
faux presence, 30,
Ferrell, Will, 93, 218, 238
Fever Pitch, 185
Fiennes, Ralph, 92, 190
Fifth Element, The, 37, 128
Fight Club, 203
Finding Nemo, 24, 27, 171, 177, 249
finite-fantasy, 217

first-run movie, 16
Fishburne, Laurence, 35, 76, 177
Flightplan, 174
Fonda, Henry, 229
Fonda, Jane, 229
Four Brothers, 37
Ford, Harrison, 117, 145, 176, 177, 188
Forrest Gump, 23, 252
Foster, Gloria, 73, 76
Foster, Jodie, 174, 182
Fox, Vivica A., 17, 35, 126, 213, 227
Foxx, Jaime, 431, 57, 159, 211, 216
Fraser, Brendan, 116, 181
Freeman, Morgan, 4, 70, 73, 112, 113, 147, 174, 177, 183
Frida, 142, 244
Friday series, 237
    Friday, 35, 129
    Friday After Next, 236
Friendly, David, 208
From Dusk Till Dawn, 126, 136
Fugitive, The, 117, 188
Fun with Dick and Jane, 186
Fuqua, Antoine, 119
Furlong, Edward, 171

G

Gates, Henry Louis, 203
genre, 12, 46, 56, 167, 208, 234, 235-37, 239, 243
Gere, Richard, 73, 79, 88, 143, 192, 239
Gertz, Jami, 183
Get Rich or Die Tryin', 37, 216, 217
Ghost, 72, 80
Giamatti, Paul, 131
Gibson, Mel, 120, 122, 127, 133, 136, 145, 170, 177, 187, 193, 240, 251
girl next door, 115, 203, 229, 243, 251
Giuliani, Rudy, 187
Glickman, Dan, 10, 29, 249, 251
Glover, Danny, 90. 127, 153, 166, 170, 177, 237, 240
Godfather, The, 39
Goldberg, Whoopi, 17, 72, 80, 96, 105
Gone with the Wind, 4, 54, 225, 248
Good Will Hunting, 165, 183, 242
Gooding, Jr., Cuba, 31, 94, 180, 204
Gonzalo, Julie, 160
Gothika, 120, 146
Gould, Alexander, 177
greatest possible audience, 11, 14, 17, 18, 21, 24, 28, 29, 65, 209, 218, 226-28

Green Mile, The, 76, 117, 129, 204
Greene, Graham, 94, 117
greenlight, 30, 35, 61, 62, 106, 136, 167, 203, 227, 236, 247
Griffin, Eddie, 37
Guess Who, 13, 34, 53, 63, 191, 207, 237
Guess Who's Coming to Dinner, 63, 191
Gyllenhaal, Jake, 173, 190
Gyllenhaal, Maggie, 61

H

Halo, 22
Hamilton, Linda, 171
Hanks, Tom, 38, 76, 81, 172, 176, 192, 204
Harada, Masato, 144
HARM theory. *See* Hollywood's Acting Rule for Minorities
Harold & Kumar Go to White Castle, 66, 236, 237
Harris, Naomie, 24, 246
Harris, Tip (also known as T.I.), 227
Harry Potter series, 21, 22, 222, 239
    Harry Potter and the Goblet of Fire, 44, 245
    Harry Potter and the Chamber of Secrets, 245
    Harry Potter and the Sorcerer's Stone, 89, 245
Hart, Kevin, 165, 170
Harvey, Steve, 37
Hasselhoff, David, 100
Hatch, Orin, 220
Hawke, Ethan, 86, 116
Hawn, Goldie, 229
Hayek, Salma, 38. 61, 65, 126, 136, 147, 158, 190
Hayworth, Rita, 38, 129
He Got Game, 126
Head of State, 235-37
Henry, Gregg, 120, 133
Henson, Taraji P., 126
Hero prototype, 163, 175, 176, 177, 194, 231, 239, 240, 241, 256, 264
Heslov, Grant, 106
Hitch, 35, 37, 72, 77, 80, 165, 169, 181, 190, 207, 238, 239, 259
Hoffman, Dustin, 117
Hollywood's Acting Rule for Minorities (HARM theory), 56, 57, 71, 145, 146, 150, 154, 159, 188, 209, 255, 259, 261, 267
Hollywood Audience, 56, 112, 223, 225, 247
Hollywood's Racial Makeup, 33, 34, 72
Hollywood Reporter, The, 25, 29, 38, 208, 215, 227

Holm, Ian, 173
Home Alone, 180, 188, 219, 239
Honey, I Shrunk the Kids, 239
Honeymooners, The, 13, 22, 37, 207, 208
Hopkins, Anthony, 93, 111, 113, 182, 183
Horner, Jack, 19
Horowitz, Winona. *See* Winona Ryder
Hoskins, Bob, 115
Hotel Rwanda, 66, 142, 244
Houghton, Katharine, 63, 191
Hounsou, Djimon, 88, 113, 222
How High, 236
How to Lose a Guy in 10 Days, 192
How Stella Got Her Groove Back, 30, 36, 167
Howard, Terrence, 120
Hu, Kelly, 65, 88, 120
Hudson, Jennifer, 4
Hudson, Kate, 4, 192, 229
Huffington, Arianna, 228
Hulk, 22 176
Hunt, Helen, 183, 193
Hunted, The, 148, 153
Hurricane, The, 112, 142
Hustle & Flow, 37, 126

I

I, Robot, 35, 37, 44, 65, 153, 207, 219, 230, 231, 233, 240
Ice Age series
    Ice Age, 18
    Ice Age 2, 24
Ice Cube, 35, 37, 40, 236, 237
identification process, 170, 171, 191, 203, 223, 226, 2227, 228, 229, 234, 235, 236, 239, 240, 242, 245, 247, 250, 252
Idlewild, 37
Inaba, Carrie Ann, 100
Incredibles, The, 26, 80, 170, 171
Independence Day, 37, 44, 126, 166, 182, 207
Inside Man, 207
Insider, The, 40
Inspector Gadget, 34
Intellectual prototype, 163, 173, 179-83, 187, 256, 264
Internet Movie Database, The (IMDB), 65, 245
Interpreter, The, 166, 248
Intolerable Cruelty, 55, 90
Invincible, 165
Island, The, 186
Italian Job, The, 24, 36

J

Jackman, Hugh, 62, 88, 120, 132
Jackson, Samuel L., 80, 113, 115, 121, 153, 237, 241, 246
Jadakiss, 36
James, Kevin, 80
Jar Jar Binks, 26, 246
Jaws, 24, 199, 222
Jazz Singer, The, 4, 35, 97, 226
Jerry Maguire, 180, 204
Jewish, 65, 66, 67, 68, 97, 106, 186, 251
Jezebel, 129
Jim Crow, 128
Johansson, Scarlett, 61, 186
Johnson, Anne-Marie, 84
Johnson, "The Rock" Dwayne, 106, 128, 182
Johnson Family Vacation, 37, 174-75, 237
Jolie, Angelina, 88, 190, 229, 248
Jones, Angus T., 172
Jones, James Earl, 243, 250
Jones, Russell G., 115
Jones, Tommy Lee, 118, 121, 148
Josie and the Pussycats, 17
Joy Luck Club, The, 242
Jumanji, 153
Jungle Fever, 126
Jurassic Park series, 19
    Jurassic Park, 22, 169, 180, 219, 245, 246
    Jurassic Park III, 19, 170
Juwanna Man, 128

K

Karate Kid, The, 73
Kaufman, Charlie, 44
Keaton, Diane, 192
Kebbel, Arielle, 170
key art, 215-17
Kidman, Nicole, 41, 248
Kill Bill: Vol. 1, 35, 76, 86, 127, 170, 171, 213
King Arthur, 40
King's Ransom, 208
Kingdom Come, 17, 36, 167
Kline, Kevin, 236
Knightley, Keira, 40
Knowles, Beyoncé, 37, 65
Kramer vs. Kramer, 241
Kruger, Diane, 184
Ku Klux Klan, 57, 112, 226
Kuhn, Judy, 136
Kung Fu, 72
Kutcher, Ashton, 63, 64, 117, 119, 146, 191

L

La Bamba, 142
Landau, Martin, 236
Lane, Diane, 61
Lara Croft Tomb Raider: The Cradle of Life, 22, 88
Larby, Ahmed Ben, 122
Last Action Hero, 153
Last Boy Scout, The, 126
Last Holiday, 37, 151
Last King of Scotland, The, 4, 134, 227
Last of the Mohicans, The, 82, 179
Last Samurai, The, 35, 82, 86, 144, 165, 179, 204, 216, 263
Latino archetpyes
    Angel, 77
    Background Figure, 90
    Comic Relief, 105
    Menace to Society, 116
    Physical Wonder, 135
    Utopic Reversal, 148
Lawrence, Martin, 37, 128, 150, 151, 153, 159, 166, 207, 237, 238
Lean on Me, 142
Lee, Ang, 4
Lee, Bruce, 34
Lee, Spike, 35, 36
Legally Blonde series
    Legally Blonde, 189
    Legally Blonde 2, 228
Legend of Bagger Vance, The, 77, 207
Leguizamo, John, 105, 128
Leigh, Janet, 229
Leoni, Téa, 79, 186
Lester, Adrian, 173
Lethal Weapon series, 98, 153, 177, 237, 240
    Lethal Weapon 2, 166, 240
    Lethal Weapon 4, 99, 114, 127, 166, 170, 186, 240
Li, Jet, 32, 114, 115, 127, 130, 240
Lil' Kim, 37
Lilo & Stitch, 26, 27, 171,
Lion King, The, 21, 23, 96, 105, 243
Lister, Tommy "Tiny," 117, 129
Liu, Lucy, 61, 86, 88, 120, 127, 133, 190
LL Cool J, 17, 37, 152
Lloyd, Jake, 184

Lohman, Alison, 61
Loken, Kristanna, 167
Lone, John, 114
Long, Justin, 160
Longest Yard, The, 37, 112, 128, 137
Looters. See Trespass
Lopez, Jennifer, 61, 64, 65, 72, 73, 79, 126, 190
Lord of the Rings (LOTR) series, 23, 179, 223, 259
    Lord of the Rings: The Fellowship of the Ring, 179, 228
    Lord of the Rings: The Two Towers, 245
    Lord of the Rings: The Return of the King, 245
Loren, Sophia, 67
Lost in Translation, 28, 86, 101, 185
Love & Basketball, 36, 167
Love Jones, 36, 167
Low Down Dirty Shame, 153
Lucas, Josh, 92, 182
Ludacris, 37, 120

M

Mac, Bernie, 235, 237
Madagascar, 37
Madea's Family Reunion, 128, 159
Madsen, Virginia, 132
Maestro, Mía, 92
Magneto, 23, 62
Maguire, Tobey, 107, 176, 180, 181, 194, 204
Maid in Manhattan, 65, 91, 129, 190
mainstream culture, 22, 24, 28, 45, 63, 220, 252
mainstream injection, 28
mainstream movie
    general definition, 11
    mainstream movie factors, 16
        A-list talent, 20
        full-length release, 16
        large box office sales, 19
        large production/mktg. costs, 17
        mainstream media exposure, 21
        widespread distribution, 16
    mainstream movie bonus factors, 22
        academy award nomination/win, 25
        long lead time, 24
        paraphernalia, 23
        promotional tie-ins, 23
        spinoff, 22
        spunoff, 23
        theme park rides, 24

mainstream pipeline, 21, 28, 29
Major League Baseball (MLB), 22, 187
major movie studio, 11, 19, 30, 191, 219, 229
Major Payne, 153
Malco, Romany, 101
Malcolm X, 35, 142, 244
Malibu's Most Wanted, 106, 179
Malik, Art, 123
Maltin, Leonard, 11
Man, The, 153, 237
Man On Fire, 73, 77, 78, 91, 120, 145, 149, 151, 153, 165, 166, 207, 230, 233
Manchurian Candidate, The, 13, 203
Mandela, Nelson, 25
Mandvi, Aasif, 107, 154
Manipulator prototype, 163, 178, 184, 185, 186, 187, 194, 256, 264
Mapother, William, 176
Marin, Cheech, 96, 105
Martin, Ricky, 40
Martin, Steve, 80, 172, 236
masking, 45, 67, 106
Matrix, The series, 73
    Matrix, The, 76, 177
    Matrix Reloaded, The, 217
Mazzello, Joseph, 180
McConaughey, Matthew, 61, 113, 192
McDaniel, Hattie, 4, 52, 54
McGregor, Ewan, 186
Me, Myself & Irene, 102, 175
Means, Russell, 82, 136
Meet the Fockers, 13, 72, 105, 117, 180
Men in Black, 24, 37, 44, 98, 122, 153, 219, 230
Menace to Society archetype, 12
    Asian, 114
    Black, 115
    Latino, 116
    Other, 121
Mendes, Eva, 65, 126, 158, 238
Method Man, 236
Metoyer, Patricia Heisser, 2
Metro, 153
Middle Eastern, 33, 39, 40, 106, 122, 123, 138, 142
Milchan, Arnon, 203, 204
Million Dollar Baby, 4, 73
Minority Cycle of Movie-Making, 166, 167, 218
Minority Report, 189, 216, 219, 232
minstrel, 97, 98, 102
minstrelsy, 97, 98
Miracle, 223
Miracle on 34th Street, 4

Missing, The, 39, 45, 118, 120, 179
Mission: Impossible series
    Mission: Impossible, 177, 216
    Mission: Impossible III, 15
Mississippi Burning, 53
Mitchell, Radha, 78, 149
Mixon, Jerod, 102
Mizota, Diane, 100
Mo'Nique, 37, 153, 227
Monster, 25
Monster's Ball, 4, 25, 37, 115, 117, 124, 126, 132, 146, 159, 166, 180, 204
Monster-in-Law, 65
Monsters, Inc., 27
Montalban, Ricardo, 38, 129, 140
Moore, Demi, 80
Moore, Joel, 160
Moore, Julianne, 61
Moore, Michael, 221
moral compass, 221
Moreno, Antonio, 129
Morgenstern, Joe, 70
Morita, Pat, 73
Mortal Kombat, 22
Morton, Joe, 166, 171
Mos Def, 37
Motion Picture Association of America (MPAA), 10, 29, 41
Mr. 3000, 237
Mr. Deeds, 164
Multi-facial, 68
Mummy, The series
    Mummy, The, 138, 181, 182
    Mummy Returns, The, 24, 182
Murphy, Eddie, 26, 27, 28, 37, 102, 106, 120, 128, 153, 180, 181, 229, 237, 246, 247
Murray, Bill, 101
My Big Fat Greek Wedding, 23
Myers, Mike, 27, 100, 102, 247

N

Nakamura, Shichinosuke, 144
National Security, 153
National Treasure, 184
Native American, 33, 39, 42, 43, 45, 46, 65, 74, 82, 94, 109, 117, 118, 122, 136, 142
Neeson, Liam, 26, 111

Nelly, 37, 137

Newton, Thandie, 120
Nicholson, Jack, 187, 192
Night at the Museum, 39, 135, 219, 237
Norris, Chuck, 161
Novarro, Ramon, 129
Nutty Professor series, 37, 237
    Nutty Professor, The, 128, 207
    Nutty Professor II: The Klumps, 128, 174

O

Ocean's Eleven series
    Ocean's Twelve, 130
    Ocean's Thirteen, 131
Ochoa, Jesús, 91, 149, 153
O'Connor, Isabell, 90
Office of the UN High Commissioner for Refugees (UNHCR), 248
Oh, Sandra, 131
Okonedo, Sophie, 65, 66, 126
Old School, 93
one-way culture sharing, 74, 76, 82
Oscar. *See* Academy Award
Osment, Haley Joel, 152
Other archetypes
    Angel, 80
    Background Figure, 93
    Comic Relief, 106
    Menace to Society, 121
    Physical Wonder, 136
    Utopic Reversal, 151
Otto, Miranda, 174
Out of Time, 145, 153
Owen, Clive, 120, 135, 190

P

Pallana, Kumar, 81, 82
Paltrow, Gwyneth, 61
pararealistic movie, 221
parity, 260, 262
Party, Politics & Movies, 220
Passion of the Christ, The, 28, 251
Paxton, Bill, 183
Payback, 120, 126, 133
Pearl Harbor, 19, 31, 35, 87, 222
Pelican Brief, The, 190
Peña, Elizabeth, 80

Penn, Kal, 66, 236, 237
Penn, Sean, 248
Perry, Tyler, 35, 128, 159
Phat Girlz, 227
Physical Wonder archetype
    Asian, 130
    Black, 132
    Latino, 135
    Other, 136
Pianist, The, 132
Pink Panther, The, 13, 37
Pinkston, Ryan, 170
Pirates of the Caribbean series, 40, 223
    Pirates of the Caribbean: Dead Man's Chest, 24, 245, 246
    Pirates of the Caribbean: At World's End, 13
Pitt, Brad, 75, 159
Planet of the Apes, 134
Plowright, Joan, 172
Pocahontas, 39, 136
Poitier, Sidney, 63, 191
Police Academy, 153
Pompeo, Ellen, 93
Poseidon, 92, 182
Preacher's Wife, The, 36, 37, 167, 242
premium of proportion, 54, 58, 59, 113, 125, 159, 163, 212, 214, 238
Preston, J.A., 54
Pretty Woman, 126, 192, 203
Pride & Prejudice, 40
The Program, 249
Proof of Life, 119
protective stereotype, 111-13
prototype
    general definition, 163
    categorical definitions
        Assumed Affluent, 164
        Family-Tied, 169
        Hero, 175
        Intellectual, 179
        Manipulator, 184
        Romantic, 189
Pulp Fiction, 128, 129, 242
Punisher, The, 171
Pursuit of Happyness, The, 142
Pyle, Missi, 161, 170

Q

Qin, Shaobo, 130, 131
Quaid, Dennis, 173, 182
Queen Latifah, 35, 37, 65, 72, 80, 152, 172, 236, 237

R

race, 33
Race Doctor, The, 5, 8, 9, 128, 267
racial capital, 41, 58-61, 68, 86, 91, 107, 109, 111, 113, 122, 142, 146, 151, 157, 158162, 182, 211, 212, 214, 217, 238, 243, 257
racial requirement, 34, 35, 40, 86, 87, 92, 118
Radcliffe, Daniel, 89
Raimi, Sam, 156, 227
Rainmaker, The, 90
Ray, 41, 42, 211, 216, 244
Rebecca of Sunnybrook Farm, 73
Red Corner, 143
Redman, 236
Reeves, Keanu, 76, 177
Reid, Tara, 17
Remember the Titans, 145
Rent, 126
Resident Evil, 22
Rhames, Ving, 26, 117, 128, 129, 177, 242
Richards, Ariana, 180
Rising Sun, 98, 144, 166
Rivera, Emilio, 148, 153
Robbins, Tim, 112
Roberts, Julia, 126, 178, 190, 192
Robinson, Bill "Bojangles," 73, 78
Rock, Chris, 37, 99, 112, 153, 170, 235, 237, 240
Rodríguez, Freddy, 92
Rodriguez, Robert, 66
Rojecki, Andrew, 212
Romantic prototype, 163, 189, 192. 256, 264
Romeo Must Die, 37, 130
Romero, Cesar, 129
Romijn, Rebecca, 62, 88
Root, Stephen, 160
Rosewood, 53
Rossum, Emily, 180, 190
Rules of Engagement
Runaway Jury, 40
Rush Hour series, 153, 237
    Rush Hour, 37, 127, 151, 153
    Rush Hour 2, 13, 98, 114, 259

Russell, Kurt, 182
Ryan, Meg, 119, 192
Ryder, Winona, 68

S

sacrificial sofa, 211, 214, 238, 262
Sahara, 23, 129, 219
Saldaña, Zoë, 63, 64, 191
Sandler, Adam, 79, 100, 112, 137, 168, 187, 238
Santiago, Ray, 105, 180
Sarandon, Susan, 79
Saving Private Ryan, 166, 172
Scary Movie, 128, 237
Schindler's List, 222
School for Scoundrels, 128
Schumacher, Tom, 96, 105
Schwarzenegger, Arnold, 167, 175, 204, 209, 250
Schweig, Eric, 82, 118, 120
Scicolone, Sofia Villani. *See* Sophia Loren
Scorpion King, The, 106, 128, 182
Scott, Sean William, 74, 75, 97
Screen Actors Guild (SAG), 42, 43, 47
Seabiscuit, 194, 223
Selena, 142
Seven Years in Tibet, 75
Shahi, Sarah, 93, 94
Shalhoub, Tony, 122
Shall We Dance?, 72, 73, 79, 170
Shanghai Noon, 237
Shark Tale, 190, 207
Shawshank Redemption, The, 112
Shea, Jack, 198
Sheen, Charlie, 67
Sheen, Martin, 67
Showgirls, 126
Shrek series, 23, 26, 27, 37
    Shrek 2, 24, 102, 245, 246, 247
    Shrek the Third, 13, 23
Shyamalan, M. Night, 152, 154
Sideways, 131, 219
Siege, The, 122
Silence of the Lambs, The, 111, 158, 182
Simpsons Movie, The, 23-25
Sin City, 120, 126, 135, 153, 190
Sinbad, 153
Sinbad: Legend of the Seven Seas, 26, 27
Sinclair, Madge, 243
Singh, Dalip, 137
Singin' in the Rain, 4

Six Degrees of Separation, 128
Sixth Sense, The, 152, 180, 219
Sky High, 181
Sleepless in Seattle, 192
Smart, Jean, 172
Smith, Arjay, 173, 181
Smith, Jada Pinkett, 17, 35
Smith, Will, 12, 35, 37, 44, 72, 77, 80, 128, 150, 151, 153, 166, 181, 190, 207, 229, 230, 233, 237, 238
Smits, Jimmy, 90, 91
Snipes, Wesley, 35, 128, 132, 144, 216, 240
Snoop Dogg, 37, 106
Snow Dogs, 94
Something's Gotta Give, 192
Soul Food, 30, 158
Soul Plane, 37, 38, 103, 104, 153, 165, 170, 214
Spanglish, 77, 79
Spider-Man series, 21, 22
    Spider-Man, 165, 171, 209
    Spider-Man 2, 22, 107, 181
    Spider-Man 3, 13
Spielberg, Steven, 219, 226, 229
Spy Kids, 66, 67
St. Augustine, 14, 15
St. Elmo's Fire, 67
Stallone, Sylvester, 175
Stand and Deliver, 142
Star Wars series, 23, 24, 131
    Episode I - The Phantom Menace, 26, 180, 184, 222, 245, 246, 250
    Episode II - Attack of Clones, 90
    Episode III - Revenge of the Sith, 199
    Episode IV - A New Hope, 91
Starsky & Hutch, 37
Stealth, 203
Stepford Wives, The, 210
stereotype, 34, 54
Stewart, Kellee, 63
Stiller, Ben, 39, 97, 105, 160, 207, 238
Stone, Oliver, 206
Stone, Sharon, 202
Stormare, Peter, 175
Striptease, 126
Suarez, Jeremy, 171, 180
Sum of All Fears, The, 177
Superman Returns, 13, 22, 44, 176
Swank, Hilary, 61
Swordfish, 126, 132, 209

T

Tagawa, Cary-Hiroyuki, 144, 166
Talladega Nights: The Ballad of Ricky Bobby, 218, 237
Talk to Me, 142
Tarzan, 21
Tavare, Jay, 118
Taxi, 37, 98
Taylor, Christine, 160
Tejada, Jo Raquel *See* Raquel Welch
Temple, Shirley, 78, 97
Terminal, The, 81
Terminator series
    Terminator 2: Judgement Day, 24, 166, 170, 171
    Terminator 3: Rise of the Machines, 167, 218
Terrero, Jessy, 38, 103
There's Something About Mary, 175
Theron, Charlize, 25
Thomas, Jonathan Taylor, 243
Thornton, Billy Bob, 132, 175
Three Kings, 40
Thurman, Uma, 76, 86, 213, 242
T.I. *See* Tip Harris
tipping point, 206, 207, 229
Titanic, 17, 193, 204, 205, 218, 245, 247, 259, 266
To Wong Foo Thanks for Everything, Julie Newmar, 128
Tomei, Marisa, 187
Total Recall, 204, 250
Traffic, 4, 115, 153
Training Day, 4, 37, 40, 86, 116, 126, 145, 153, 158, 207
Travolta, John. 132, 242
Trejo, Danny, 117, 135
Trespass, 209
Troy, 218, 259
True Lies, 123, 170
Tucker, Chris, 37, 98, 127, 128, 151, 153, 237, 238
Tudyk, Alan, 160, 230, 232
Twister, 24, 183
Two Can Play That Game, 30, 36, 167
Tyler, Liv, 176, 238

U

ugly American, 86, 107
umbrella image, 215
unclean hero, 144, 145
Unger, Deborah Kara, 133
United Nations (UN), 166, 248
United Nations Educational Scientific and Cultural Organization (UNESCO), 250
Unleashed, 115, 240
Utopic Reversal archetype, 57
    Asian, 143
    Black, 146
    Latino, 148
    Other, 151

V

Valenti, Jack, 41, 199, 201, 249
Valentino, Rudolph, 129
Valleta, Amber, 190
Vaughn, Vince, 106, 160, 166, 168
Vega, Paz, 77, 79
Velez, Lupe, 129
Vin Diesel, 68
visibile continuum, 116, 117
Voight, Jon, 229
Vosloo, Arnold, 138

W

Wahlberg, Mark, 40
Waiting to Exhale, 36, 167
Walken, Christopher, 168
Wall Street, 67
Wallace & Gromit in The Curse of the Were-Rabbit, 27
Wangchuk, Jamyang Jamtsho, 75
War of the Roses, 241
War of the Worlds, 44, 174
Ward, Sela, 173
Warhol, Andy, 254
Washington, Denzel, 4, 35, 73, 78, 91, 94, 112, 116, 120, 122, 145, 149, 153, 181, 190, 207, 229, 233, 237, 239
Watanabe, Ken, 204
Waterworld, 218, 259
Watts, Naomi, 61
Wayans, Damon, 153
Wayans, Keenan Ivory, 153
Wayans, Marlon, 128, 153, 237
Wayans, Shawn, 128, 153
*Wedding Crashers*Wayans, 44, 106, 166, 168, 238
Wedding Planner, The, 61
Welch, Raquel, 67
What Women Want, 193
What's Love Got to Do with It, 142
Whitaker, Forest, 4. 134, 227

White prototypes, 163
- Affluent, 164
- Family-Tied, 169
- Hero, 175
- Intellectual, 179
- Manipulator, 184
- Romantic, 189

White balance, 158, 159, 194
White Beauty Standard, 63-66, 136, 190, 239
White, Betty, 173
White Chicks, 53, 128, 153, 237
White, Michael Jai, 240
Wiesz, Rachel, 181
Wild Wild West, 44, 153, 207
Williams, Chris, 160
Williams, Robin, 183
Willie, Roger, 80
Willis, Bruce, 86, 135, 154, 175, 176, 240
Wilson, Owen, 106, 166, 168
Wilson, Woodrow, 38
Windtalkers, 80
Winslet, Kate, 193
Witherspoon, Reese, 189, 228
Wolverine, 23, 62
Wood, The, 36, 167
Wood, Elijah, 179
Wood, Evan Rachel, 118
world-stop scene, 184-87, 192
World Trade Center, 176, 206
Writers Guild of America (WGA), 45-47

X

X-Men series, 23, 216
- *X-Men*, 207
- *X2: X-Men United*, 62, 88, 120
- *X-Men: The Last Stand*, 13, 216

xXx series
- *xXx*, 68
- *xXx: State of the Union*, 37

Y

You Got Served, 37
You've Got Mail, 192
Yukai, Diamond, 101
Yulin, Harris, 116
Yun-Fat, Chow, 74, 75
Yune, Rick, 114

Z

Zellweger, Renée, 88, 190, 192, 204
Zeta-Jones, Catherine, 62, 82, 90, 93, 132
Zoolander, 97
Zorro series
- *Legend of Zorro, The*, 62
- *Mask of Zorro, The*, 62, 92, 119

ABOUT THE AUTHOR

Frederick W. Gooding, Jr. (PhD, Georgetown University) is an Associate Professor within the Honors College at Texas Christian University in Fort Worth, TX. Gooding critically analyzes race within mainstream media, effectively contextualizing problematic patterns based upon their historical roots. As such, Gooding's best-known work thus far is *You Mean, There's RACE in My Movie? The Complete Guide to Understanding Race in Mainstream Hollywood*, which has been utilized in high schools and universities nationwide. Also the co-editor of *Stories from the Front of the Room: How Higher Education Faculty Overcome Challenges and Thrive in the Academy*, Gooding has stayed focused on the practical applications of equity with his historical contribution, *American Dream Deferred: Black Federal Workers in Washington, D.C., 1941-1981*, which carefully details the growth and struggles of black federal workers in the postwar era.

Gooding's latest work, *Black Oscars: From Mammy to Minny, What the Academy Awards Tell Us about African Americans*, expands his reach into pop cultural studies by analyzing African American Academy Award winners and how their narratives reflect and reinforce larger American history.

May we all continue to hold out hope for a "Hollywood ending"...

FOR MORE INFORMATION

For more information about racial analysis within mainstream media and other product offerings from *The Race Doctor*, visit online at:

www.theracedoc.com

Thank you for reading *You Mean, There's RACE in My Movie?*

You will NEVER see movies the same way again . . .

www.ingramcontent.com/pod-product-compliance
Lightning Source LLC
Chambersburg PA
CBHW080530170426
43195CB00016B/2518